D1694414

Rosetta

Rosetta

Elena Reygadas

BOM
DIA
BOA
TARDE
BOA
NOITE

sextopiso

For Lea and Julieta

For Luciano

Sharing	29
Sourdough country bread	31
Ramón-flour bread	35

I Beginnings 39

Cocopaches and nasturtium	42
Pickled Kumiai oysters, horseradish, borage flower, and samphire	45
Snails, habanero, red onion, and lime	49
Sweet shrimp aguachile	51
Burrata, anchovies, citron, buckwheat, and lemon basil	53
Endives, beets, orange, and pink pepper	57
Ingredients	**63**
Fennel, citrus, tarragon, and pomegranate	77
Yellowtail amberjack, muscatel plum, Asian pear, and red onion	79
White mole, carrots and charcoal oil	81
Pen shell scallops, vanilla, habanero, tangerine, and jicama	84
Quelites, avocado, lemon, and chicatana ants	87
More Than Food	**91**
Pickled sardines, farro, orange, celery, peppermint, and kalamata olives	97
Soft-shell crab, manila mango, habanero, and jicama	101
Persimmons, herbs, ricotta, lemon, and pistachios	102
Chicatana ant mole, pickled cucumbers and purslane	105

II Grains 111

Grains	117
Corn tamal, celery root, and smoked butter	121
Potato gnocchi, Ramonetti cheese, grape tomatoes, and smoked eel	126
Potato gnocchi with chaya and hoja santa	129
Farro, lobster and fennel	131
Beef tongue risotto with cilantro	134

Our Pasta	**145**
Fresh Pasta	147
Ricotta ravioli, lemon, and lemon thyme	148
Smoked beet tortelli, sheep's milk cheese, and sorrel	149
Mesquite tagliatelle with wild mushrooms	152
Buckwheat ravioli with 'nduja and burrata	156
Tagliolini, sea cradle, zucchini, and bottarga	158
Tagliatelle, sausage and chile de árbol ragù	163
Pápalo pappardelle with duck ragù	167

III Animals

171

Mahi-mahi, lentils, carrots, parsley, and peppermint	184
Sea bass, potatoes, hoja santa, squash vine, and squash blossoms	186
Beef sweetbreads, plums, yogurt, pomegranate, and zaatar	190
Our Suppliers	**197**
Wagyu beef tips, sorrel, lemon, and fennel frond	208
Black cod, endives, cauliflower, celery, golden raisins, and pine nuts	211
Suckling pig, achiote, and smoked sweet potato	213
Grouper and romesco	218
Rock cod, green romesco, bok choy, and mizuna	220
Pork neck, black romesco, and turnip flowers	222
Rabbit, carrots, and lovage	224
Scorpionfish, chorizo, and tomatoes	229
Red snapper, tamarind, and habanero	231
Quail, farro, dates, and mustard leaves	234
Cider-braised pork, apples, and elderberries	239
Chuck tail flap, avocado leaf, smoked zucchini, and chayotes	242
Striped black bass, pineapple, cascabel pepper, sorrel, tarragon, and xoconostle	244
Well-being	**249**

IV Endings 253

Bread and cheese	259
Amaranth bread	260
Walnut raisin bread	262
Smoked meringue, sour cream, pulque, and vanilla	267
Pink mole, strawberries, raspberries, hibiscus flowers, and yogurt foam	269
Farro, Tzalancab honey, chantarelles, and goat cheese	273
Nanches, yucca flowers, sour cream, and lemon	275
Pulque, prickly pear, xoconostle, and dragon fruit	280
Chocolate and hazelnut mousse	282
Licorice ice cream, banana, and macadamia nuts	284
Barley, olive oil, and lavender	286
Fresh herbs, olive oil and rosemary ice cream	289
Nicuatole, sweet lime, and macadamia	291
Melipona honey, pollen, and chamomile	294
Mamey, pixtle, and taxcalate	297
Ice creams and sorbets	301
Coffee	**307**
Amaretti	315

V La Panadería 317

La Panadería	**325**
Berry mille feuille	328
Rosemary bun	332
Concha	336
Guava roll	338

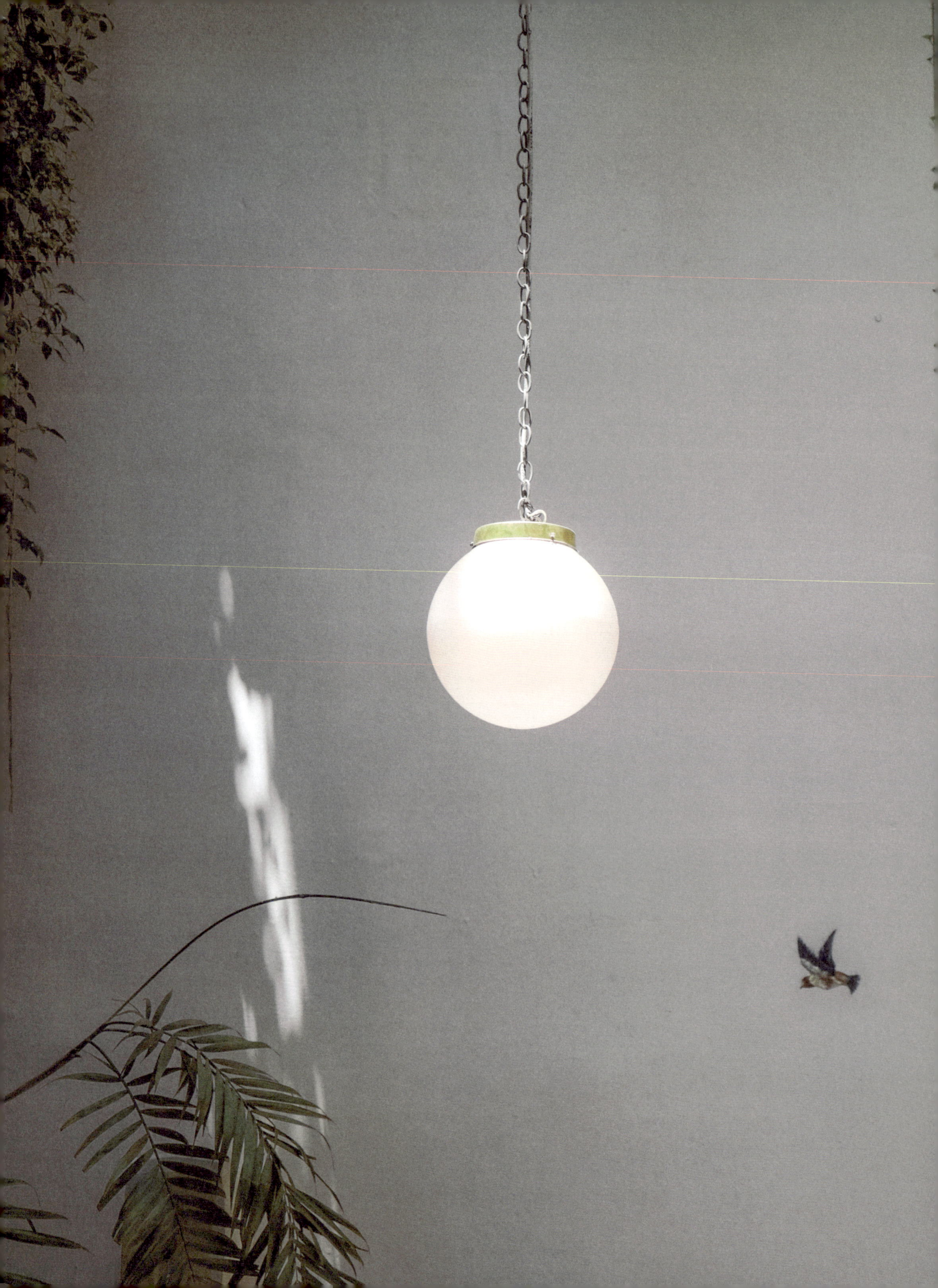

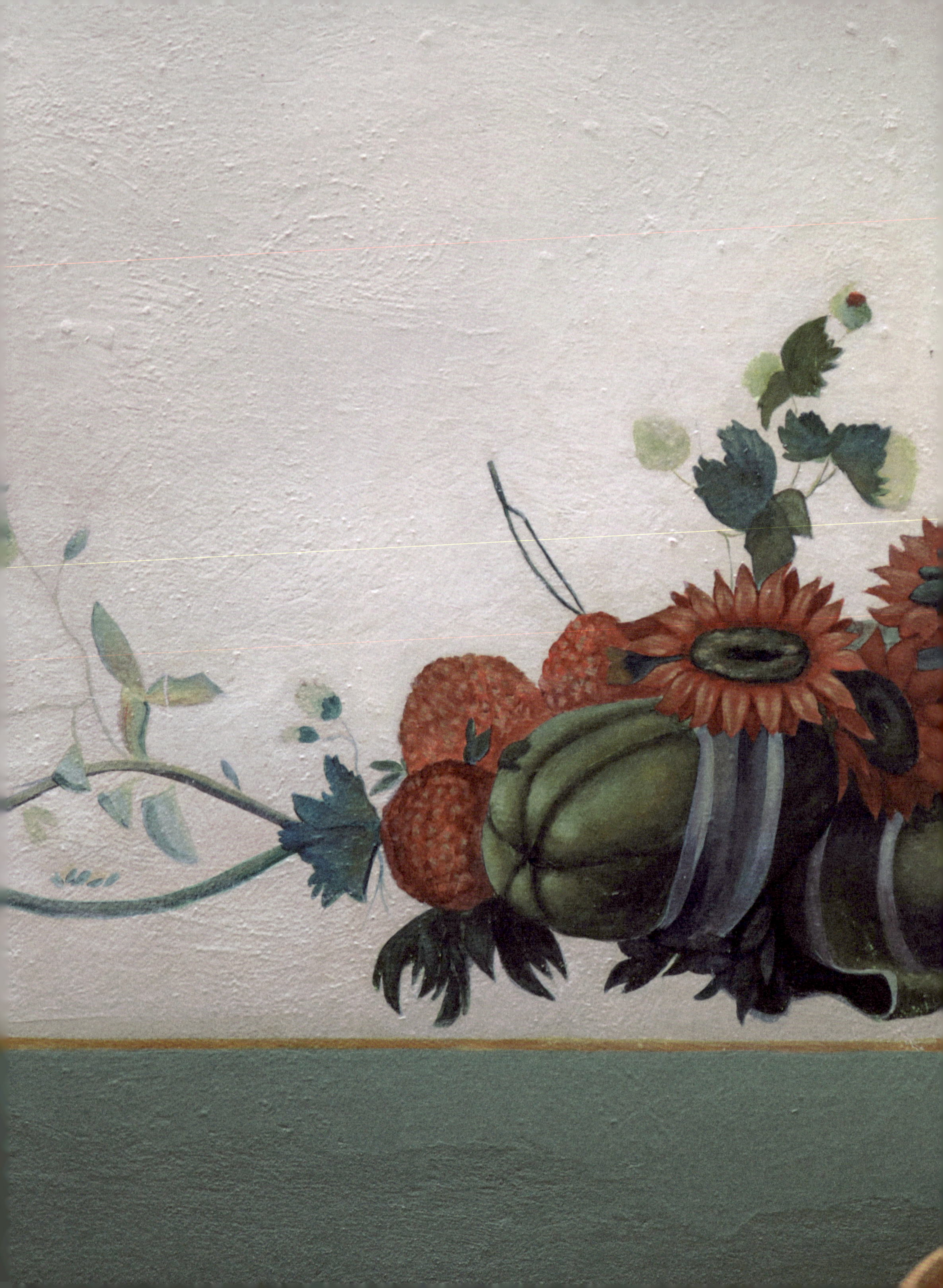

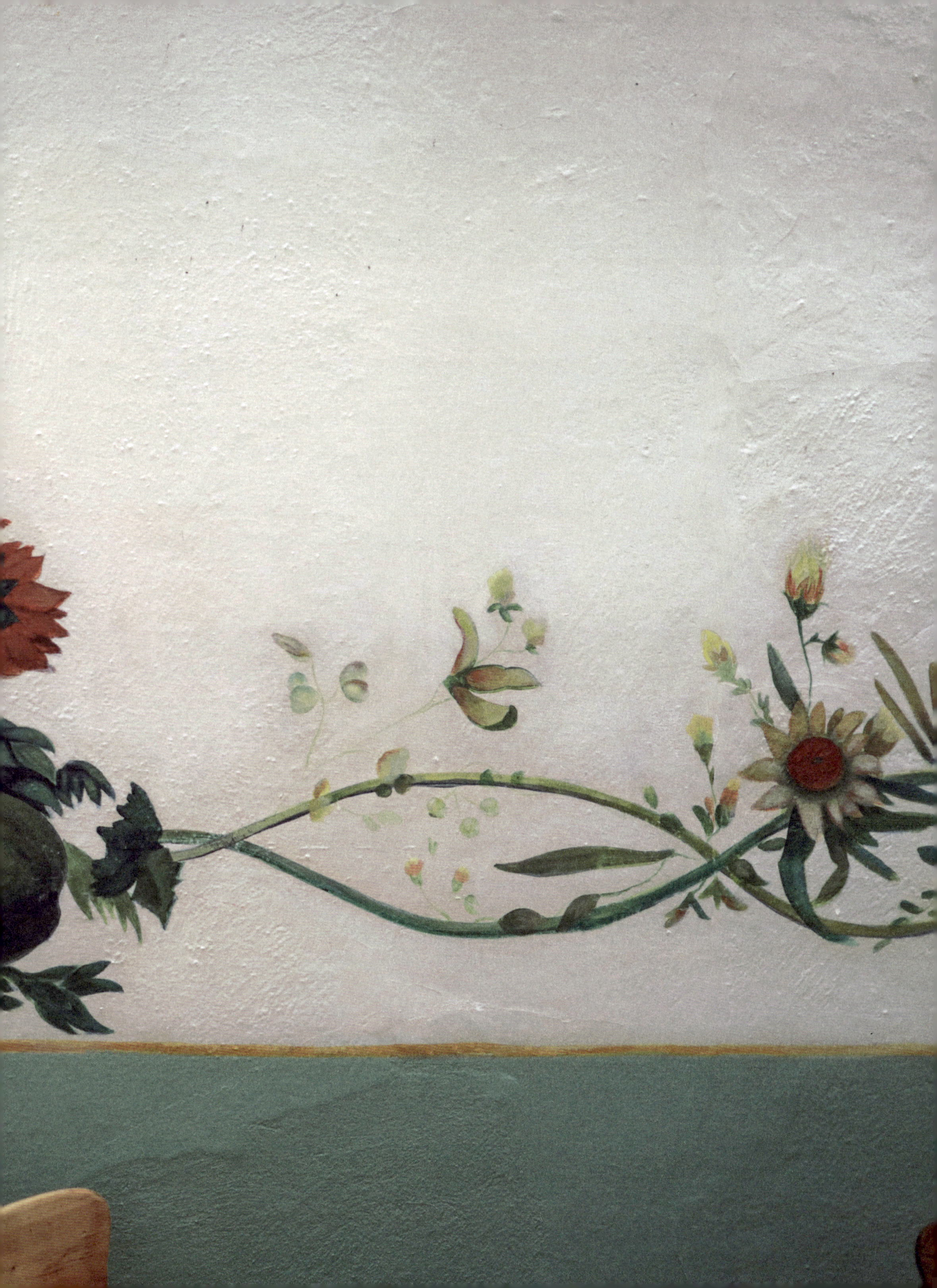

ROSETTA

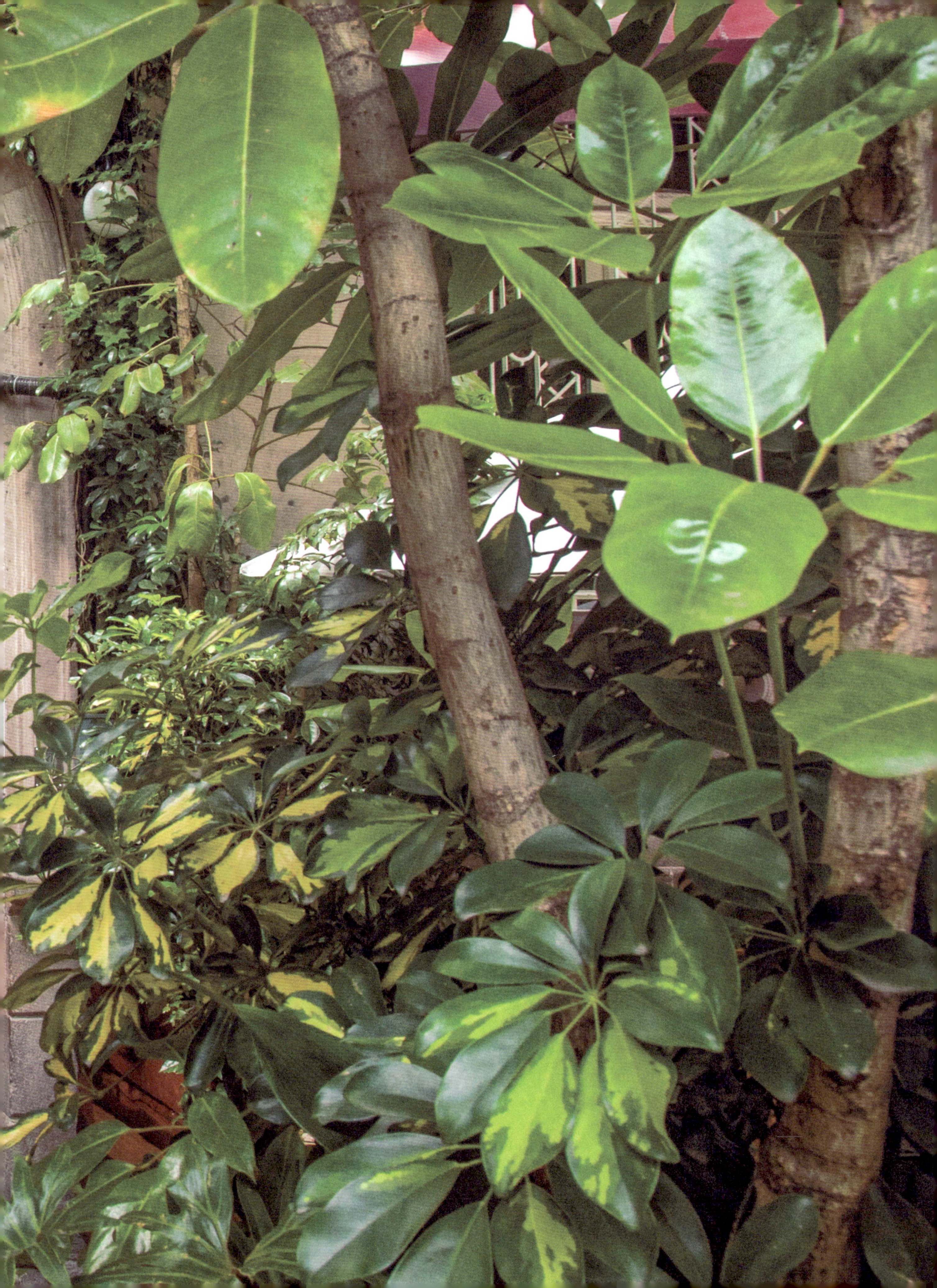

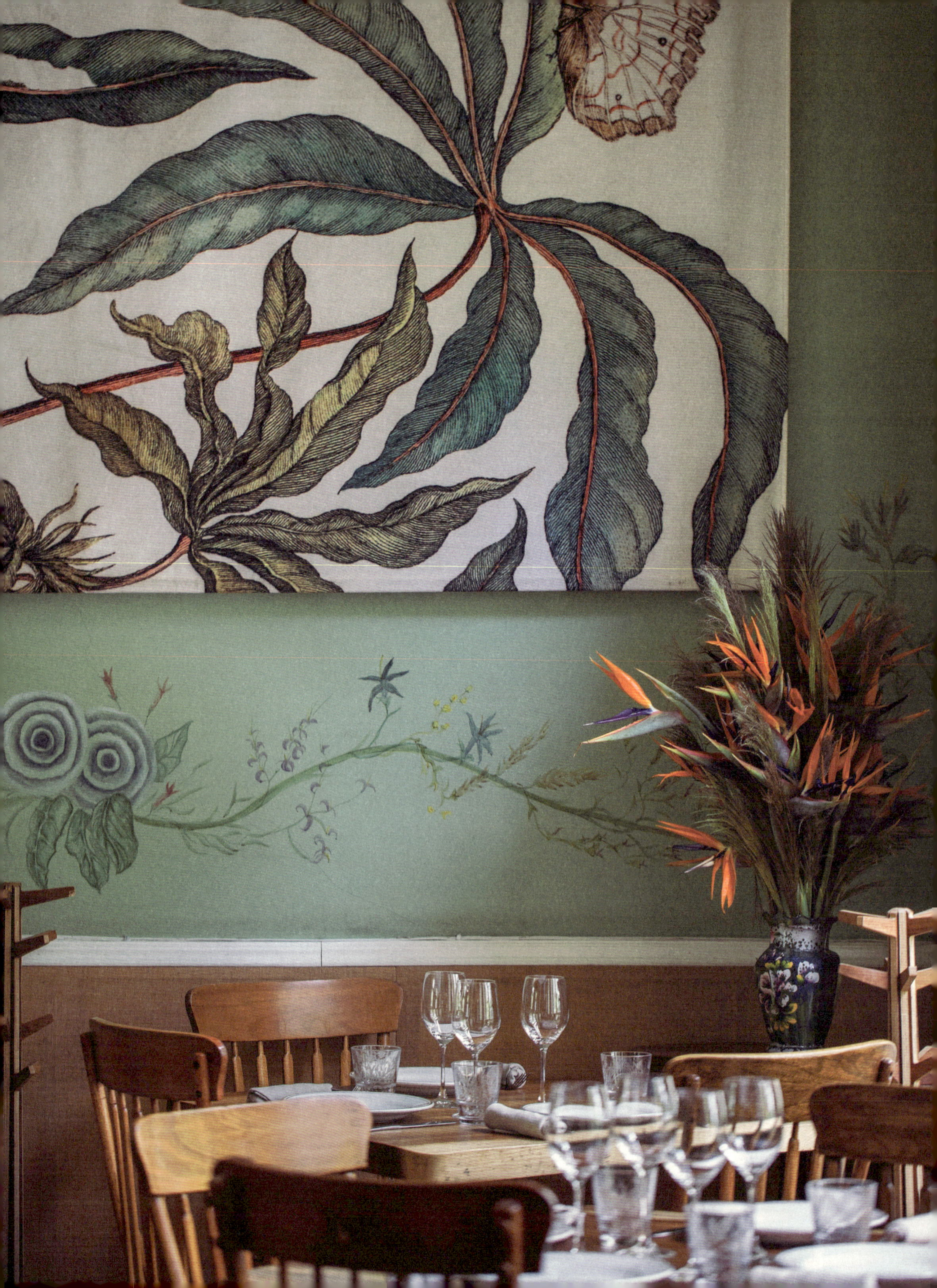

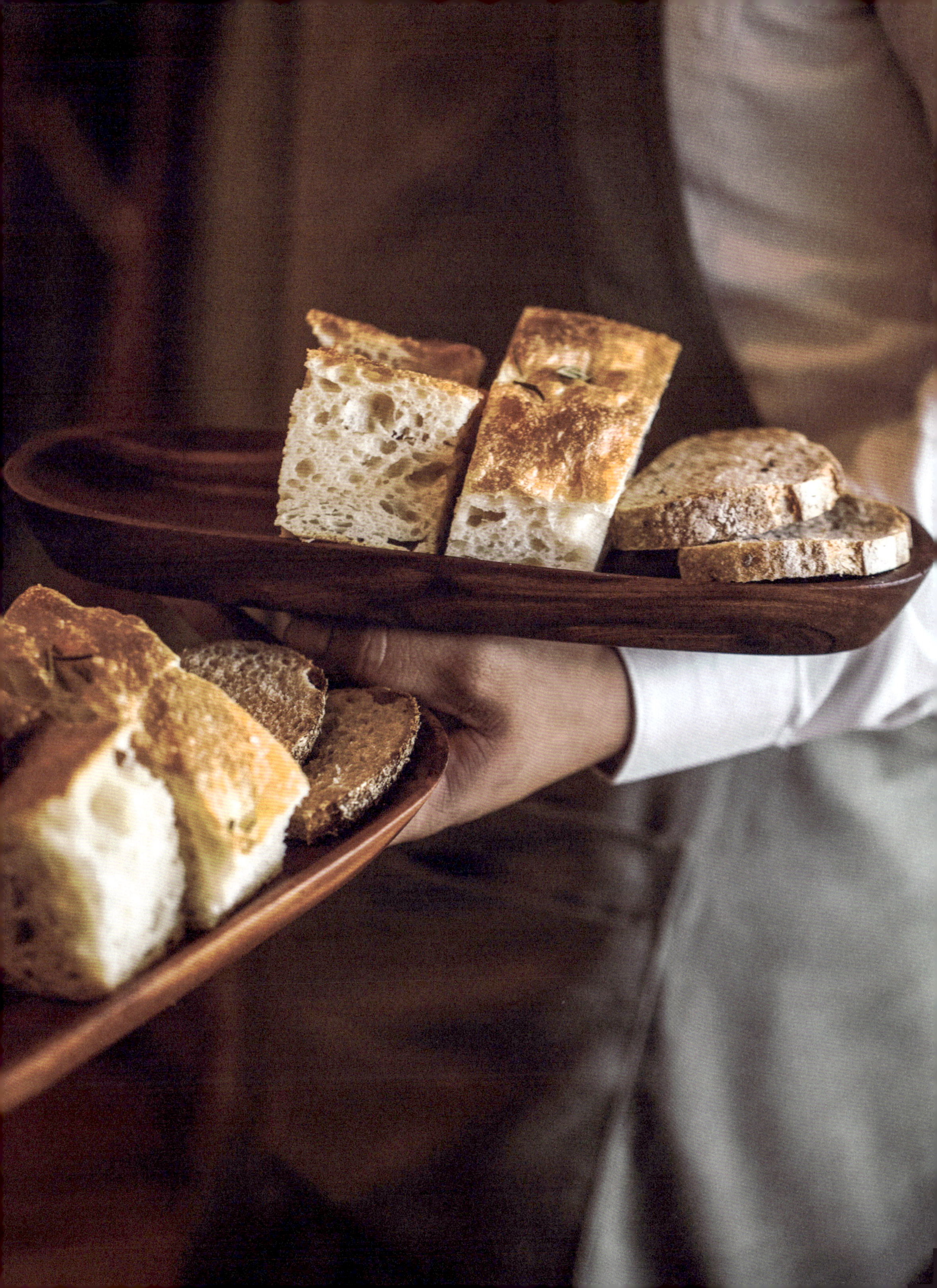

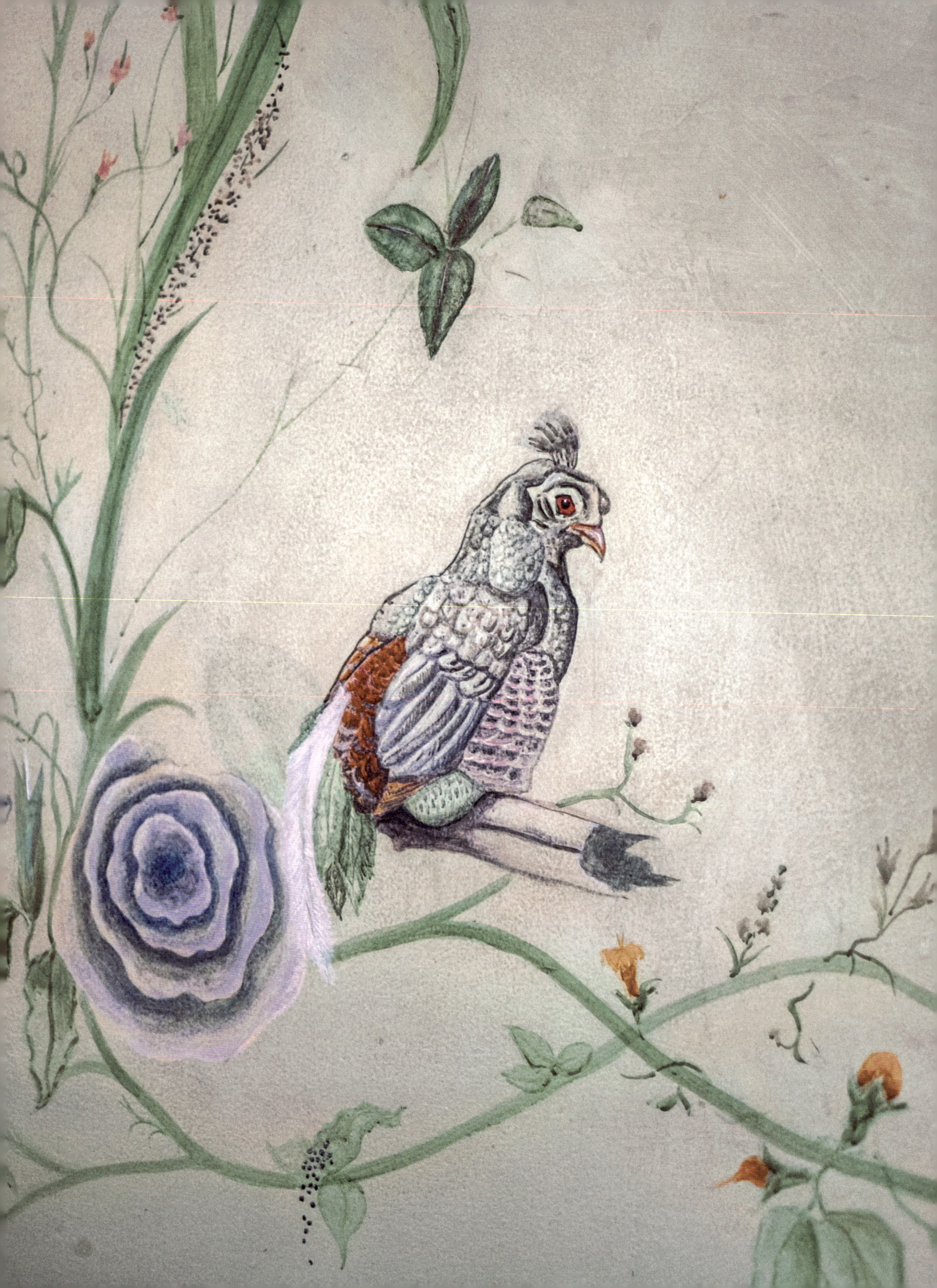

As a child, I learned that eating is a social activity grounded in sharing. Big gatherings were common in my family, attended by my cousins, my aunts and uncles, and my grandparents. Food played a key role in these get-togethers. It was the link that connected us, the trigger for conversation and companionship. The meals we ate weren't especially sophisticated; they were dishes we would all make at home. The most important thing was to gather together. Food was a pretext for doing just that.

My relationship with food was strengthened by the weekends I'd spend in the countryside, on a ranch in the state of Hidalgo, Mexico, with my parents, cousins, and friends. There, too, meals were a massive affair. In this context, I discovered a series of flavors, like pulque and bread baked in a woodburning oven, which gradually shaped my palate. In retrospect, I know I learned things on that ranch that have been essential for me—like knowing how to kill, pluck, clean, and prepare the birds we hunted.

My parents love eating, and they also love getting to know cultures and traditions through food. Our family environment encouraged me to be curious, try everything, and never fear the unknown. Food in our household changed radically after my father suffered a couple of heart attacks. We started eating more vegetables, fruits, legumes, and grains. Meat took on a secondary role. That's when I started to understand the close relationship between our health and the food we eat. As a result of this experience, I became interested in my own diet, and I even became a vegetarian for a few years.

While I'd always enjoyed cooking, I never contemplated pursuing it professionally when it was time to decide what I wanted to study in college. I saw cooking as an everyday task, something I liked doing for my friends, but not as something I'd necessarily have to learn at a university. That's why I ultimately decided to study English literature at the National Autonomous University of Mexico. But my love of cooking never went away. I spent a couple summers working in Mexico City restaurants; I learned some techniques. More than anything else, though, I learned about the rigor and discipline you need if you're going to be a cook.

When I was about to finish my degree, my brother Carlos invited me to do the catering for his crew on the shoot of *Japón*, his first film. It was a low-budget project and I had to make do as best I could. The hardest part was satisfying the preferences of both the Mexican crew members and of the foreigners: I started to understand how our tastes are conditioned by cultural and social factors. This experience reminded me—helped me discover, really—that what makes me happiest is cooking for other people. Which meant, I concluded, that cooking should be my profession.

So I started to research cooking schools. I decided to go to New York, to what was then called the French Culinary Institute, because they offered an eight-month practical course (unlike the several-year-long programs offered by other institutions). I wasn't as young as I once was, and what I wanted most was to start cooking as soon as possible.

Once I'd finished the course, I moved to London. I worked for four years at the restaurant Locanda Locatelli. There, I learned that the most important thing about cooking is your choice of ingredients: you have to respect their purity and simplicity, selecting the highest-quality products and using them at the right time of year. I realized how satisfying it was to use your hands when you cook. I loved practicing tasks that had been gradually neglected over time, like making bread and pasta from scratch.

During my time in London, where a vast quantity of food products are imported, I started to grasp the astonishing array of ingredients available in Mexico. I valued the country's animal and vegetable diversity. But it wasn't until my first daughter Lea was born that I began to seriously consider the possibility of returning home. Even while pregnant, I thought about how complicated it would be to cook professionally and be a mother at the same time. Both are profoundly demanding activities that require incredible passion. In Mexico, I'd have access to a family support network that would allow me to do both. No less important: I wanted my daughters to grow up surrounded by family, just as I did.

I returned to Mexico City and started a restaurant in an old mansion in the Roma neighborhood. It was a clandestine operation at first, serving dinner three nights a week behind closed doors. It was the perfect project for that time in my life, because I could also devote myself to being a parent. It also taught me the virtues of running a restaurant in that kind of house: how the experience of eating is shaped by the space that surrounds it. But this project slowly stopped working for me. I didn't want to have an underground restaurant; I wanted one where I could develop my cooking without limitations. The birth of Julieta, my youngest daughter, gave me the courage to open my own restaurant as I imagined it. In February 2010, just eight months after she was born, Rosetta opened its doors, a place:

To enjoy

and share

and frequent

and celebrate

and spend time together

Where the menu changes constantly

although some dishes stay the same

Where you'll find local and seasonal products

Where tradition is both questioned and upheld

Where time flies and time stops

Where you'll eat vegetables, seeds, and grains

but also fish, seafood, and meat

Where vegetables and proteins have the same status

Where we waste as little as possible and recycle what's left over

Where we make use of fruit pulp and seeds

Where we integrate wild herbs

Where we ferment bread unhurriedly

Where we make fresh pasta every day

Where you'll drink mezcal and vermouth

Where we make preserves

Where the wines aren't generic

Where people can get comfortably tipsy

Where the coffee is Mexican and freshly ground

Where the desserts are low in sugar

Where you can wipe your plate with your bread

Where mistakes happen

and are learned from

and are made again

Where we know our diners

Where both tourists and locals, men and women

of all ages, come to eat

Where you'll hear Nina Simone and Nick Cave

Where the walls are hung with tapestries and frescos

Where there are plants, flowers, and candles

Where there's closeness among people sharing a table

Where you'll eat off black clay pottery and porcelain

Where you'll sit on secondhand furniture

Where we pay attention to details

In an old house

with its own bakery

That encourages long conversations around the table after meals

That serves both pasta and mole

That supports small-scale producers

That my mother likes

and so do my daughters

This book, just like my kitchen, was born out of a desire to share. To share what we've learned over the years. To share our creative processes and show the effort we put into every dish. To share the ingredients and flavors I love most. To share our experiences as cooks. To share ideas so that others can use them and make them their own. That's when this book will make sense. That's when it will come to life.

Pan del día
- Lu - Integral con avena
- Ma - Amaranto con trigo
- Mi - Espelta y amapola
- Ju - Aceituna kalamata
- Vi - Ramón, Castaña
- Sab - Higo avellana.
        Orgánico y quinoa
- Dom - Trigo sarraceno

Mi bong
2 baguett
Sab - Dom

Doctor Di
2 espelta t
los martes

	Docena - Lu a Ju	Vie a Dom
Baguett	35	50
Bollos	30	40

Palacio
...r a Dom:
..baguett.

Masa Madre:
½ focaccia
Dom a Jue

-51: 60 birotes 200g Lu a Vi
Atlixco birotes 120g

Lu	Ma	Mi	Ju	Vi	Sab	Dom
40	40	40	45	55	80	80

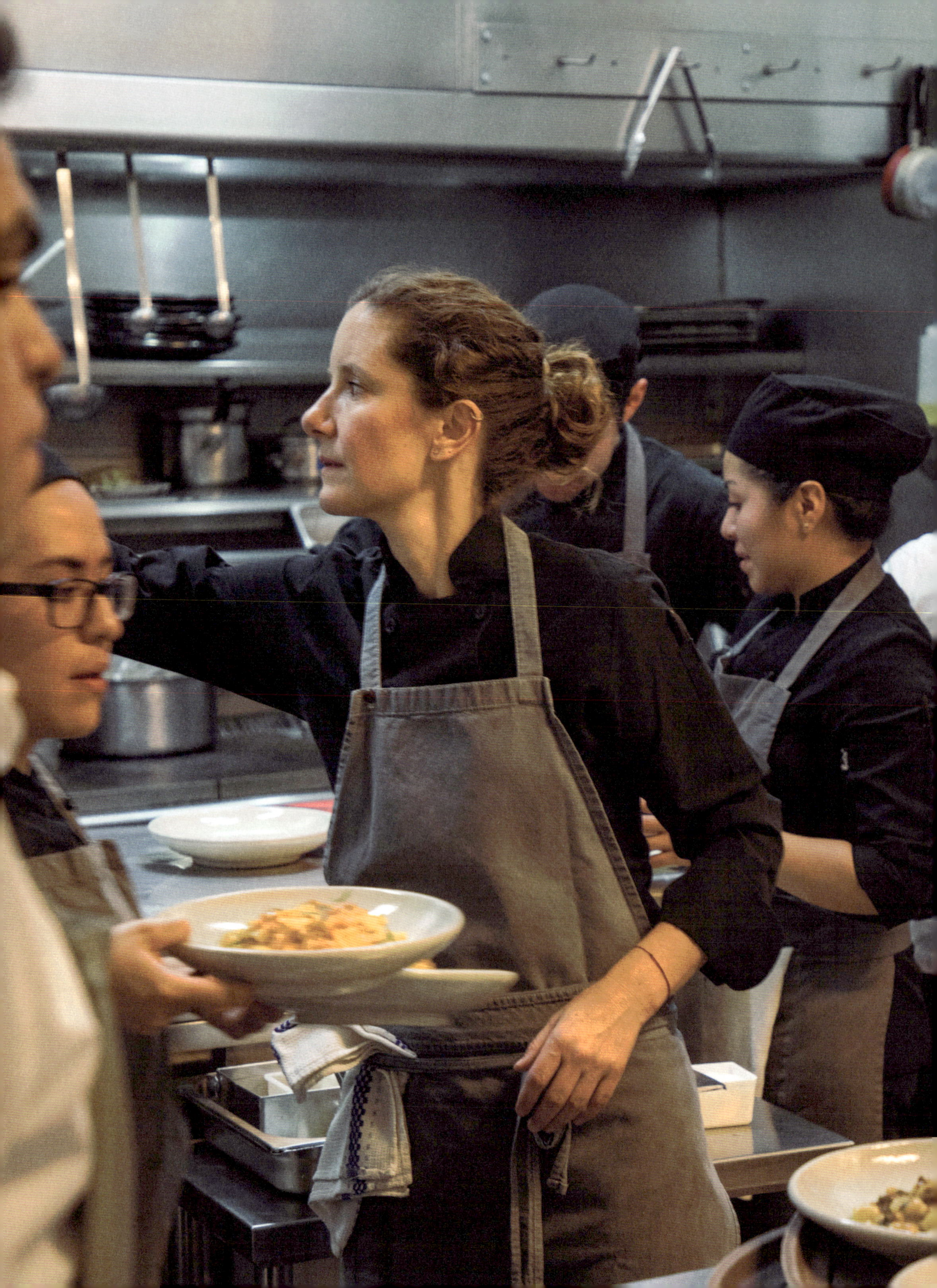

Sharing

One of my constant goals as a cook is to encourage accompaniment and coexistence through what happens or could happen around a table. I enjoy sparking pleasant moments among people, and my approach could be described as gourmet. But there's also something else I strive for: to create conversation, to prompt the exchange of ideas. And if this experience develops into dialogue, knowledge, and empathy with someone else—into a special kind of communication and communion—then that's the best possible outcome.

A meal at Rosetta begins with bread for the table. Bread, immensely symbolic, is eaten with the hands, broken, torn apart. That's how we share it. It's said that the words *company* and *companion* come from the Latin *companio*, which refers to the "act of eating from the same bread." Companions are those who share bread.

There is nothing trivial about enabling or provoking coexistence and communication. Especially now, when our contact with reality and with others is so often mediated by a screen. Even in strictly culinary terms, food today is enjoyed through the photographic documentation of each dish and its obsessive circulation on social media. When we eat, though, the three-dimensional pleasures of food can elicit profoundly sensory, even sensual reactions. And so, when we give preference to the digital image, we distance ourselves from the sensations themselves. In other words, we distance ourselves from the present, the here and now. That's why I try to make sure that every dish, every piece of bread, helps people engage in the joy of a shared experience.

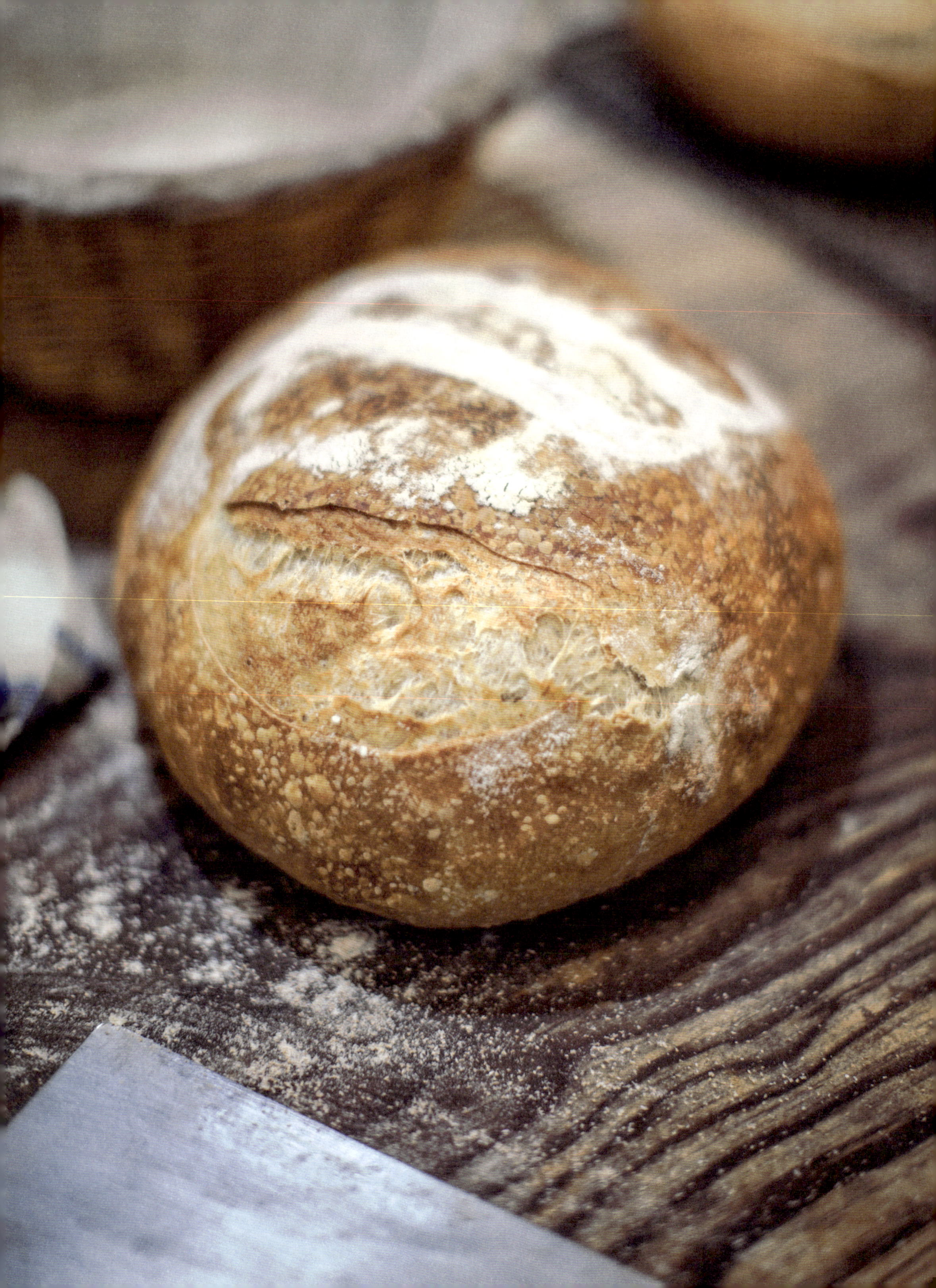

Sourdough country bread

Versatile, digestive, and long-lasting, this is one of Rosetta's most emblematic loaves. It's inspired by the French bread of old, the kind of bread that predominated before the baguette took over in the late nineteenth century. This sourdough bread is made of wheat flour, rye, sourdough starter, and salt. It's a large, firm loaf, and it ferments for no less than a full day.

My favorite kinds of bread to bake and to eat are those made with sourdough starter: a mixture of water and flour that doesn't call for artificial yeast and that undergoes a slow fermentation process, fermenting with the bacteria in the environment. The taste of this bread is both acidic and sweet. The inside of the loaf is quite different from the crust: the inner part is soft and spongy, while the crust is thick and crunchy. This kind of crust demands to be patiently and thoroughly chewed. When you chew it well, you produce saliva, which contains an enzyme that helps your body digest carbohydrates and keeps the stomach from getting irritated when you eat bread. I like how I feel when I eat sourdough: satisfied and full of energy. Besides, bread made with sourdough starter and fermented slowly is the kind of bread that tastes fresh for several days.

This is the bestselling bread in our bakery and what we put on the table at Rosetta. It's the bread that people dip in olive oil at the start of the meal, and the bread they use to wipe their plates or absorb what's left of a sauce at the end. In the kitchen, we use it a day after we bake it so that the inner part takes on a firmer consistency and can be easily toasted. We use it to make bread salads, to improve the texture of certain dishes and thicken certain sauces, and to make breadcrumbs. Bread should always be on hand and should never be thrown out.

Makes 3 pieces

1125 grams wheat flour
25 grams whole grain flour
100 grams rye flour
500 grams sourdough starter
25 grams salt
800 milliliters water
2 grams yeast

Place the flours and the salt in a large bowl.
Make a hollow in the middle of the flour and pour in the yeast and the sourdough starter.
Add the leftover water little by little, mixing it in with your fingers in a circular motion from the center outward.
Once the mixture is smooth, place the dough on a smooth surface and start to knead it, striking it lightly until the texture is even and stretchy.
Place the dough in a bowl with a lid and let it sit at room temperature for 1 hour, or until it has doubled in volume.
Divide the dough into 3 equal parts and place them on a floured wooden surface. Make each piece of dough into a ball shape.
Place each piece in a basket with a floured cloth, the smooth surface facing downward, and cover it with the cloth. Refrigerate for 24 hours.
Carefully transfer the pieces to a baking sheet with the smooth surface facing upward.
Make 3 shallow cuts on each loaf.
Bake with steam at 250°C for 30 minutes. If necessary, rotate the baking sheet after 15 minutes for even browning.

How to make a sourdough starter

120 grams water
5 large grapes, in halves
2 grams brown sugar or honey

100 grams flour
100 grams fresh fruit water

Day 1
Mix all the ingredients and store in a closed glass jar. Let sit for 24 hours at room temperature, and then, 48 hours in refrigeration.

Day 3
Add these ingredients to the mix, close the jar, and let sit for 24 hours at room temperature.

100 grams flour
100 grams water
100 grams starter from the day before

Day 4
Mix all the ingredients, and let sit in a closed jar for 24 hours at room temperature.

100 grams flour
100 grams water
100 grams starter from the day before

Day 5
Mix, and let sit in a closed jar for 24 hours at room temperature. Repeat the same process from day 6 thru 9.

200 grams flour
200 grams water
100 grams starter from the day before

Day 10
Feed the sourdough starter for the first time. Mix all the ingredientes, and let sit in a closed jar from 8 to 12 hours at 10°C-15°C.

200 grams flour
200 grams water
100 grams starter from the day before

Feed again your starter. Mix, and let sit in a closed jar from 8 to 12 hours at 10°C-15°C.

Once the 12 hours have passed, the sourdough starter is ready to use. Repeat the feeding process daily.

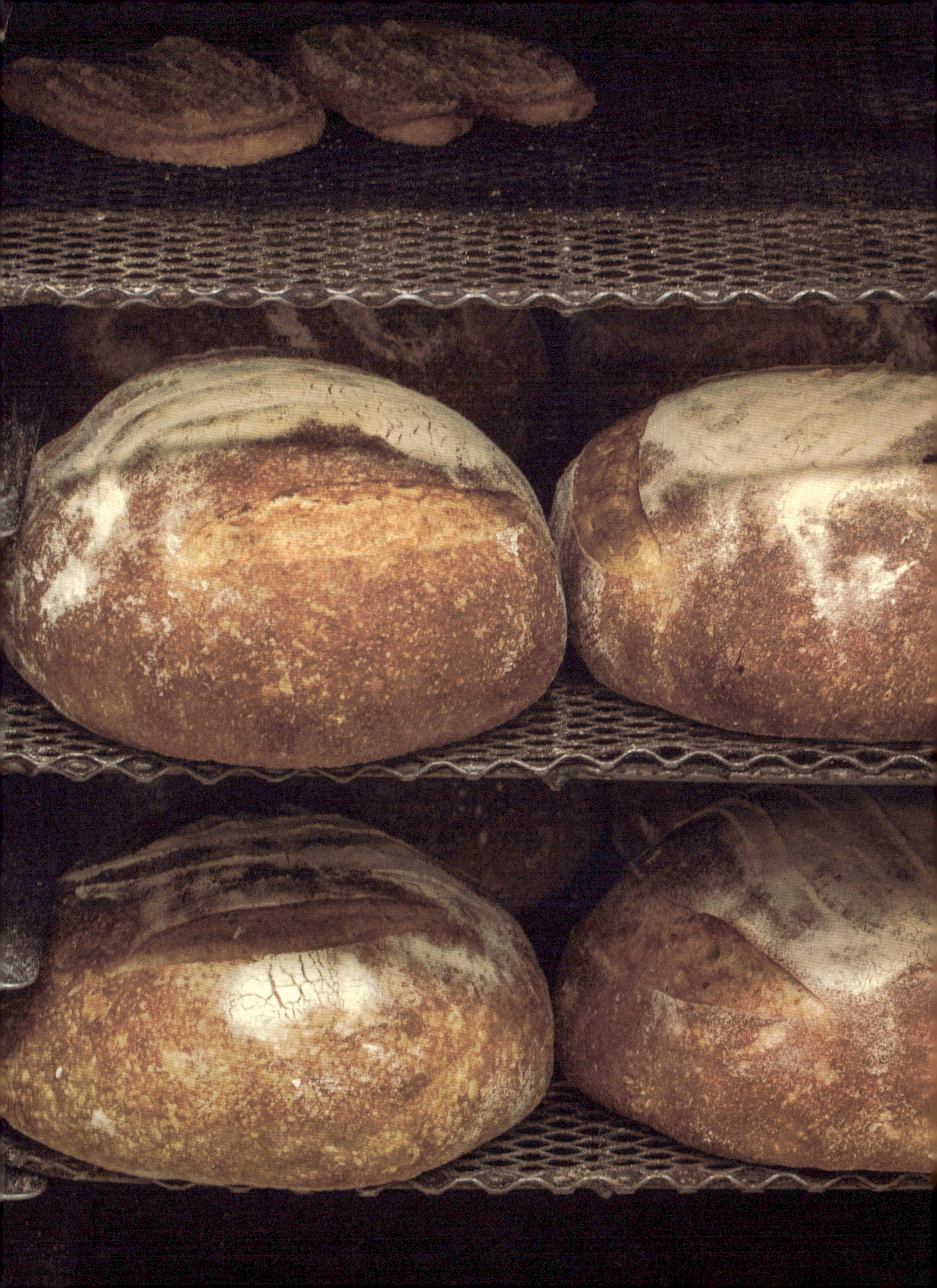

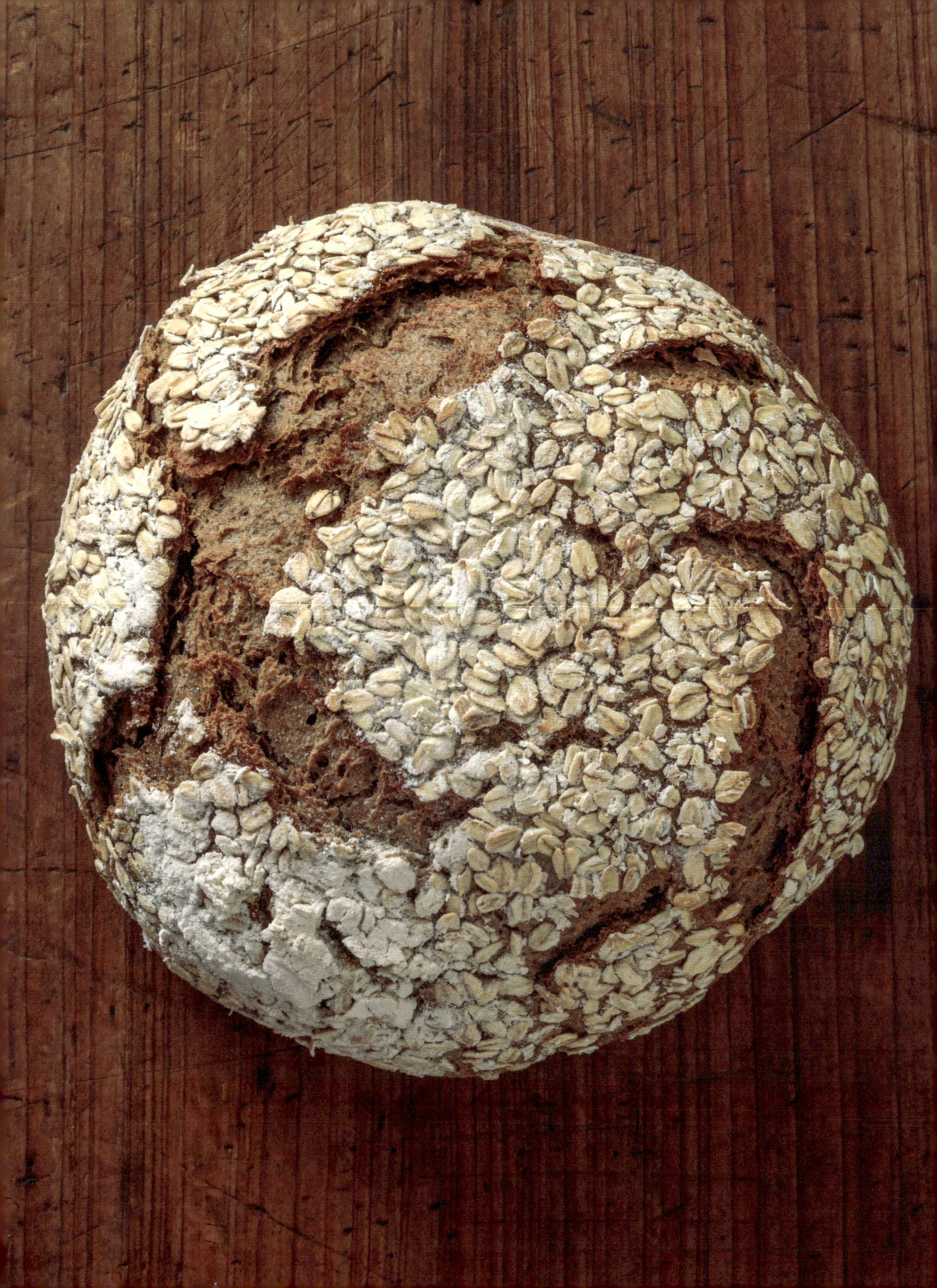

Ramón-flour bread

The Yucatán Peninsula—and the southeast region of Mexico in general—offers a vast diversity of ingredients. Traveling to this part of the country with some friends, I discovered that the ramón tree, which grows abundantly there, has a fruit that the local Mayan communities use in cooking: they dry it and grind it to make tortillas when there isn't enough corn, or they make it into a beverage that's consumed as a substitute for coffee.

Ramón isn't a grain, which means it has no gluten, so it must be combined with some sort of flour in order to ferment. At our Panadería, we mix it with wheat flour. We fold the dough only a few times so that it takes on a firm structure. The result is a dense, compact, slightly acidic bread that reminds me of German rye. It's fresh and aromatic, which makes it pair well with oysters, honey, and any kind of citric jam. What's more, ramón is full of proteins and antioxidants; we could improve our diets if we were more familiar with the fruit and consumed it more often.

Makes 3 pieces

1 kilogram high-protein wheat flour
250 grams ramón flour
25 grams salt
700 milliliters water
350 grams sourdough starter
350 grams rye starter
100 grams rolled oats

Place the flours and the salt in a large bowl, make a hollow in the middle, and pour in the sourdough starter and the water.

Mix together the flours and sourdough starter with your fingers in a circular motion from the middle outward.

Once everything is mixed together, transfer the dough to a wooden surface and start to knead it, striking it lightly against the surface until its texture is even and stretchy.

Place the dough in a bowl with a lid and let it sit at room temperature for 1 hour, or until it has doubled in size.

Press the dough to remove excess air and fold the ends inward to obtain a ball shape. Place it with its folds facing downward in the bowl, cover it, and let it sit for 30 minutes at room temperature. Repeat this process once more.

Place the dough onto a floured surface and divide it into 3 equal parts. Shape each piece into a ball.

Place the oats in a deep bowl. Take each piece of bread and dip its smooth surface into the oats so that they stick to the dough.

Place each piece in a basket with a lightly floured cloth, the oat-covered surface facing downward. Cover each piece with the cloth and let them sit for 1 hour or until they have doubled in size.

Transfer them to a baking sheet covered in parchment paper, turning over the basket so that the oats are facing upward.

Bake with steam at 260°C for 30 minutes. If necessary, rotate the baking sheet after 15 minutes for even browning.

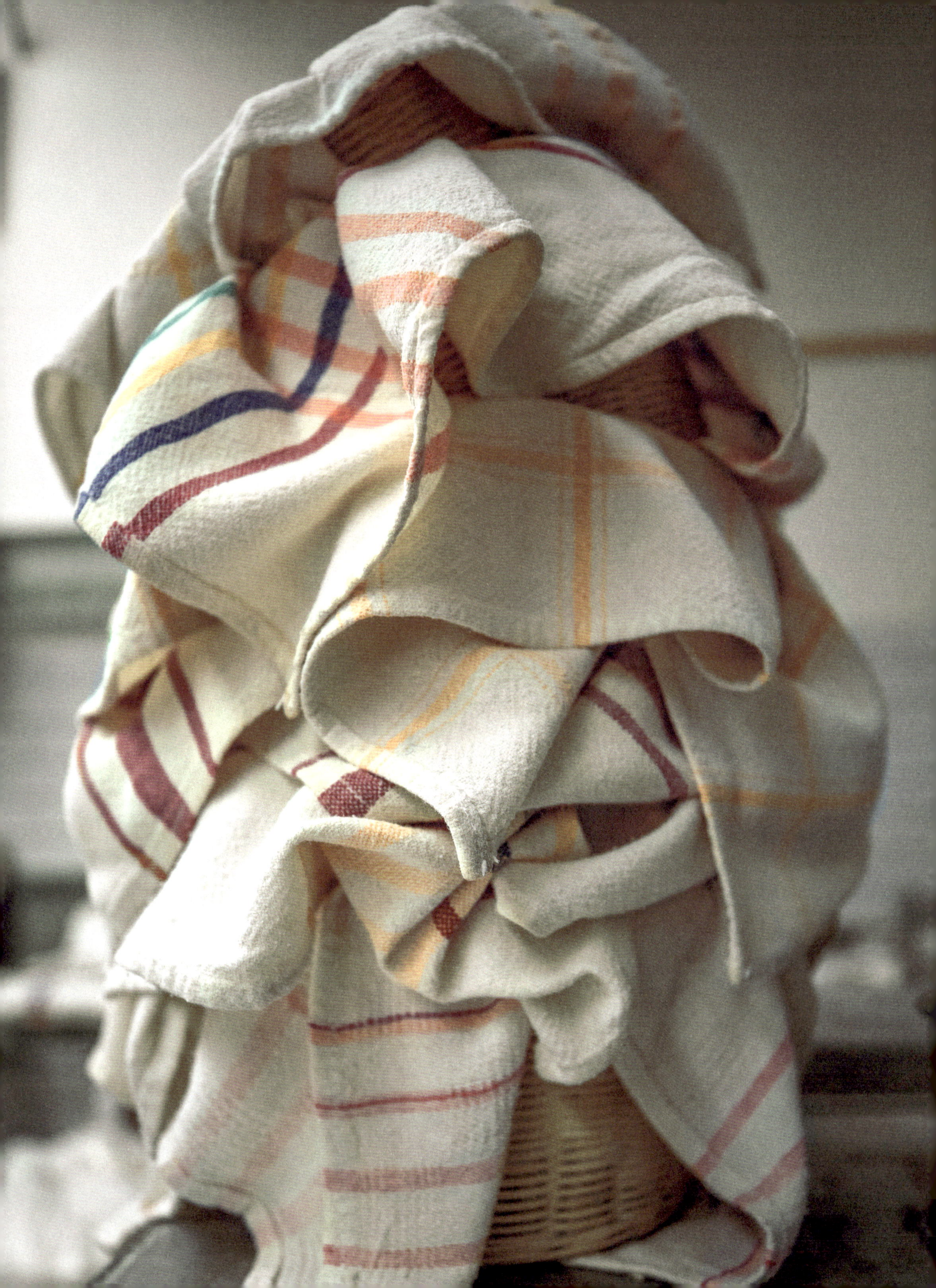

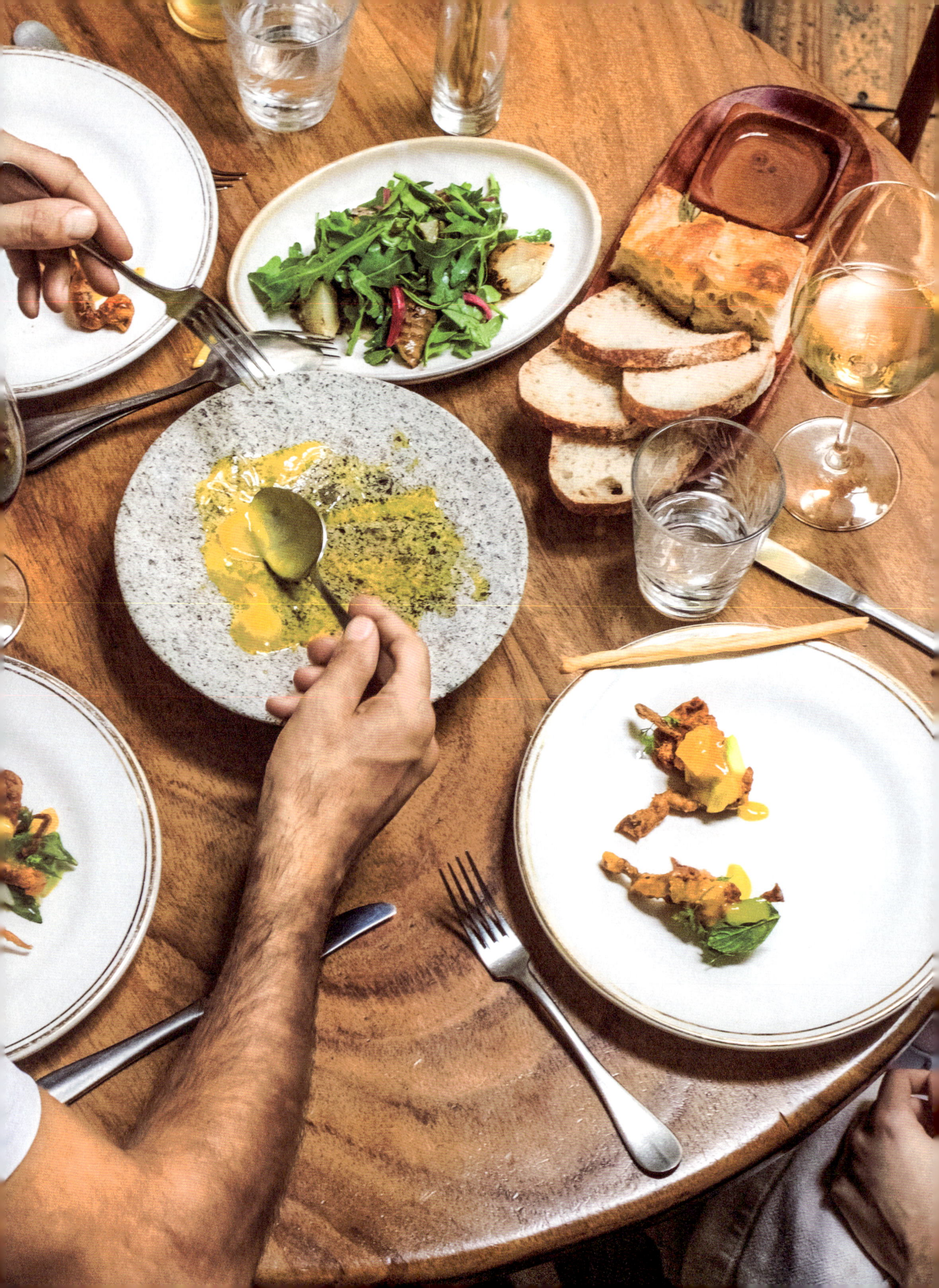

I

Beginnings

Cocopaches and nasturtium	42
Pickled Kumiai oysters, horseradish, borage flower, and samphire	45
Snails, habanero, red onion, and lime	49
Sweet shrimp aguachile	51
Burrata, anchovies, citron, buckwheat, and lemon basil	53
Endives, beets, orange, and pink pepper	57
Ingredients	63
Fennel, citrus, tarragon, and pomegranate	77
Yellowtail amberjack, muscatel plum, Asian pear, and red onion	79
White mole, carrots and charcoal oil	81
Pen shell scallops, vanilla, habanero, tangerine, and jicama	84
Quelites, avocado, lemon, and chicatana ants	87
More Than Food	91
Pickled sardines, farro, orange, celery, peppermint, and kalamata olives	97
Soft-shell crab, manila mango, habanero, and jicama	101
Persimmons, herbs, ricotta, lemon, and pistachios	102
Chicatana ant mole, pickled cucumbers and purslane	105

Cocopaches and nasturtium

Insects—protein-rich and uniquely flavored—are among the foodstuffs that have thrived in Mexico since the pre-Hispanic era. I'm especially fond of cocopaches, which live in mesquite trees in the states of Puebla, Hidalgo, and Oaxaca. In addition to their exceptional beauty, cocopaches have a different taste and texture than other insects. They're crunchy and creamy at the same time; they taste of both earth and butter. After they're caught, these insects are boiled, fried, and salted for purchase. They should be toasted in a hot pan to restore and intensify their flavor.

At Rosetta, we serve cocopaches inside nasturtium flowers, which have a pleasant spicy taste in addition to acting as a garnish. We fill these flowers with avocado purée, lemon, and a bit of chicatana ant vinaigrette to accentuate their earthy flavor.

Cocopaches make an excellent appetizer in the company of mezcal: their saltiness and the spicy nasturtium flowers whet the appetite. In Mexico, an aperitif is known as a botana. However, I think there's an important distinction between the two. While a drink is an essential element of an aperitif (vermouth, for example), the most important part of a botana is the food, although it's always accompanied by some sort of beverage (generally tequila, mezcal, or beer). The botaneo is not only the time when guests begin to develop an appetite; it's when conversation and company begin, too. The fact that the food is served at the center of the table to be shared—and that the food itself almost never calls for cutlery—encourages this.

Avocado purée

Serves 4

80 grams avocado pulp
5 grams zucchini skin
2 grams serrano pepper, seeded
15 milliliters lemon juice
20 milliliters water
1 pinch salt

Makes 120 grams
    Blend all the ingredients until they have the texture of purée.

Chicatana ant vinaigrette

90 grams chicatana ants
180 milliliters red wine vinegar
80 milliliters olive oil
10 grams salt

Makes 360 milliliters
    Clean the chicatanas, removing their wings and heads.
    Sauté them in a frying pan until they begin to release their own fat. Take care not to burn them. Spread them out on a tray to cool.
    In a food blender, grind the chicatanas with the vinegar and salt until completely blended. Add in the oil at the end.
    Place the mixture in a bowl and refrigerate.

To Serve

20 cocopaches
50 grams avocado purée
20 nasturtium flowers
10 milliliters chicatana ant vinaigrette

Brown the cocopaches in a hot frying pan.
    Place the avocado purée in a pastry bag or regular plastic bag. Close it and cut off a corner.
    Fill the nasturtium flowers with the avocado purée.
    Add a drop of chicatana ant vinaigrette on top of the purée.
    Insert the browned cocopache in the avocado so that half is inside the flower and half is outside.
    Serve immediately.

Beginnings

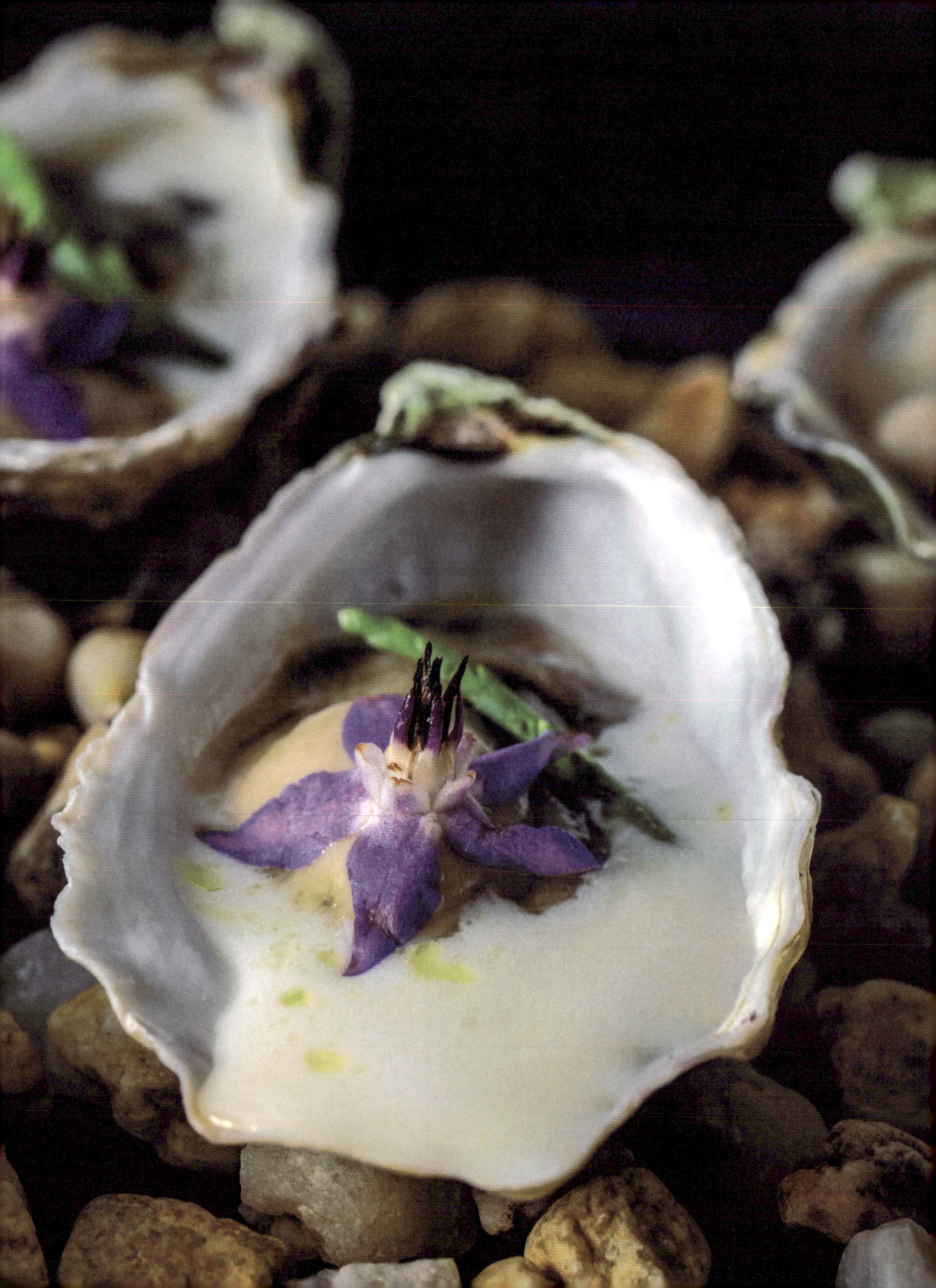

Pickled Kumiai oysters, horseradish, borage flower, and samphire

Pickling is a technique used to preserve food in vinegar, oil, and spices. We use it quite a lot at Rosetta, mostly with vegetables and seafood. In the case of oysters, pickling transforms their consistency, in addition to making them last longer and suffusing them with a vinegary aroma. When the oysters are cooked lightly in vinegar, their flesh grows firm. Different spices can be used to perfume the vinegar in the brine. For these oysters, we use not only the traditional spices (bay leaf, pepper, and clove), but also cinnamon, which gives them a spicy sweetness. Choosing the right type of oyster is crucial for pickling. The fleshy, creamy ones are best, like Kumiai oysters, which come from the San Quintín estuary in Baja California. To balance out the acidity of the brine, we combine the oysters with a yogurt-based horseradish ice cream.

Horseradish ice cream

Serves 4

560 grams yogurt
130 grams sugar
46.5 grams glucose
235 milliliters milk
7 grams salt
30 grams finely grated horseradish

Makes 1 liter

Place the milk, sugar, glucose, and salt in a saucepan, heat them until the temperature reaches 85°C, and remove them from the heat.
Add the grated horseradish and let it infuse for 15 minutes.
Blend the mixture and strain it.
Once the mixture has cooled to 40°C, whisk in the yogurt.
Refrigerate for 6 to 12 hours.
Transfer the mixture to the ice cream machine and run until smooth.

To Serve

24 small Kumiai oysters
2 whole cloves
60 milliliters white vinegar
10 black peppercorns
2 grams whole cinnamon
2 bay leaves
100 milliliters olive oil
4 grams garlic
48 grams horseradish ice cream
8 grams samphire
8 grams parsley
24 borage flowers

Clean the oysters, setting aside the juices. Remove them from their shells, making sure to clean off any sand or bits of shell.

Place them in a bowl with their juices and refrigerate.

For the brine, heat the vinegar with the cloves, peppercorns, cinnamon, and bay leaves. Bring to a boil, remove from the heat, and let it sit.

Heat the olive oil in a saucepan with the garlic. Fry until before the garlic starts to brown.

Remove the pan from the heat and remove the garlic from the oil.

With the heat still on, strain the vinegar into the oil and emulsify with a whisk.

Add the oysters to the still-heating mixture and let them steep for approximately 5 minutes without letting them cook.

Add a third of the oyster juice to give the mixture a salty taste and lower the temperature. Let it cool in the refrigerator.

Prepare the shells, cleaning them of any spots, and let them cool in the freezer for 5 minutes.

Remove the shells from the freezer and place 4 grams of horseradish ice cream inside each one.

In each shell, add a cold oyster and ½ teaspoon brine, then add the samphire, the parsley, and the borage flowers.

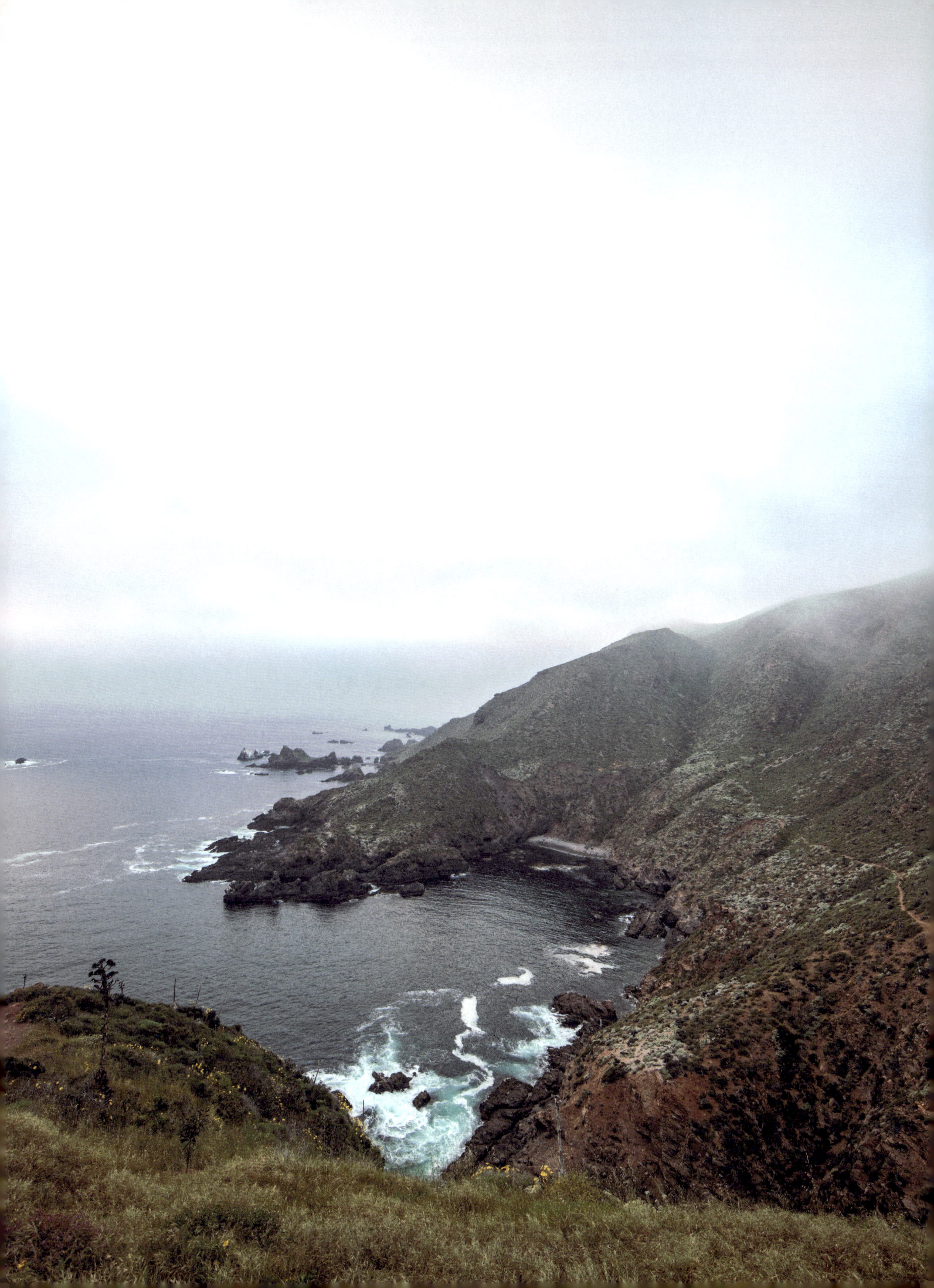

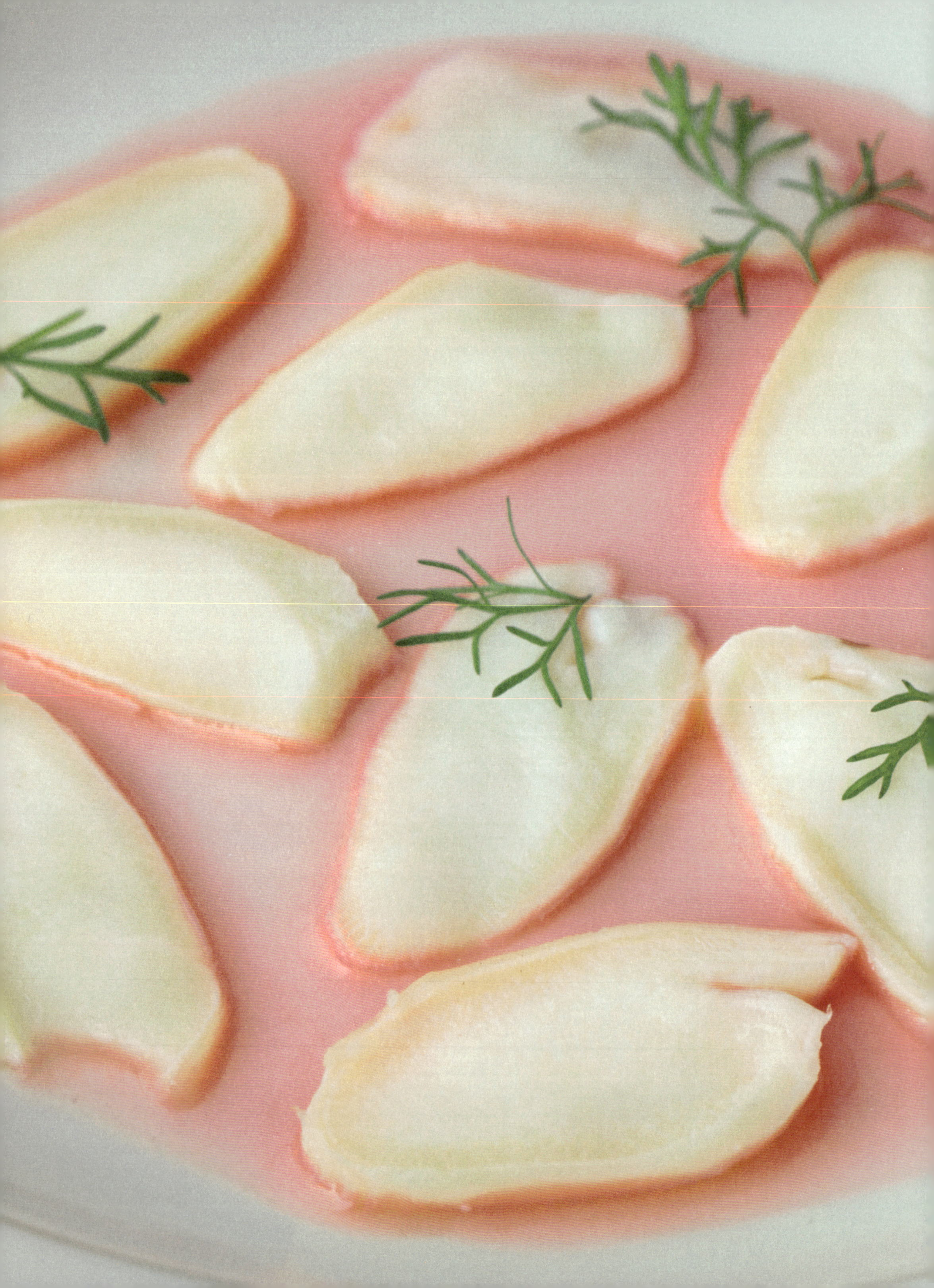

Snails, habanero, red onion, and lime

At Rosetta, we like to know where our ingredients come from. When possible, we also like to get to know the people who produce them. For example, when we use snails, we use the Machachán variety, also known as the white snail, which comes from the Pacific Ocean. It's an absolute delicacy, its flavor is sweet, its texture firm. With shellfish as delicate as these snails, we prefer them to speak for themselves, so the ingredients accompanying them shouldn't overshadow their taste.

Both to respect the snail's fine flavor and to exalt it, we serve them in a pink juice made by steeping habanero pepper and red onion in lime. One might think that these two ingredients would overpower the snails. Surprisingly, though, the steeping process draws out their flavor and eliminates the burning sensation we associate with them. In this way, three flavors that would initially overwhelm each other come into coexistence; in fact, they even reinforce one another.

Serves 4

200 milliliters lime juice
120 grams julienned red onion
2 snails
4 grams coarse salt
7 grams green habanero pepper
40 milliliters olive oil
20 cilantro leaves

Mix the lime juice with the red onion. Refrigerate and allow them to infuse for at least 2 hours or until the onion has released its color into the juice.

Clean off the snails with lots of water. Using a knife, remove the skin of the snails and set aside only the softest meat.

Take a very sharp knife and cut each snail into slices approximately 2 millimeters thick.

Spread the slices of snail meat onto wax paper and season with coarse salt on both sides.

Arrange the slices of snail meat in shallow bowls.

Slice the habanero pepper down the middle and seed it. Squeeze the pepper lightly to extract the oils that contain its scent, immerse it in the lime juice and onion, and remove it after 2 minutes. If you want a spicier juice, let the pepper soak for longer.

Strain the lime and red onion mixture and cover the snail slices with juice.

Add a few drops of olive oil and the cilantro leaves onto each plate.

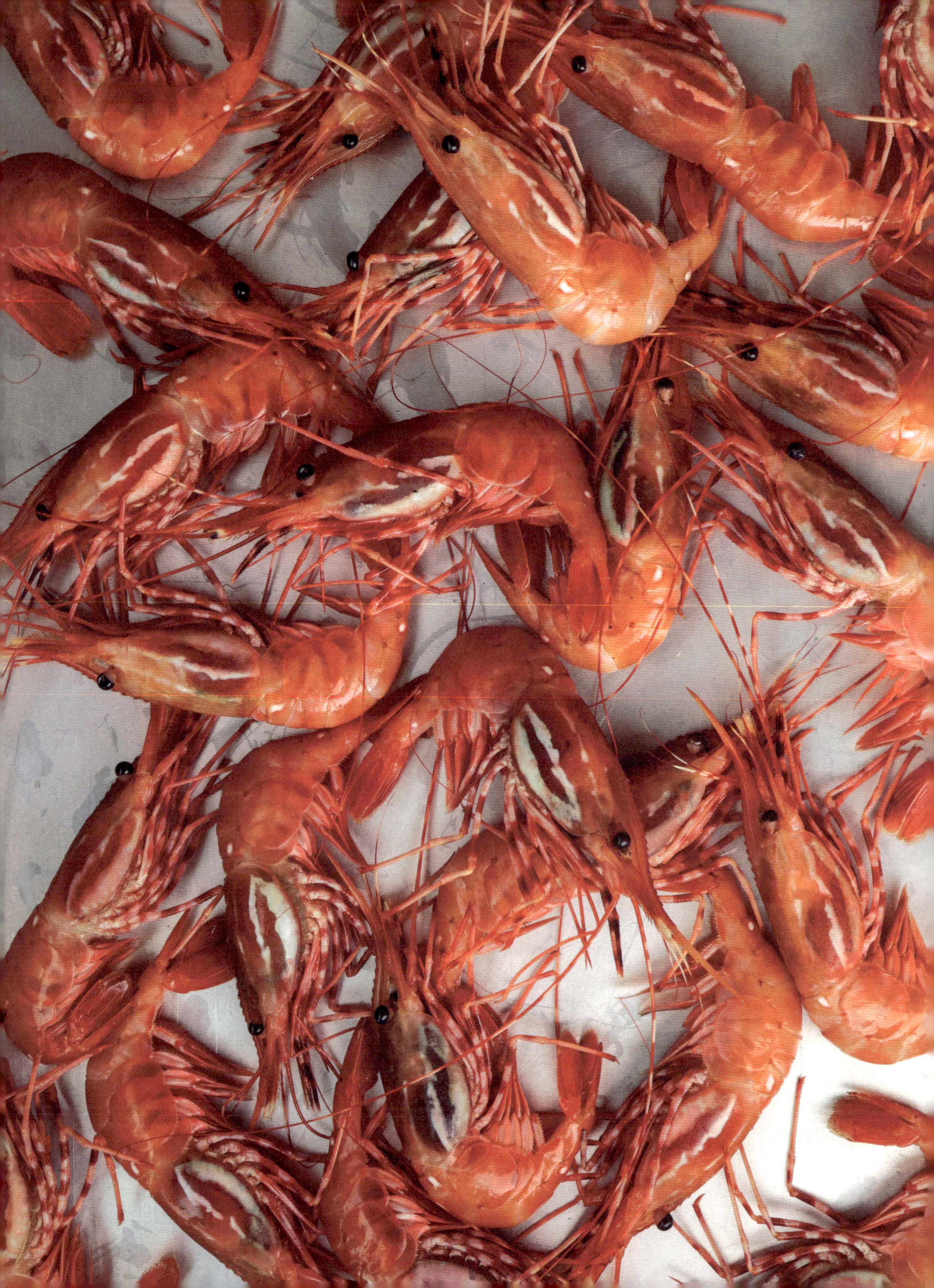

Sweet shrimp aguachile

The sweet shrimp is easy to identify because of its intense red color and its size: it's substantially larger than farmed or shallow-water shrimp. Its flavor is incredibly sweet, but it has a buttery taste that distinguishes it from other varieties. This kind of shrimp can be eaten completely raw. Since it lives in the depths of the ocean, where the water is far colder than at the surface, its flesh is fatty and delicate.

On the Mexican coasts, raw shrimp is typically eaten as an aguachile: a dish that involves cooking and serving seafood in lime juice with hot pepper. We make this popular dish at Rosetta, but we've adapted it so that the sweet shrimp's delicate flavor won't be overwhelmed by the intense acidity and spiciness that characterize an aguachile. We achieved this by mixing the aguachile with another traditional recipe: caldo de camarón (shrimp broth), made by boiling the heads and shells, which is actually where the shrimp's most prominent flavor is found. We serve the sweet shrimp raw, in this mixture of aguachile and broth. In this way, the taste and delicate consistency of the shrimp are preserved—at the same time as the acidity, spice, and sweetness awaken our taste buds and help us perceive the subtle layering of flavors.

Kumquats in syrup

Serves 4

75 grams sugar
100 milliliters water
100 milliliters green lime juice
150 grams kumquats

Makes 100 grams

Make a syrup out of the sugar, water, and lime juice, heating them in a pot over low heat and then letting the mixture cool.

Transfer the syrup to a hermetically sealed bag along with the halved kumquats.

Submerge the bag for 3 minutes in a pot of boiling water.

Remove the bag from the pot and submerge it in ice water to stop the cooking process.

Remove the skin from the kumquats and julienne it very finely.

Shrimp broth

800 grams clean shrimp shells and heads
8 grams peeled garlic
60 grams white onion
80 grams peeled carrots
8 grams parsley stalks
2 liters water

Makes 1 liter

Wash the shrimp heads thoroughly, removing the content and leaving only the shell.

Place the garlic, onion, carrots, and parsley stalks into a pot. Cook over medium heat until they start to brown.

Add the shrimp heads and shells and cook for 5 minutes. Add the water and let it boil for 20 minutes.

Blend the contents of the pot, then return the mixture to the pot and let it reduce by half. Strain and cool.

Lemon shrimp stock

1 gram charred habanero
12 milliliters lemon juice
50 milliliters shrimp broth
1 pinch salt

Makes 60 milliliters

Wash and seed the charred pepper. Blend all the ingredients, gradually adding in the pepper.

Orange juice reduction

800 milliliters orange juice

Makes 200 milliliters

In a small pot add the orange juice in medium heat. Let it reduce to a quarter.

To Serve

280 grams sweet shrimp
2 grams salt flakes
30 milliliters lemon juice
80 grams kumquat skin in syrup
2.5 grams peppermint
50 milliliters lemon shrimp stock
20 milliliters olive oil
200 milliliters of orange juice reduction

Wash the shrimp, removing their heads and shells.

Use a knife to make a cut along the underside, butterfly them, and cut them into fourths. Season with salt flakes and lemon juice.

Arrange the shrimp on a plate and add the kumquat skin, peppermint, and spicy shrimp juice.

Add a few drops of olive oil and the orange juice reduction.

Burrata, anchovies, citron, buckwheat, and lemon basil

After spending a summer in southern Sicily, I developed a taste for anchovies. Their intensely aquatic, fermented flavor makes them perfect for seasoning; they give a strong jolt of umami to many dishes. To make this burrata, we dilute anchovies with oil and a little cream. In this way, their taste isn't overpowering, but they still provide their characteristic salinity and flavor. In this case, they also contrast with the sweet creaminess of the burrata.

Citron is another spectacular ingredient. It looks like a bright yellow grapefruit, and although it doesn't have much juice and is extremely bitter, the scent of its thick, coarse skin is exquisite: an aroma somewhere between lemon and lime, both sweet and citric. Its albedo—the spongy white tissue under the skin of citrus fruits—is what makes it so special: it's thick and not very bitter, which allows us to use the entire fruit. We soak half the slices in bittersweet vinegar, cooking the other half gently in a light syrup.

Toasted buckwheat lends this dish a pleasing crunch, and lemon basil gives it a hint of herbal acidity.

Anchovy sauce

Serves 4

88 grams anchovies
10 grams egg yolk
75 milliliters olive oil
100 grams heavy cream

Makes 260 grams

Heat the anchovies in a double boiler and use a fork to make sure they dissolve completely.

Beat the egg yolk and gradually stream the oil. Add in the dissolved anchovies and beat the mixture.

Finally, add in the heavy cream and continue to beat until the sauce is creamy.

Citron in syrup

35 grams sugar
100 milliliters water
2 thin slices citron

Makes 2 slices

Make a syrup with the water and sugar and let cool.
Add the lemons to the still-warm syrup.
Let the syrup cool, remove the liquid, and cut each slice into 8 triangles.

Beginnings

Citron in vinegar

15 milliliters white wine vinegar
15 milliliters water
2 slices citron

Makes 2 slices

Mix the vinegar with the water.
Add the citron slices to the mixture. Leave them there for 2 hours.
Strain the mixture so that only the citron slices are left. Cut each slice into 8 triangles.

To Serve

80 milliliters anchovy sauce
4 pieces burrata
1 pinch salt flakes
12 grams fried farro
15 milliliters olive oil
2 slices citron in syrup
2 slices citron in vinegar
4 grams lemon basil leaves

Spoon some anchovy sauce into the center of each plate and spread it out lightly. Place a burrata piece on top of it; sprinkle a few salt flakes; add fried farro and olive oil; and, finally, add the citron in syrup and citron in vinegar, alternating between the two.
Add lemon basil leaves.

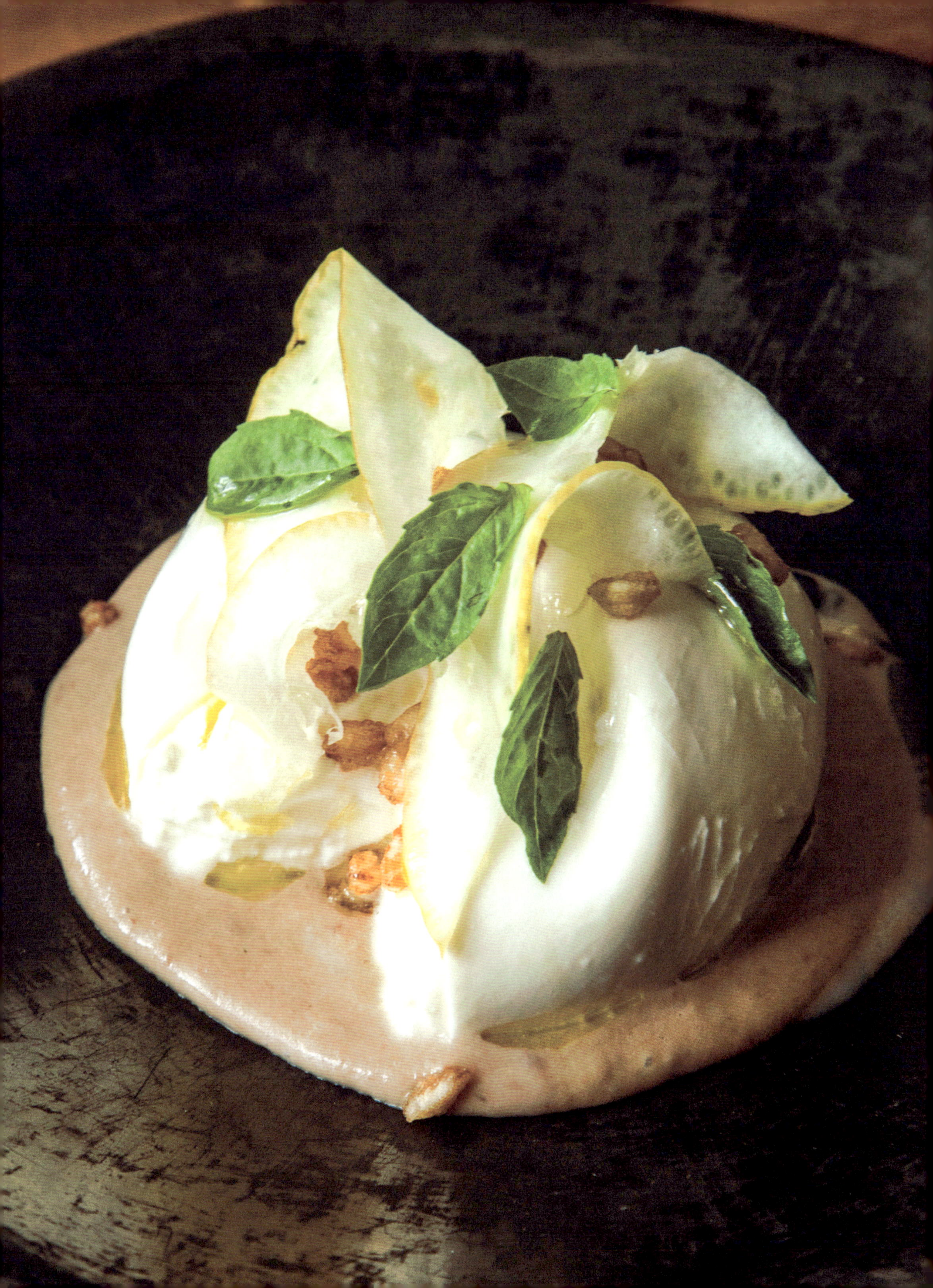

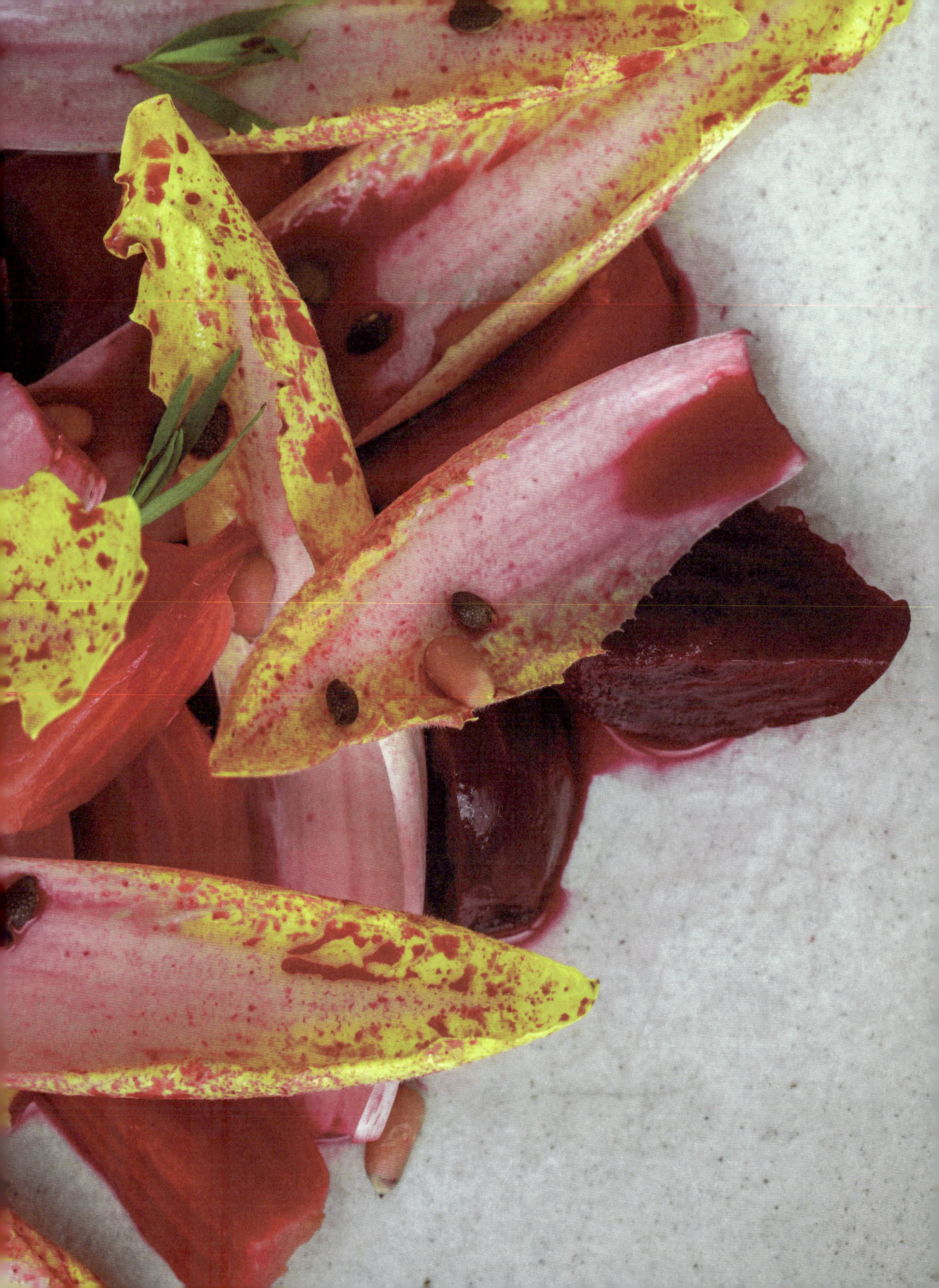

Endives, beets, orange, and pink pepper

This dish came about when we dissected the recipe for pink mole. We realized that what distinguishes it from other moles are the spices, especially pink pepper, and beet. We took these elements and turned them into a vinaigrette. Which became, in a way, a liquid distillation of the pink mole, in both flavor and color.

Based on this vinaigrette, we decided on the other ingredients that would make up the dish. Because it's spiced, sweet, and acidic, vinaigrette calls for bitterness—which we found in endives. With endives alone, however, the result was too light; beets gave it a greater consistency and density. The orange diluted the high concentration of the vinaigrette, softening its acidity at the same time. The pink pine nuts added a fatty touch—and I'd almost call them a natural fit, because they're also an ingredient in the pink mole. The passion fruit seeds contributed texture; tarragon, anise-flavored freshness.

Pink pepper vinaigrette

Serves 4

200 grams beets sliced in cubes
500 milliliters white wine vinegar
20 grams pink pepper
5 grams cumin seeds
10 grams cloves
10 grams cumin seeds
2 grams dried thyme
2 dried bay leaves
1 pinch of salt
1 piece of chipotle
200 grams red beet, peeled and diced into cubes
250 milliliters water

Makes 1 liter

Warm the vinegar over low heat in a small covered pot. Pour the warm vinegar over the beets and let them rest for 20 minutes.

Place the beets and the water in a pot and cook for 20 minutes over low heat.

Combine both mixtures in a bottle and shake well. Refrigerate.

Beginnings

To Serve

160 grams red beets
160 grams pink beets
2 oranges
20 grams pink pine nuts
2 grams passion fruit seeds
200 grams endives
4 grams fresh tarragon
80 milliliters pink pepper vinaigrette
40 milliliters olive oil
2 grams fleur de sal

Place the beets in a baking pan, 5 centimeters deep, with 1 centimeter of water. Bake at 180°C for 1 hour or until well cooked.

Remove the beets from the oven, peel them, and cut them into fourths or eighths, depending on the size. Set them aside until needed.

Remove the skin from the orange wedges with a very sharp knife, then cut the wedges down the middle.

Toast the pine nuts in the oven at 180°C for 3 minutes. Repeat this process with the passion fruit seeds.

Cut 1 centimeter off the end of the endives so you can separate the leaves from the stalk and place them in a bowl. Season the endives with salt and pink pepper vinaigrette, then mix them well with your hands.

Arrange the endives on a plate along with the beets, orange wedges, pink pine nuts, and passion fruit seeds.

Add the fresh tarragon, the rest of the vinaigrette left in the bowl with the endives, the salt and a few drops of olive oil.

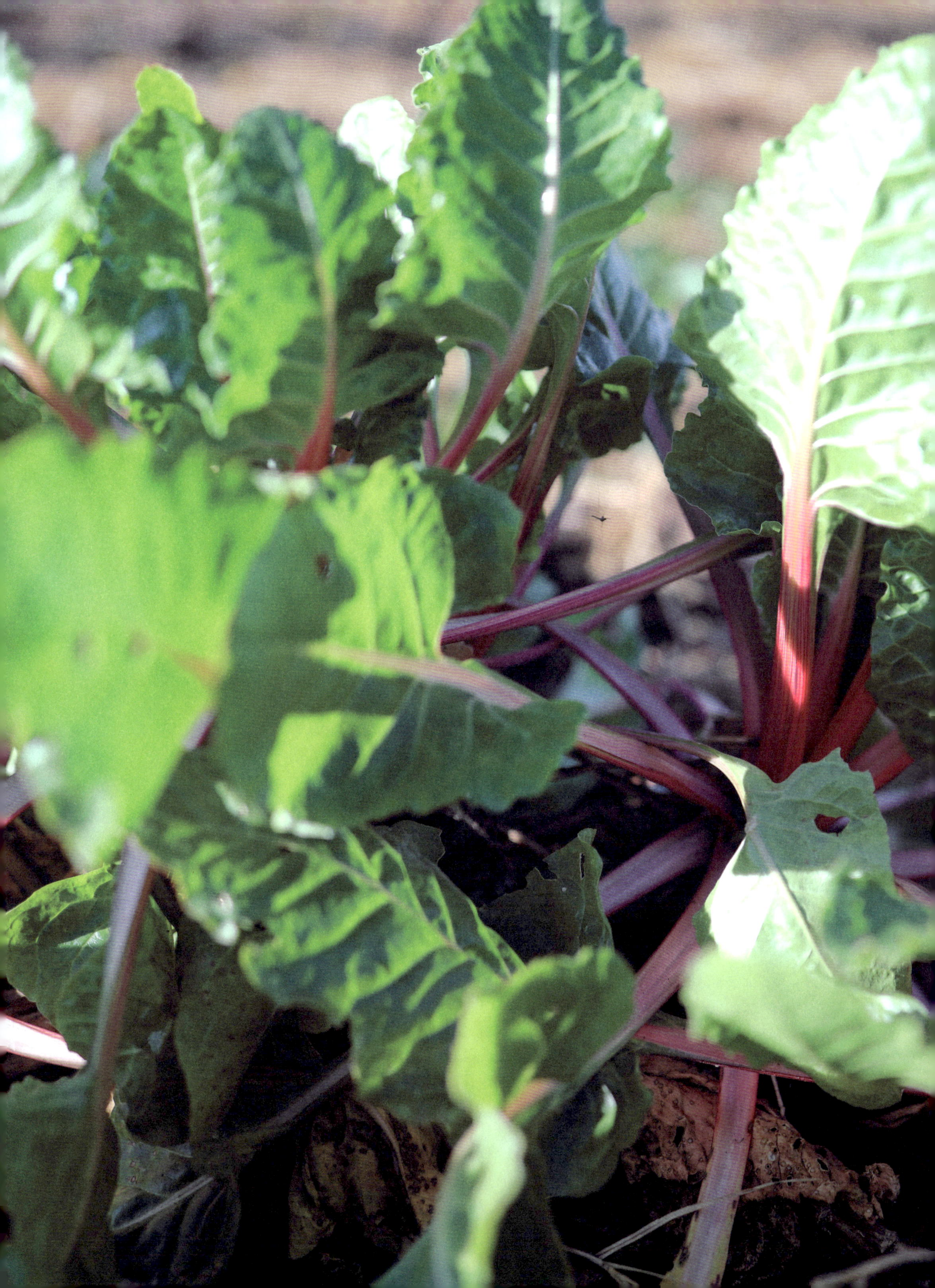

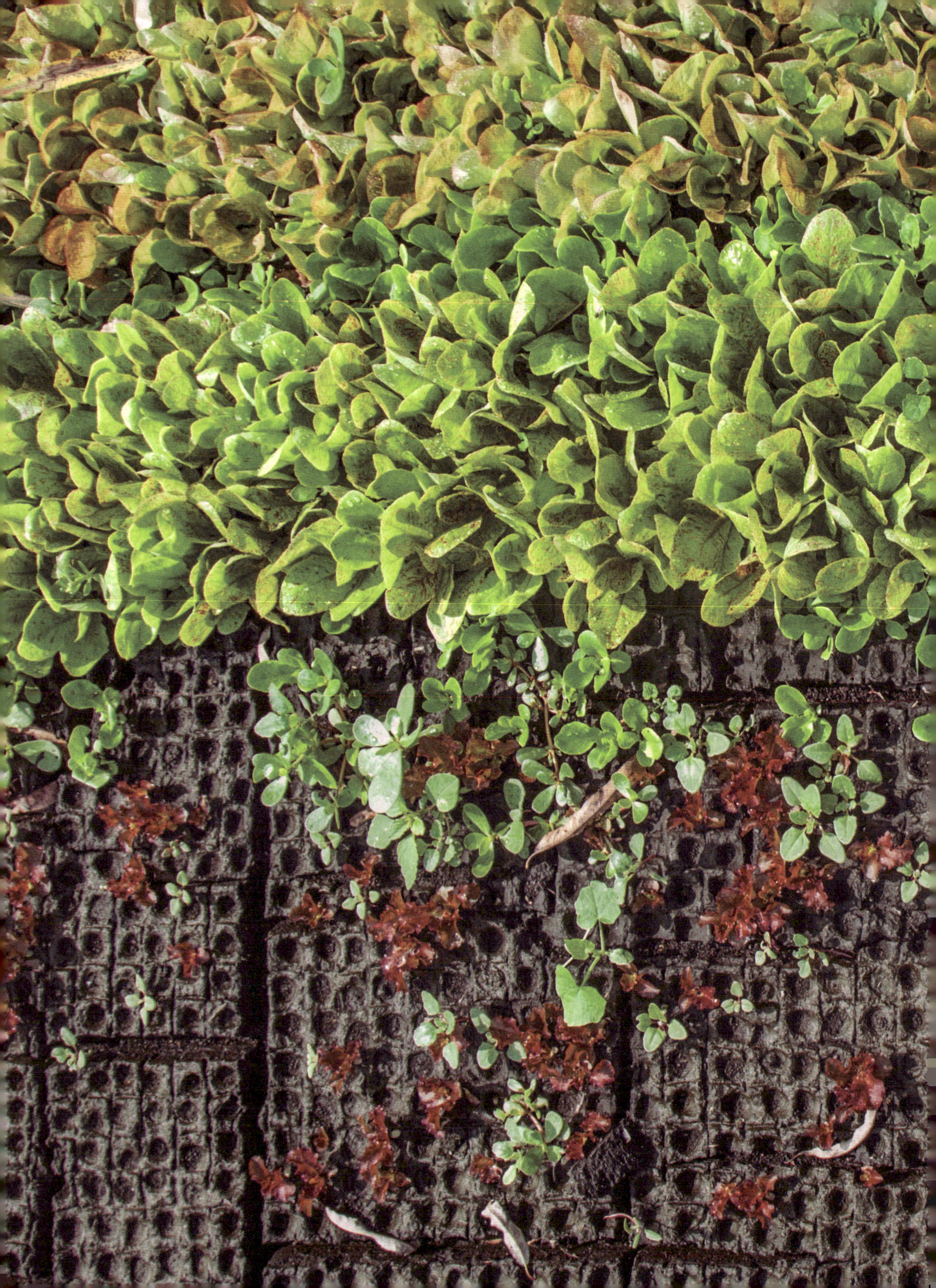

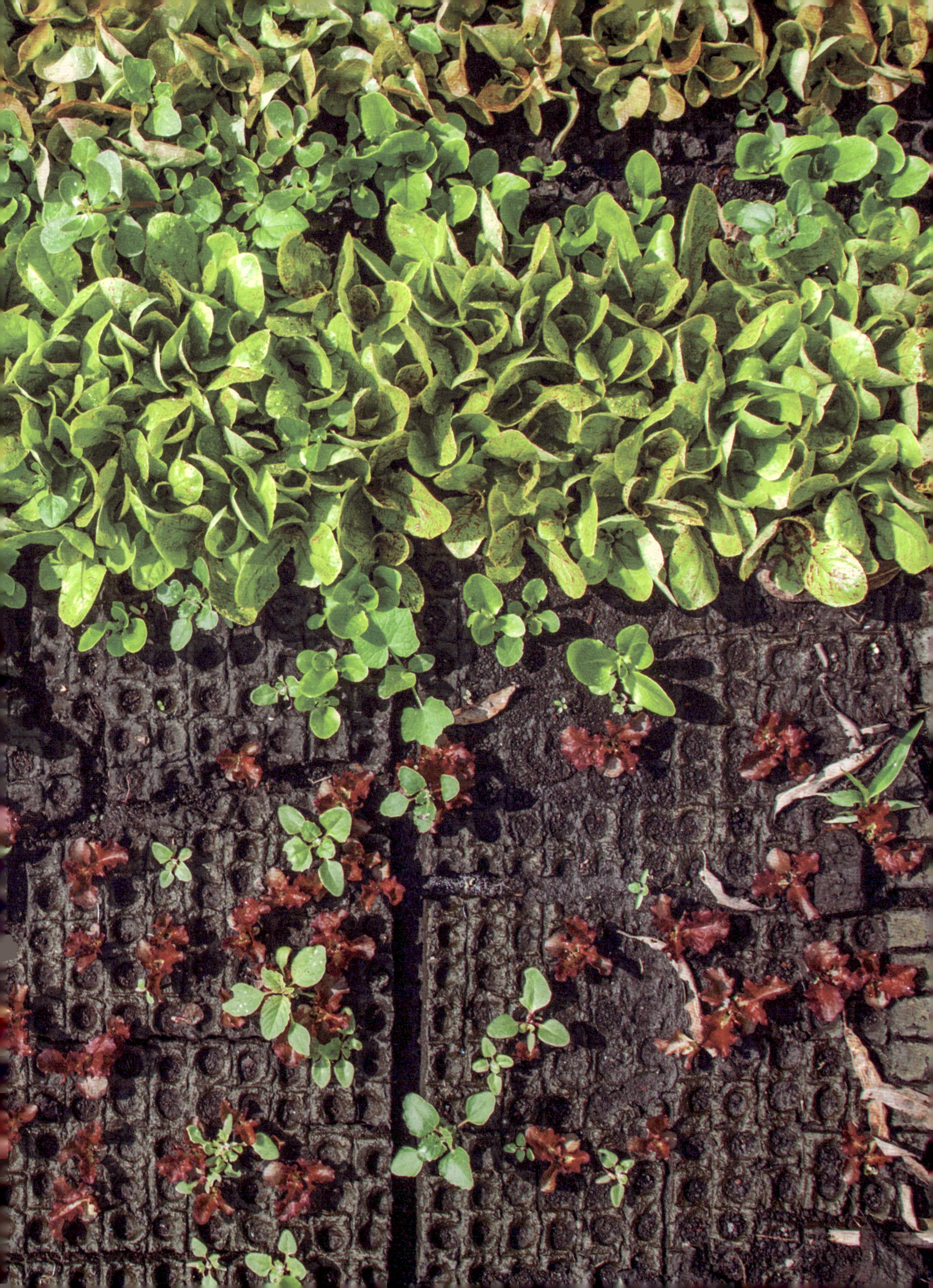

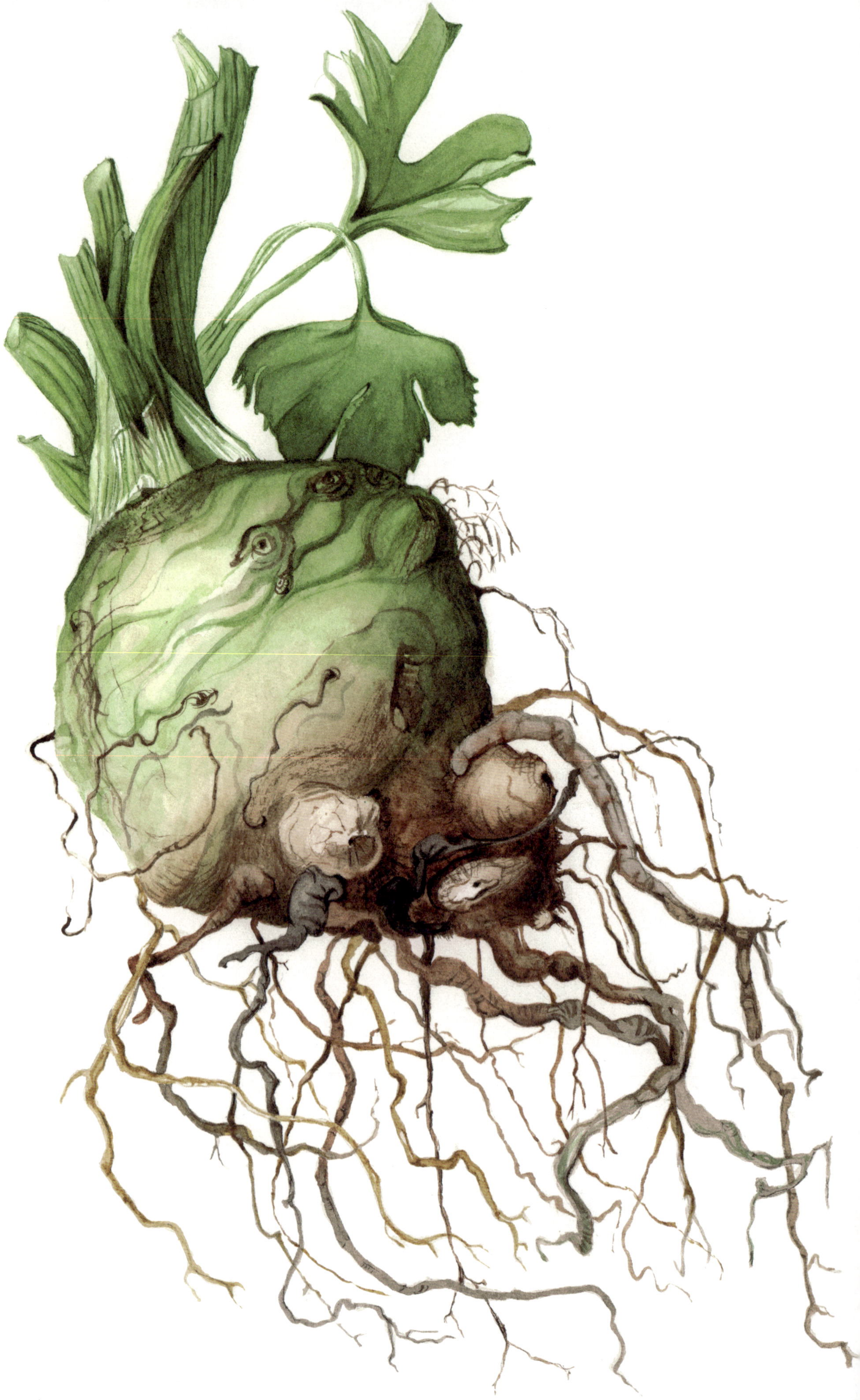

Ingredients

For me, nothing is more important than ingredients. Not even technique. When I cook, I want the ingredients to shine; I don't want to hide them away. I want to focus on their flavor and seek to accentuate it. When I come up with a new dish, I almost always imagine it based on a specific ingredient, exploring its different possibilities. Then I explore its affinities with other ingredients. I make combinations, trying to ensure that no single ingredient overwhelms another.

At Rosetta, we respect ingredients not only in terms of their flavor, but also in terms of their natural cycles. We understand that not all ingredients are available twelve months of the year. We have to learn about the lifetime of each one: to know at what point or during what season it's best consumed. We don't like forcing nature to do anything. And we don't expect our ingredients to always be exactly the same, as if they were made in a factory. In fact, we love observing how ingredients vary in flavor, size, color, and texture, depending on the weather or the conditions of the soil where they grew. Their natural variability stimulates our creativity.

We use local ingredients because we want to respect their flavor and freshness; because we're concerned about the environment; and because we want to collaborate with small-scale producers. It's problematic to import ingredients from far-away places because they deteriorate in transit: as time passes, their flavor wanes and their nutritional properties are diluted. Besides, importation often entails a serious carbon footprint, especially when products are transported in a short time span.

My definition of "local" is a non-restrictive one. As I see it, "local" doesn't necessarily mean endemic products. Its meaning is nearly literal: ingredients grown and produced across the land we call Mexico. Over the years, I've tried to depart from traditionally Mexican elements and make use of other ingredients that aren't commonly associated with our country.

One of the driving forces behind my work is to find little-known or under-used ingredients and to share them through my cooking. I want to somehow broaden people's palates while simultaneously encouraging biodiversity. I work, in my own context, to be part of the resistance against the industrialized and globalized food market, which tends toward homogeneity, poor nutrition, and labor exploitation.

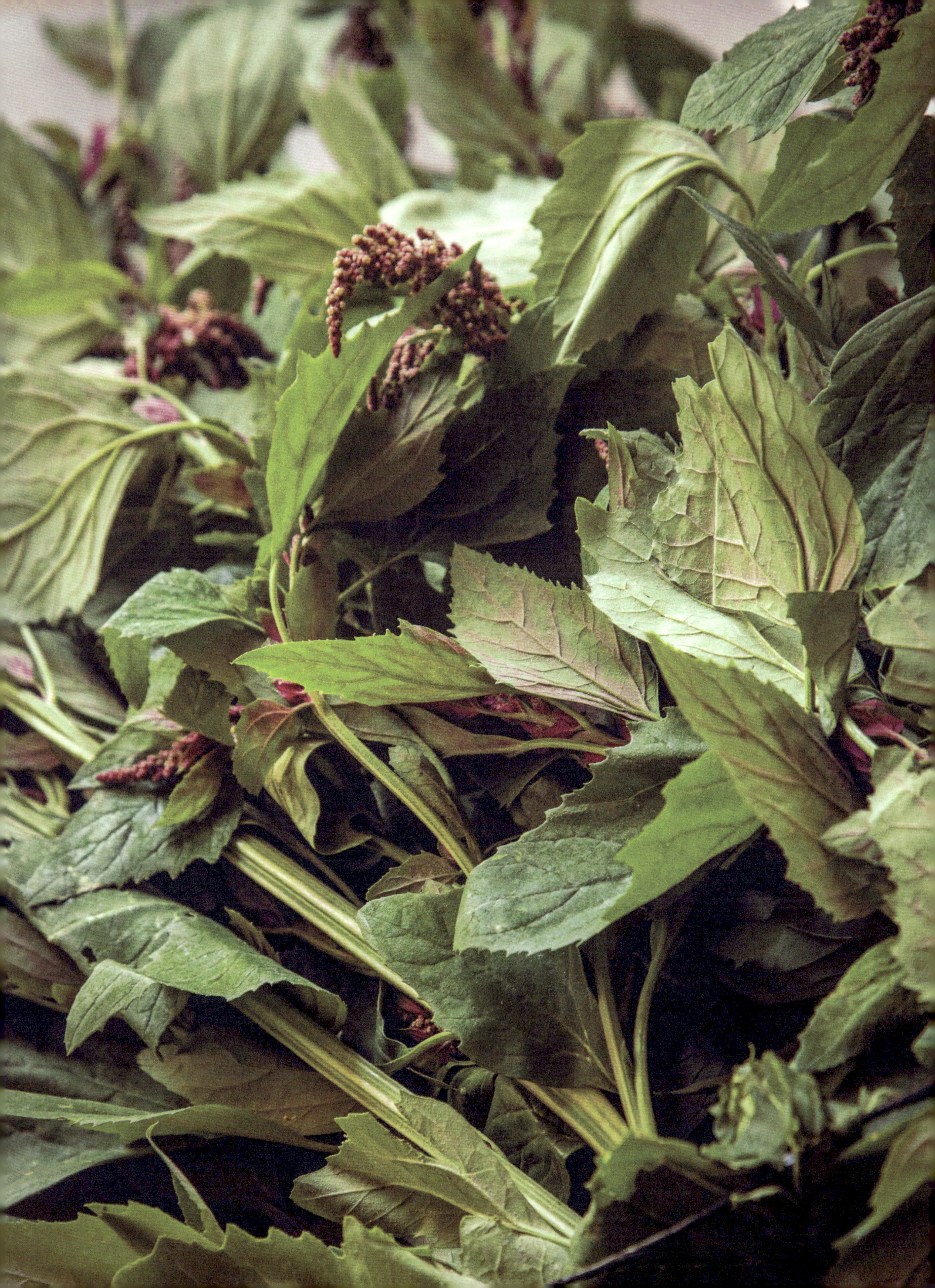

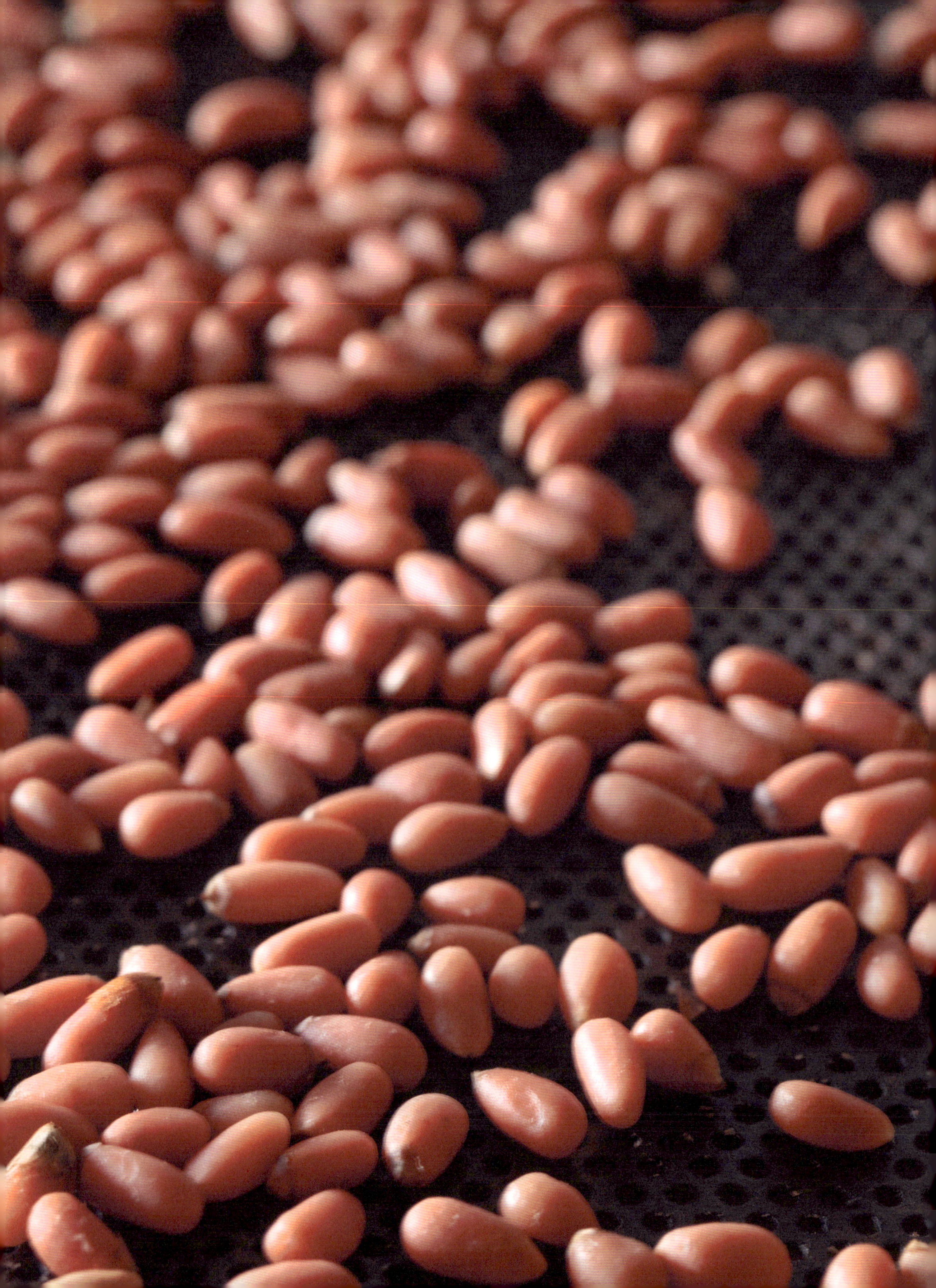

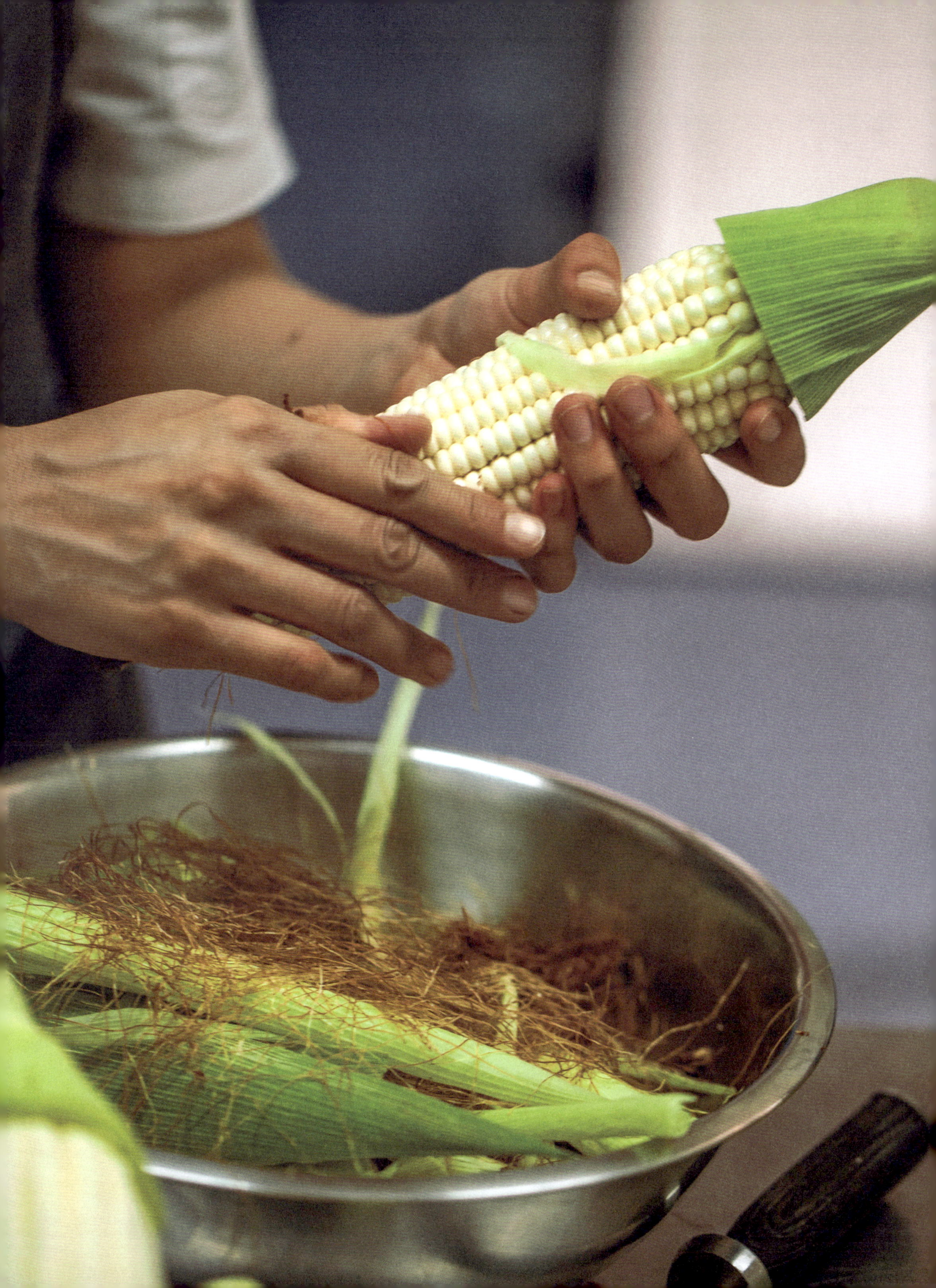

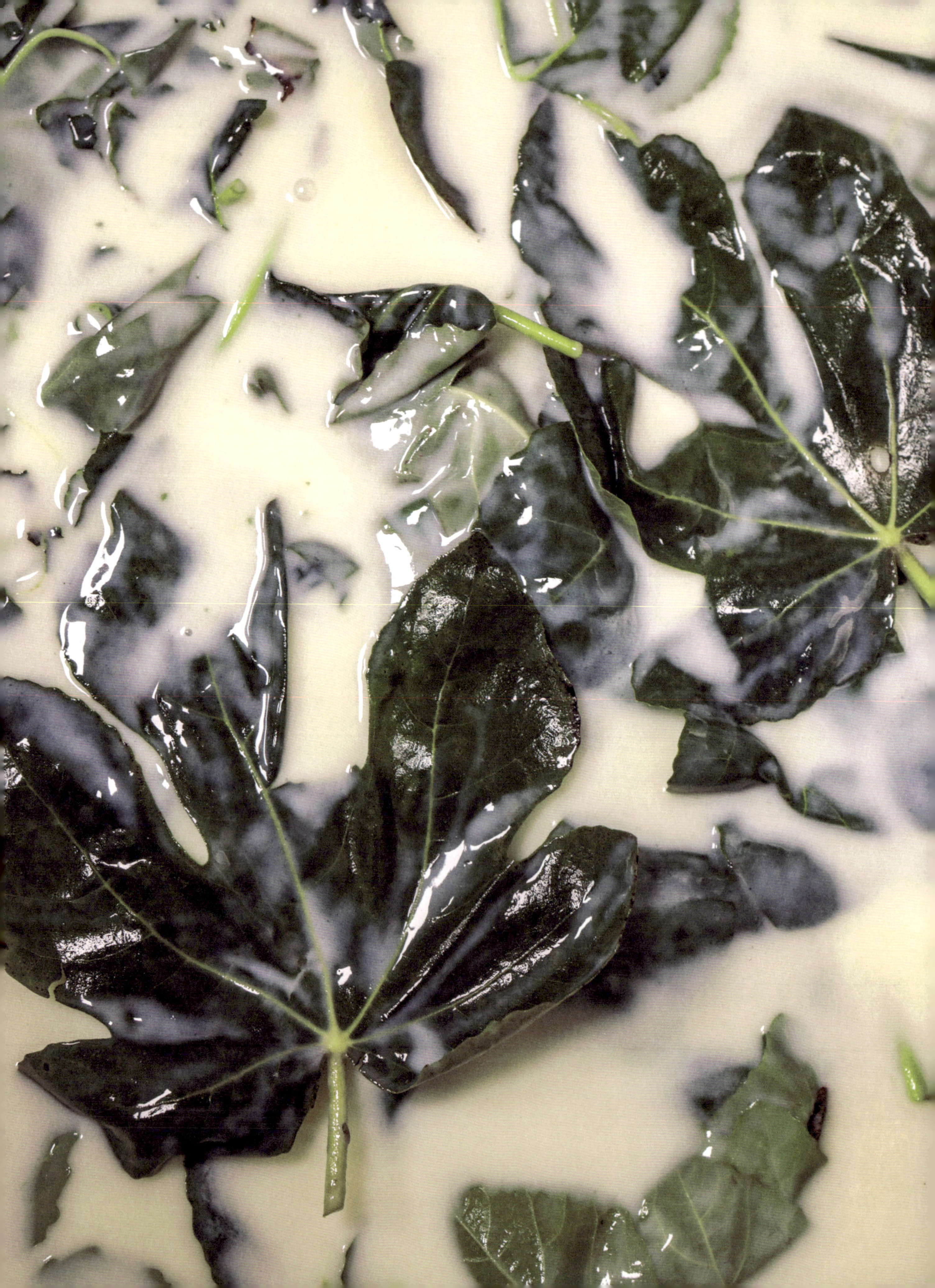

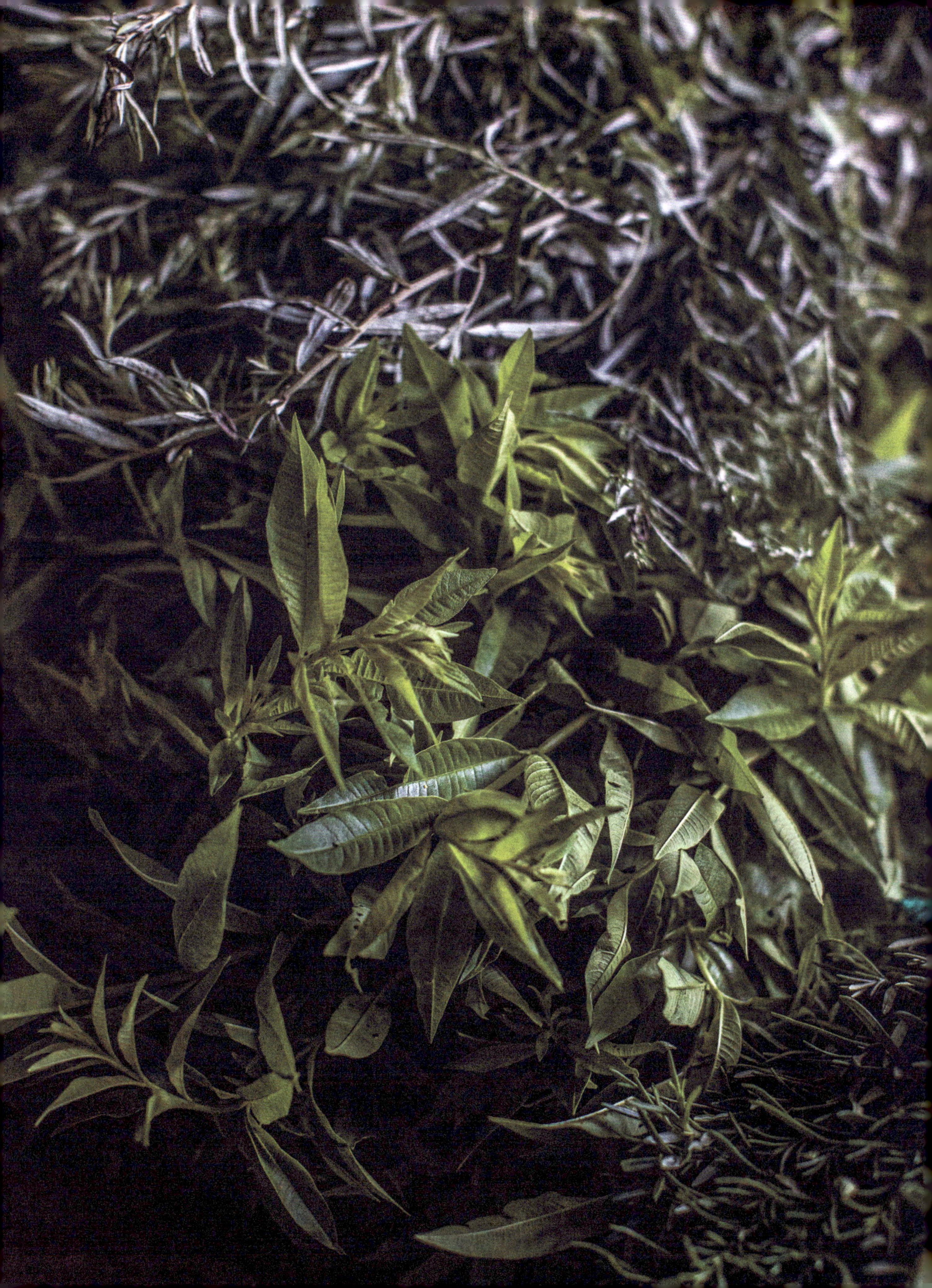

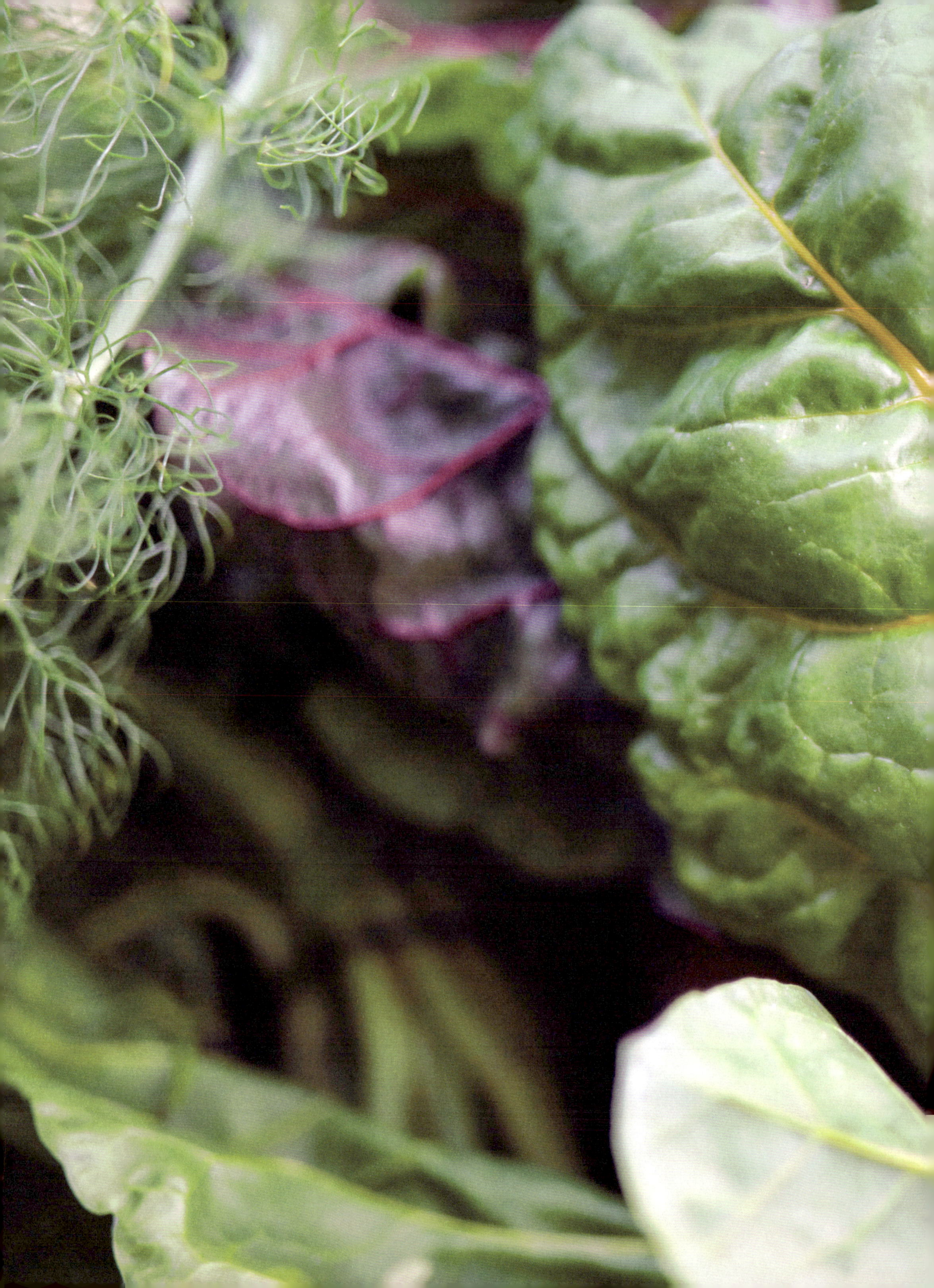

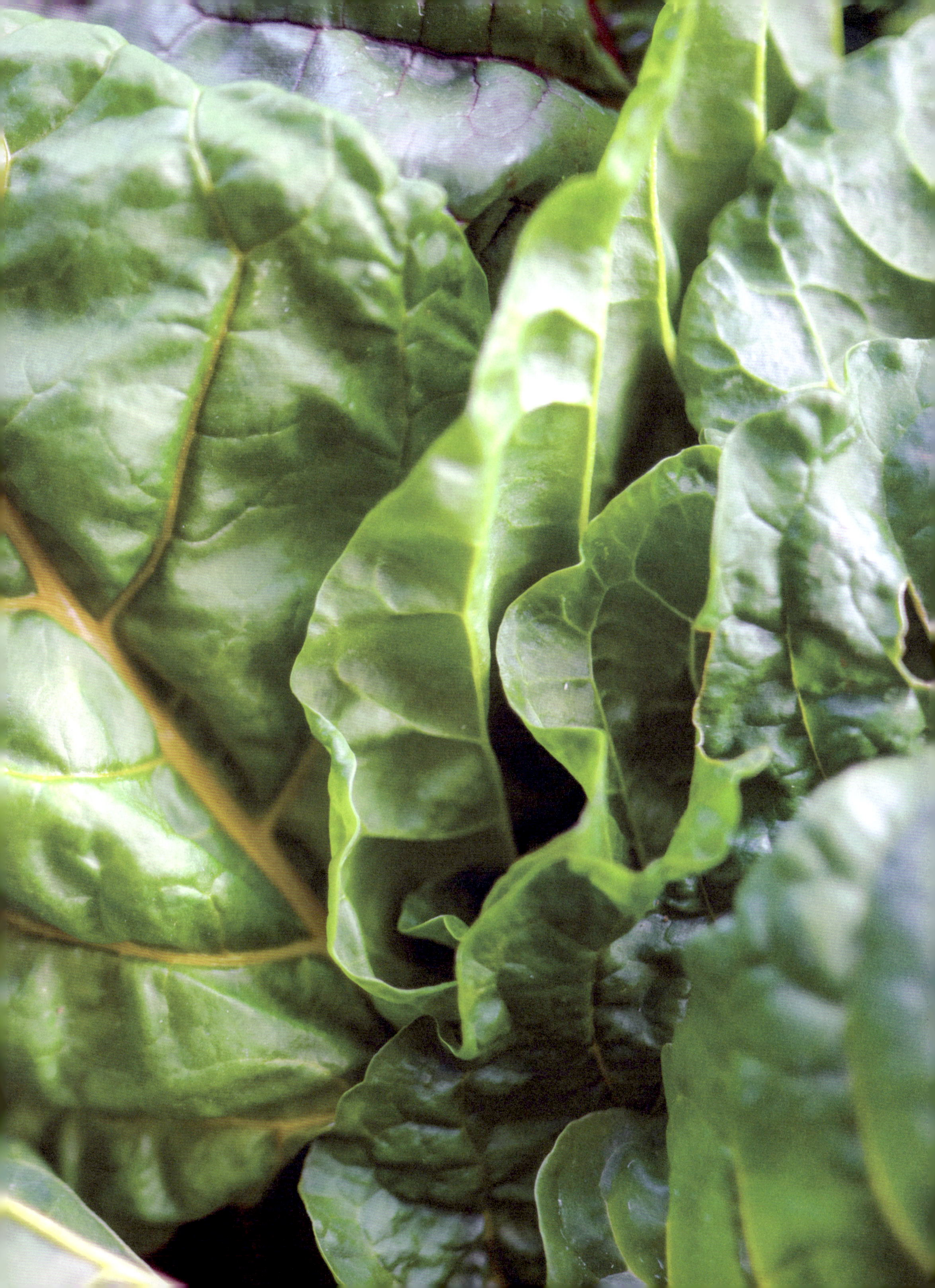

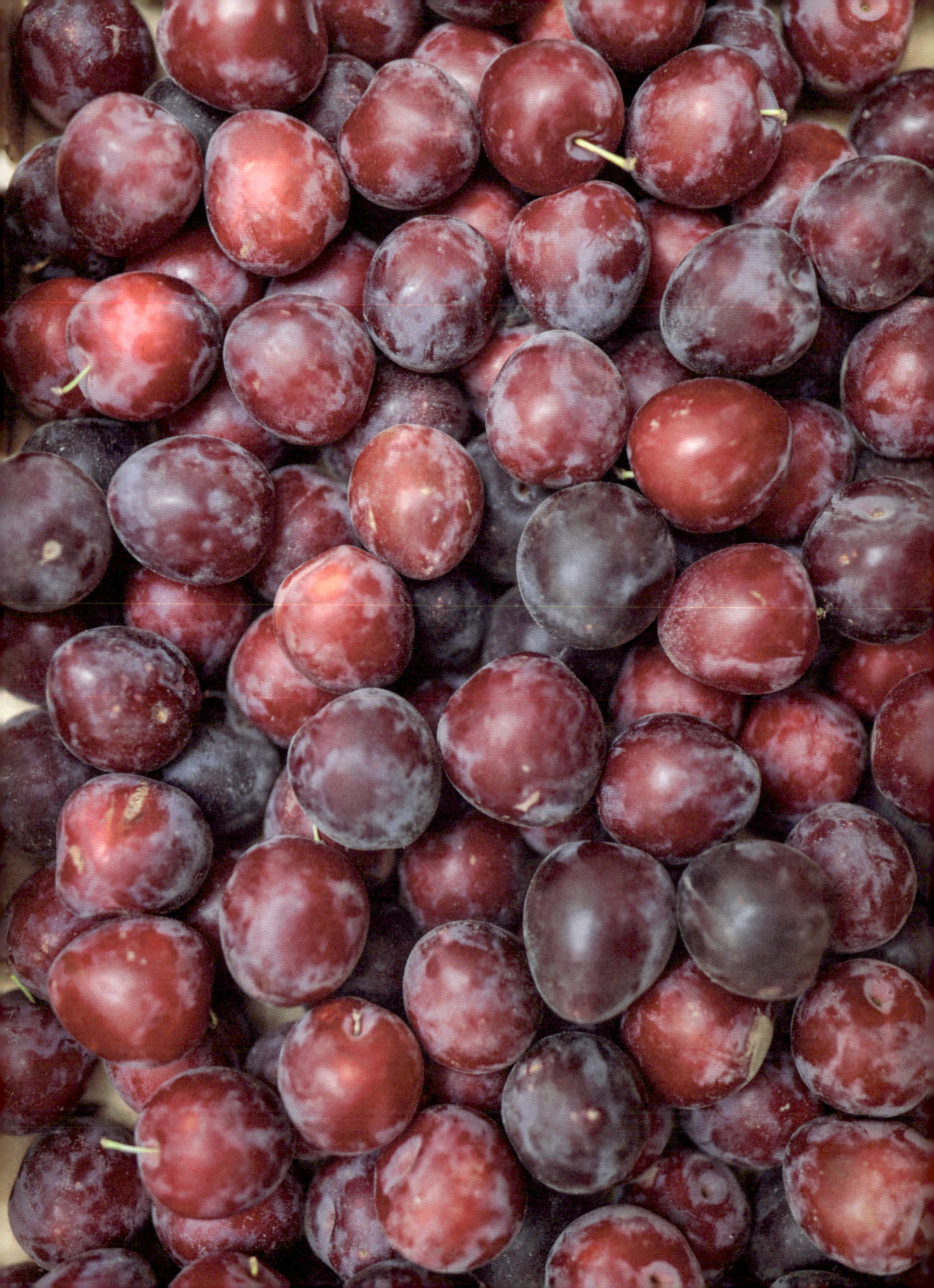

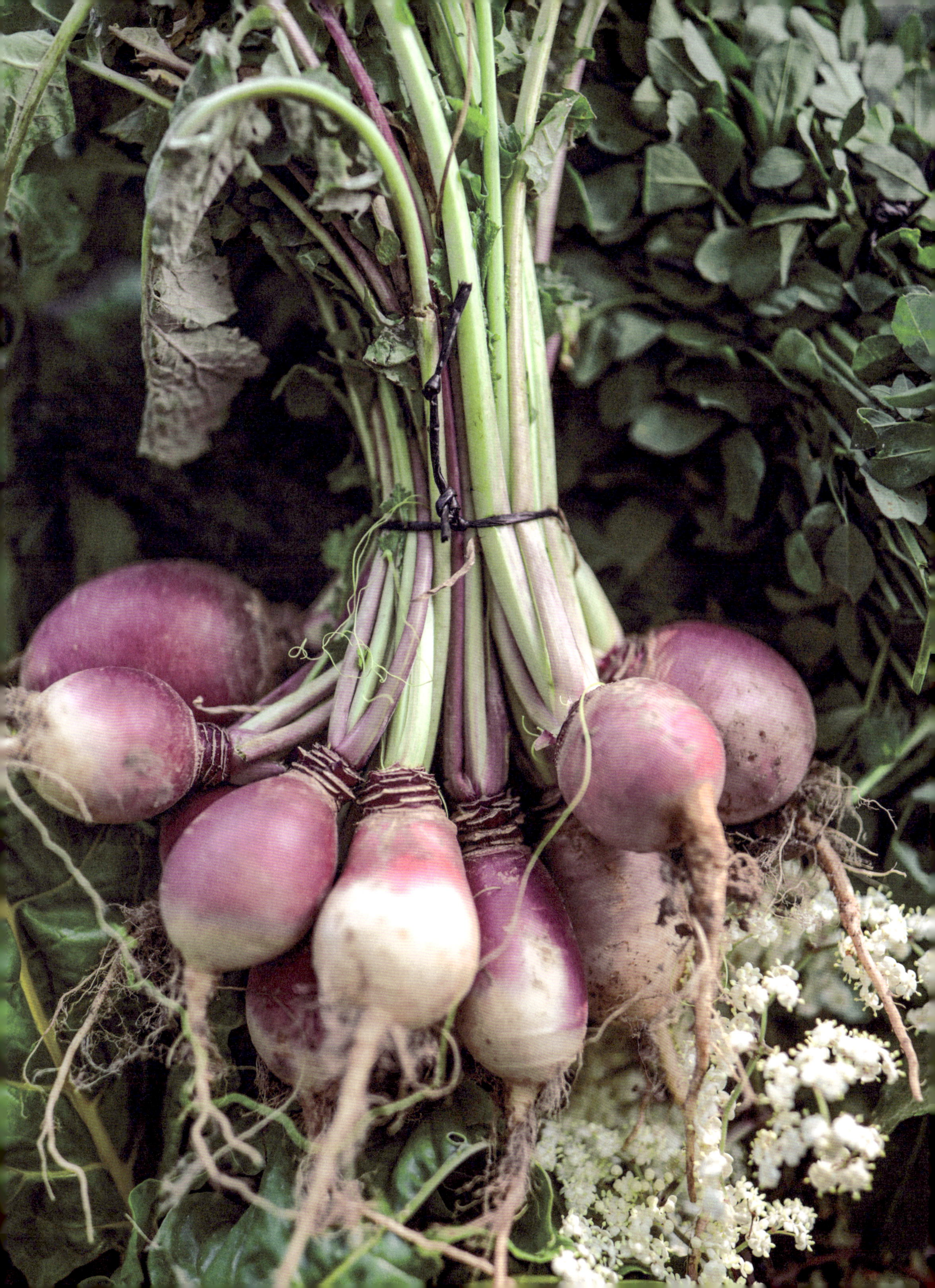

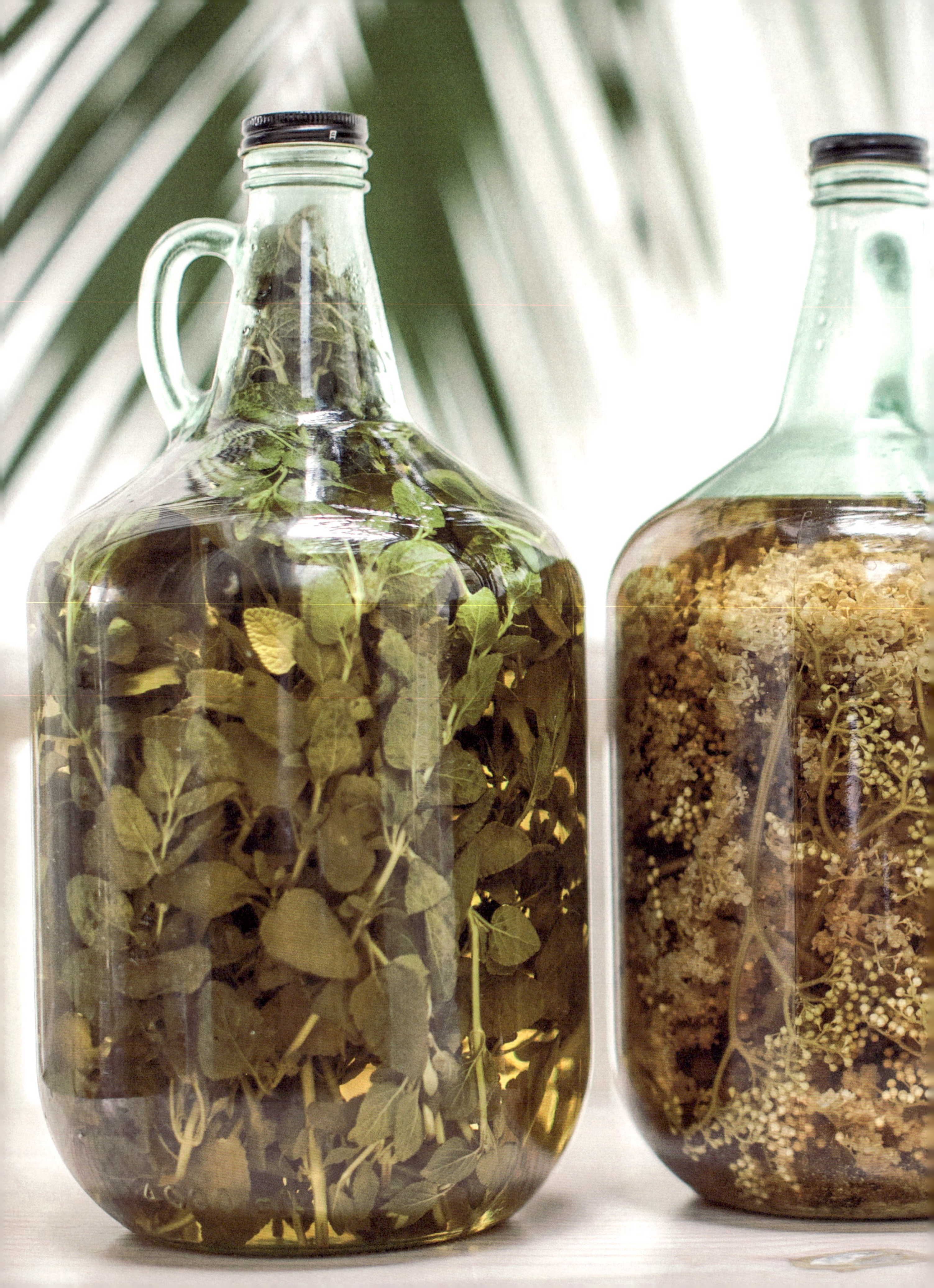

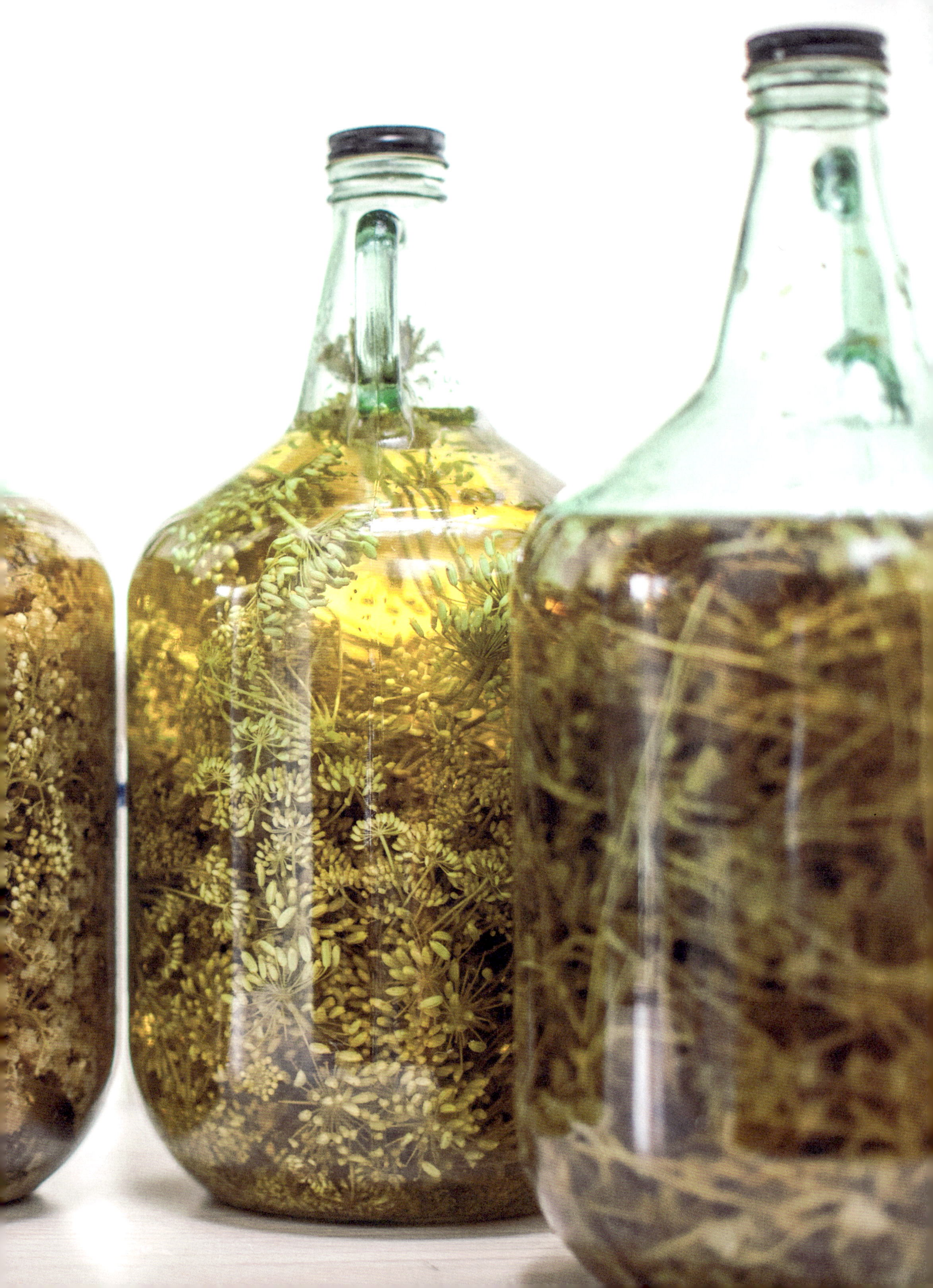

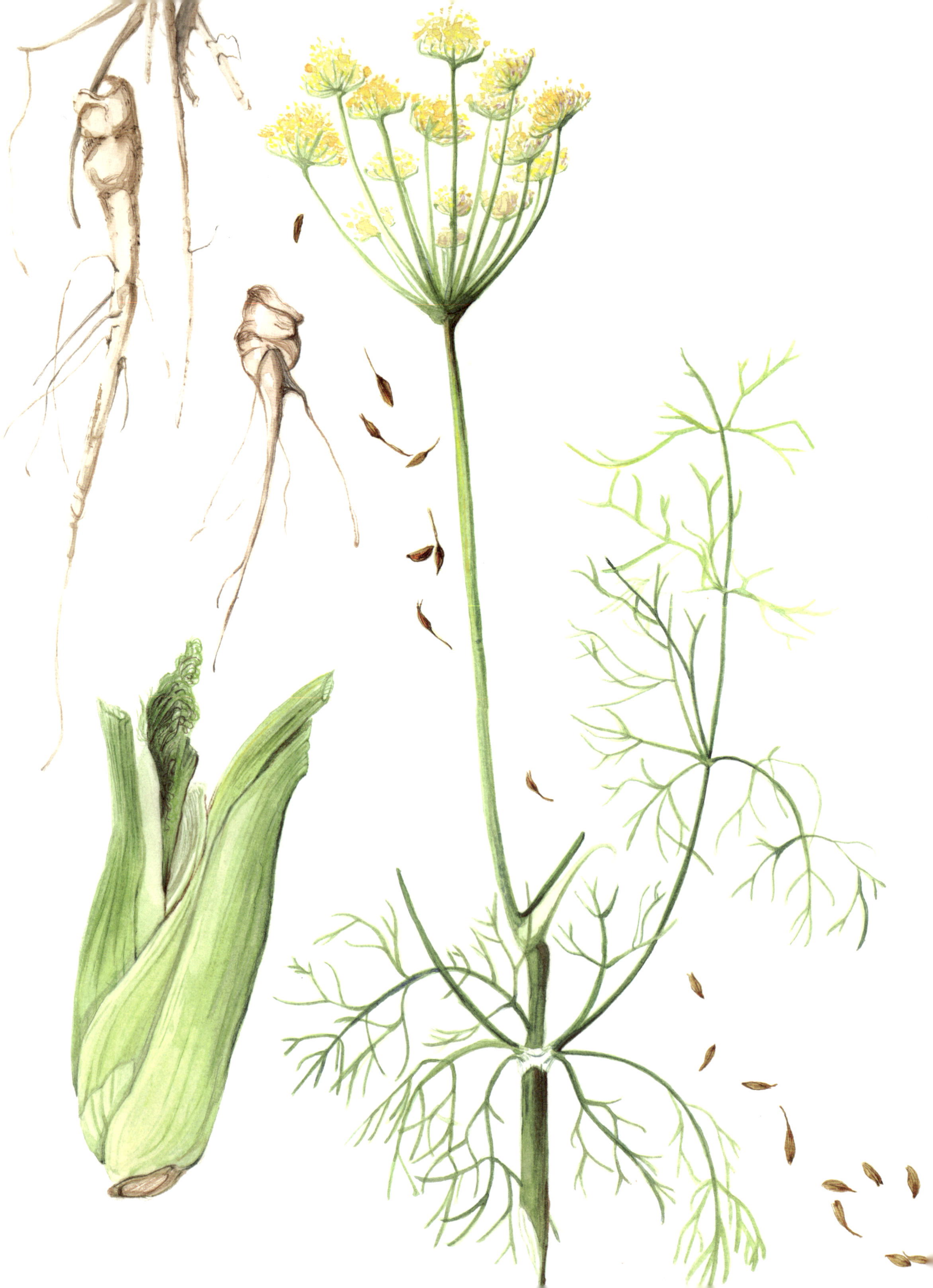

Fennel, citrus, tarragon, and pomegranate

Fennel is hard to find in Mexico. It's gotten easier in recent years, though, thanks to a handful of small-scale producers who are making the effort to grow it (much to my excitement!). This vegetable is often used in Italian cuisine. In fact, it was in working with Italian chefs that I discovered its versatility: the whole thing can be used, from the flower to the root. I feel strongly about making full use of our products and wasting as little as possible.

Serves 4

50 milliliters olive oil
190 milliliters chardonnay vinegar
60 grams butterhead lettuce
120 grams orange, peeled and cut into wedges
160 grams grapefruit, cut into wedges with no skin
720 grams fennel
80 milliliters lime juice
8 grams salt
20 milliliters chardonnay vinegar
40 grams red pomegranate seeds
1 gram fresh tarragon

Sweet and sour vinaigrette

Makes 240 milliliters

Mix the vinegar and the oil. Reserve.

Wash and cut the lettuce into large pieces.

Use a sharp knife to peel the oranges and grapefruit, removing the inner skin. Dig the knife into each segment to remove the wedges.

Use a mandoline slicer to cut the fennel into thin slices. Place them in a bowl and dress with lime juice and salt. Dress the lettuce with the sweet and sour vinaigrette and add it to the fennel, mixing everything together with your hands.

Arrange half the orange and grapefruit slices on the plate, placing the lettuce and fennel on top of them. Add the rest of the orange and grapefruit wedges, the pomegranate seeds, and the tarragon.

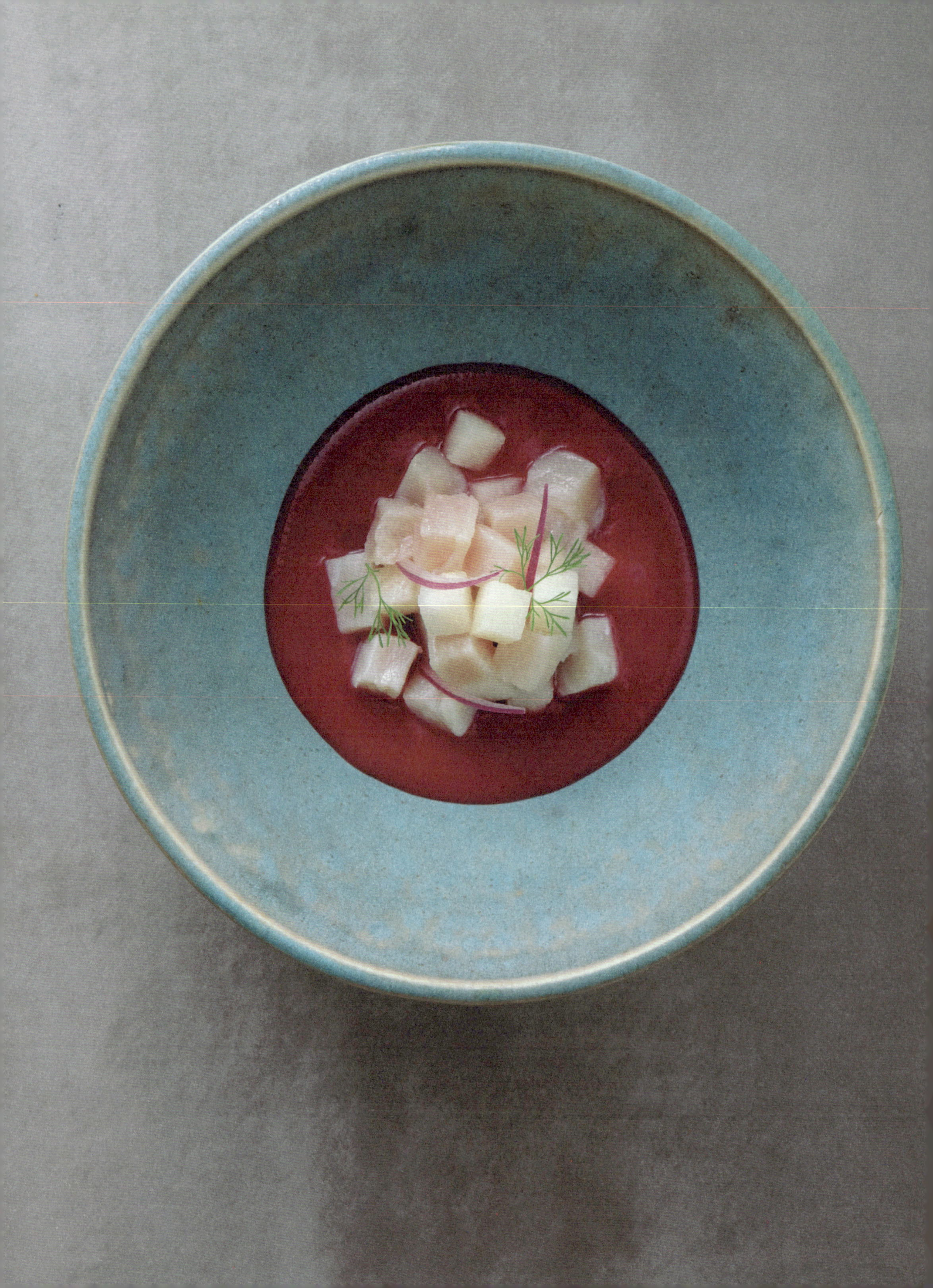

Yellowtail amberjack, muscatel plum, Asian pear, and red onion

Using fruit in the savory world is risky, even suspicious. During the 1980s, the tables of many restaurants brimmed with meat and fish dishes in sauces so sweet they tasted like jam. This trend crept into people's home cooking, too. I remember how my mother bathed the wild ducks caught by my father in powerfully sweet blackberry liqueurs. Although the result was pleasant and tasted good, the fad ultimately had a negative effect: it led to the belief that fruit must be incorporated into dishes as a sweet element. By contrast, I like to explore flavors in fruit that are much more complex than mere sweetness. Some fruits are distinctly acidic, others have a touch of bitterness, and still others are earthy-tasting.

Fruit is ever-present in the Rosetta kitchen. We use it in different stages of ripeness, depending on the degree of acidity or sweetness we need. This dish, for example, calls for muscatel plums that aren't very ripe yet, so they're more acidic than sweet. To reduce their sweetness even further, we serve them in a sauce that contains vinegar, habanero pepper, and lime. In this way, the muscatel plum functions as an acidic element that contrasts with the yellowtail amberjack, a relatively fatty fish.

As for the Asian pear, we chose this fruit for its consistency and the effect it causes more than its flavor per se. Like the plum, it serves to dilute the fattiness of the yellowtail amberjack. But its porosity also means that it absorbs the added lime and salt and refreshes the whole dish. No less important is the fact that the pear and the yellowtail amberjack are similar in color; in what becomes a monochromatic dish, it's hard to tell one ingredient from the other.

Plum sauce

Serves 4

250 grams muscatel plums
75 milliliters sweet and sour white wine vinegar
45 milliliters lime juice
4 grams habanero pepper

Makes 360 milliliters

Make a small cut across the top of the plums. Place them in a saucepan with boiling water for 1 minute. Use a slotted spoon to remove them from the water and place them in a bowl of ice water to stop the cooking process.

Skin the plums, cut them in half, and remove the pits.

Blend the plums until they're completely crushed.

In a bowl, add the plums, white wine vinegar, lime juice, and pepper (cut in half and seeded). Leave the habanero in the bowl for a couple minutes or until the contents are as spicy as you like.

To Serve

320 grams yellowtail amberjack, cubed
4 grams salt (pinch)
40 milliliters lemon juice
100 grams peeled Asian pear
120 milliliters plum sauce
4 grams cilantro
10 grams julienned red onion

Season the cubes of yellowtail amberjack with salt and lemon, then add the Asian pear (cubed).

Spoon a bit of plum sauce onto the middle of each plate. Arrange the yellowtail amberjack mixture on top of the sauce.

Add the cilantro leaves and julienned red onion.

White mole, carrots and charcoal oil

We learned how to make white mole from Víctor Jiménez, who has been the kitchen manager at Rosetta since we opened. He is a perfectionist and absolutely passionate about cooking. White mole is a traditional dish in various parts of the country. The dish is "white" because it's served to the bride and groom at their wedding. Several different versions of this mole exist. We make a variation of the one from Ometepec, Guerrero, where Víctor grew up.

The defining characteristic of this mole is that its ingredients are very clear not only to the eye, but also to the taste buds. I like it because it contains fruit and it isn't as dense as other moles, which basically consist of nuts and peppers. Its heat and aroma come more from the spices than from the pepper. We serve it with sweet tubers, like carrots, which attenuate the spices.

Finally, we splash the mole with a smoky oil we learned to make from Diego Hernández Baquedano, the chef at the restaurant Corazón de Tierra, when we cooked a dinner together. This oil is none other than a hot log, completely charred and then blended with safflower oil. Its roasted flavor evokes rural hearths where people still cook over a wood fire and not on a gas stove.

This dish is true to two of mole's characteristic features beyond its special flavor: it's always prepared by a group of people, usually for a celebration, and the method is passed along orally. Mole is, in the very best sense of the word, a collective recipe.

White mole

Serves 4

White mole
100 grams whole almond
50 grams peeled sunflowers seeds
100 grams white pine nuts
50 grams white chocolate
7 grams green habanero pepper
7 grams guero peppers
100 grams breadcrumbs
100 grams apple
200 grams plantain
50 grams white onion
4 grams fresh hoja santa
150 grams golden raisin
8 grams garlic
1 grams clove
5 grams cinammon stick
5 grams anise seeds
5 grams cilantro seeds
15 grams refined salt
5 grams fennel seeds
2.5 grams black pepper
500 grams cauliflower
1 litrer almond milk
100 grams cacao butter

Charcoal oil
25 grams charcoal
250 milliliters olive oil

Fermented carrots
150 grams carrots
330 rainbow carrots
220 grams coarse salt
20 milliliters olive oil

240 grams white mole
400 grams fermented carrots
5 milliliters charcoal oil

Makes 500 grams
  Wash and cut the habanero into fourths.
  Place the cloves, anise, cilantro seeds, black pepper, and fennel seeds in a frying pan, leaving them for 1 minute over low heat or until they start to become fragrant.
  Put the spices, the cinnamon and the hojasanta into a cooking mesh and make a knot.
  Place the chicken stock and the milk into a saucepan, then add the apple, plantain (cubed), cauliflower, habanero, güero pepper, breadcrumbs, and the cooking mesh with the spices. Cook over medium heat for 20 minutes.
  Remove the cooking mesh and drain it well. Blend the rest of the ingredients.
  In a saucepan, heat the butter and the olive oil and sauté the onion and garlic until they get golden. Add the almonds, pine nuts, and sunflower seeds. Lastly, add the golden raisins.
Cook until they start to brown, then blend them.
  Combine the two hot mixtures. Finally, add the chocolate and the salt.

Charcoal oil

Makes 250 milliliters
  Take the clean piece of wood and put it on the fire until completely charred. Once it has lit up , remove it and blend it with the olive oil until it dissolves.

Fermented carrots

Makes 400 grams
  Place the regular carrots in a saucepan and cover with coarse salt. Bake at 200°C for 25 to 30 minutes, depending on their thickness. Remove from the oven, let cool for 10 minutes, and remove the excess salt. Repeat this process with 160 grams of the rainbow carrots, baking only for 10 to 15 minutes.
  Take the remaining carrots and place them directly on the charcoal until they're cooked inside.
  Slice all the carrots (unpeeled) into ribbons and dress them with a little olive oil.

To Serve

Heat the mole, spooning some onto the center of each plate. Arrange the carrots on top of the mole and drizzle with a little charcoal oil.

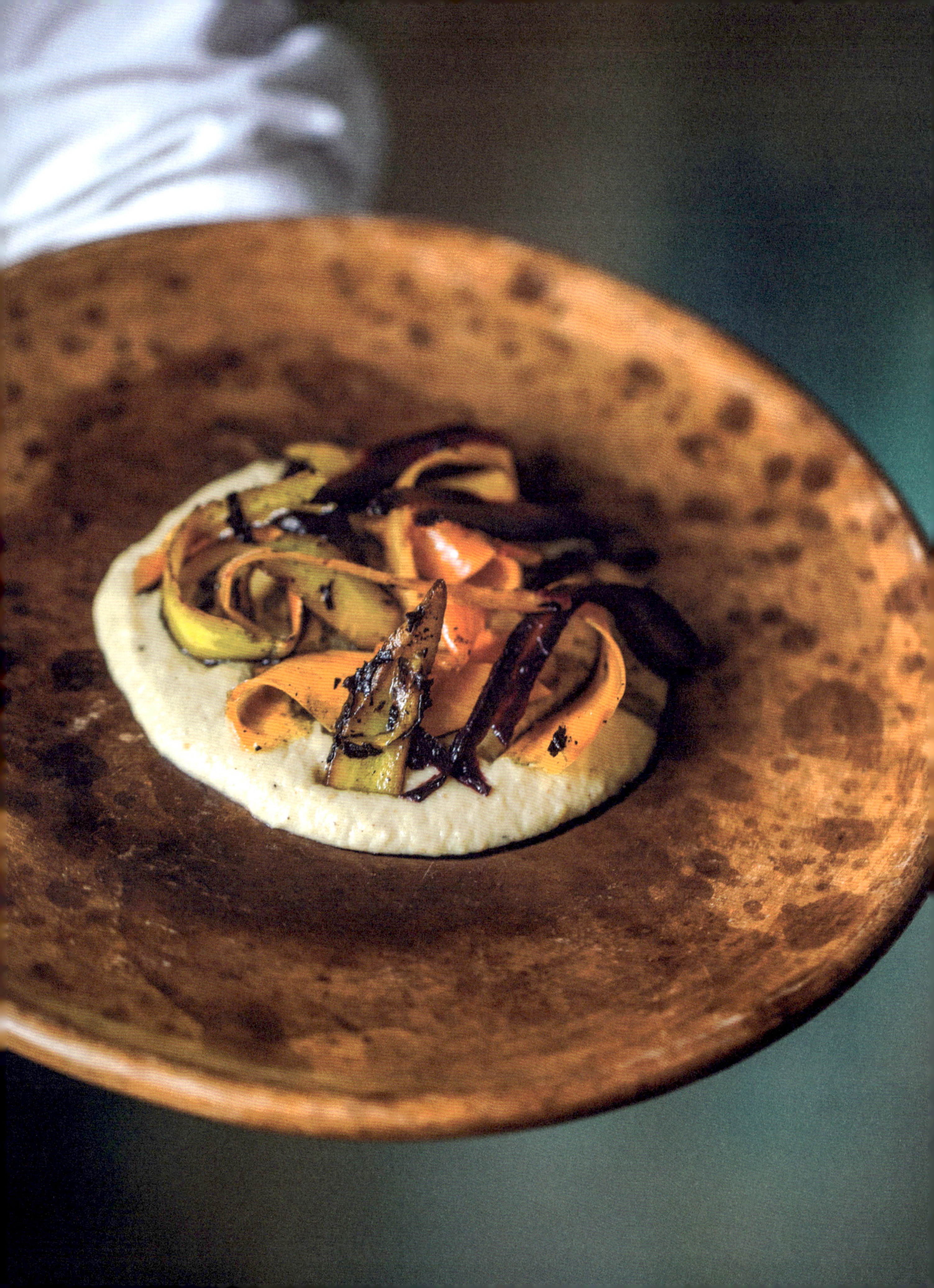

Pen shell scallops, vanilla, habanero, tangerine, and jicama

Vanilla is a sweet spice that comes from the pods of a tropical orchid. The kind we use at Rosetta is from Papantla, Veracruz. It's a carefully tended vanilla, which is reflected in the thickness, taste, and freshness of the pods.

Vanilla is normally used in desserts. However, when combined with habanero and something acidic, it yields a sweet dressing that makes our mouths water from the first spoonful. In my opinion, a jolt of acidity is essential in cooking: it enlivens food and ensures that a dish doesn't grow tiresome after a few bites. We make constant use of vinegars, marinated with herbs or spices. One of the most special kinds is the one we use in this dish, given the unusual combination of the vanilla's sweetness with the vinegar.

The vanilla pods are cut down the middle and left to steep in the vinegar in a cool, dry place for at least twelve hours (the longer the better). The vinegar takes on the flavor and aroma of the vanilla and its acidity diminishes, which makes it an ideal accompaniment to soft mollusks, like the pen shell scallop. This vinegar can also be used with other shellfish, fatty fishes, and fruits like strawberries and persimmons.

Pickled lemon

Serves 4

1 lemon
15 grams coarse salt
80 milliliters water
40 grams sugar
120 milliliters lemon juice
120 milliliters olive oil

Makes 20 grams

Cut the lemon into fourths and place them in a bowl.
Add the coarse salt and mix so that the entire lemon is coated in salt. Let sit for 5 minutes.
Place the lemon in a hermetic container. Add the lemon juice, water, and sugar, then close. Place the container in the oven for 15 minutes at 180°C.
Let the container cool at room temperature, then let it sit for 7 days to continue the fermentation process.
Once this period of time has passed, transfer the lemon to a new container and cover it with olive oil.
Refrigerate.

Citrus and vanilla aguachile

¼ vanilla pod
10 milliliters sweet and sour white wine vinegar
½ habanero pepper
45 milliliters lime juice
200 milliliters tangerine juice

Makes 250 milliliters

Make a crosswise cut along the vanilla pod and use a knife to remove the seeds. Place the seeds and the pod in a hermetic container with the sweet and sour white wine vinegar. Let the mixture steep for at least 12 hours and remove the pod before using it.
Place the habanero pepper directly on the fire until completely charred; that is, until its skin has totally carbonized. Cut it in half and remove the seeds.
In a bowl, place the habanero pepper, lemon juice, tangerine juice, and marinated vanilla vinegar.
Let the mixture steep for approximately 1 hour or until the juice is as spicy as you like. Strain and refrigerate.

To Serve

320 grams scallops
60 grams jicama
120 grams pickled lemon
1 pinch salt flakes
60 milliliters lemon juice
250 milliliters citrus and vanilla aguachile
30 milliliters olive oil
1 sprig lemon thyme

Make thin crosswise cuts, approximately 2 millimeters thick, along the scallops. Lay out the scallops on wax paper and refrigerate.
Cut the jicama as thick as the pen shell scallops, cutting small 1-centimeter triangles from each side. Place the jicama in a bowl of cold water and set aside.
Remove the pulp from the pickled lemons and dice the peel into very small cubes.
Season the scallops with salt and lemon juice.
Arrange the scallops on the plate and bathe in the citrus and vanilla aguachile. Add a few drops of olive oil, the pickled lemon peel, the triangles of jicama, and some thyme leaves.

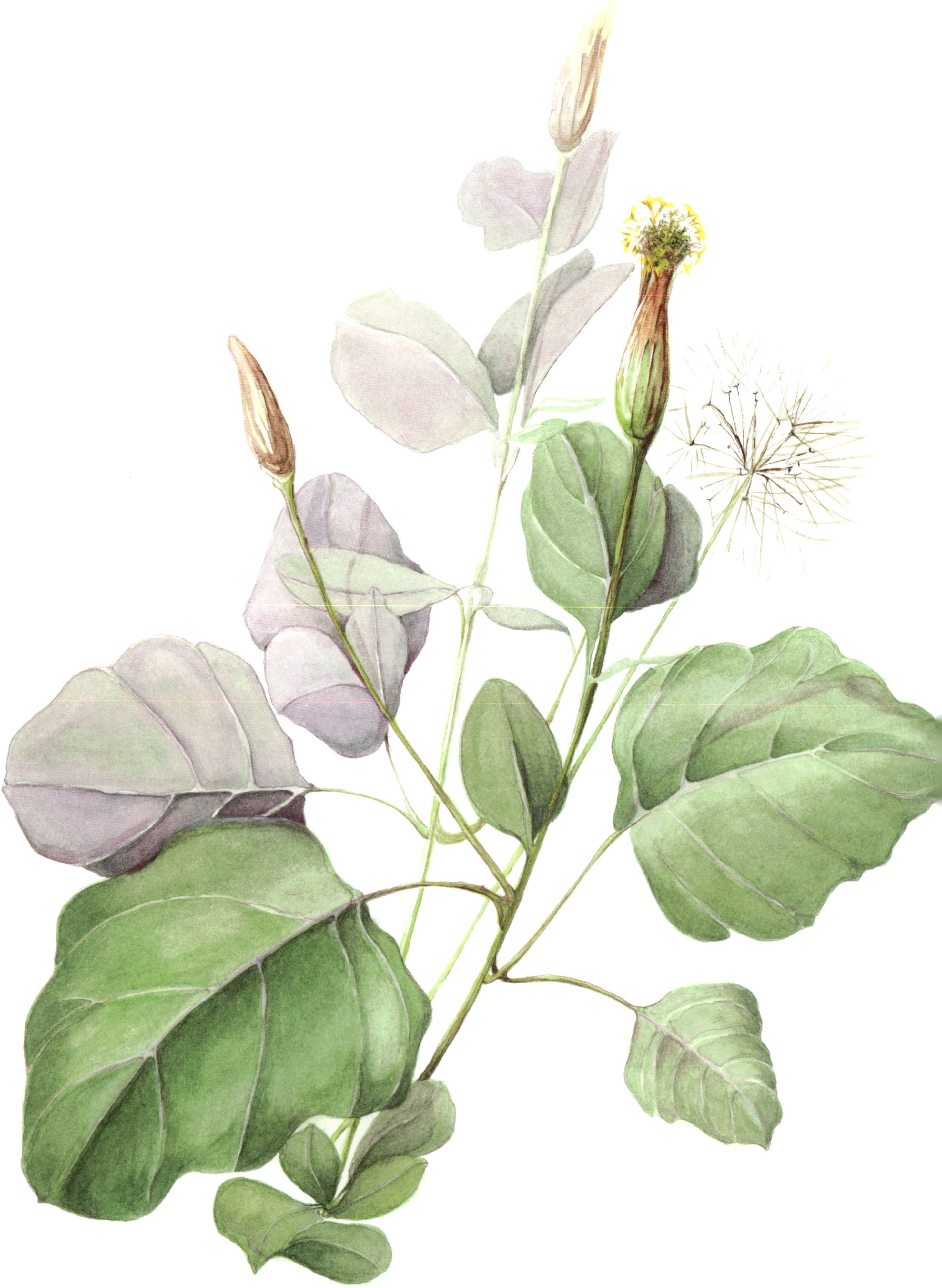

Quelites, avocado, lemon, and chicatana ants

Late May, early June: when the first rains of the year descend on central Mexico, cooks rejoice. The first rains bring us mushrooms, chicatana ants, quelites, and wild herbs rich with the taste of damp earth. For a long time, such herbs were dismissed as mere weeds and consumed only by those who had little to eat—but they're pure abundance, full of nutrients and flavor.

One of our primary suppliers is a ranch in Mexico State. Once a week, they send us the vegetables and herbs that were ready for harvest. We don't make any specific requests; they send us what they have and we make use of it. This exchange means that we plan our dishes around the ingredients we have on hand. In one harvest, greens like quelites were especially plentiful: we found ourselves with varieties such as quelites cenizo, pápalo, nasturtium, watercress, and purslane. We mixed them all together, adding avocado for greater consistency, lemon juice to refresh the herbs, and chicatana ant vinaigrette to accentuate the earthy taste.

The combination of these rich flavors transports me to the place where these herbs come from: a nearly virgin landscape teeming with undergrowth, far from chemical fertilizers and single-crop farming. I hope these lands—and, in turn, these kinds of flavors—will always be with us.

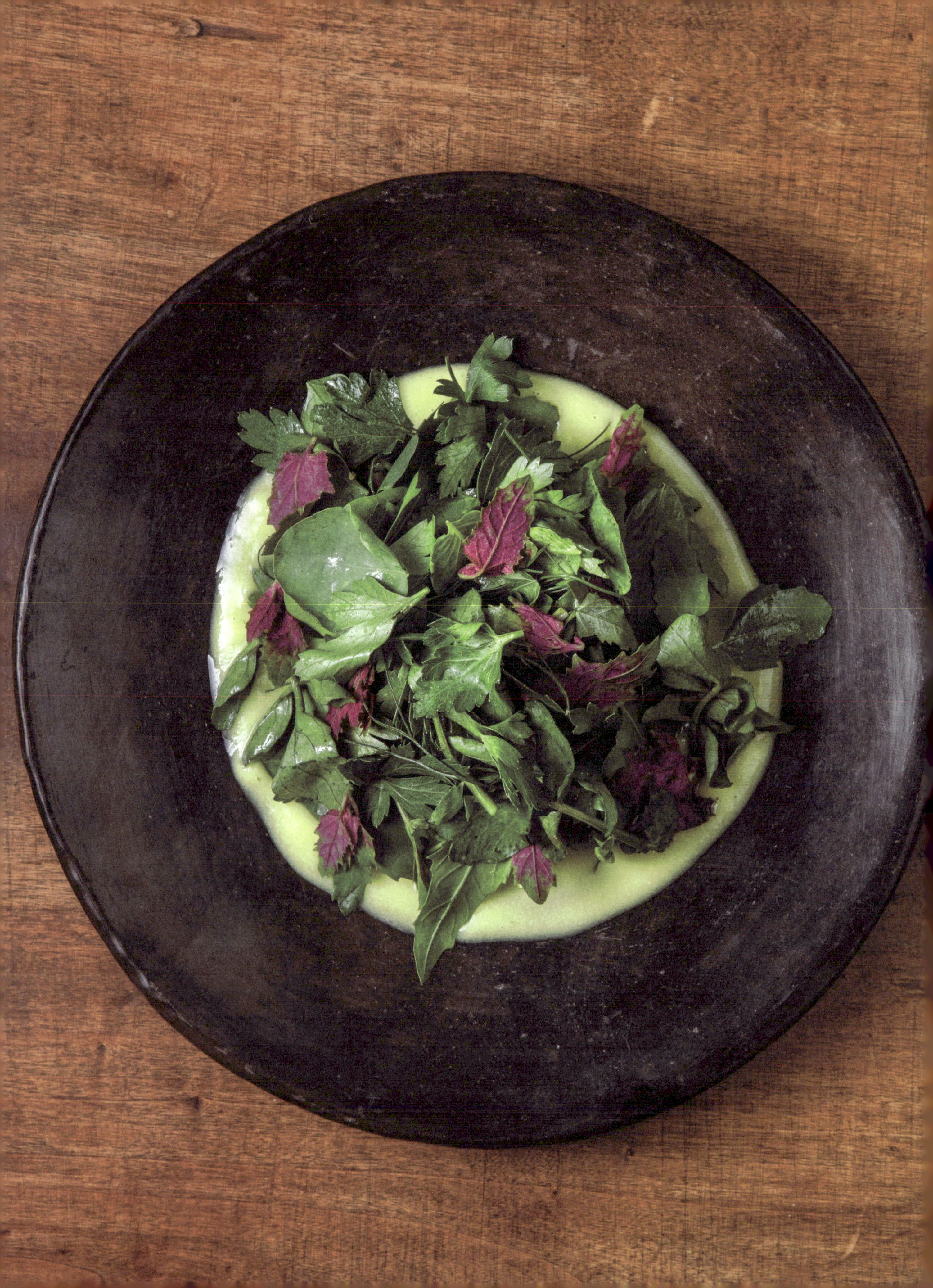

Avocado purée

Serves 4

200 grams avocado pulp
50 milliliters water
22 milliliters lime juice
3 pinch salt
5 grams zucchini skin

Makes 250 grams

Blend the zucchini skin with the lime juice, water, and salt. Add the avocado and blend until the texture becomes firm.

Chicatana ant vinaigrette

160 grams chicatana ants
760 milliliters red wine vinegar
320 milliliters olive oil
30 grams salt

Makes 1 liter

Wash the chicatanas, removing their wings and heads.
Sauté them in a frying pan until they begin to release their own fat. Take care not to burn them. Spread them out on a tray to cool.
In a food processor, crush the chicatanas with the red wine vinegar and salt until they're completely ground up. Add the olive oil at the end so that it blends in, too.
Transfer the mixture to a bowl and refrigerate.

Lemon vinaigrette

750 milliliters olive oil
200 milliliters lemon juice

Makes 950 milliliters

Place the lemon juice in a bowl and stream in the olive oil, whisking the mixture. Once everything is well mixed, transfer to a bowl.

To Serve

40 grams quelite cenizo
35 grams watercress
10 grams pápalo
10 grams nasturtium leaves
1 gram fennel frond
25 grams parsley
80 grams avocado purée
40 milliliters chicatana ant vinaigrette
10 milliliters lemon vinaigrette
6 grams salt

Strip the leaves off all the herbs, mix them together in a bowl, and refrigerate.
Place a spoonful of avocado purée in the middle of each plate, then add a little chicatana vinaigrette in lines across the purée.
Dress the herbs with the lemon vinaigrette and salt, then arrange them on top of the purée.

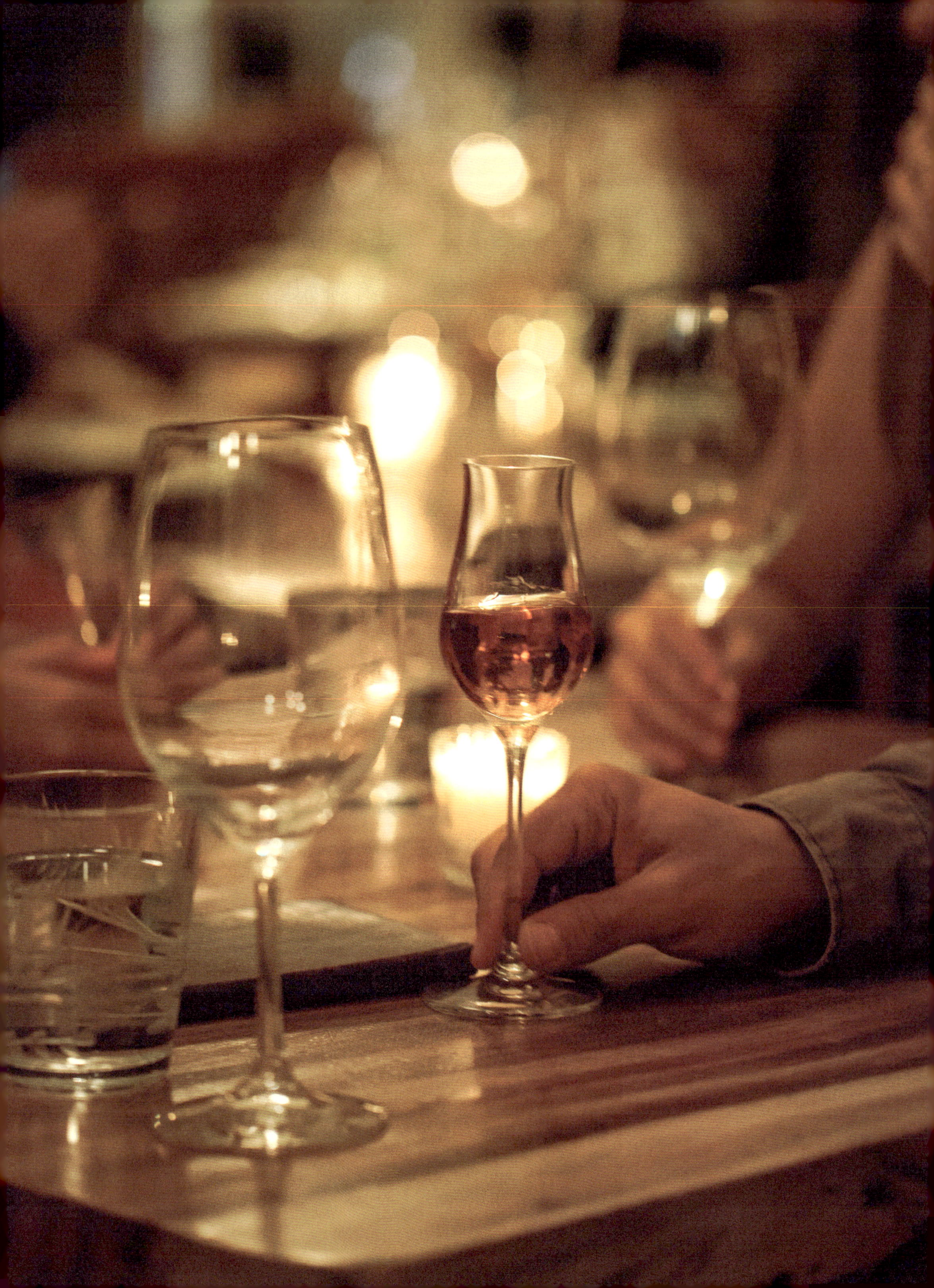

More Than Food

Every decision you make in a restaurant, a place where people go to have an experience, affects that experience in a crucial way. Most of all, there's the question of what you cook and put on the plate. But there are also the materials and the arrangement of certain spatial elements. Every decision has an effect on everything else: how and where you organize the tables, for instance, or how wide and how long they are. I like smaller tables, where there isn't much distance between the people sharing them, because I think they encourage more intimate conversations.

Instead of offering a long tasting menu, ours is à la carte, with the option of small sharing plates, which also changes the restaurant experience. It influences not only how you eat, but also how conversations are held: I know my favorite meals are the ones where you keep talking long after you've finished eating.

The logic of the tasting menu isn't my logic: I don't like interrupting conversations every time a new dish arrives. Besides, I think that part of the excitement of eating at a restaurant is the freedom to choose what you eat in the first place. Not to mention the enormous symbolic weight of sharing food with others.

I try to create dishes that can be clearly understood, dishes in which each and every ingredient can be identified. Dishes that don't hide anything. I never strive for preciosity when I plate food. Harmony, yes; beauty, yes; but never excess or purely ornamental elements.

At Rosetta, we strive for warmth, for a complete experience, for a specific objective: to create an environment. Music is an important part of this goal: I put on the same music I listen to with friends at home. Decor is also key: we want to convey a warmth and comfort that encourages our guests to stick around. The sobremesa—which in Spanish refers to when people linger to keep chatting over a beverage even after they've finished their meal—is a source of great satisfaction.

I decided that Rosetta would occupy an early twentieth-century mansion because I thought its architecture could generate an intimate environment and evoke a touch of nostalgia. It's important to adapt to your surroundings, to your space. To offer continuity to the place's original vocation. With Rosetta, I feel strongly about letting the house speak for itself, never getting in the way of what it wants to express. My goal, rather, is to help its own discourse carry on, enriching it however I can. I don't want to put up a fight; I want to give it free reign. I strive for an aesthetic that harmonizes or dialogues with the physical space. The idea is to create an experience, and interior design is essential to that goal. We seek to create a harmonious setting.

In a restaurant, beyond the originality of the concept or the idea behind a dish, beyond technical prowess or flavor, there are always other forces at work.

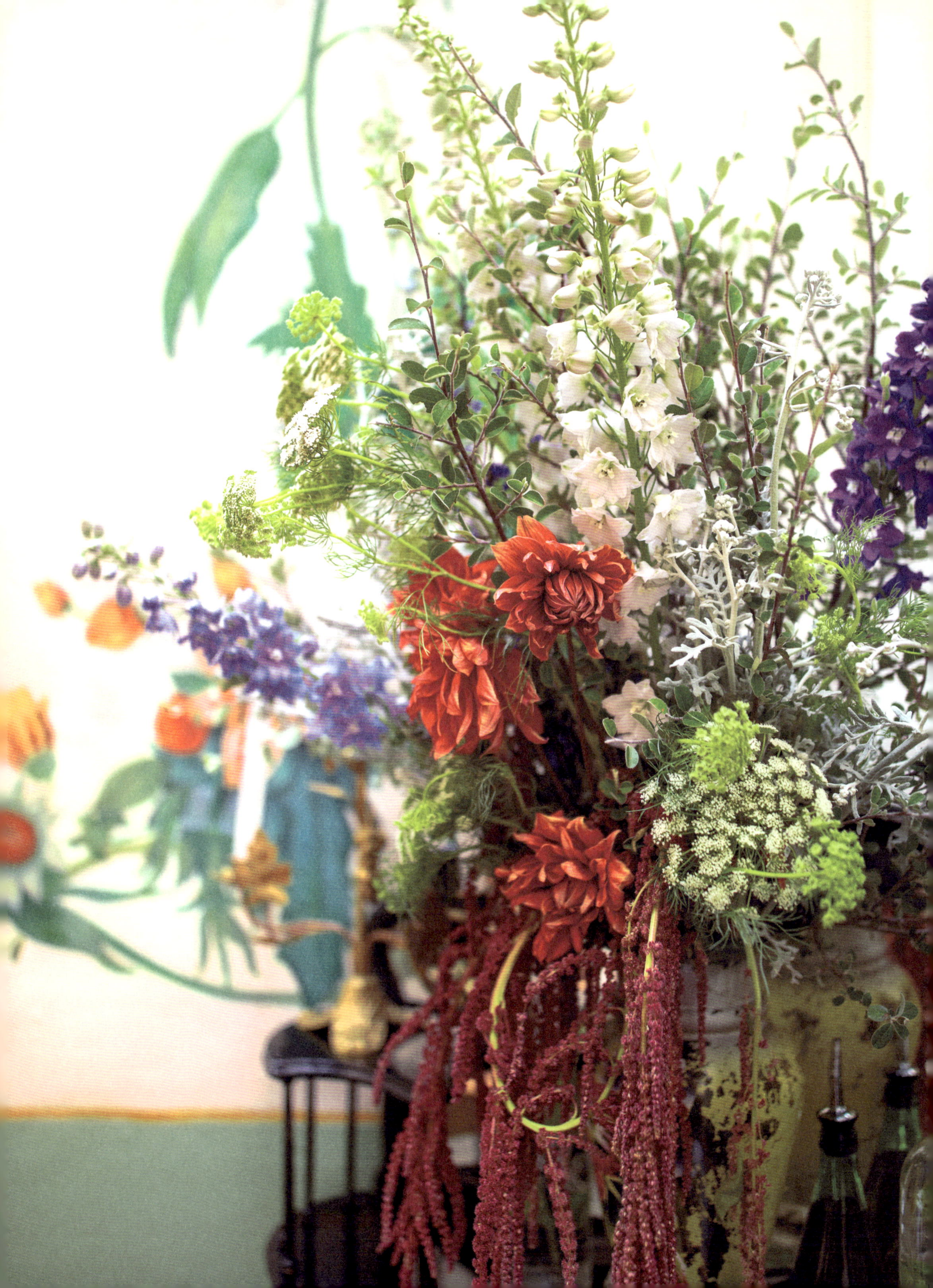

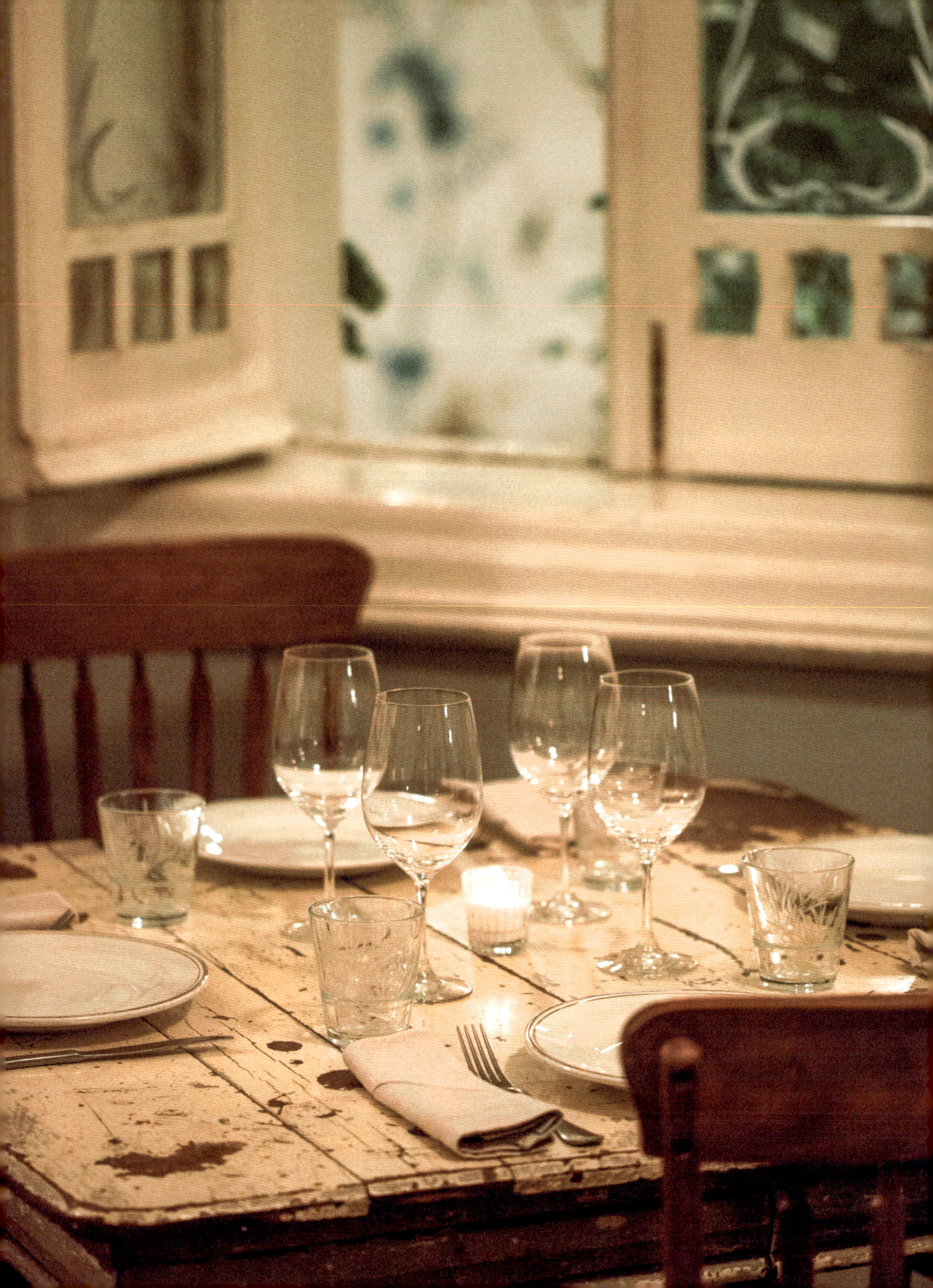

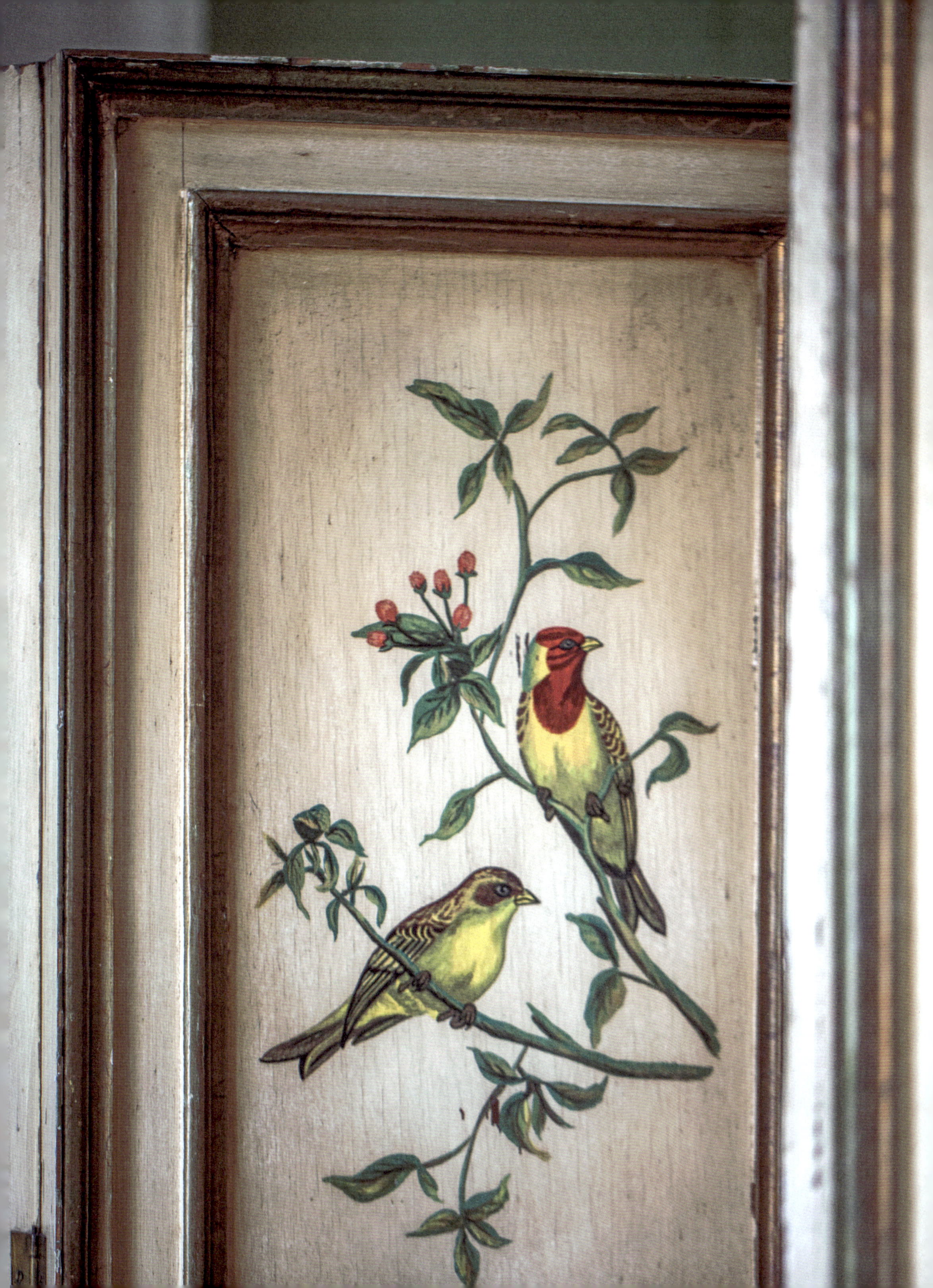

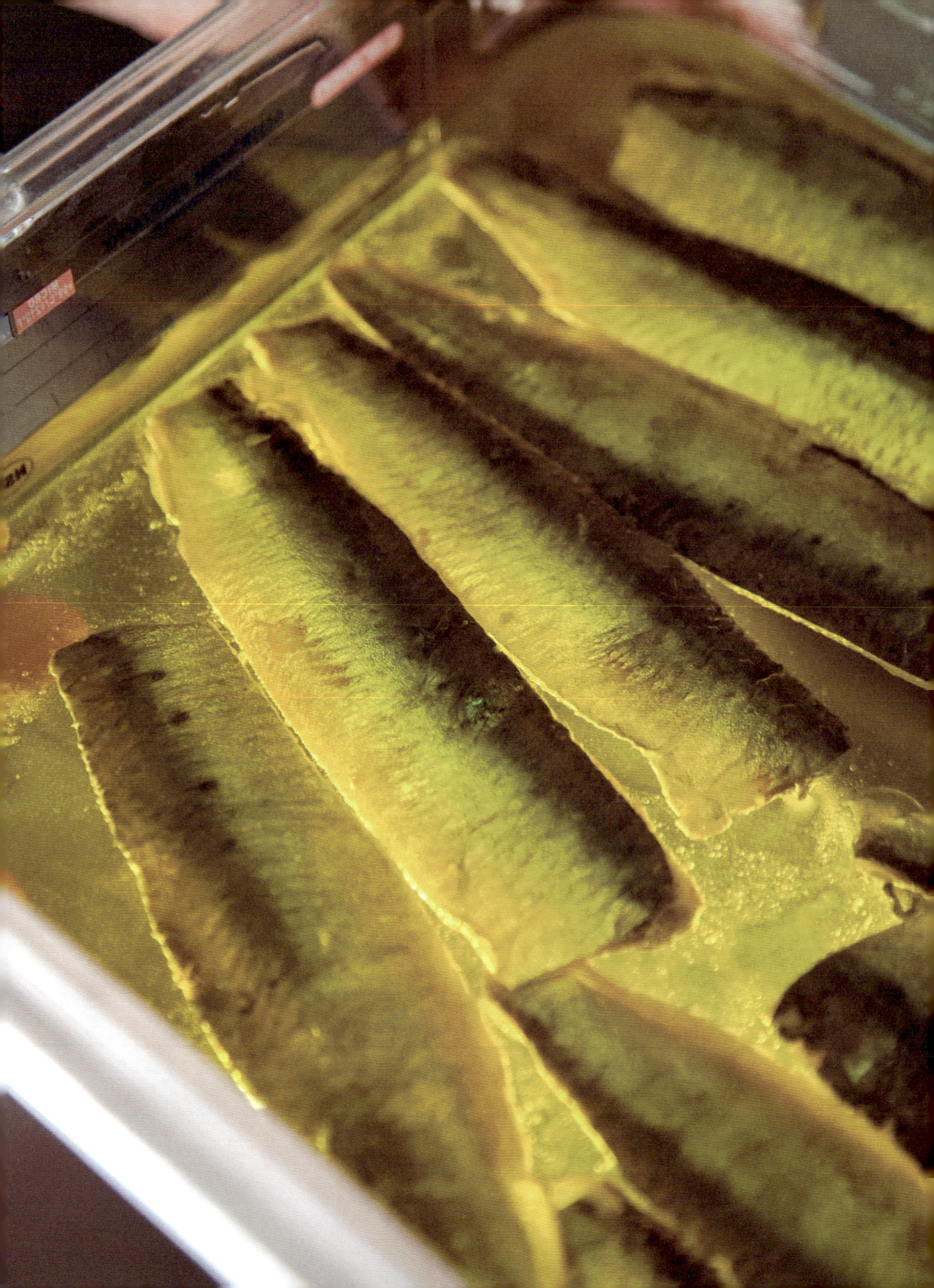

Pickled sardines, farro, orange, celery, peppermint, and black olives

The sardine is a fantastic fish. Its skin and texture are very delicate, but its flavor has a lot of character. Cooking with fresh sardines, far from their place of origin, is a luxury: their high blood density makes them extremely perishable, and they're difficult to transport without harming the fish. For many years, sardines were primarily available as a canned food. In addition, sardines have become a food source for bluefin tuna, exported to Japan. This is why we only occasionally come into contact with fresh sardines in Mexico City.

The day sardines arrive at Rosetta, we grill half of them and pickle the other half. We remove the fillets from the bones, taking care not to harm their silvery skin. Then we pickle them with salt, sugar, and some acidic ingredient, which not only increases their flavor, but also gives them a firmer consistency and keeps them fresh a little longer.

This recipe makes use of orange and vinegar. The sardine releases its aquatic flavor as it's pickled, producing an acidic, sweet, and salty liquid we use to cover the farro that accompanies it. Farro, a grain like barley, has the perfect spongy consistency to absorb this marinade. Besides, the other ingredients we combine with the farro add freshness to the sardines. This is a dish of Mediterranean flavors. Sardines are found in many kitchens in that region. In fact, Ensenada is located at the very same latitude as the lower part of the Mediterranean Sea.

Pickled sardines

Serves 4

800 grams sardines
48 grams fleur de sel
55 grams sugar
100 milliliters lemon juice
95 milliliters orange juice
55 grams lemon zest
65 grams orange zest
15 milliliters white wine vinegar
150 milliliters olive oil

Makes 400 grams

Remove the scales from the sardines. Carefully remove the fillets.

Combine the sugar and salt and completely cover the sardine fillets with this mixture. Set aside for 30 minutes, then rinse.

In a deep bowl, combine the lemon and orange juices with the zest of both fruits and the vinegar, then place the sardine fillets into this mixture. Let sit for at least 12 hours.

Remove the sardine fillets from the juice, transfer them to a bowl, and cover them with the olive oil.

Cooked farro

160 grams farro
400 milliliters water
6 grams salt

Makes 320 grams

Put the water and the farro in a pot and cook over medium heat for 15 to 20 minutes.

Add the salt and cook for another 2 minutes.

Spread out the farro on a tray, pour a little olive oil over it to keep it from sticking, and cover with plastic wrap.

To Serve

260 grams orange
55 grams celery
10 milliliters olive oil
35 milliliters chardonnay vinegar
310 grams cooked farro
10 grams black olives
10 grams fennel frond
160 grams pickled sardines
1 pinch salt
10 grams peppermint

Peel and cut the orange into wedges, removing the skin with a sharp knife.

Peel and dice the celery into very small cubes.

Mix the olive oil and chardonnay vinegar in a bowl or bottle.

Mix the farro with the orange wedges, celery, olives, and the chopped fennel frond.

Dress with the vinaigrette and salt, then mix together.

Tear the peppermint leaves into pieces with your hands and add them to the mixture.

Arrange the pickled sardine fillets on top of the farro mixture.

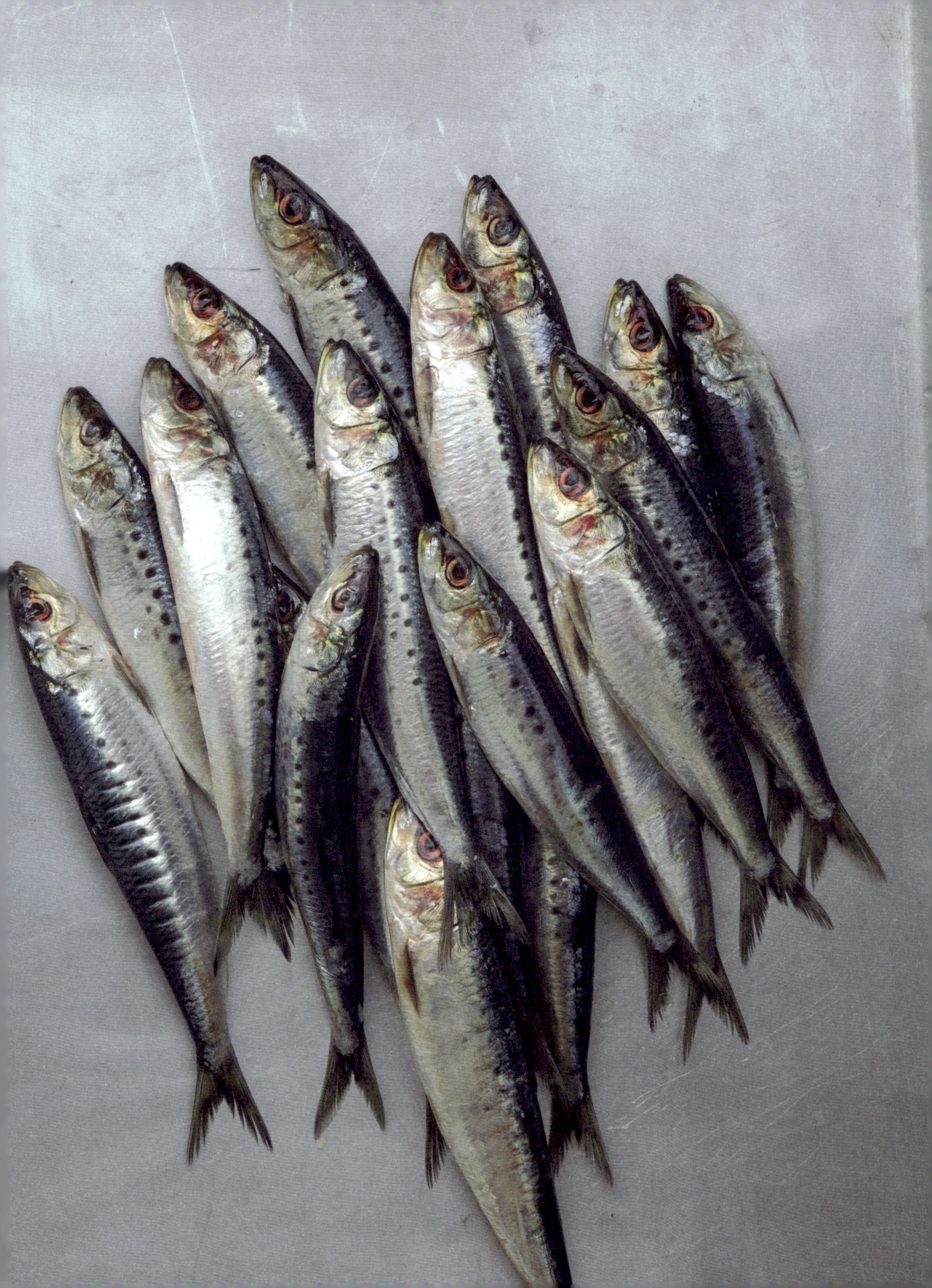

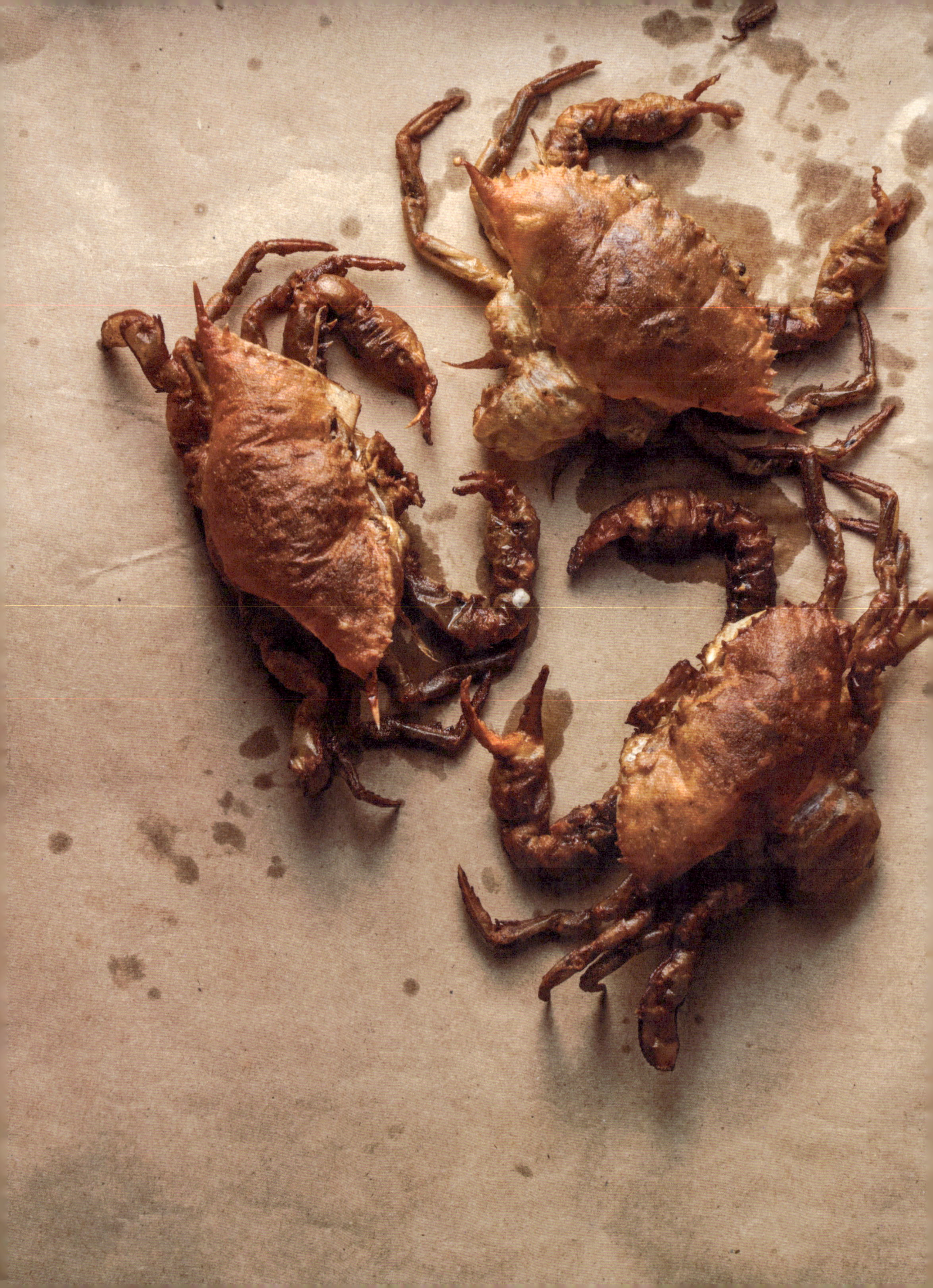

Soft-shell crab, mango, habanero, and jicama

A crab is called "soft-shell" when the animal has shed its hard shell and can be eaten whole. This dish is remarkably simple: all we need to do is cover the soft-shell crabs with a mixture of wheat flour and chickpea flour, fry them in abundant hot oil, and eat them right away.

Manila mango purée

Serves 4

200 grams manila mango pulp
100 milliliters lemon juice
1 habanero pepper

Makes 200 grams
  Blend the mango pulp with the lemon juice and transfer the mixture to a bowl.
  Cut the habanero pepper in half and seed it. Add it to the mango purée and leave it submerged there for 20 minutes or until the mixture is as spicy as you like.

Peppermint and cilantro salad

80 grams clean jicama
60 grams cucumber
10 grams red onion
200 grams peeled orange wedges
10 grams peppermint leaves
32 mililiters lemon
2 grams salt
4 grams cilantro leaves

Makes 380 grams
  Cut the jicama and the cucumber into similarly sized pieces.
  Mix the jicama, cucumber, orange, cilantro, and peppermint with the lemon juice and a pinch of salt.

To Serve

250 grams chickpea flour
250 grams wheat flour
8 pieces soft-shell crab
3 liters vegetable oil
300 grams manila mango purée
300 grams peppermint and cilantro salad

Mix the two flours together, cut the crabs down the middle, and bread them. Fry them at 180°C for 1 minute.
  Lay them out on paper towel to remove the excess fat and serve them immediately.
  Place a spoonful of mango purée on each plate, followed by a little salad and the crab pieces. Finally, add a bit more salad on top.

Persimmons, herbs, ricotta, lemon, and pistachios

A persimmon is beautiful and delicious when it ripens until its color is a deep, translucent orange; when it's soft, semi-liquid, and sweet inside; when the only thing you have to do is remove the stem and suck out the pulp.

It's tricky to buy persimmons in this state. As happens with other delicate fruits, persimmons aren't sold ripe: when they are, they fall apart, they don't look very appetizing, and they don't last long. That's why it's important to let them ripen for a few days after purchase in the cardboard box they come in, waiting for the tannic taste of their skin to disappear. In this sense, persimmons teach us patience: every ingredient has an ideal time for consumption.

At Rosetta, we like to use the Japanese variety of persimmons: kaki. They're conical and their lower end is pointy. They appear in the last and first months of the year. We serve them with ricotta and a mix of herbs, especially shisho, which also comes from Japan. All of this is unified by the fresh perfume and acidity of lemon.

Serves 4

1 gram tarragon
20 milliliters white wine vinegar

Tarragon vinegar

Makes 20 milliliters

Place the tarragon sprig into the white wine vinegar and let it marinate for at least 24 hours. Then strain it. This process produces tarragon vinegar (which you'll be able to use in many other dishes).

Lemon jello

30 milliliters water
50 grams sugar
2 lemons
5 grams gelatin sheets
120 milliliters lemon juice

Makes 240 grams

Zest the lemons and set aside the shavings.
Place the water and sugar in a small pot and keep on a low heat until the temperature reaches 85°C.
Add the lemon zest and let it sit for 2 minutes.
Strain and add the previously hydrated gelatin.
Once the gelatin has dissolved, add the lemon juice all at once and beat energetically.
Transfer to a container and refrigerate.

Lemon ricotta

160 grams ricotta cheese
1 pinch salt
10 milliliters olive oil
2 grams lemon zest

Makes 165 grams

Mix all the ingredients in a bowl and set aside.

To Serve

1 sprig tarragon
20 milliliters tarragon vinegar
40 milliliters olive oil
1 gram fresh tarragon
4 grams peppermint
160 grams lemon ricotta
320 grams persimmons
10 milliliters lemon juice
40 grams peeled pistachio
8 shisho leaves, chopped
8 grams peppermint
160 grams sorrel
1 pinch salt
40 grams lemon jello

Transfer the tarragon vinegar to a bowl. Little by little, add the olive oil, beating the mixture vigorously.
Strip the leaves off the tarragon and the peppermint.
Place three spoonfuls of lemon ricotta in the middle of each plate.
Cut the persimmon into six wedges, then cut those in half. Dress them with lemon juice and arrange three pieces in the center of the cheese.
Scatter chopped pistachios over the persimmons and the ricotta cheese.
Mix all the herbs together and dress lightly with the tarragon vinegar and the salt. Make sure not to overdress the herbs or their leaves will wilt.
Place a little more cheese on top, then more herbs on top of the cheese.
Finally, distribute little bits of lemon jello across the plate, as well as more pistachios.

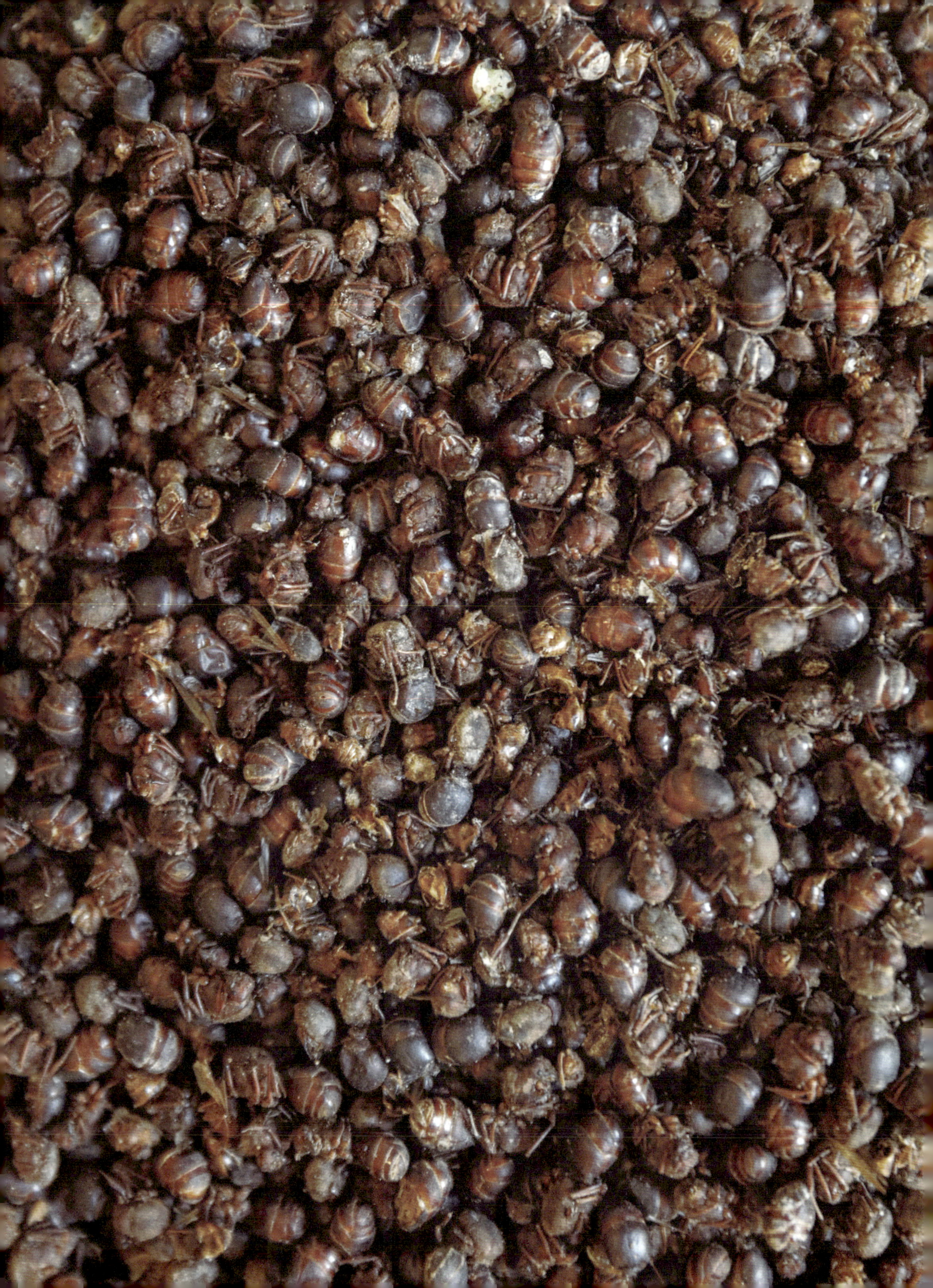

Chicatana ant mole, pickled cucumbers and purslane

My mom makes black mole empanadas covered with sugar and cinnamon. I've loved them since I was a little girl. She'd make them for massive dinner parties: she loved bringing together friends and family. The special thing about the dish was eating mole without chicken; it was just wrapped in puff pastry. Even today, I usually eat moles without animal protein, accompanying them either with vegetables or simply a good tortilla.

A couple years ago, we started to serve light variations of traditional moles at Rosetta: we added unusual vegetable pairings, like beets; reduced the fat and spiciness; and even incorporated them into desserts, omitting the garlic and onion and increasing the chocolate.

We arrived at chicatana ant mole while searching for a dish that would feature wild mushrooms as the main attraction. This kind of mole is typical to the states of Guerrero and Oaxaca, and it's rarely served without pork or turkey. Mushrooms seemed like an almost natural choice: both mushrooms and chicatanas appear with the rains, and nature is so wise that almost everything that grows close together, out of the same ground, goes well together. But it wasn't until we added cucumbers that the dish really started to shine. The creaminess of the mole, added to the earthy strength of the chicatanas, calls out for something to lighten and refresh it. Lo and behold, the wonderful cucumber unexpectedly achieves this feat. The cucumber doesn't stand out for its flavor, but rather for its freshness and texture. We further refreshed the mole by pickling some of the cucumbers in vinegar. Then came the purslane leaves to intensify the dish's aqueous side, diluting the density of the mole even more.

Chicatana ants have a flavor that was new to me until recently. I was amazed to learn about these flying ants and their transformation into a seasoning. When I tried the sauce, though, I found it so spicy that I wasn't really captivated by the flavor. Months later, we started experimenting with different ways to use chicatanas so that their taste would come through more clearly. In this way, we developed the vinaigrette we serve with cocopaches, nasturtium flowers, and avocado. The chicatanas play a much more prominent role in the mole. In addition to the flavor, paradoxically, they provide the animal protein

I'd sought to avoid. In fact, it's a singular form of animal protein from our country: unique, noble, and under-explored.

Chicatana ant mole

Makes 500 grams

Toast the oregano, thyme, star anise, cumin seeds, cinnamon, peppers, and cloves in a frying pan, stirring constantly for 5 minutes, until they start to become fragrant; then set aside.

Roast the tomatillos, tomatoes, onion, and garlic in the oven at 220°C for 15 minutes or until the skin darkens in color and everything is fully cooked.

De-vein the peppers, rinse them with plenty of water, dry them thoroughly, and fry them in the lard until well browned.

In a frying pan, toast the sesame seeds, pumpkin seeds, peanuts, pecans, and almonds until lightly browned.

In another frying pan, roast the chicatanas over medium heat, sautéing them constantly for 5 to 10 minutes, or until they're very crunchy and start to give off an earthy fragrance.

Blend all the spices until they make a powder. Then add the tomatillos, tomatoes, peppers, onion, garlic, and a little chicken stock, blending until they form a stiff paste. Add the chopped chocolate and the seeds, then blend again until all the ingredients are smooth and fully mixed.

Finally, add the chicatanas and the salt and blend again until they're completely mixed into the mole. Add the rest of the broth, mix, and set aside.

Charred Persian cucumbers

Makes 200 grams

Wash the cucumbers with cold water, dry well, and char them directly on the fire until dark in color. While they're still hot, transfer them to the vinegar so they can marinate. Let them cool at room temperature before cutting the cucumbers down the middle, then diagonally into 3 equal parts.

Lemon cucumbers in vinegar

Makes 150 grams

Wash the cucumbers with cold water, dry them well, and put them into a bowl with the warm vinegar. Let cool at room temperature.

Cut the cucumbers in 4 or 6 wedges.

To Serve

Spoon the chicatana ant mole onto the middle of each plate. On top of it, add some pieces of Persian cucumber and some lemon cucumber quarters. Finally, add the purslane leaves.

Serves 4

Chicatana ant mole
1 gram oregano
1 gram thyme
1 gram star anise
1 gram cumin seed
1 gram whole cinnamon
1 gram peppercorn
1 gram black pepper
1 gram clove
10 grams tomatillo
85 grams tomatoes
15 grams white onion
4 grams garlic
6 grams ancho pepper
7 grams pasilla pepper
7 grams guajillo pepper
21 grams lard
4 grams sesame seeds
2 grams green pumpkin seeds
2 grams peanuts
2 grams pecans
2 grams whole almonds
70 grams chicatanas
12 grams Mexican chocolate
300 milliliters chicken stock
3 grams salt

Charred Persian cucumbers
400 milliliters white wine vinegar
200 grams Persian cucumbers

Lemon cucumbers in vinegar
150 grams lemon cucumbers
350 milliliters chardonnay vinegar

480 grams chicatana ant mole
200 grams charred Persian cucumbers
150 grams lemon cucumber in vinegar
20 grams purslane leaves on tiny sprigs

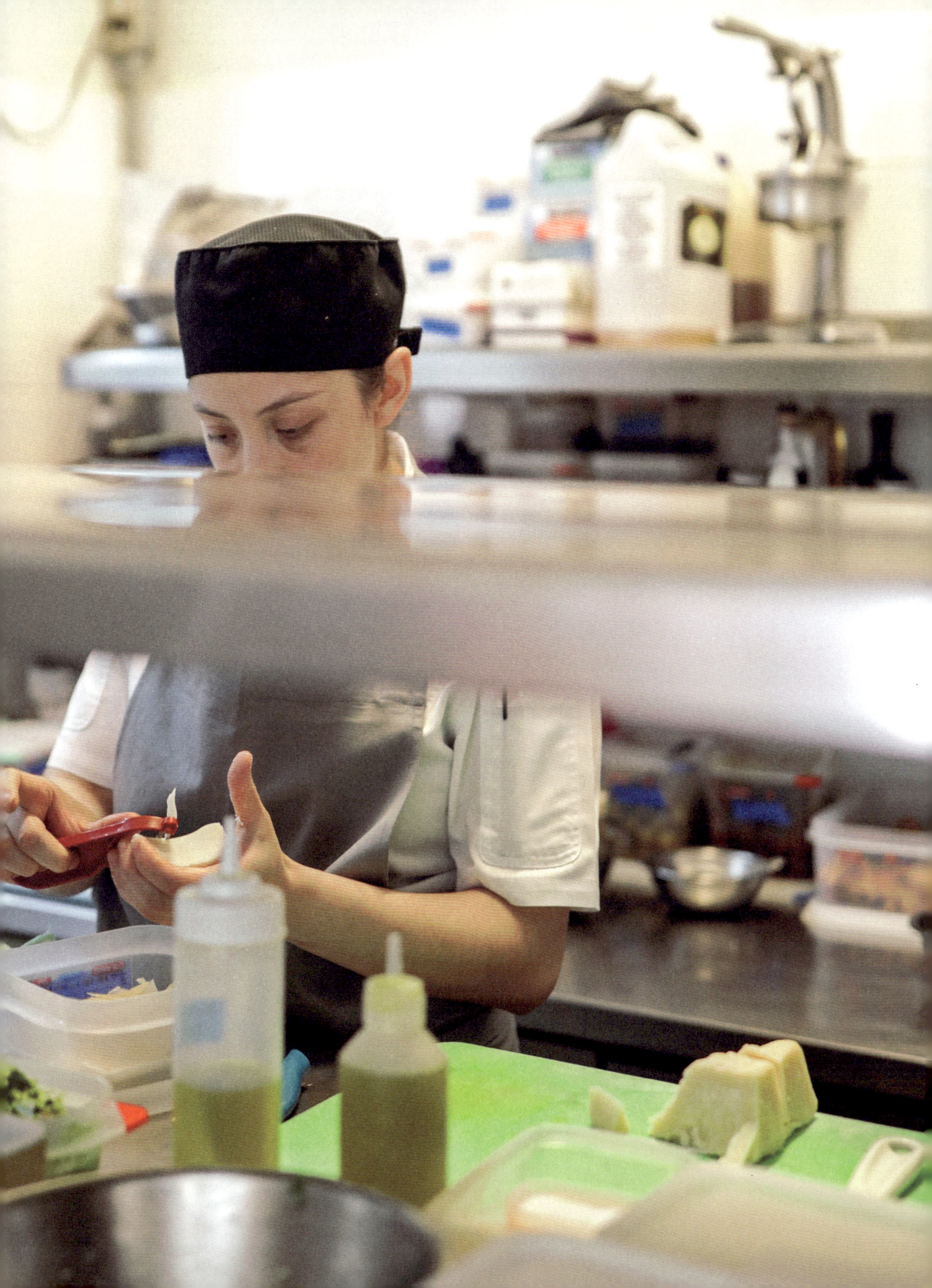

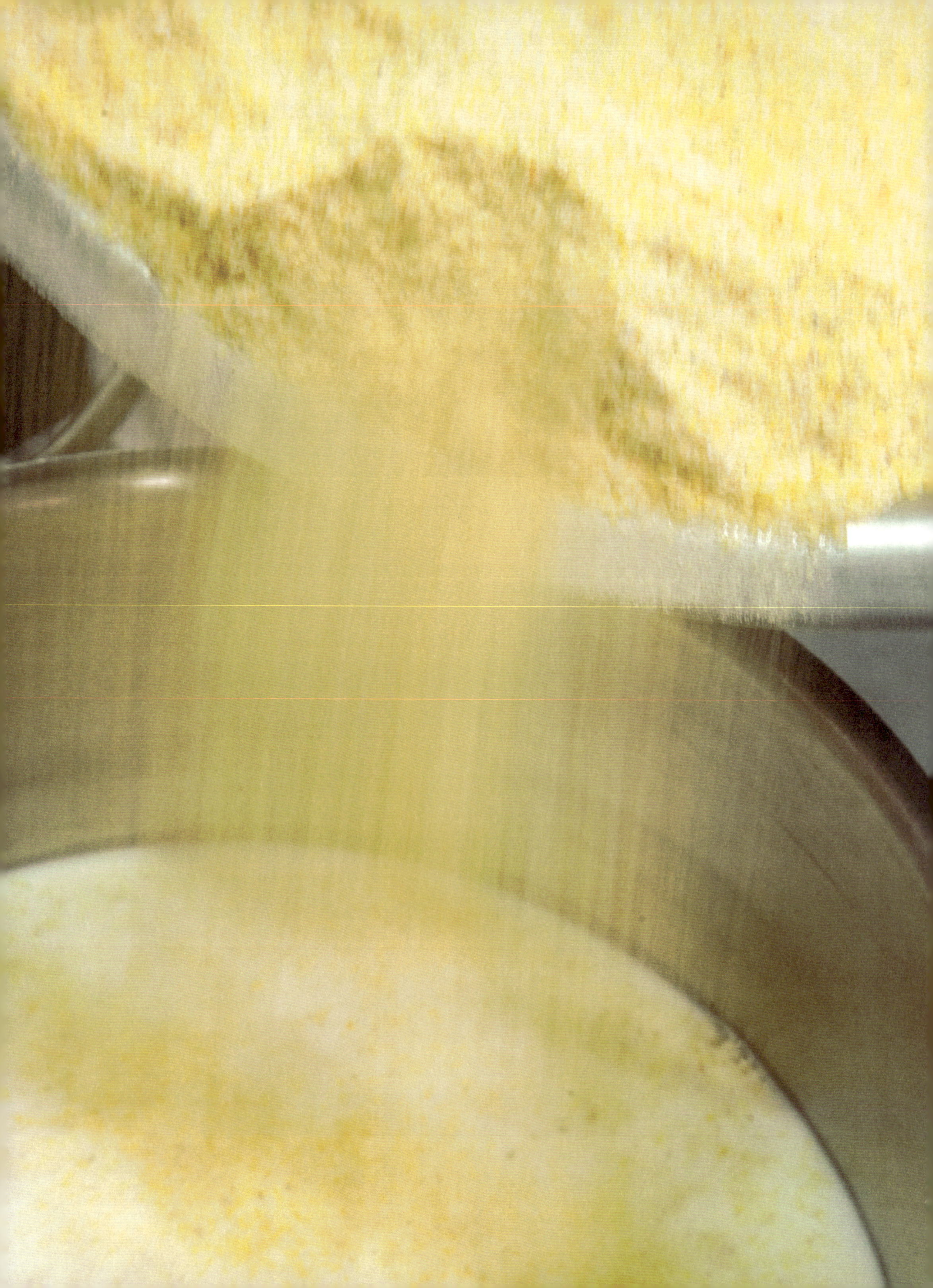

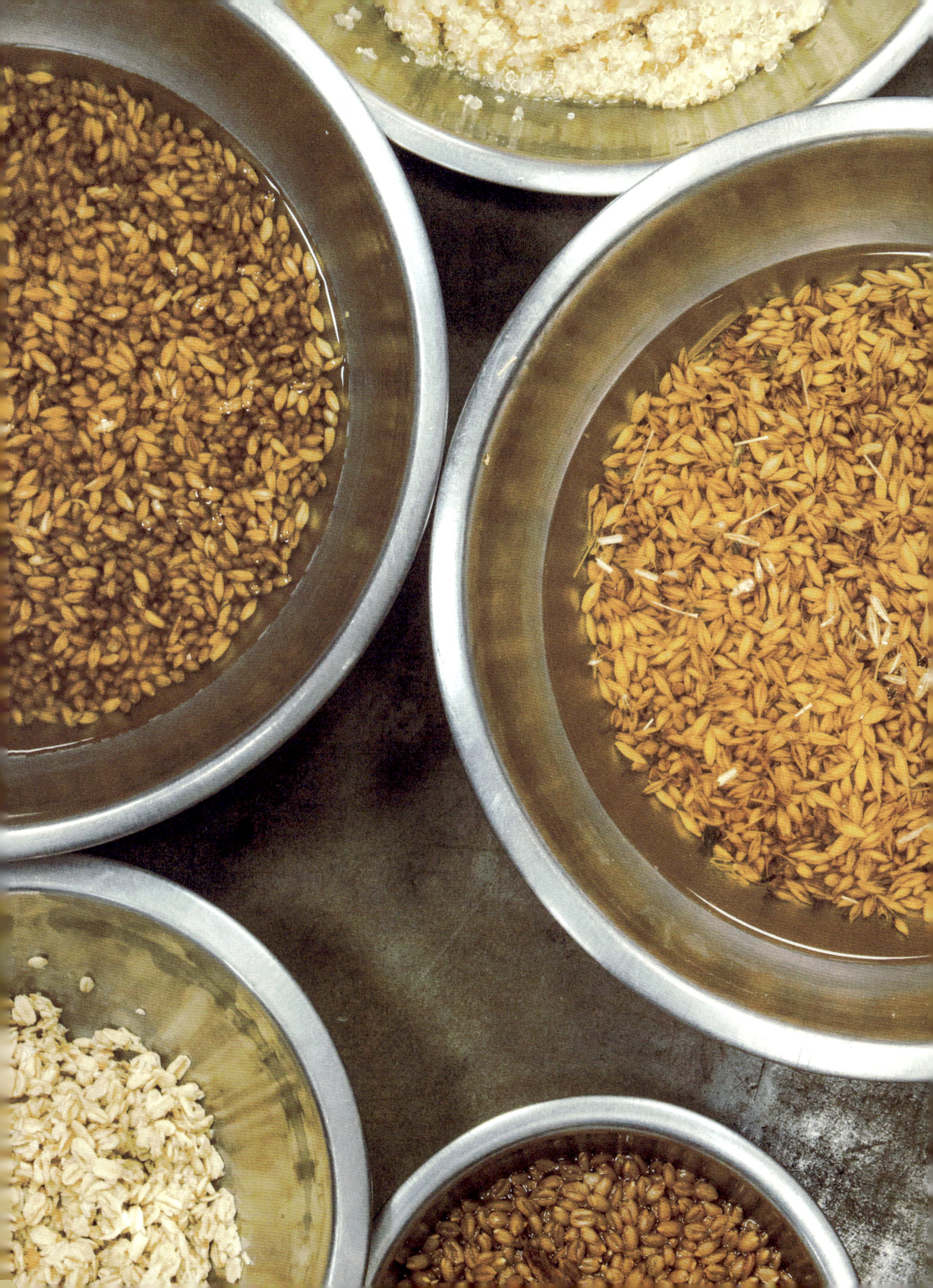

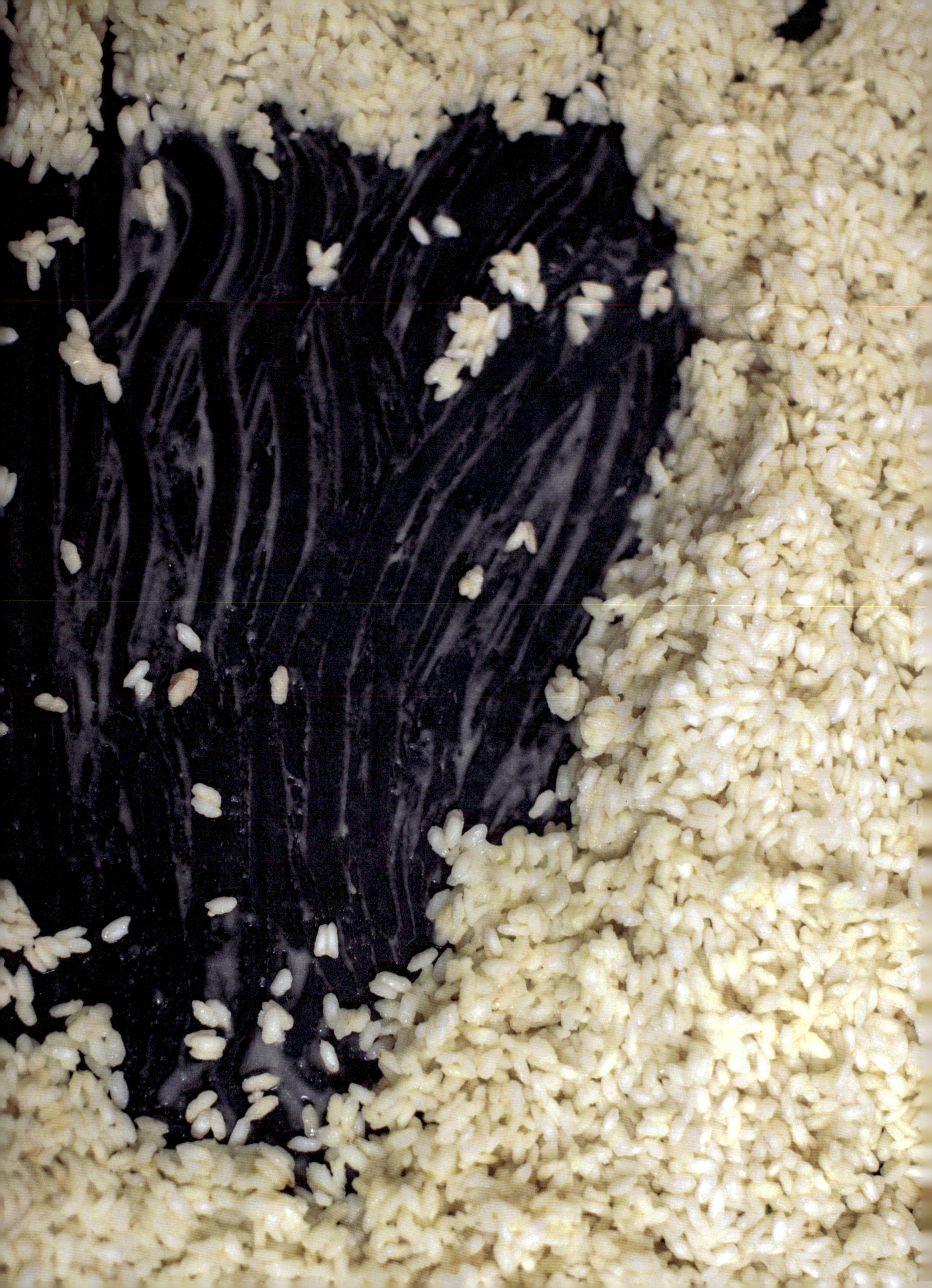

II
Grains

Grains	**117**
Corn tamal, celery root, and smoked butter	121
Potato gnocchi, Ramonetti cheese, grape tomatoes, and smoked eel	126
Potato gnocchi, chaya and hoja santa	129
Farro, lobster and fennel	131
Beef tongue risotto with cilantro	134
Our Pasta	**145**
Fresh Pasta	147
Ricotta ravioli, lemon, and lemon thyme	148
Smoked beet tortelli, sheep's milk cheese, and sorrel	149
Mesquite tagliatelle with wild mushrooms	152
Buckwheat ravioli with 'nduja and burrata	156
Tagliolini with sea cradle, zucchini, and bottarga	158
Tagliatelle with sausage and chile de árbol ragù	163
Pápalo pappardelle with duck ragù	167

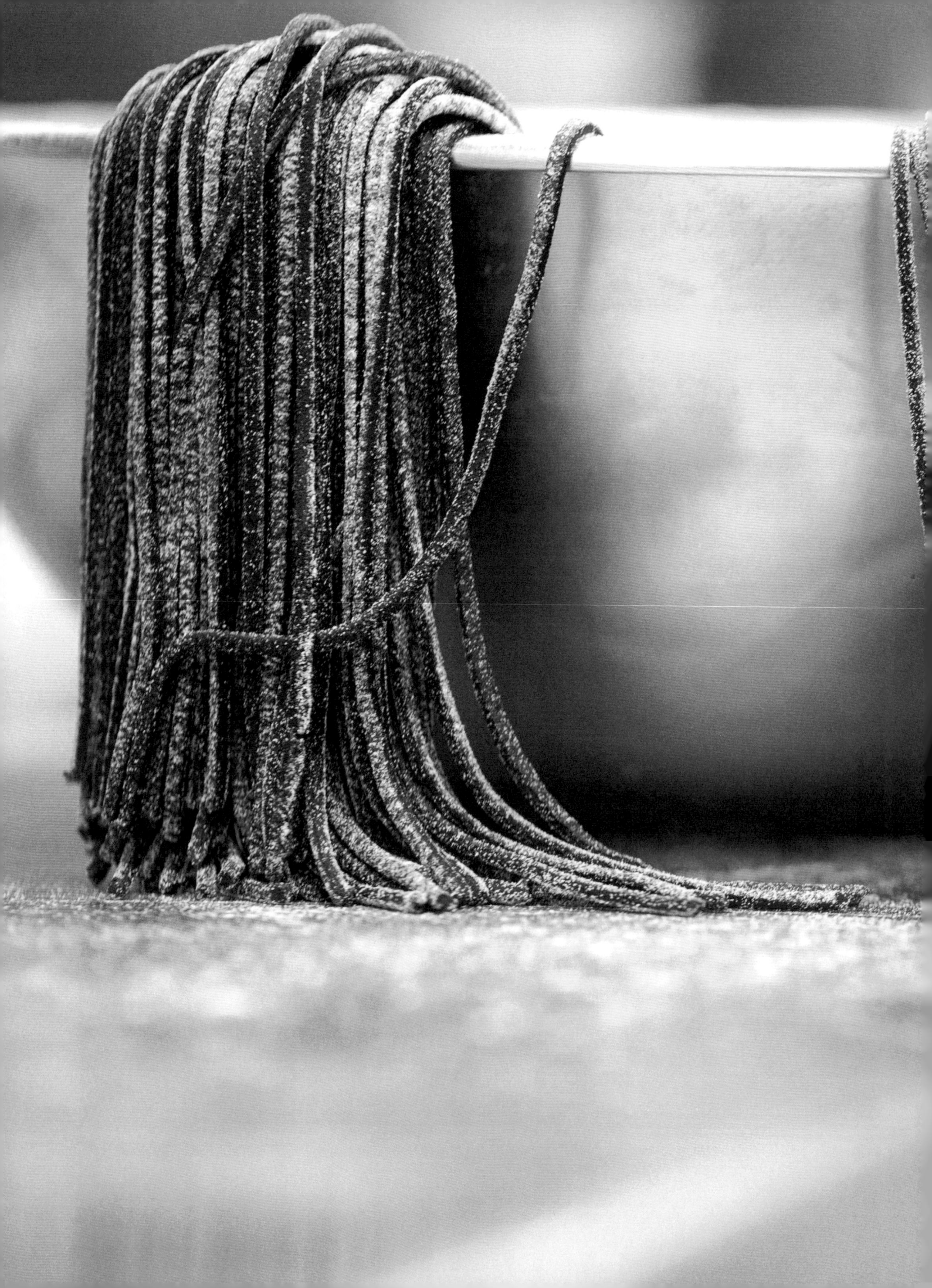

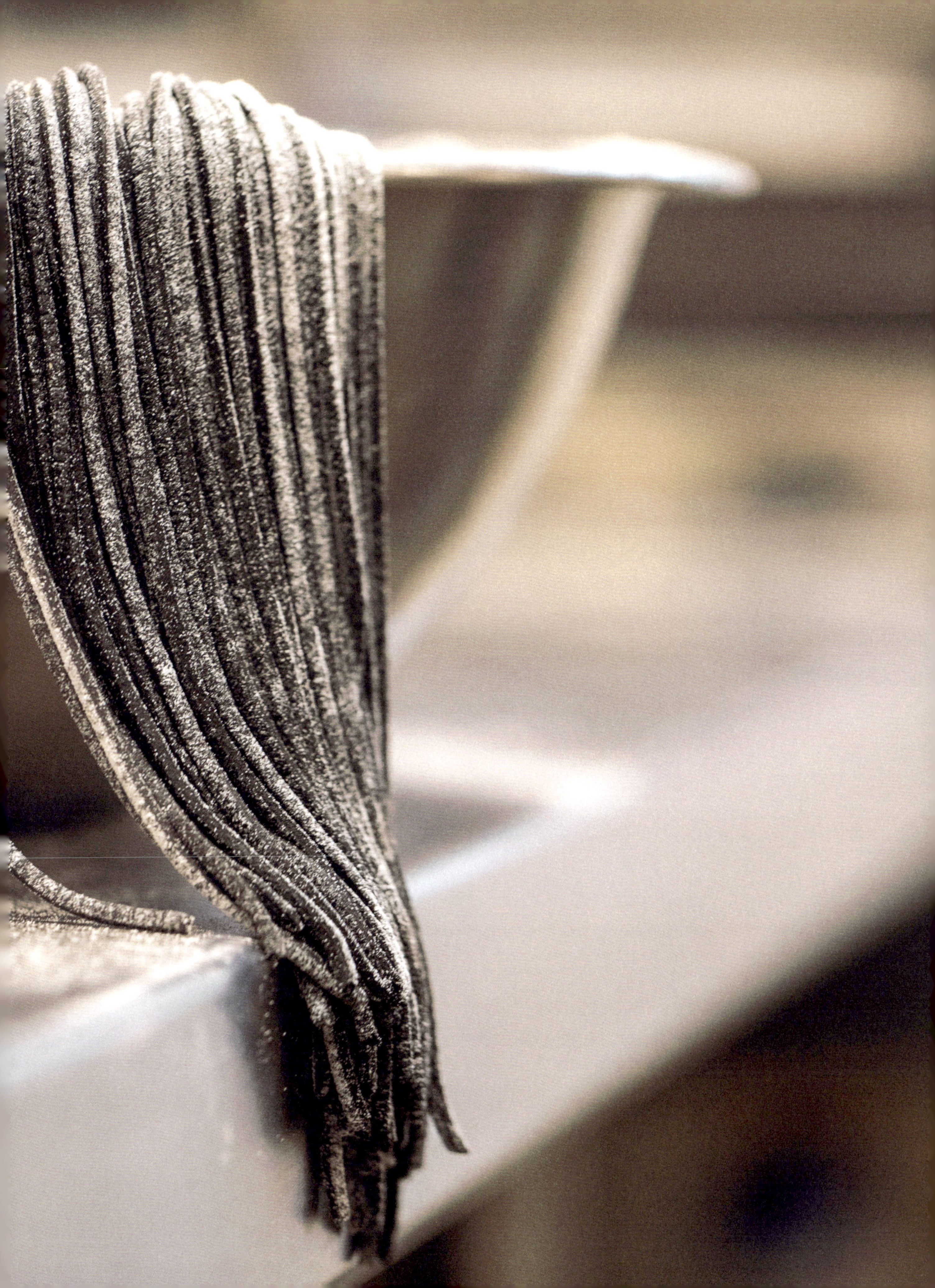

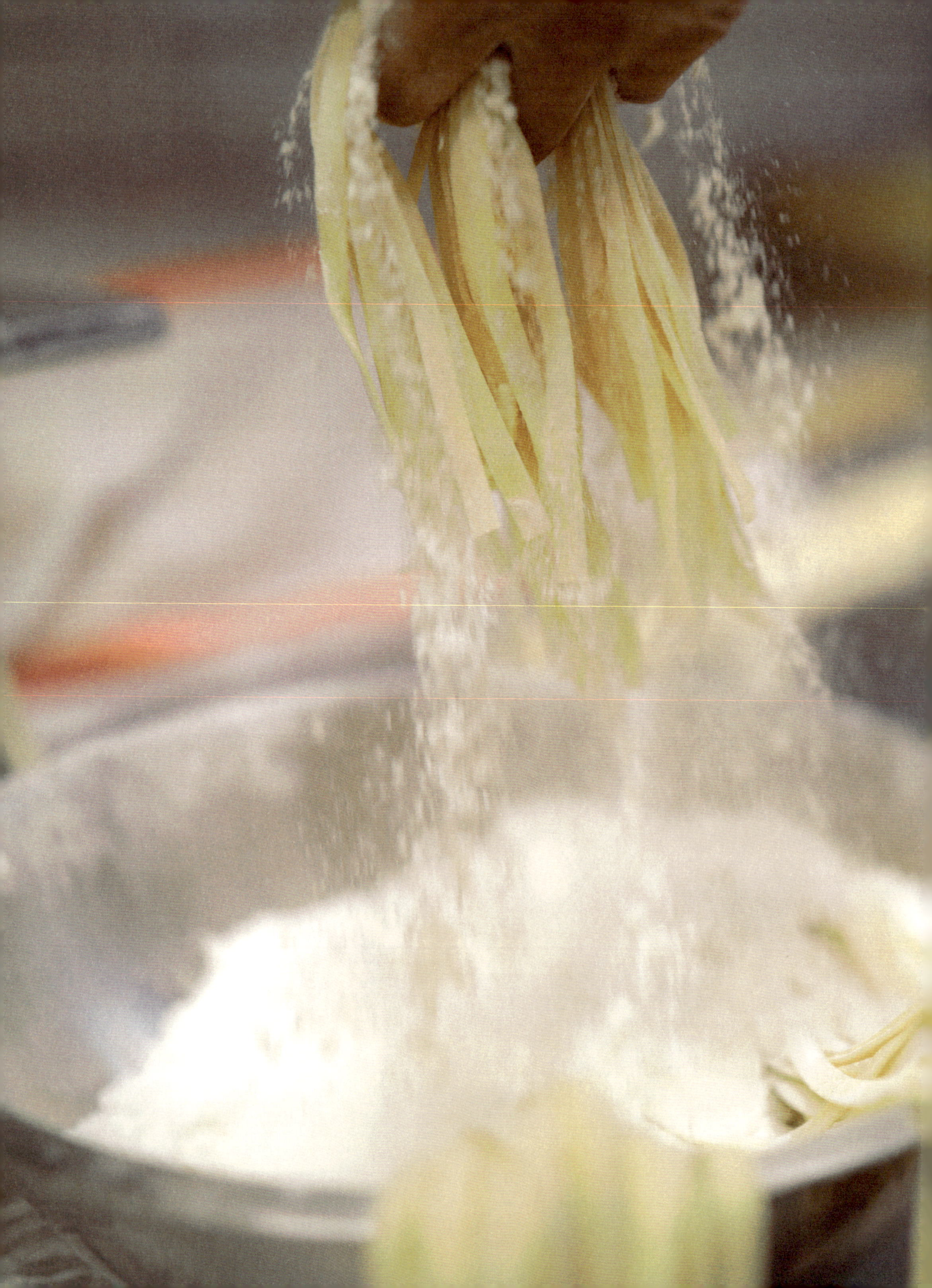

Grains

Grains have been humans' primary foodstuff for centuries. However, the discourse in recent decades has demonized them, associating them with poor diet and obesity. But grains aren't necessarily harmful to our health. The problems are rooted in the various industrial and chemical processes applied to grains today, which strip them of many nutritional properties.

Here's an example. To prolong the time span in which wheat can be sold without spoiling, the wheat germ is removed; wheat germ is an element containing certain oils that make wheat more perishable. This element, though, also contains most of the nutrients in wheat. And so, for purely commercial reasons, wheat has lost not only much of its flavor, but most of its nutritional content, too. Other grains have been affected by similar processes, as well as by the incorporation of pesticides, fertilizers, and other genetically modified organisms (GMOs).

I encourage the consumption of grains that haven't been altered by these industrial, chemical, and genetic processes I've mentioned above. This is my position for several reasons. Beyond their flavors and unique textures, grains contain important minerals, vitamins, proteins, and amino acids; they're a great source of carbohydrates and fibers; and they're low in fat. In my kitchen, therefore, we've sought out nutritional, unmodified, sustainably produced, and uniquely flavored grains.

Grains play an essential role at Rosetta. We use them to make pasta, bread, tamales, soups, and desserts. We pay as much attention to them as to the ingredients accompanying them; we never treat them as a means to an end. Without a doubt, grains like wheat, corn, oats, rye, buckwheat, farro, rice, and amaranth—as well as fruit- or legume-based flours like ramón and mesquite—are a cornerstone of my cooking.

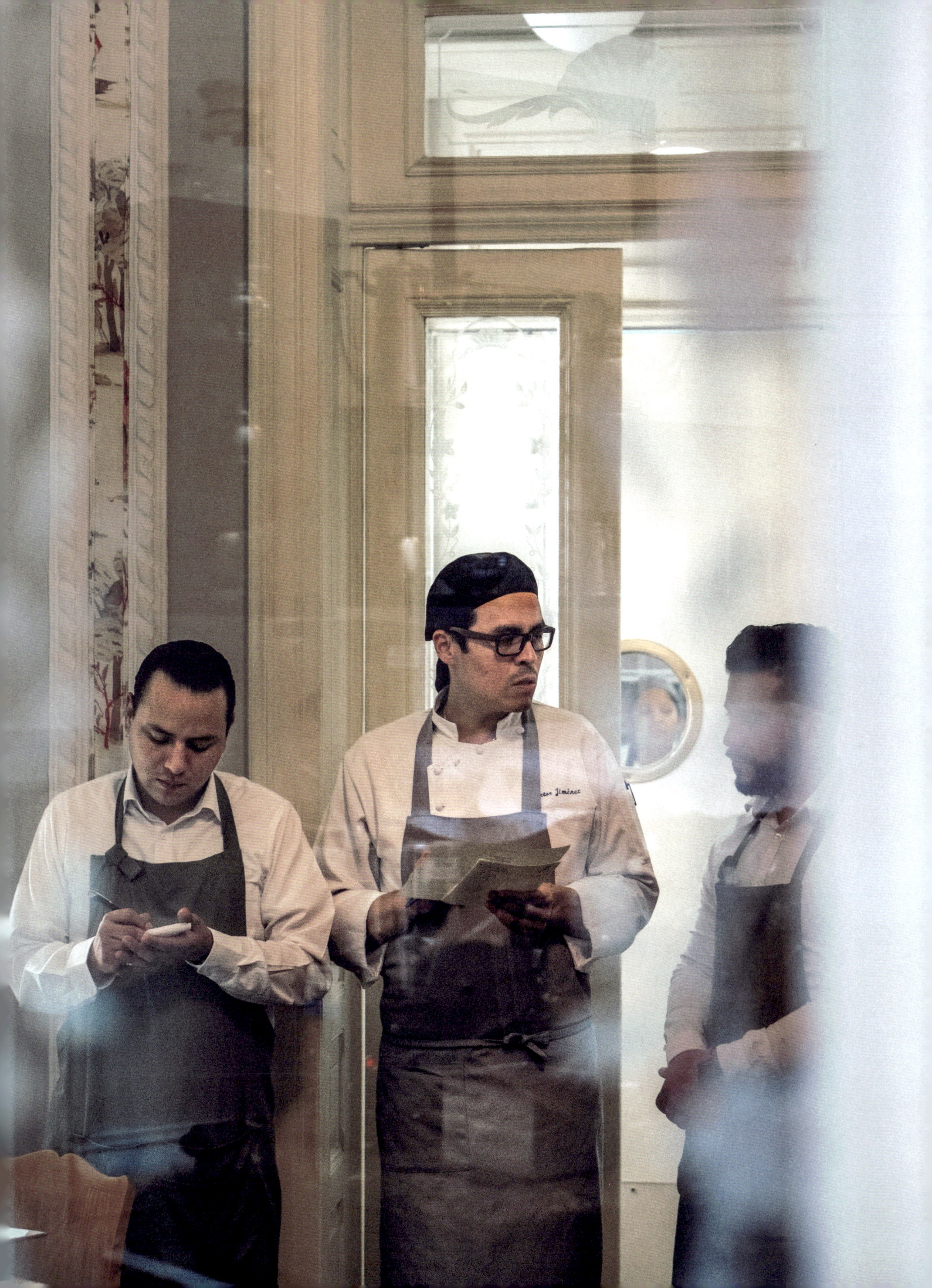
Jiménez

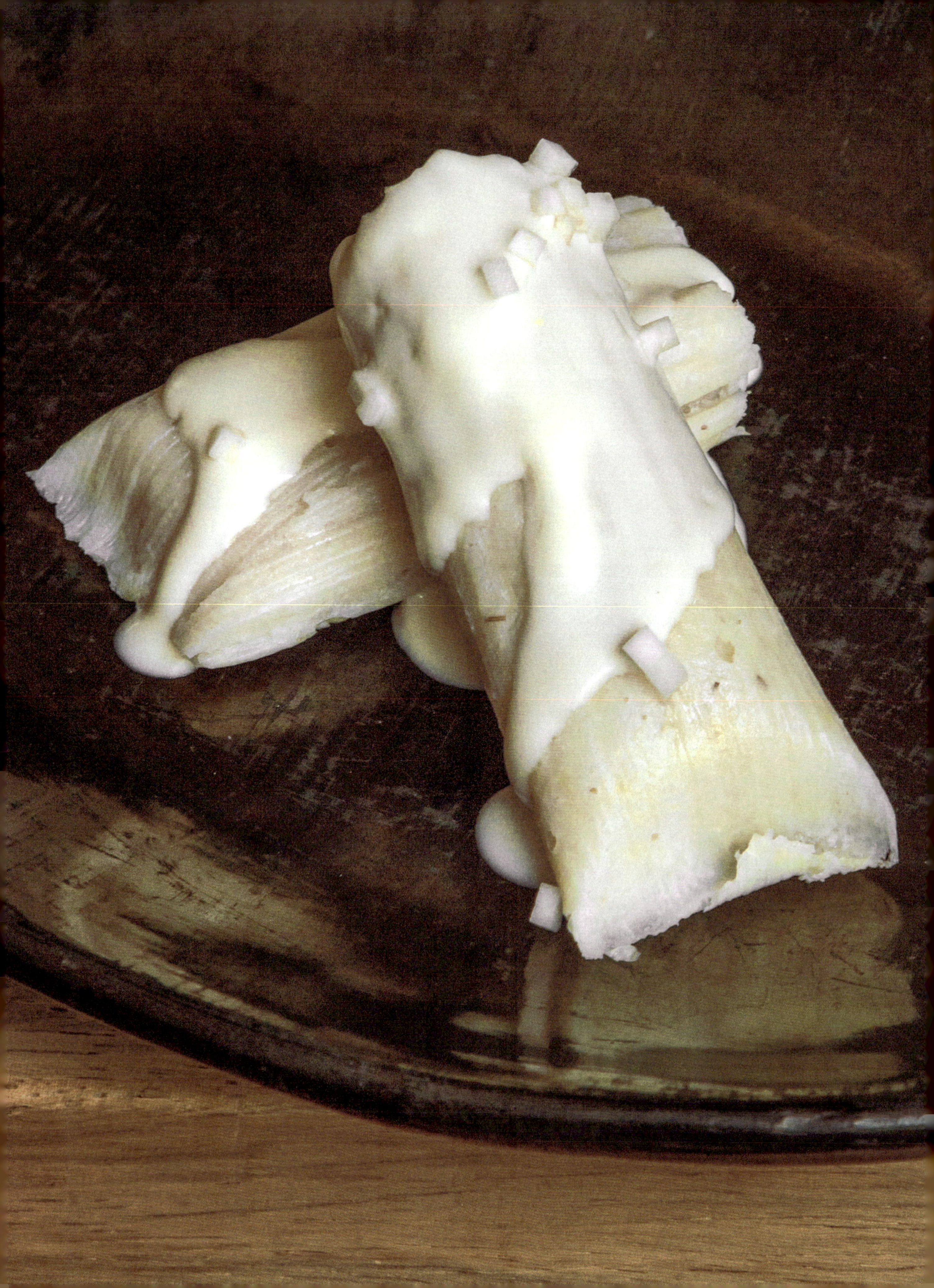

Corn tamal, celery root, and smoked butter

I'm crazy about tamales: I think they're the most exquisite kind of simplicity. The combination of corn masa with another ingredient, wrapped in cornhusk (or banana leaf), makes for a complete meal. Delicious and restorative, tamales are also easy to transport and to eat. In my opinion, the very highest form of tamal is the one made of sweet corn or elote. It's made with kernels of corn right off the cob, instead of using corn cooked with water and quicklime (nixtamalizado). This makes it softer and lighter than other tamales. When you make it, the sweet corn shouldn't be completely ground—not only so that you can feel the texture of the kernels when you take a bite, but also so that their consistency remains dense without being completely compacted.

Corn tamales don't usually come with a filling like other tamales. For this one, though, we add a little celery root purée for more thickness. Celery root is a creamy root with a note of freshness that's rarely found in other root vegetables. We also add a bit of smoked butter on top of the tamal. This final touch evokes the traditional means of cooking tamales: in a pot over a wood fire.

Since pre-Hispanic times, tamal-making has been a woman's task—as is true of almost all food, both in Mexico and in the rest of the world. Women have historically been relegated to the kitchen. Our work has been underappreciated, made invisible. Paradoxically, cooking is an effective way to combat this discrimination.

Celery root purée

Serves 4

155 grams celery root, peeled
½ sprig rosemary
2 grams garlic
100 milliliters water
40 milliliters milk
25 milliliters heavy cream

Makes 250 grams

Cut the celery root into medium-sized chunks.
Place the celery root, along with the rosemary sprig and the garlic, on a deep tray with a bit of water, making sure not to completely cover the celery root. Cover the tray with aluminum foil.
Bake for 45 minutes at 100°C.
Remove from the oven and blend the celery root only. Gently heat the milk and the cream and add them gradually to the purée while blending. Keep blending until the purée is smooth.

Smoked butter sauce

120 milliliters heavy cream
60 grams butter
15 grams mesquite chips
200 grams charcoal

Makes 120 grams

There are various techniques for smoking butter. Two are quite practical. The first way involves placing a tray with wood shavings into a household oven, along with the product you want to smoke. It's important to seal the oven well so that the smoke doesn't escape. The second way involves setting the product to smoke on a grill, tossing wood shavings into the coals and immediately covering the grill to keep in the smoke.

Smoke the cream and the butter. Let them sit for approximately 2 minutes or until the wood shavings have stopped burning and are no longer giving off smoke.

Set aside the smoked cream and butter for 30 minutes.

Transfer the cream to a pot and cook over low heat until it's reduced by half.

Once the cream has been reduced, add the butter little by little and whisk the sauce.

Set aside in a warm place.

Tamales

420 grams corn kernels (approximately 4 cobs of corn)
7 grams salt
13 grams sugar
100 grams vegetable shortening
40 grams celery root purée

Makes 8 tamales

Wash the corn, discard the silk, and set aside the husks. Cut from top to bottom to de-kernel the corn and set aside the kernels.

Using a blender, crush the corn kernels with the salt and sugar until they start to mix together. Don't over-blend.

Melt the butter in a pot over medium heat.

In a bowl, combine the corn mixture with the shortening.

Take a corn husk: in the middle, place a spoonful of corn purée, then spread a spoonful of celery root purée, followed by another spoonful of corn purée. Fold the husk so that it's closed on top and open on the bottom, giving shape to the tamal.

In a pot approximately 30 centimeters in diameter, place the corn kernels at the bottom and cover them in water. On top of them, arrange a few corn husks to serve as a base.

Arrange the tamales vertically, with their openings pointing upward. Stuff the remaining leaves into the gaps so that the tamales won't fall.

Place a couple more husks on top of the tamales and cover the pot.

Cook over medium heat. Once the water starts to boil, reduce to low heat for 20 minutes. Remove from the burner and keep the tamales hot in the pot until ready to serve.

To Serve

8 tamales
120 grams smoked butter sauce
20 grams raw celery root, diced into ½-centimeter cubes
1 pinch salt flakes

Remove the husk from each tamal and place two in the center of each plate.

Bathe each tamal in smoked butter sauce, add the celery root cubes, then sprinkle a pinch of salt flakes onto the tamales.

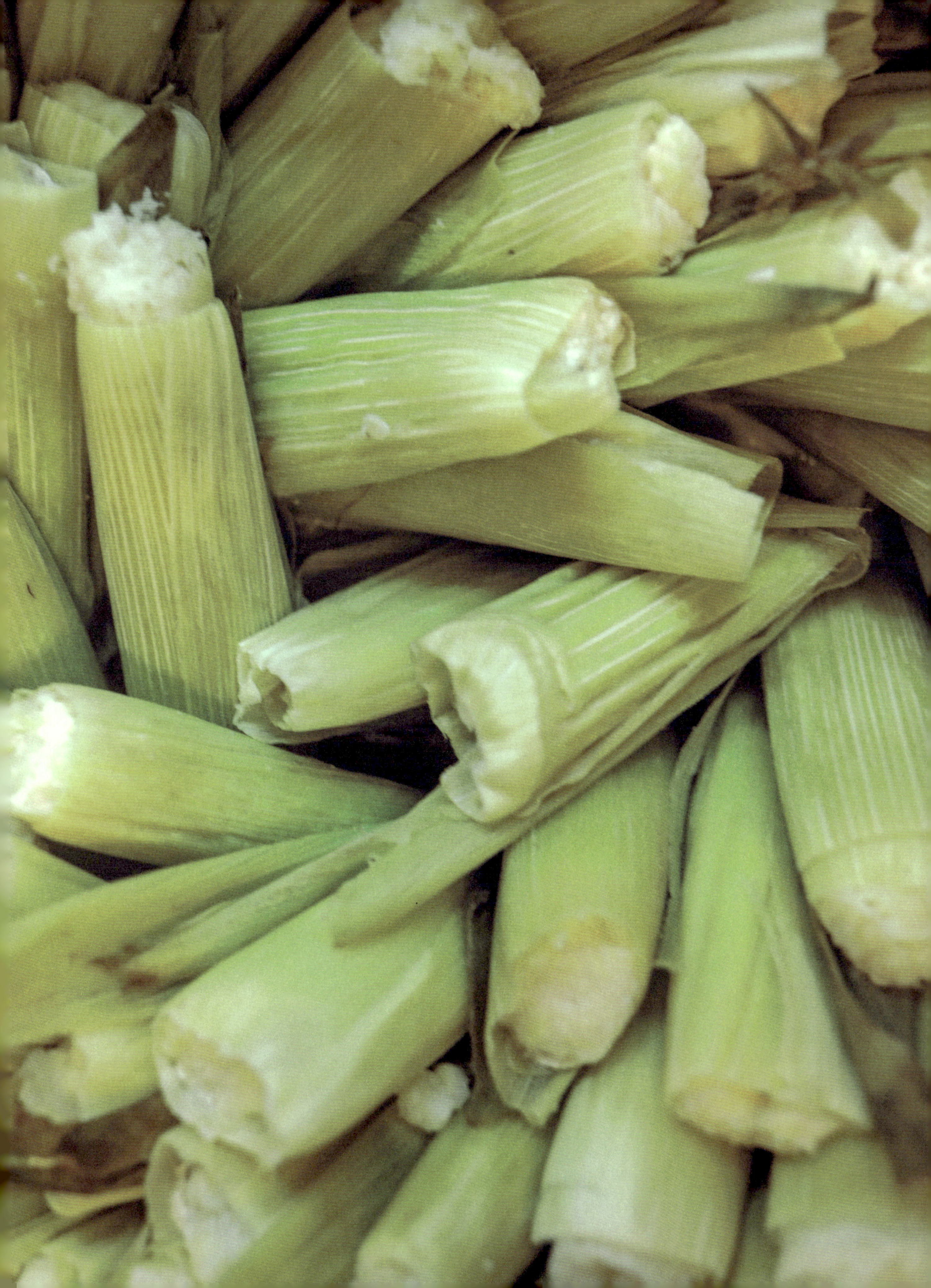

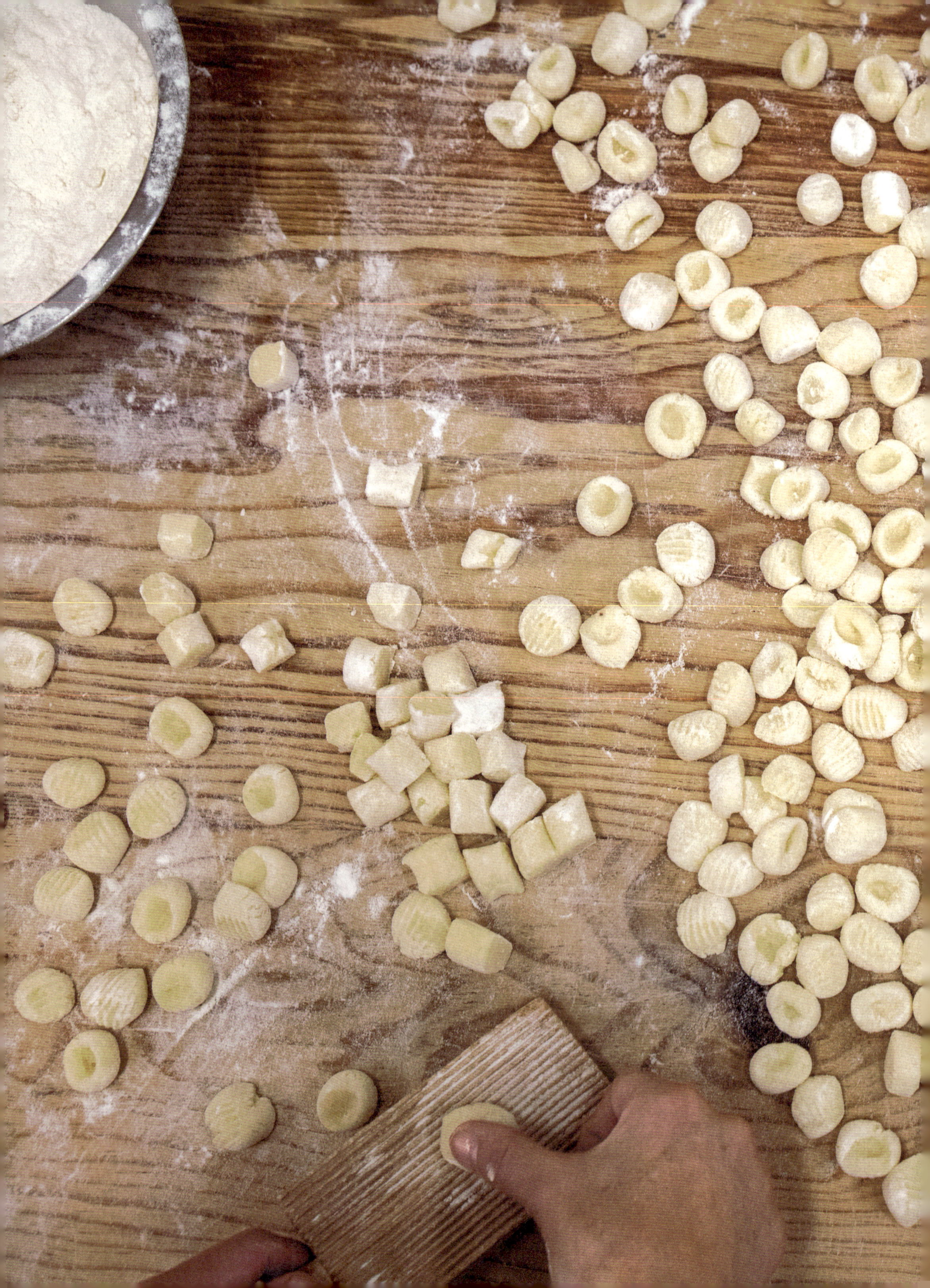

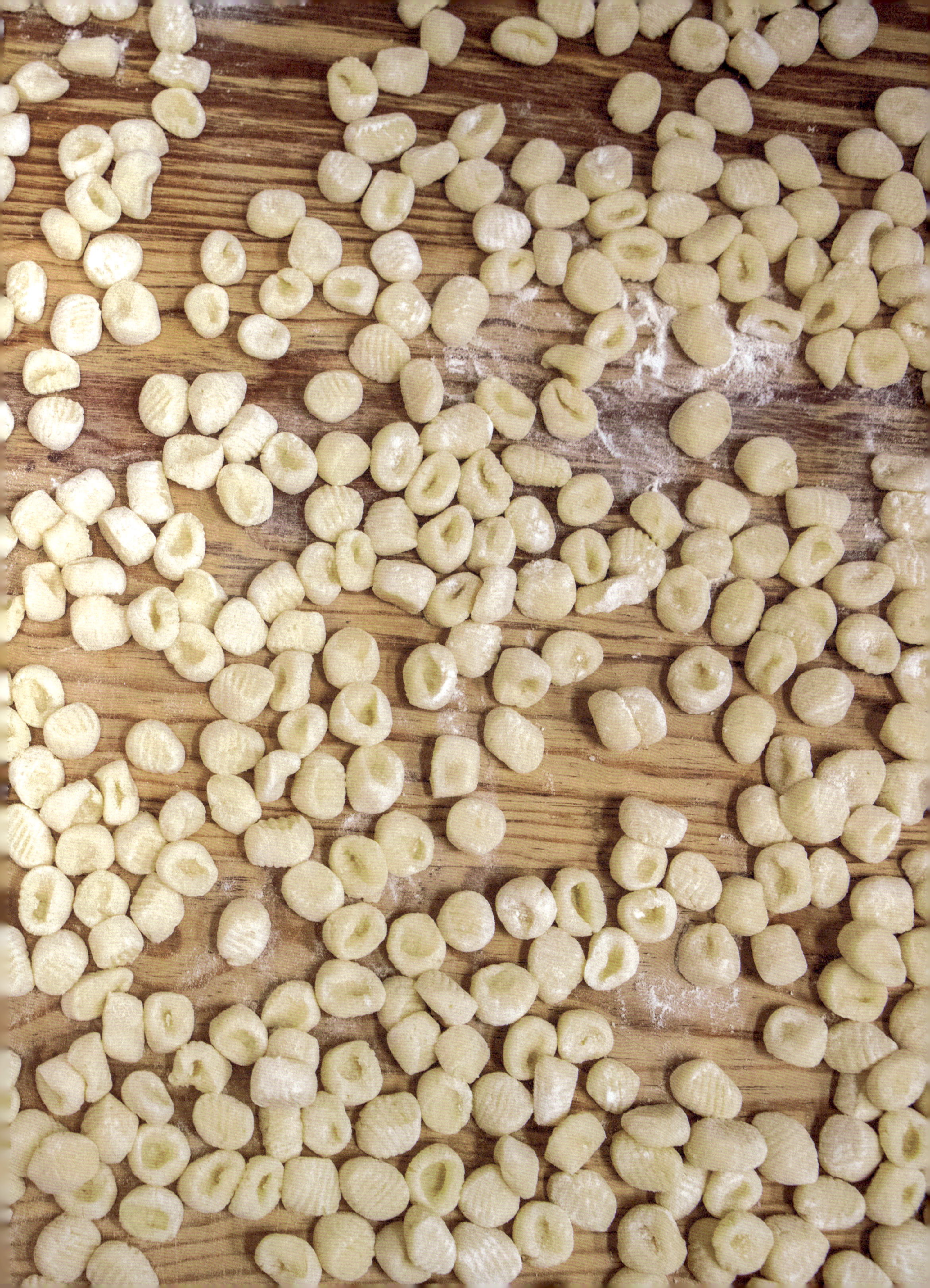

Potato gnocchi, Ramonetti cheese, grape tomatoes, and smoked eel

Unfortunately, many people are familiar with industrialized potato gnocchi—the packaged kind you can make in a couple minutes. Fortunately, though, handmade potato gnocchi are the exact opposite. While the former are compact and chewy and taste like plastic, the latter are spongy, melt in your mouth, and taste like baked potato.

It's relatively easy to make potato gnocchi at home. At Rosetta, we've learned some key details over the years that can be taken as practical advice. You need to find potatoes that still have a little earth on them. And they should be more or less the same size, so they'll cook evenly. Once the water starts to boil, you should lower the heat so that the water boils gently; this keeps the potato skin from breaking and makes sure they don't get wet on the inside. The potatoes should be well cooked, though not overcooked: you should be able to insert a knife into them with no effort, but without the potatoes coming apart. You'll need to work quickly: the potato shouldn't get cold (that's why it's best to make this recipe in a group and with less than a kilo and a half of potatoes in each batch). When it comes to making the potato purée, you should use a press or fine strainer. Try to add the minimum amount of flour to the mixture.

On the Rosetta menu, we generally serve potato gnocchi accompanied by different sauces and ingredients. We've served them, to mention just a few, with Ramonetti cheese, grape tomatoes, and smoked eel; with lamb ragù; with chaya and hoja santa; with artichokes; with oxtail; with butter and sage; with lobster and herbs; with fish and eggplant; with broccolini and anchovies; with asparagus, tarragon, and lemon; with bacon and peas; and with wild mushrooms.

Potato gnocchi

Serves 4

600 grams potatoes
70 grams eggs
5 grams salt
130 grams flour

Makes 650 grams

Place the potatoes in a saucepan and cover them with water at room temperature. Salt the water. When the water reaches a boil, lower the heat and let the potatoes cook until well done, making sure the skin doesn't break. Peel the potatoes and put them through a food mill or fine potato press. Add the egg, the salt, and the flour to the pressed potatoes. Mix with your hands or a wooden spoon until everything is well combined. Wrap the dough in a cloth.

Take a bit of the potato dough. On an ideally wooden surface, make long cylinders, about 1.5 centimeters in diameter.

Cut the cylinders into 1-centimeter-long pieces and press each one with a gnocchi board or a fork. You can also leave them unmarked. Place the gnocchi on the back of a floured tray so that they won't stick together while you finish shaping them.

Baked grape tomatoes

100 grams grape tomatoes
5 grams salt
20 milliliters olive oil
3 grams fresh thyme
½ clove garlic

Place the tomatoes on a baking sheet with the salt, olive oil, fresh thyme, and ½ garlic clove cut in two. Bake for 10 minutes at 230°C or until they start to brown.

To Serve

2 liters water
30 grams sea salt
80 grams butter
100 grams Ramonetti cheese in cubes
600 grams potato gnocchi
40 grams grated sheep's milk cheese
40 grams Parmigiano Reggiano, grated
120 milliliters pasta water
100 grams smoked eel
4 grams fresh thyme
100 grams baked grape tomatos

Put a saucepan of water on the stove, bring to a boil, and add the salt.

Put the butter and the Ramonetti cheese in a frying pan.

Pour the gnocchi into the saucepan with the boiling water. Once they start to float, remove them from the water and add them to the frying pan with the cheese sauce.

Add the sheep's milk cheese, the parmesan, and a little of the pasta water.

Serve the gnocchi in deep dishes, adding the baked grape tomatoes and dressing with their juice. Add the eel, after cutting it into little squares, and add a bit of fresh thyme.

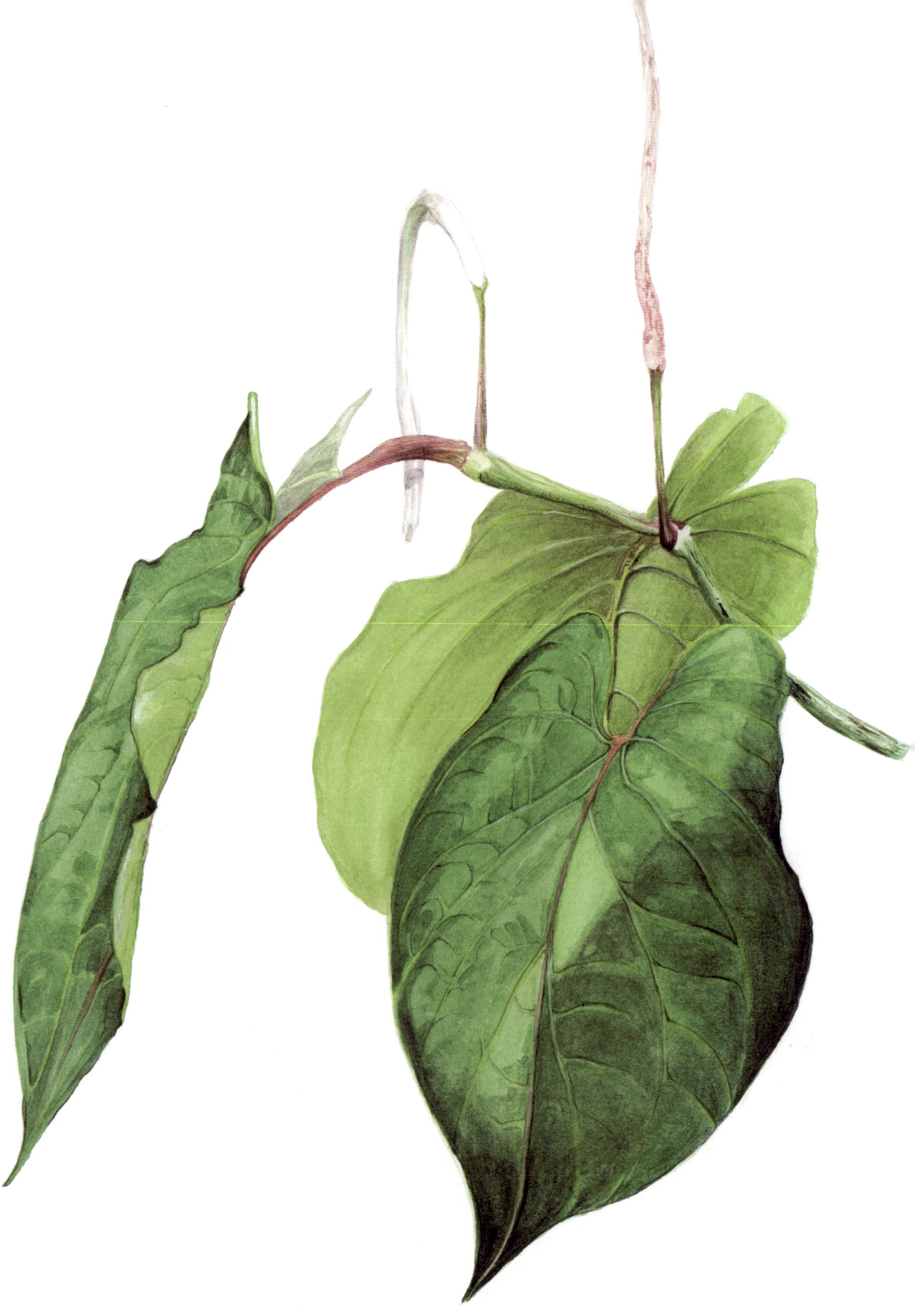

Potato gnocchi, chaya and hoja santa

To accompany these potato gnocchi, we make an herb-based sauce starring the hoja santa leaf. This anise-flavored herb grows in central and southern Mexico. Its velvety leaf is usually served with corn-based dishes (like tamales and quesadillas), beans, and fish—often as a wrapper, because it can grow to be up to 30 centimeters long. For this dish, we mix the hoja santa with basil, parsley, and chaya. The basil adds sweetness and fragrance; the parsley adds freshness. The chaya, though it has a gentle flavor, intensifies the green color of the herbs with its high chlorophyll content. This is an iron- and protein-rich bush that grows abundantly on the Yucatan Peninsula, where it has been a basic element of the Mayan diet for hundreds of years.

When these herbs are combined, blanched, and ground together, we come up with a thick, bright green paste we then mix with pine nuts, pumpkin seeds, parmesan cheese, and olive oil to obtain the sauce we serve with the gnocchi. The dish is a variation on the classic Genovese pesto made with basil, pine nuts, and parmesan. However, with the addition of the hoja santa and the chaya, this one has a stronger anise flavor than the original. Moreover, by incorporating local herbs that are different from the usual ones, we preserve their use and grant them new possibilities as ingredients.

Hoja santa pesto

Serves 4

40 grams pine nuts
30 grams pumpkin seeds
60 grams parsley
60 grams basil
60 grams hoja santa
30 grams chaya
4 grams garlic
4 grams salt
140 milliliters olive oil
100 grams Parmigiano Reggiano

Makes 500 grams

Toast the pine nuts in a frying pan with a little olive oil and salt. Set aside to cool. Repeat the process with the pumpkin seeds.

In a pot of boiling water, blanch the herbs separately and then blend them together with the garlic, salt, and olive oil.

Add in the parmesan until the mixture is smooth and uniform.

Pour into a bowl and lightly cover with olive oil. Refrigerate if you don't intend to serve immediately.

Potato gnocchi

600 grams potatoes
70 grams egg
5 grams salt
130 grams flour

Makes 650 grams

Place the potatoes in a saucepan and cover them with water at room temperature. Salt the water. When the water reaches a boil, lower the heat and let the potatoes cook until well done, making sure the skin doesn't break. Peel the potatoes and put them through a food mill or fine potato press. Add the egg, the salt, and the flour to the pressed potatoes. Mix with your hands or a wooden spoon until everything is well combined. Wrap the dough in a cloth.

Take a bit of the potato dough. On an ideally wooden surface, make long cylinders, about 1.5 cm in diameter.

Cut the cylinders into 1-centimeter-long pieces and press each one with a gnocchi board or the back of a fork. You can also leave them unmarked. Place the gnocchi on the back of a floured tray so that they won't stick together while you finish shaping them.

To Serve

2 liters water
30 grams sea salt
230 grams hoja santa pesto
40 milliliters olive oil
40 grams sweet corn
600 grams potato gnocchi
120 milliliters pasta water
80 grams Parmigiano Reggiano
10 grams toasted pumpkin seeds

Boil a pot of water with the sea salt.

Transfer the hoja santa pesto into a bowl, along with the olive oil. Cook the corn kernels briefly in the pot of boiling water, strain them, and add half of the Parmigiano Reggiano add them to the pesto. Put the gnocchi into the same pot. Once they start to float, remove them and transfer them to the bowl with the corn and the pesto, adding a bit of the pasta water to loosen the herb paste and mix well.

Serve the gnocchi in deep dishes, scattering the other half of the parmesan cheese and pumpkin seeds on top.

Farro, lobster and fennel

The strength of this dish isn't the much-prized lobster tail, but rather the lobster coral, heads, and shells. We use the coral (a semi-liquid sac that contains the unfertilized roe) to make a butter with a strong lobster-y taste. We use the heads and shells to make a concentrated lobster broth, sweet and intense in flavor.

We then use this lobster broth to hydrate the farro, a kind of sweet-tasting, firm-textured wheat. While farro has been consumed for centuries, this grain has become better known in recent years as an alternative to standard wheat. Let's not forget that wheat began to be drastically modified in the twentieth century in order to make it more economically productive and profitable, which has diluted its flavor and nutritional value. Since it hasn't been genetically modified, farro still contains a substantial amount of nutrients, and it has a wonderful flavor. I like using it for all of these reasons. We cooks shouldn't only consider how ingredients taste; we must also think about their nutritional qualities and the environmental and social consequences of consuming them.

Serves 4

800 grams lobster heads and shells
10 milliliters safflower oil
10 grams shallots
20 grams parsley stalks
40 grams carrots, cubed
20 grams tomato paste
2 liters water

Lobster broth

Makes 1 liter

Wash the lobster heads and shells, rinse them, and cut them in half.

Heat the oil in a saucepan and add the heads and shells, along with the shallots, parsley stalks, and carrots, until the heads are bright red in color.

Add the tomato paste and let the mixture cook over medium heat, making sure it doesn't burn.

Add the water and reduce the heat to low. Let the contents reduce for an hour, then remove from the heat and strain.

200 grams farro
500 milliliters water
5 grams salt

Cooked farro

Makes 400 grams

Set a pot of water to boil and cook the farro over medium heat, covered, for 15 to 20 minutes.

Add the salt and boil for 2 more minutes.

Drain the farro and lay it out on a tray. Add a bit of oil so it won't stick.

Once the farro is cool, cover it with plastic wrap to keep it from drying out.

Pickled fennel

40 grams olive oil
250 grams fennel
5 grams salt
50 milliliters chardonnay vinegar
40 milliliters water

Makes 250 grams
    Heat oil in a frying pan.
    Dice the fennel into little triangles and sauté them in hot oil until transparent.
    Add the salt, the vinegar, and the water. Let the liquid evaporate completely and remove it from the heat.

Coral butter

85 grams butter
15 grams lobster coral (roe)

Makes 100 grams
    Let the butter sit at room temperature until it has the texture of a cream or ointment.
    Heat the coral in a frying pan over low heat. Crush it until it's entirely ground up.
    Add the butter and whisk the mixture until it's uniform and coral-colored.

Garlic oil

150 milliliters extra-virgin olive oil
50 grams garlic, finely minced

Makes 200 milliliters
    Add the garlic to the oil and let it infuse for at least 48 hours before use. Keep in a cool place or refrigerate.

Tomato sauce

200 grams tomatoes
½ garlic clove
1 pinch salt
10 milliliters olive oil

Makes 150 grams
    Use a knife to cut an X across each tomato. Place them in boiling water for 30 seconds and remove. Transfer them to a bowl of ice water to stop the cooking process. Remove the skin, cut them into 4 pieces each, remove the seeds, and set aside.
    Sauté the garlic with the tomato seeds, then add the tomatoes. Remove from the heat and blend.
    Return to the burner, add salt, and boil until the sauce thickens a bit.

To Serve

8 milliliters olive oil
240 grams lobster tail
5 grams salt
60 milliliters white wine
400 grams cooked farro
400 milliliters lobster broth
20 milliliters lemon juice
5 grams lemon zest
8 grams fennel frond
200 grams pickled fennel
60 grams tomato sauce
40 grams coral butter

Heat the oil and garlic in a frying pan without browning.
    Quickly sear the lobster, adding a bit of salt and the white wine.
    When the wine starts to evaporate, remove the lobster before it cooks completely.
    In the same frying pan, add the previously cooked farro, the lobster broth, the fennel frond, the pickled fennel, the tomato sauce, and the lemon juice and zest.
    Return the lobster to the pan and finish cooking it along with the other ingredients.
    Add the coral butter to thicken it.
    Serve in a deep dish and add the fennel frond on top.

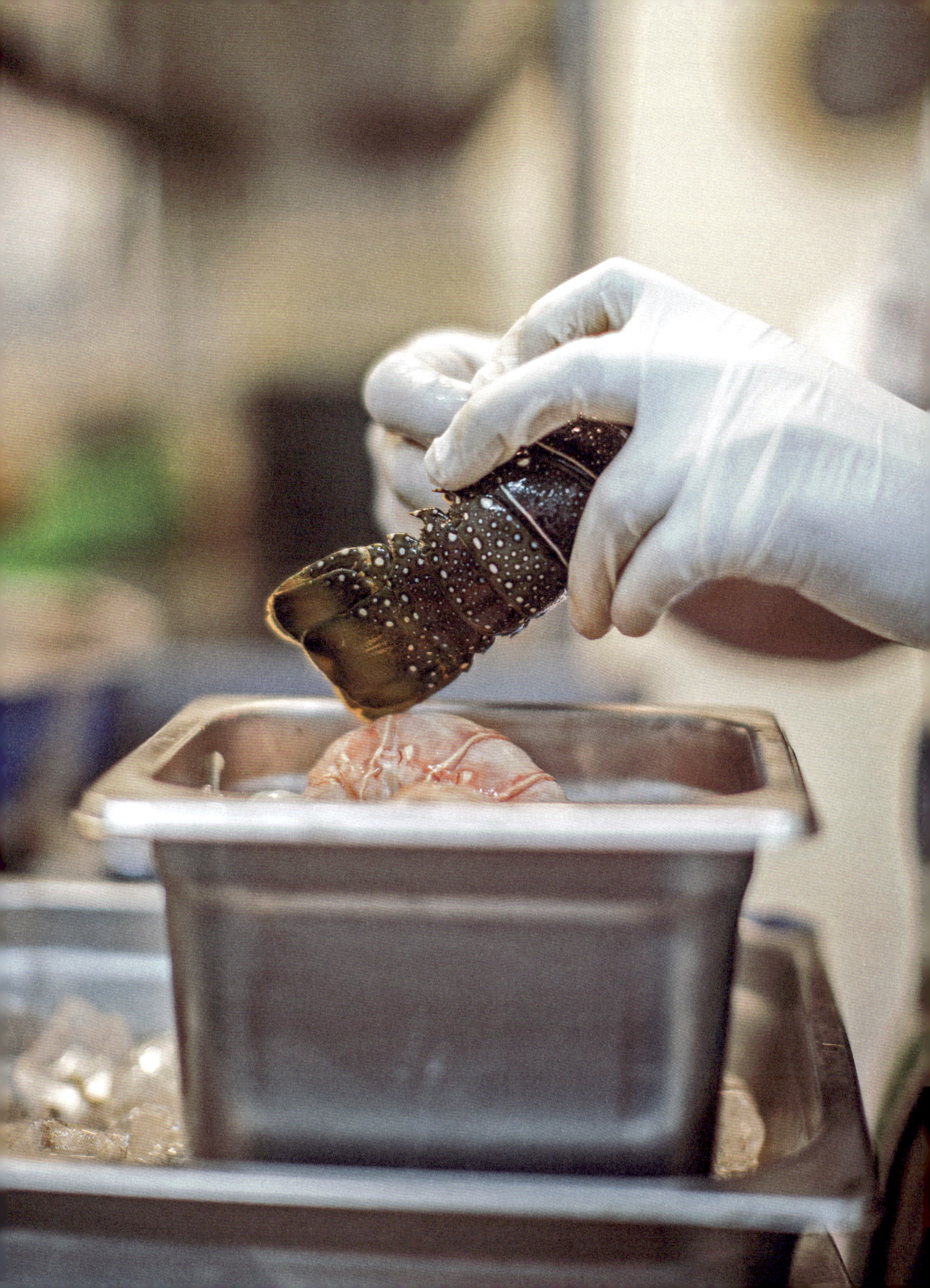

Beef tongue risotto with cilantro

In the process of writing this book, I've realized how delicate and defining it is to name a dish on a menu. I should have named this one "Birria risotto and beef tongue." But I didn't. I thought it might not be as appealing if I used the term "birria," a traditional meal from Jalisco that's made by cooking goat meat with peppers and spices. Perhaps I was wrong; maybe it would have been even more popular if I had. What I know for sure, however, is that the names of dishes—just like the titles of works of visual art or movies—influence their reception.

There is a longstanding debate about birria. About how to make it, yes, but also about which ingredients to use. We make a hybrid at Rosetta: we use the traditional goat meat, and we also incorporate beef tongue. In this way, our birria is less dense and its scent is less powerful. The goat-meat flavor is subtly maintained, but the experience of the peppers and spices is stronger, especially the cumin. We make the risotto with the broth yielded by preparing the birria. When it's done, we add cubes of beef tongue and a bit of cilantro. This dish ultimately tastes like birria, but faintly, because it's mitigated by the risotto. I find that certain especially strong flavors, like birria, are better perceived when they reach us indirectly, through other ones.

Lamb broth

Serves 4

500 grams lamb bones
80 grams white onion, quartered
20 grams garlic, unpeeled and halved
50 grams carrots, sliced
70 grams celery stalk, sliced
4 grams whole peppercorns, lightly toasted
1 gram bay leaves
3 liters water

Makes 1 liter

Place the bones on a baking sheet and bake for 30 minutes at 235°C.
Place the bones in a saucepan.
Lower the oven heat to 180°C. Lay out all the vegetables on the same baking sheets and bake for 30 minutes, shifting them around every 10 minutes.
Add the vegetables and the fat on the baking sheet to the bones.
Add the pepper, the bay leaves, and the water.
Cook over medium heat. Once it reaches a boiling point, reduce heat to low and cook until the liquid has reduced by half. Strain and set aside the broth until ready to use.

Tongue broth

Tongue broth
20 milliliters olive oil
50 grams veal bones
50 grams lamb bones
300 grams beef tongue
150 grams white onions
450 milliliters lamb broth
20 grams celery
20 grams carrots
2 bay leaves
1 gram thyme
5 grams garlic
5 grams cascabel pepper
5 grams ancho pepper
1 gram cumin seed
1 gram nutmeg
1 gram juniper berries
1 gram allspice
1 pinch salt

White stock
500 grams chicken carcass
50 grams celery
50 grams white onion
50 grams carrots
1 gram juniper berries
4 liters water

Shaved beef tongue
250 grams beef tongue
5 grams salt
20 grams white onion, minced
10 grams celery, minced
1 bay leaf
1 gram thyme
½ garlic clove
10 grams carrots, peeled and thickly sliced
1 liter water

Makes 250 milliliters

Put a little oil in a frying pan over high heat. Brown the veal and lamb bones and remove.

Place the tongue to cook in a saucepan along with the lamb broth. Add 100 grams of onion, the celery, the carrots, the bay leaves, the thyme, and the bones.

In another saucepan, place the rest of the onion and sauté with the ancho and cascabel peppers, the cumin seeds, the nutmeg, the juniper, the allspice, and the salt. Blend together with a little of the tongue broth. Add it to the saucepan with the tongue and cook over low heat until it has reduced by half. Strain and set aside.

Peel the tongue and remove excess fat from the back side. Cut it into 1-centimeter cubes and set aside until ready to use.

White stock

Makes 1 liter

Wash the chicken carcass with plenty of water, drain it, and lay it out on a baking tray.

Bake at 230°C for 15 minutes. Remove and drain excess fat. Turn the pieces over and bake them again for 30 more minutes.

Wash and cut the vegetables into 4 pieces each. Along with the chicken carcass, transfer them to a large pot of water and cook over high heat. When it reaches the boiling point, reduce the heat to low.

Skim the fat off the stock every 20 minutes. Let it cook for 1 hour, or until it has reduced to ¼ its original volume. Remove from the heat, let sit for 30 minutes, and strain.

Shaved beef tongue

Makes 160 grams

Place the tongue, along with the rest of the ingredients, into a saucepan of boiling water. Cover and cook over medium heat for 3 hours.

Insert a knife into the thickest part of the tongue to make sure it's fully cooked. If blood comes out or if you struggle to insert the knife, let it cook a little longer.

Remove the tongue from the water and peel it. Remove excess fat from the back side.

Once it's clean, let the tongue cool at room temperature, covering it with plastic wrap to keep it from drying out. When it has cooled off, slice the cooked tongue into very thin shavings with a sharp knife.

Garlic oil

150 milliliters extra-virgin olive oil
50 grams garlic, finely minced

Makes 200 milliliters
   Add the garlic to the oil and let it infuse for at least 48 hours before use. Refrigerate or keep in a cool place.

Chile de árbol sauce

30 grams basil
40 grams salted capers
3 grams sugar
3 grams salt
100 grams tomatoes, quartered
150 milliliters olive oil
100 grams dried chile de árbol

Makes 550 grams
   Strip the leaves off the basil.
   Mix all the ingredients together in a bowl and refrigerate overnight.
   Blend the mixture until the texture is thick.

Risotto

86 grams butter, cubed
25 grams white onion, cut into small cubes
250 grams Arborio rice
75 milliliters white wine
320 milliliters white stock
120 milliliters tongue broth
180 grams tongue, cut into ½-half-centimeter cubes
20 grams cilantro
5 grams fresh marjoram leaves
10 milliliters garlic oil
10 grams chile de árbol sauce
160 grams shaved beef tongue

Melt 25 grams of butter in a saucepan, then add the onion. Once the onion starts to become transparent, making sure it doesn't brown, add the rice. Toast it for several minutes, once again ensuring that it doesn't brown, and add the white wine. Stir constantly with a wooden spoon until the wine has evaporated. Add a bit of the white stock and tongue broth, just enough to cover the rice, still stirring constantly. Once the rice has absorbed all the liquid, add more. Keep stirring to remove the starch from the rice. Repeat this process for 14 minutes.
   Add the cubed tongue, the chopped cilantro, the fresh marjoram leaves, the rest of the butter, the garlic oil, and the chile de árbol sauce to taste. Using a wooden spoon, stir vigorously so that the ingredients are well mixed.
   Heat the shaved beef tongue in a frying pan.
   Serve the risotto in deep dishes, adding a little cilantro and the sliced tongue.

8.400 lengua Birria
Zanah. 336
Ajo 84
Tomill. 8
Laurel 8
Anis 168
~~Canela~~
C Blanca 752
Sal pra ~~420~~ 42 gr

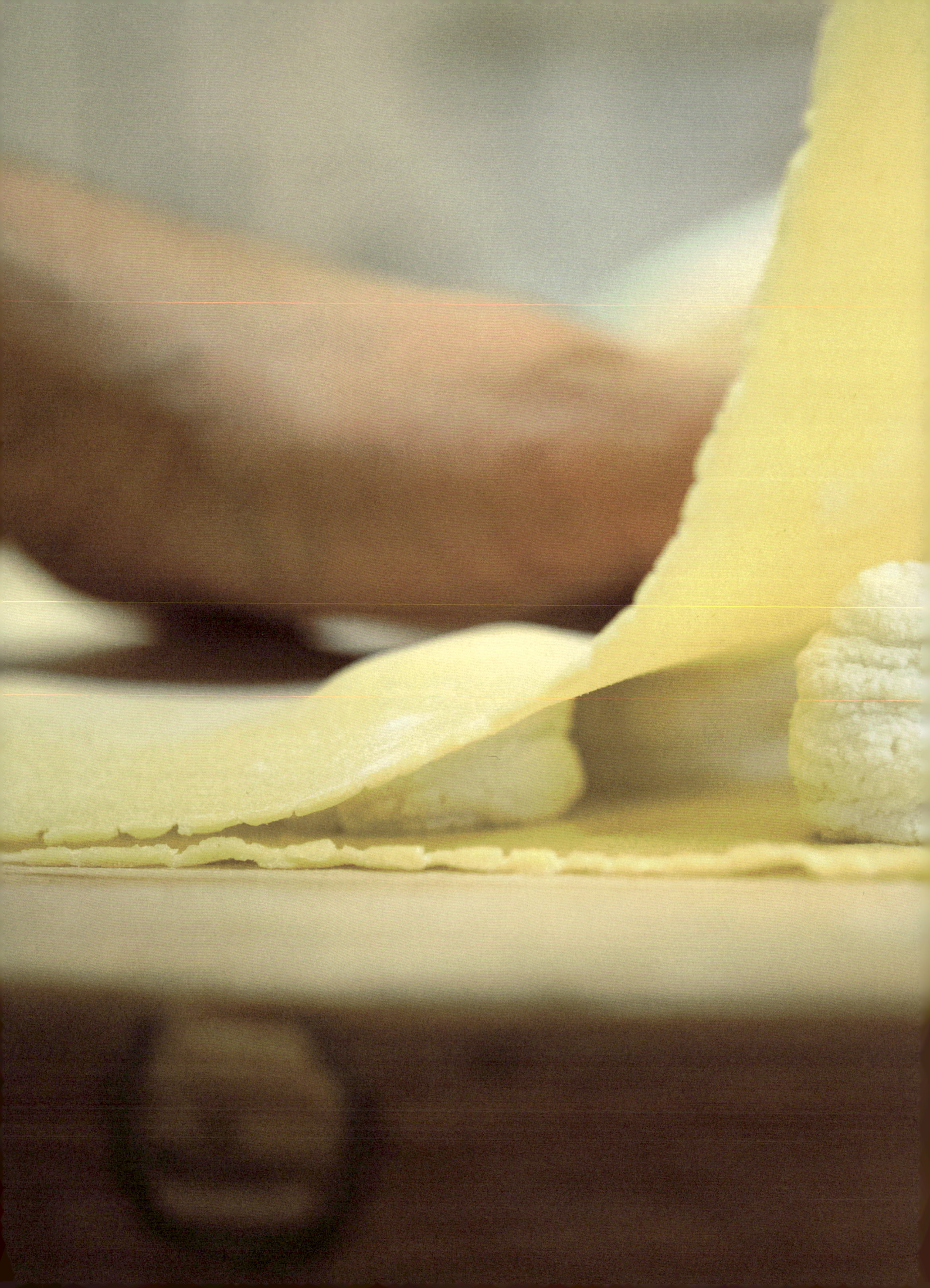

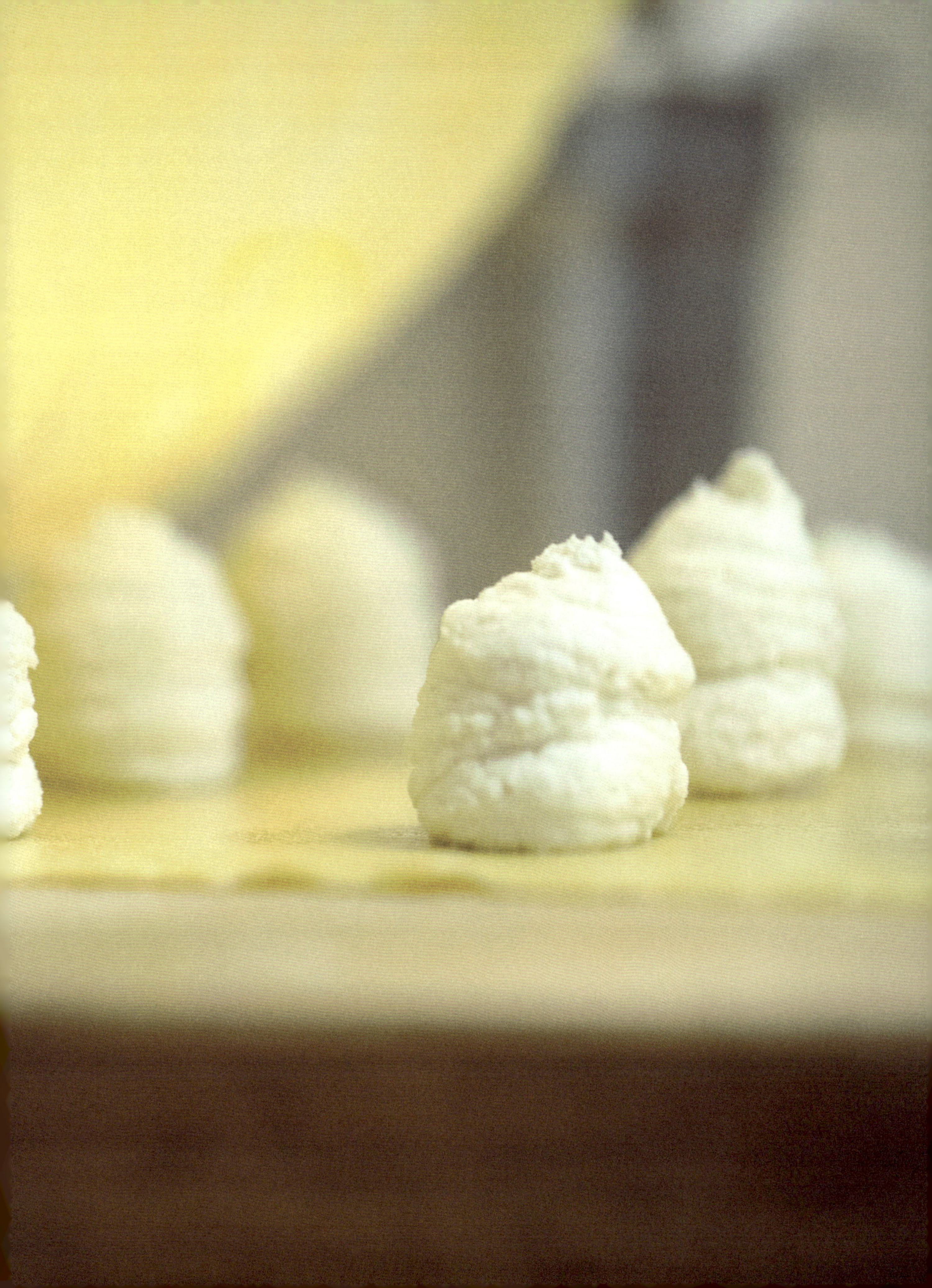

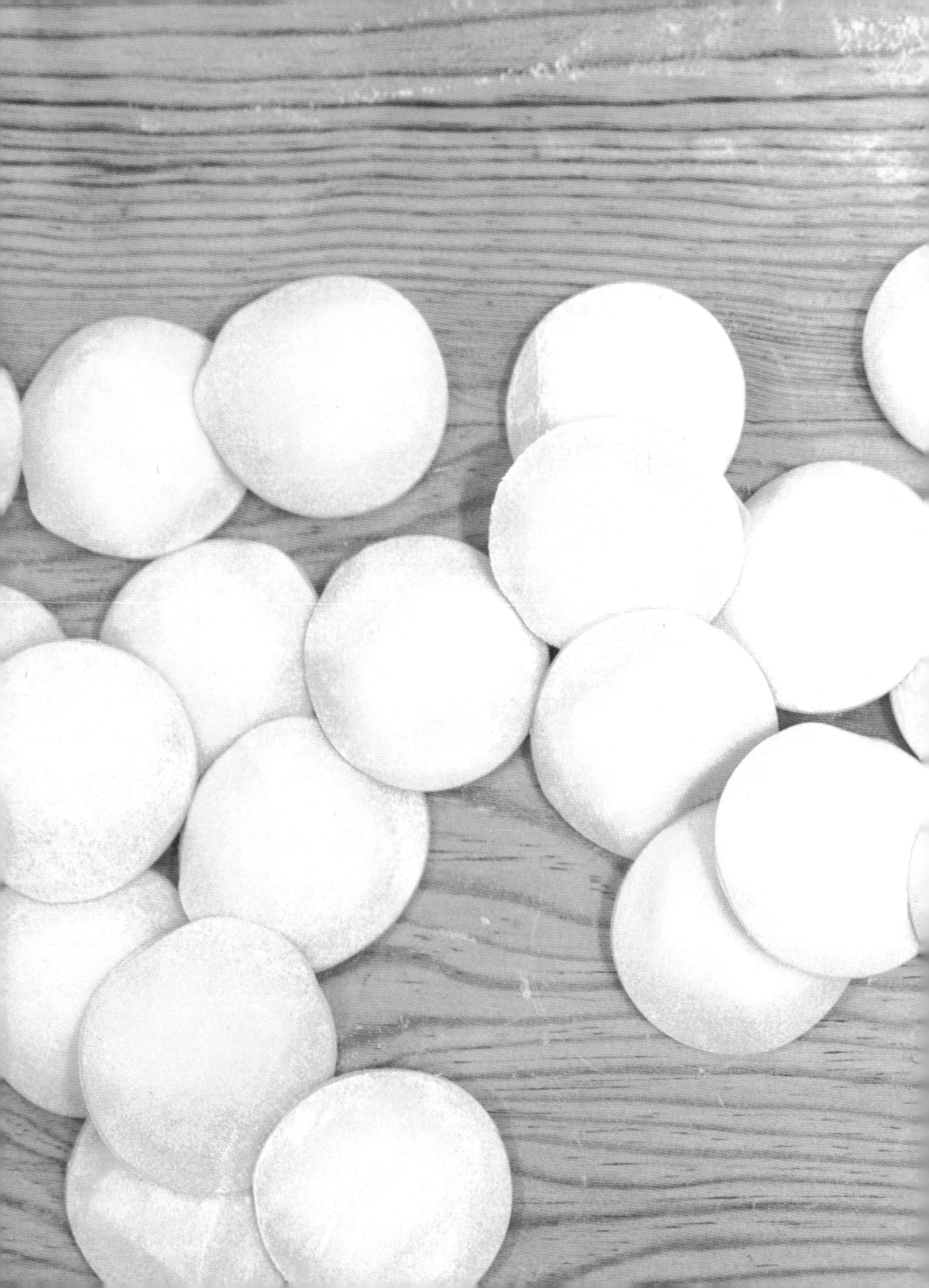

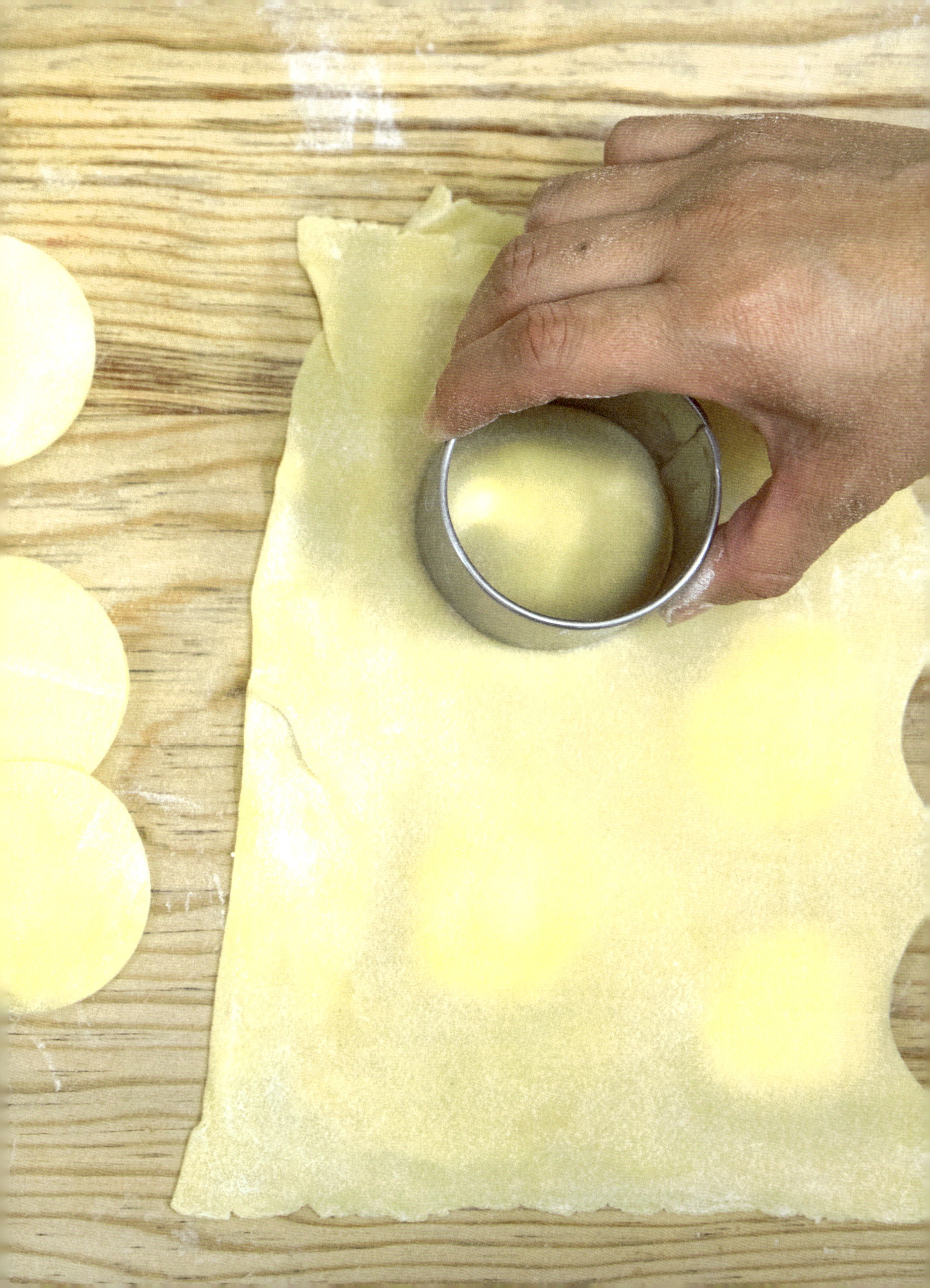

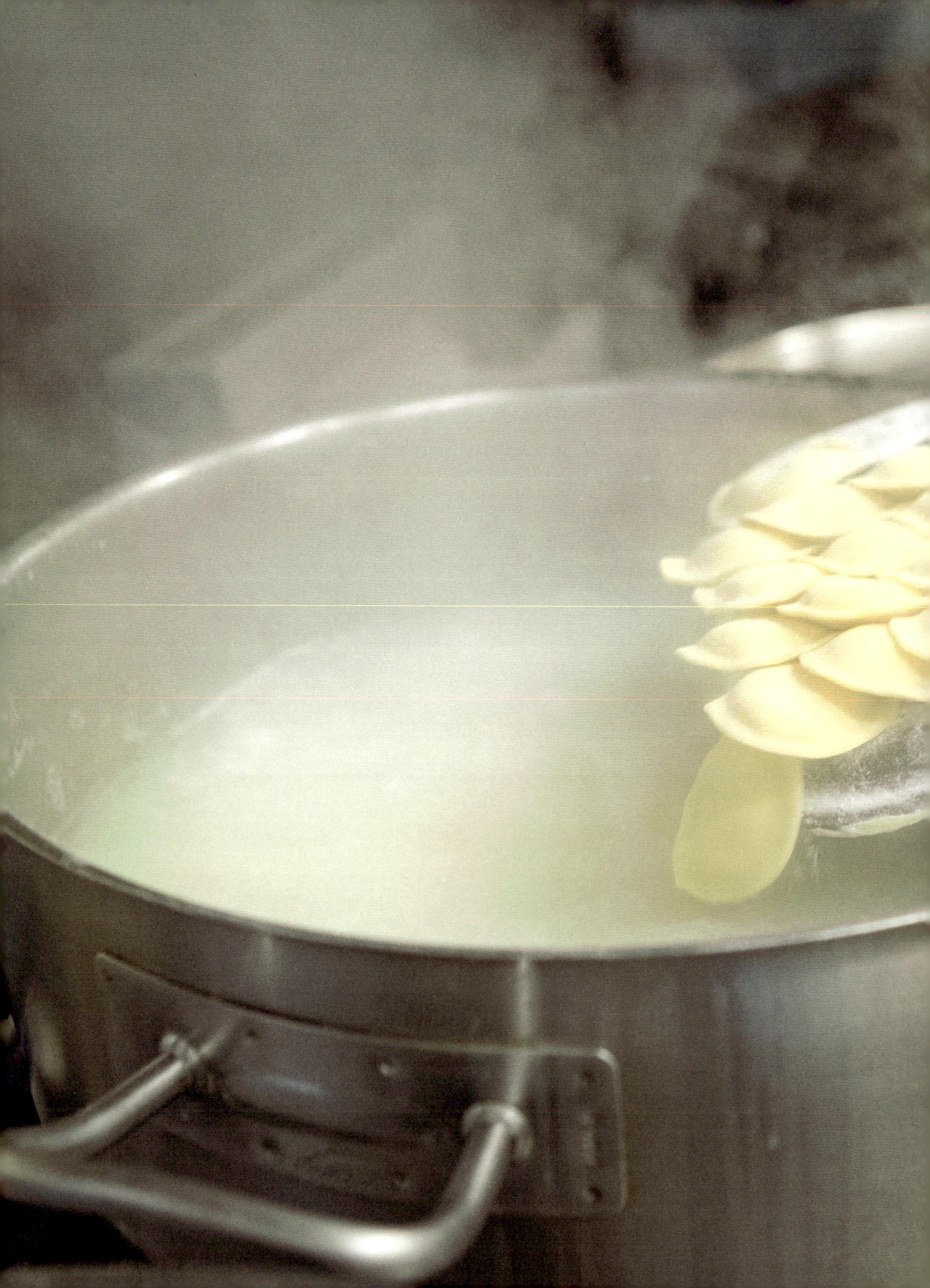

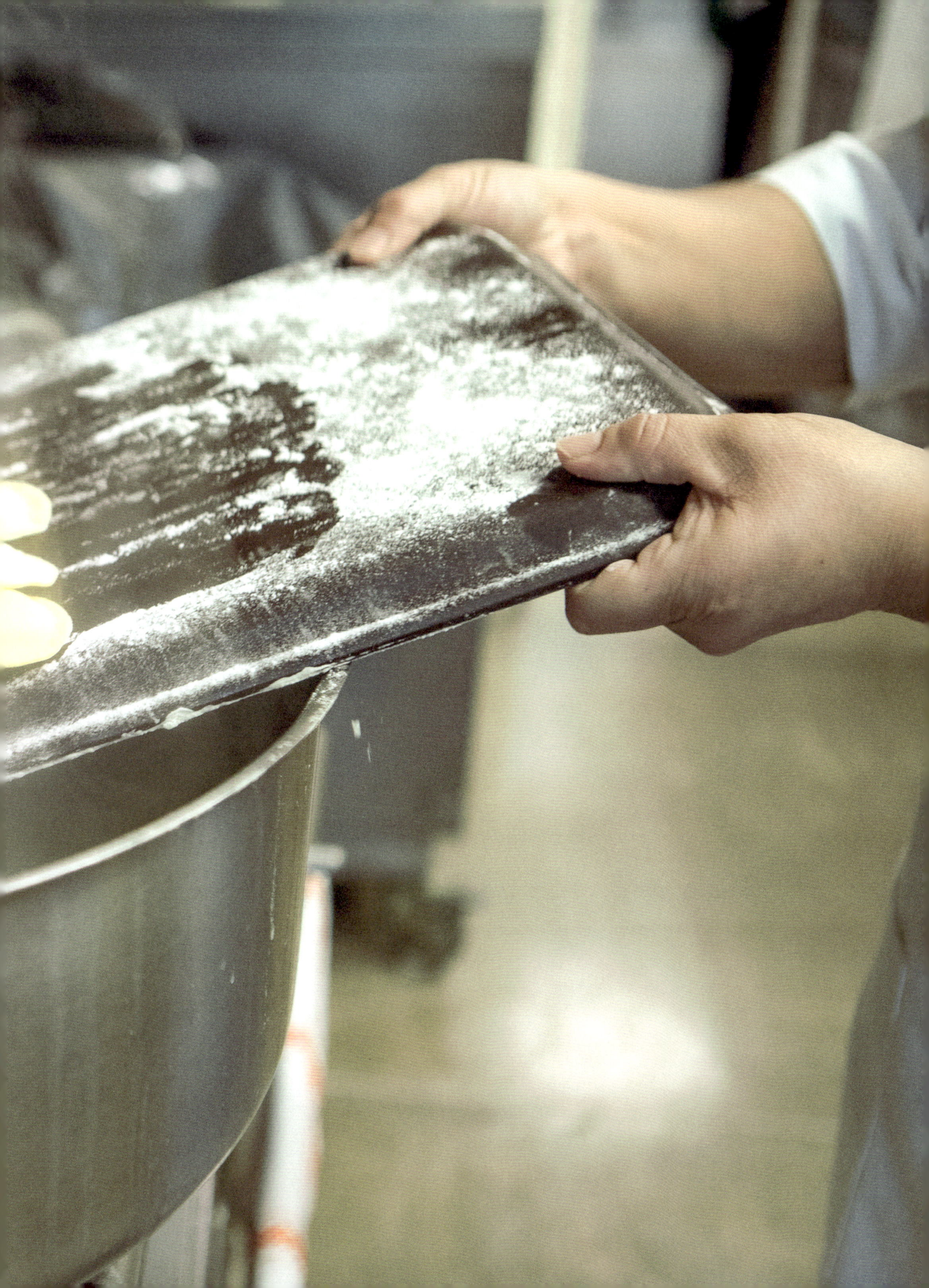

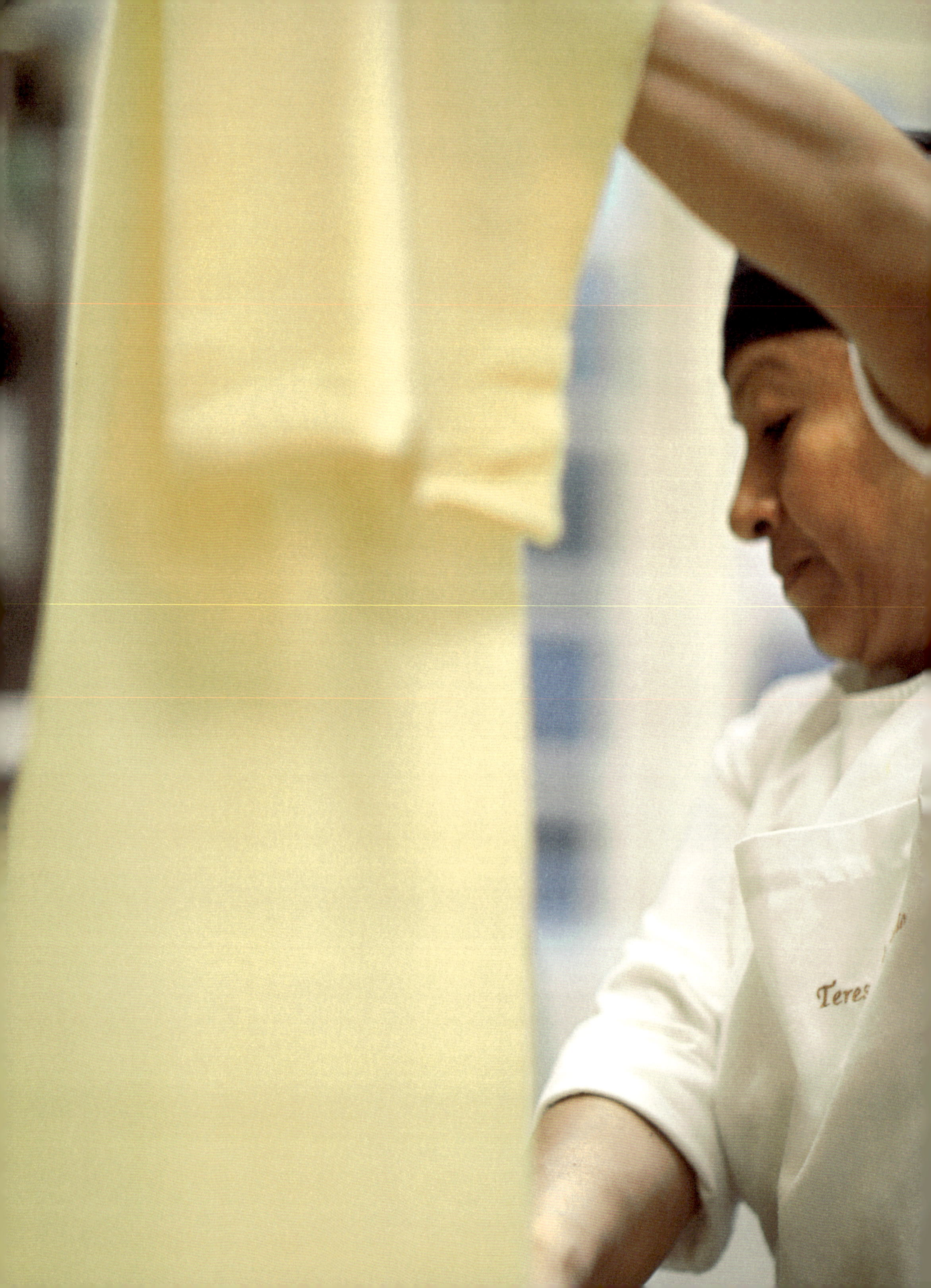
Teres

Our Pasta

At Rosetta, pasta is always fresh. We make it from scratch every morning. And we make it manually, without the use of any electrical appliances. Otherwise, we wouldn't be able to come up with pasta that's both smooth and firm. Besides, making our own pasta allows us to ensure its quality and freshness. It's laborious and time-consuming, which is why fewer and fewer restaurants are making it. We think it's essential to keep this practice alive. First of all, because we want everything to be homemade at Rosetta. And second, because pasta is one of the cornerstones of my cooking. I love it because I see it as a dish in itself; because its flavor changes with even the slightest variations in shape and size; because it's incredibly versatile; and because it's the ultimate comfort food.

Attention to detail is key when you make and cook pasta. Some of the most important details for us are: using lots of egg yolks in making the pasta; cooking the pasta in plenty of salted water; never adding oil to the water when the pasta is cooking; never rinsing the pasta with cold water; letting the pasta finish cooking in a pan with the sauce that will accompany it, so that it can absorb the flavor of the sauce; and using some of the pasta water when it's time to add the pasta to the sauce.

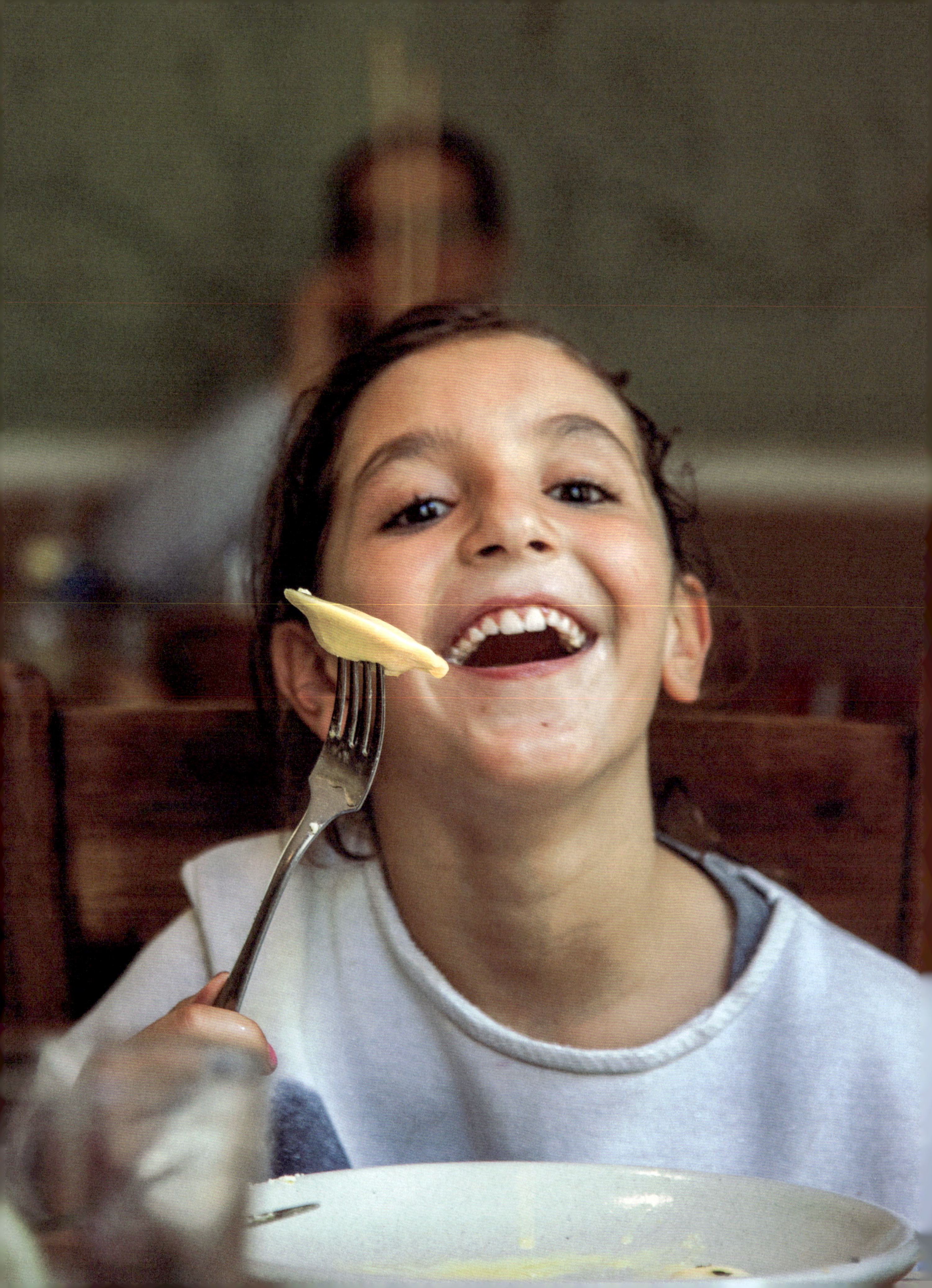

Fresh Pasta

340 grams 00 flour
3 grams salt
5 milliliters extra-virgin olive oil
135 grams egg yolks
17 grams egg whites

Makes 500 grams

Pour the flour into a large bowl and add the salt. Make a hollow in the middle and add the oil, the yolks, and the whites.

Using your fingers, incorporate the wet ingredients into the flour until everything is well mixed. If the pasta mixture is very dry, add a little more egg white.

Cover the pasta mixture with plastic wrap and refrigerate it for 2 hours.

Flatten the pasta mixture with a rolling pin until it's about 1 centimeter thick.

Adjust the settings of your pasta-rolling machine. You'll start with the widest possible opening, gradually reducing the thickness every time you run the pasta through the machine with one hand and holding it in your other hand.

Set the rollers to the second-thinnest opening and run the pasta through again. Keep running it through until you reach the slenderest opening. Fold the pasta strip into three parts. Start to run the pasta through again, but in the opposite direction, so that the fold is perpendicular to the roller.

Repeat this process once more until the pasta is smooth and glossy. Roll it one more time from the thickest to the thinnest openings, until the pasta is 1.5 millimeters thick. Immediately cut the sheet into the thickness or the shape you want, which will keep it from drying out.

Ricotta ravioli, lemon, and lemon thyme

Rosetta has served these ravioli since the very beginning. They're incredibly simple, and their flavors have become emblematic of the restaurant. Ricotta and lemon make for a subtle combination of fat and acidity. The lemon perfumes and refreshes the ricotta without overwhelming its sweet, creamy, milky flavor; the two contrasting tastes respect and complement each other. This pairing of ingredients, which also appears in desserts like the cannoli and the cassata siciliana, originates in southern Italy, home both to ricotta cheese and to a broad range of citrus fruits. When Rosetta opened its doors, we offered a dessert made with yogurt and lemon that was similarly inspired. The dessert, in turn, was what led us to concoct this pasta dish. The ricotta-filled ravioli are bathed in a butter emulsion with lemon juice and zest. The butter transports the citrusy fragrance, and its acidity makes the butter less greasy. Finally, we add a bit of lemon thyme, a thyme variant with a gentle flavor, both lemony and herbal.

Ricotta ravioli

Serves 4

500 grams fresh pasta sheets
600 grams ricotta cheese
olive oil

Makes 24 pieces

Lay out a pasta sheet and glaze half with egg.

Pour the ricotta into a pastry bag and distribute the cheese in little 20-gram mounds. Leave enough room between them that they won't stick together when it's time to cut them.

Cover with the other un-glazed half of the pasta sheet. Seal with your fingers to push out the air and cut with a cookie-cutter approximately 5 centimeters in diameter.

If you don't serve them immediately, blanch and refrigerate them in a bowl of ice water. Dry with a cloth, glaze them with a bit of olive oil to keep them from sticking together, and refrigerate.

To Serve

2 liters water
30 grams sea salt
200 grams butter
30 milliliters lemon juice
24 pieces ricotta ravioli
8 grams lemon zest
4 grams lemon thyme

Boil water in a large pot. When it reaches a boil, add the salt.

Melt the butter in a frying pan and pour in the lemon juice little by little, whisking constantly until the mixture has emulsified.

Add the ravioli to the boiling water. Once they start to float, remove them from the water and add them to the frying pan with a little of the pasta water. Let them boil for 1 minute in the pan.

Serve, adding lemon zest and lemon thyme.

Smoked beet tortelli, sheep's milk cheese, and sorrel

Smoked foods are a staple in my kitchen. Smoking is a simple method that doesn't call for major technical complexities and allows for the discovery of new flavors in the ingredients. It gives them another dimension without radically altering them, as other more sophisticated techniques do. Cooks have been using transformative techniques like smoking and pickling for a long time, generally for preserving food. I'm interested in exploring how these techniques change flavors. In this dish, for instance, the beet is less sweet than normal: the smoking process, which lightly dries out the beets, not only reduces their sweetness, but also accentuates their earthy flavor. And so, with a simple gesture, we convert the well-known combination of beets and goat cheese into something that tastes completely different.

Smoked beet purée

Serves 4

600 grams beets
35 grams shallots
95 grams butter
2.5 grams fennel seeds
3 grams salt
1 gram ground black pepper
50 grams fine sourdough breadcrumbs
5 grams mesquite chips
200 grams charcoal

Makes 500 grams

Peel the beets and cut them into medium-sized chunks.
Place the fennel seeds on a cheesecloth and make a knot. Put it into a pot of water and add the beets. Heat until the beets are well cooked.
Heat butter in a frying pan, then add the shallots. When they start to brown, add the breadcrumbs. Finally, add the cooked beets, salt, and pepper.
Blend the mixture until it has the texture of a purée, then transfer it to a bowl.
Turn on the smoker with the mesquite chips and put the bowl of purée inside. Let it smoke for approximately 5 minutes or until the shavings are no longer burning or giving off smoke.

Fresh beet pasta

70 grams smoked beet purée

Makes 500 grams

Follow the steps (p. 147) to make fresh pasta, substituting 70 grams of egg yolk for 70 grams of smoked beet purée.

Smoked beet tortelli

500 grams fresh beet pasta sheets
400 grams smoked beet purée
3 eggs

Makes 24 pieces

Cut a pasta sheet lengthwise down the middle so that you're left with two strips. Beat the eggs. Take one of them and glaze it with egg. In the center of this strip, place little 15-gram mounds of smoked beet purée, leaving about 3 centimeters of room between them.

Make vertical cuts to form squares and fold each one in half to make a triangle. Push out the air and seal them with your fingers. Take two points of the triangle and bring them toward the center to shape the tortelli.

Repeat the same process with the rest of the pasta.

If you don't serve them immediately, blanch and then cool them in a bowl of ice water. Remove them, dry them with a cloth, and glaze them with a bit of oil. Refrigerate.

Dried beets

½ beet

Makes 20 grams

Slice the beet as thinly as possible, ideally with a mandoline slicer. Spread the slices onto a tray with parchment paper and bake for 1 hour at 80°C. Make sure that the slices are completely dry.

Keep in a dry place.

Sorrel broth

60 grams sorrel, without stalk
2 ice cubes
20 milliliters water
1 pinch salt

Makes 80 milliliters

Blend all the ingredients together until the mixture is smooth and uniform.

To Serve

2 liters water
30 grams sea salt
40 grams butter
120 grams creamy sheep's milk cheese
80 milliliters water
24 pieces beet tortelli
280 milliliters olive oil
40 milliliters sorrel broth
20 grams dried beets

Boil water in a large pot. When it reaches the boiling point, add the salt.

Put butter in a saucepan until it melts. Add the goat cheese and the water until it heats, making sure it doesn't reach a boiling point.

Add the tortelli to the boiling water. Once they start to float, remove them from the water and arrange them on a hot plate with a little olive oil.

Pour the mixture of melted creamy cheese into deep dishes. Use a spoon to drip the sorrel broth onto the cheese. Distribute the tortelli in the bowls and add the chopped dried beets and olive oil.

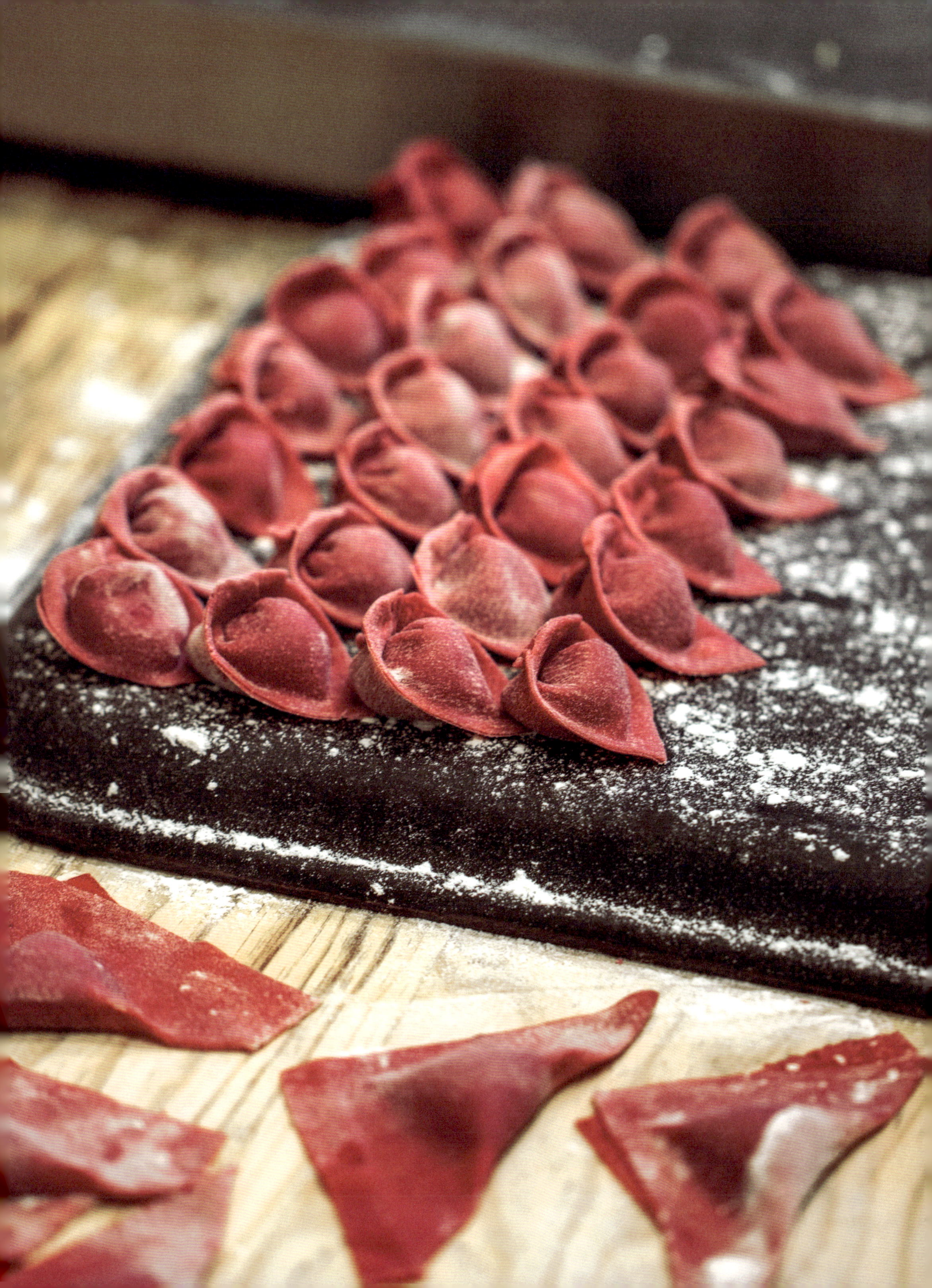

Mesquite tagliatelle with wild mushrooms

Wild mushrooms remind us of how closely we're connected to our surrounding environment, and how directly its natural cycles affect us as living organisms. The emergence of mushrooms depends on the rain. And not only that: the amount of rain also determines the varieties of mushrooms that emerge.

We serve this pasta throughout the mushroom season, which spans more or less from June to October. We use different kinds of mushrooms during this period, following the rhythm of the season itself. In the beginning, we use more clavito and señorita mushrooms. Later, porcini and yemita mushrooms. Toward the end, morels and chantarelles. This is a changing dish, then, and its different versions fluctuate with the weather.

Wild mushrooms, perhaps because of their relationship with the rain, have always struck me as a comforting ingredient. For this dish, I wanted to pair them with mesquite, a tree-shaped legume that grows in certain arid regions of Mexico, and which I consider another ideal ingredient for chilly, rainy days. Its flavor reminds me of tobacco and caramel with a mineral note. We incorporate it into the pasta-making process as a flour, made from its seeds. In this way, mushrooms and mesquite come together and form a dish that is directly linked to the climate and to the environment.

Mesquite tagliatelle

Serves 4

50 grams mesquite flour

Makes 500 grams

Follow the steps (p. 147) to make homemade pasta, substituting 50 grams of flour for 50 grams of mesquite flour. Once the sheets have been formed, cut with a tagliatelle cutter or a sharp knife, add a little flour to your hands, and roll the pasta, making little nests with the strands. Cover the pasta with plastic wrap or transfer it to a hermetic container and refrigerate.

White butter

10 milliliters chardonnay vinegar
1 gram shallot, minced
20 grams heavy cream
1 gram ground black pepper
250 grams butter, cubed

Makes 250 grams

Combine the white wine vinegar and the shallot in a pot. Heat until the vinegar has almost entirely evaporated. Add the heavy cream and the ground pepper. Boil for 2 minutes.

Turn off the heat, but don't remove the pan from the burner. Gradually add the butter with one hand, whisking with the other. Continue whisking until the butter is completely mixed in.

Keep the butter in a warm place.

To Serve

4 liters water
40 grams coarse salt
120 grams butter
4 grams garlic, finely minced
320 grams wild mushrooms: porcini, yemita, señorita, and clavito
5 grams salt
4 grams ground black pepper
100 milliliters white wine
480 grams mesquite pasta
240 milliliters pasta water
8 grams parsley, finely chopped
80 grams Parmigiano Reggiano
60 grams white butter
4 grams chives, chopped

Heat water in a large pot over high heat. When it reaches a boil, add the salt.

Fry the butter and the garlic in a frying pan. Once the garlic has just started to brown, add the sliced mushrooms, the salt, and the pepper. Let the ingredients start to fry over medium heat and sauté them a bit.

Add the white wine and let it evaporate completely. Add a little more butter to the mushrooms and cover them for approximately 3 minutes.

Add the pasta to the salted boiling water. Once it starts to float, remove it from the water and add it to the frying pan with the mushrooms, along with a bit of the pasta water. Add the chopped parsley and let it boil for a few minutes.

Shake the pan several times so the contents shift around. Lower the heat to medium, add the parmesan and the white butter, and toss a little more adding more pasta water for a creamier sauce.

Add chopped chives and serve.

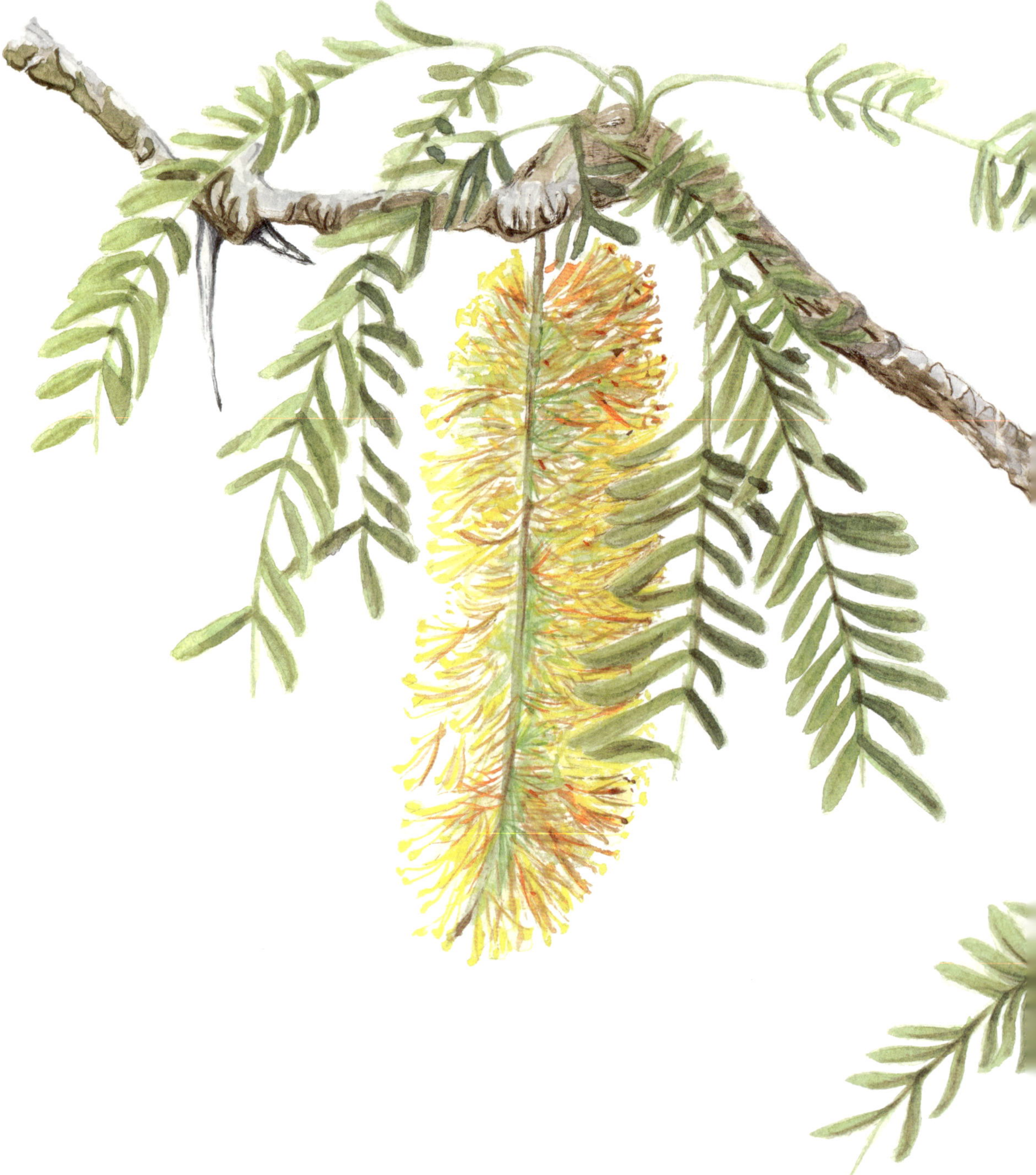

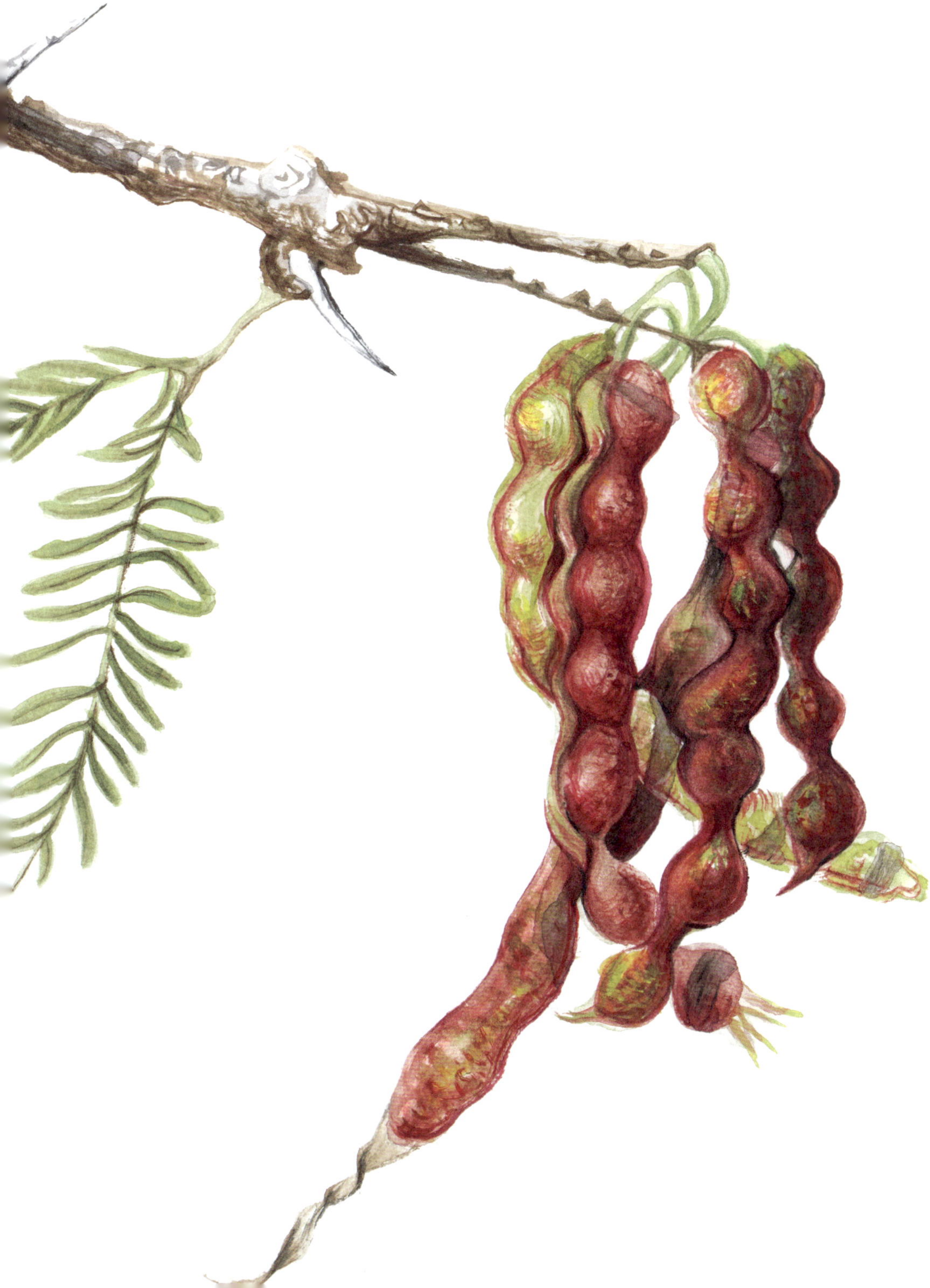

Buckwheat ravioli with 'nduja and burrata

'Nduja is my favorite cold meat. Unlike others, its smoky, peppery flavor makes it more refreshing than salty. It's also spreadable, which makes it more versatile for cooking. It's made by mixing pork fat and meat with peppers and spices, then smoking it. It comes from Calabria, a region in southern Italy, home to certain peppers that lend the meat its signature taste of spicy fat. To keep this dish from getting too heavy, we combine the 'nduja with béchamel sauce. We use this mixture to fill the ravioli, which we make with buckwheat flour (a grain with a slightly acidic flavor that means it pairs well with fats and smoked products). We sprinkle a little burrata on top to refresh the palate and attenuate the oiliness and spice of the 'nduja.

Serves 4

50 grams buckwheat flour

Buckwheat pasta

Makes 500 grams

Follow the steps (p. 147) to make fresh pasta, substituting 50 grams of flour for 50 grams of buckwheat flour.

60 grams butter
60 grams wheat flour
72 milliliters milk
5 grams salt
5 grams ground nutmeg
72 grams white onion, finely minced
1 gram ground cloves

Béchamel sauce

Makes 250 grams

Melt the butter in a saucepan and add the onion. When it starts to become transparent, add the flour and let it cool for a couple of minutes. Add the milk and the rest of the ingredients, whisking continually. Cook over medium heat. When it reaches a boil, remove from the burner.

'Nduja ravioli

100 grams 'nduja
250 grams béchamel sauce
50 grams Parmigiano Reggiano, grated
500 grams buckwheat pasta sheets

Makes 28 pieces

Mix the 'nduja with the béchamel and the parmesan in a bowl, then transfer to a pastry bag.

Cut a pasta sheet lengthwise down the middle so that you're left with two strips. Take one of them and glaze it with egg. In the center of this strip, place little 15-gram mounds of the 'nduja and béchamel mixture, leaving about 3 centimeters of room between them.

Take the ends of the pasta strip and fold them upward so that they cover the filling. Press with your fingers to push the air out and seal it. Make vertical cuts to form rectangular ravioli.

Repeat the same process with the rest of the pasta.

If you don't serve them immediately, blanch and then cool them in a bowl of ice water. Remove them, dry them with a cloth, and glaze them with a bit of oil. Refrigerate.

Dried blood orange

½ blood orange

Makes 15 grams

Cut the blood orange into the finest slices possible. Lay out the slices on a baking sheet and bake for 1 hour at 80°C. Make sure the slices are completely dry.

Set aside in a hermetic container with no humidity.

To Serve

2 liters water
30 grams coarse salt
35 grams butter
60 milliliters grapefruit juice
120 milliliters burrata whey
28 'nduja ravioli
40 grams Parmigiano Reggiano
200 grams diced burrata
15 grams dried blood orange

Bring the burrata whey to a boil in a saucepan, then remove from the heat.

Heat the butter in a frying pan. Add the grapefruit juice and the burrata whey, mixing well until they emulsify. Let them boil for 1 minute.

Boil water in a large pot. When it reaches a boil, add the salt. Add the ravioli to the salted boiling water. Once they start to float, remove them from the water and add them to the grapefruit emulsion.

Place the ravioli on the plates. Bathe them with the emulsion, adding the parmesan, burrata, and dried blood orange, previously cut into pieces.

Tagliolini, sea cradle, zucchini, and bottarga

This dish is the sum of two very special products: the sea cradle and bottarga. The so-called sea cradle is a mollusk consumed on Mexico's Pacific Coast. It's generally considered a "subsistence" product; that is, one consumed locally by fishermen and their families. I think of the sea cradle as a hybrid, both in its flavor and in its consistency, between the lobster and the crab. Its taste is subtle, and we accent it with a butter made with lemon and bottarga, another incredible ingredient.

Bottarga is the roe of salted, sun-dried fish. It's prepared in different parts of the Mediterranean. The most delicately flavored kind comes from Sardinia, Italy, using the variety of fish called grey mullet. The grey mullet is lightly smoked before drying. Bottarga tastes intensely of the sea, and using small quantities helps reaffirm the muted flavor of the sea cradle. In a way, the bottarga acts as a seasoning: it brings the sea cradle to life.

Tagliolini

Serves 4

Makes 500 grams

Follow the steps (p. 147) to make fresh pasta and cut it into 20-centimeter-long sheets. Use a tagliolini cutter, or fold the pasta sheet into three sections and cut thin strips with a sharp knife.

Flour your hands and roll the pasta, making little nests. Cover with plastic wrap and refrigerate.

Julienned zucchini

200 grams zucchini
5 grams salt

Makes 160 grams

Remove the pulp and seeds from the zucchini, keeping the skin (which should be ½-centimeter thick) and some pulp.

Cut the zucchini into strips the size of the pasta.

Season the strips with salt and transfer them to a strainer for 15 minutes. Refrigerate until ready to use.

Fumet

200 grams fish bones
50 grams white onion, quartered
50 grams celery, cut into chunks
50 grams fennel, cut into chunks
20 grams parsley stalks
20 grams leeks, thickly sliced
30 grams ginger, peeled and cut into large chunks
1.5 liters water

Makes 1 liter
Wash the fish bones thoroughly.
Put all the ingredients in a deep saucepan and cook over high heat.
Once the water reaches a boil, reduce heat to low and cook for 30 minutes. Remove from the heat and strain twice.

Bottarga butter

14 grams bottarga
300 grams butter, cut into small pieces
10 milliliters fumet

Makes 320 grams
Finely grate the bottarga and keep it covered.
Place the butter in a saucepan over medium heat. Once it starts to melt, add the fumet and whisk. Once the butter is half-melted, remove it from the burner, add the grated bottarga, and keep whisking until completely melted and incorporated. Reserve.

Chile de árbol sauce

50 grams salted capers
30 grams basil
3 grams sugar
3 grams salt
300 grams tomatoes, quartered
150 milliliters olive oil
100 grams dried chile de árbol, seeded

Makes 550 grams
Strip the leaves off the basil.
Mix all the ingredients in a bowl and refrigerate overnight.
Blend the mixture until thick.

To Serve

4 liters water
40 grams sea salt
320 grams bottarga butter
8 grams chile de árbol sauce
160 grams julienned zucchini
320 grams sea cradle
4 grams salt
260 milliliters fumet
480 grams tagliolini
8 grams lemon zest
40 milliliters lemon juice

Boil water in a saucepan. When it reaches a boil, add the salt.
Transfer the bottarga butter to a frying pan. Add the chile de árbol sauce, the zucchini, and the cubed sea cradle, seasoning with salt. Sauté, then add the fumet.
Transfer the tagliolini to the boiling water. Once it starts to float, remove it from the water and pour it into the frying pan with the bottarga butter.
Let the pasta cook in the sauce for a few minutes so that it can absorb the liquid. While you add the broth and lemon zest, toss the mixture in the pan, shaking it back and forth until the sauce is creamy.
Grate more bottarga to taste and serve.

Grains

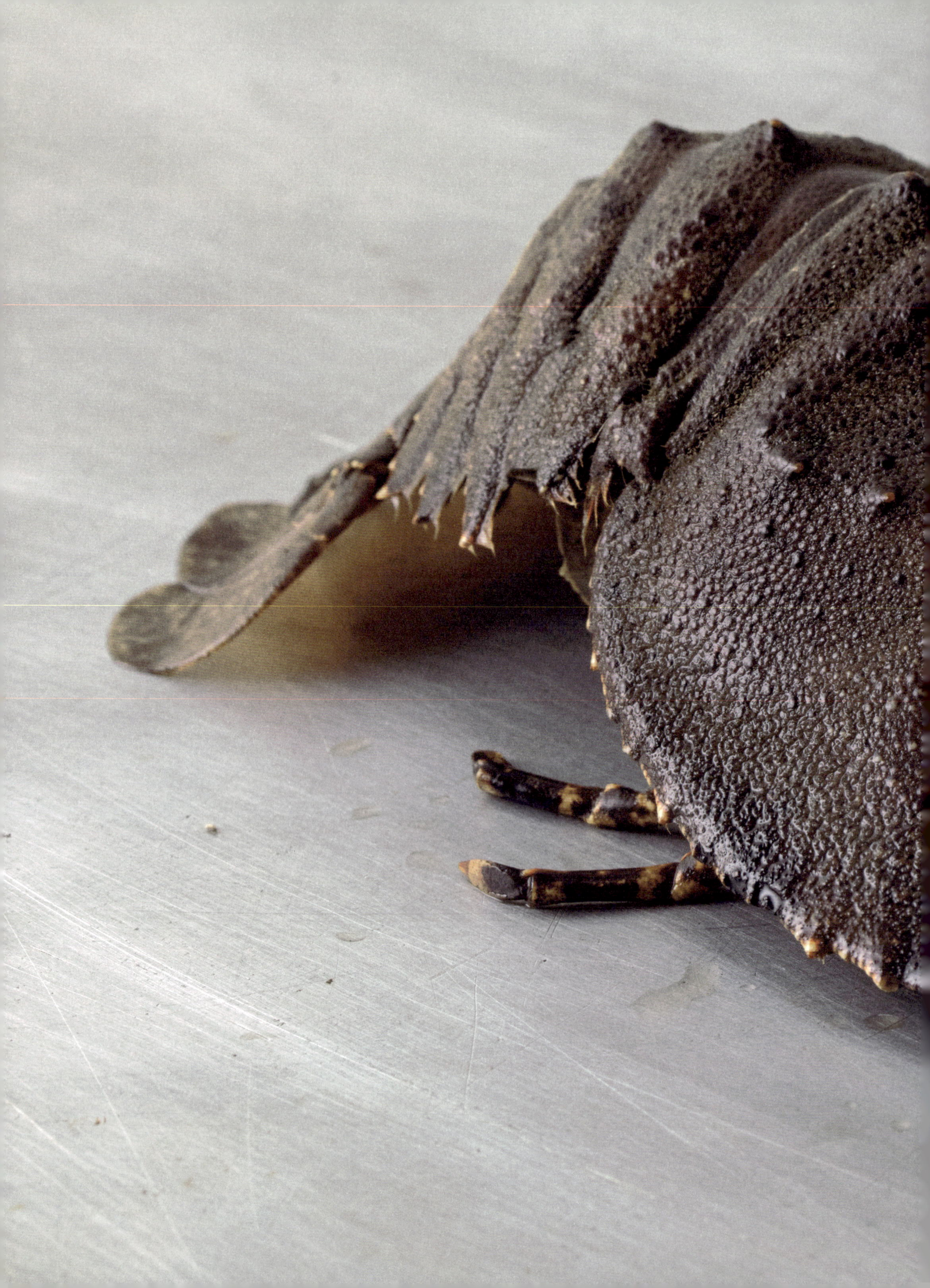

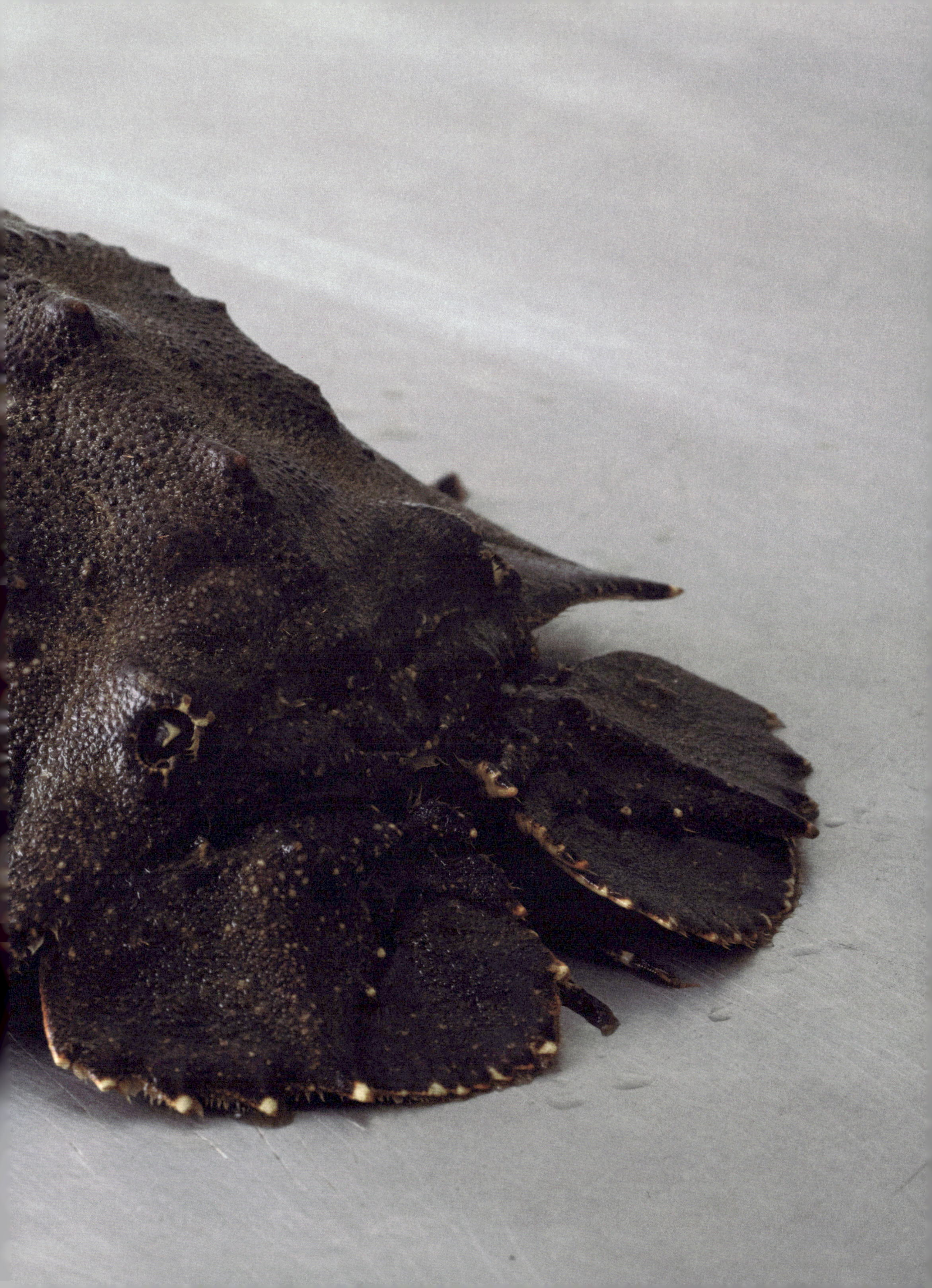

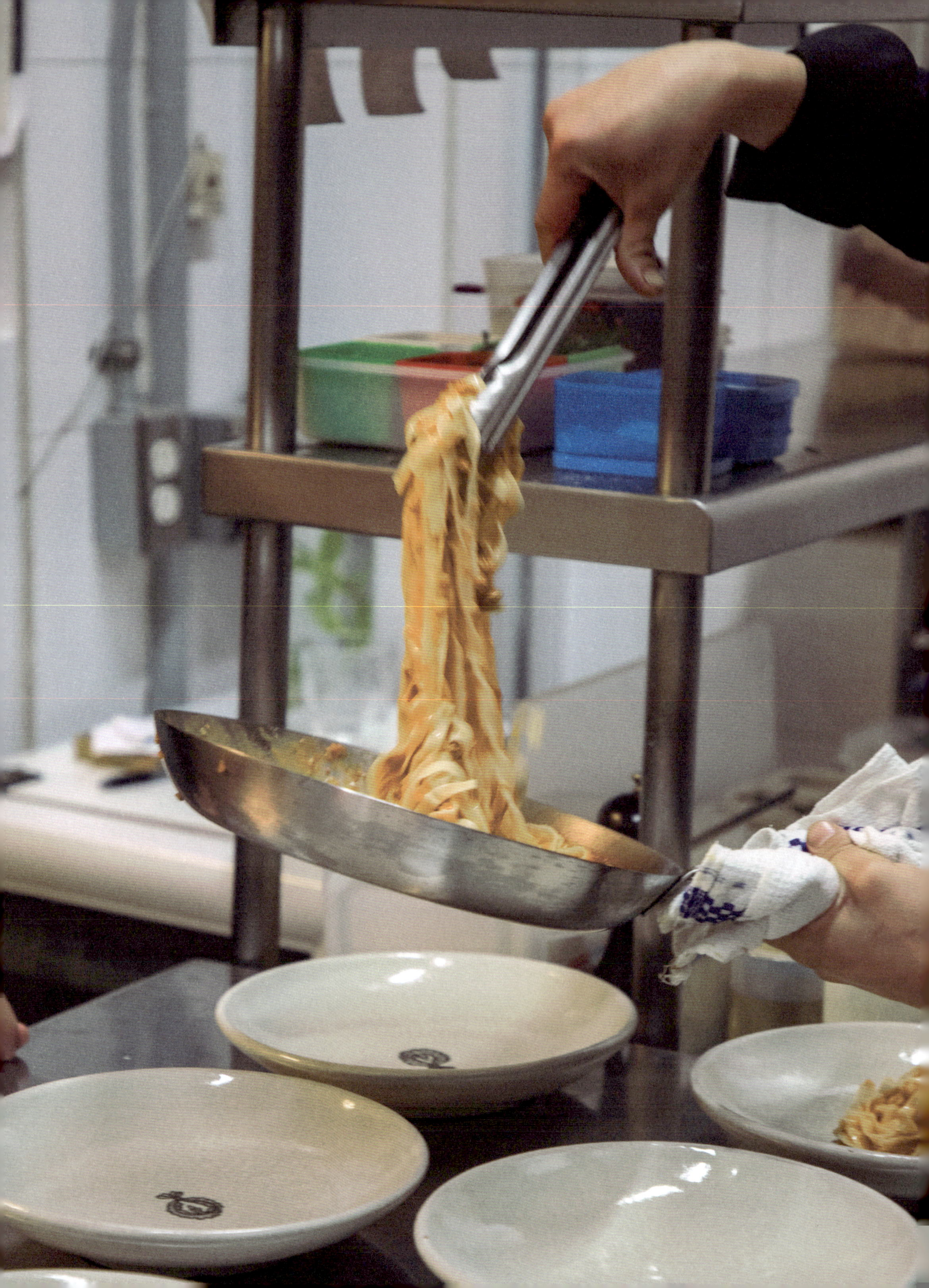

Tagliatelle, sausage and chile de árbol ragù

Those of us who work as professional cooks are often unable to eat with our families, since our schedules tend to overlap with mealtimes. To keep from missing out on this important family experience, I have my daughters eat at Rosetta several times a week after school. For me, this is a way to be close to them, and it's also a way to show them what I do for a living. To share it with them.

Someone recently asked Lea, my oldest, if she liked Rosetta. She said yes. And when they asked her why, she simply said "Because it's my mom's restaurant." She's one of my finest critics. She gives me constant feedback. Sometimes, on days off from school, she spends her mornings in the pastry section, making cupcakes. Then she sets up a little stand by the front door and sells them.

Julieta, my youngest, likes eating the same dishes over and over again, and she has her own special vocabulary for them. When she eats tortellini with poultry broth (although she prefers them without the broth; she says it burns her tongue), she calls them "noses." As for ravioli, she calls them "flying saucers"—because that's what they look like, she explains. And she's very proud of a dessert she claims to have invented herself. It involves vanilla ice cream mixed with meringue, berries, and whipped cream. She says the name "whipped cream" is ridiculous: it should be called "foam" instead, because it's tall and puffy and because cream, after all, is something you put on your skin.

Tagliatelle

Serves 4

Makes 500 grams

Follow the steps to make fresh pasta. Once you have a pasta sheet, cut it into approximately 1-centimeter strips.

Tomato sauce

800 grams tomatoes
120 milliliters olive oil
1 garlic clove
8 grams salt

Makes 600 grams

Heat the olive oil. Crush the garlic clove and add it to the pan. Once the olive oil has turned an intense golden brown, remove the garlic.

Cut the tomatoes into medium-sized chunks. Add them, along with the salt, to the oil. Cover and let cook for 8 minutes. Remove from the heat. Run the mixture through a food mill.

Sausage ragù

400 grams Italian sausage
80 milliliters olive oil
70 grams carrots, minced
100 grams onions, minced
60 grams celery, minced
2 grams dried chile de árbol, seeded
13 grams garlic
430 grams tomato sauce

Makes 500 grams
    Use a fork to mash the sausage.
    Heat the oil in a pot and fry the sausage. Add the carrots, the onions, and the celery, cooking over low heat.
    Cover the pot so the contents cook but don't brown.
    Blend the chile de árbol until it turns to powder, then add the garlic.
    Once the vegetables have cooked for 10 minutes, add the chile de árbol paste and cook for 10 more minutes. Then add the tomato sauce, cover, and cook for 20 minutes, stirring constantly.

White stock

500 grams chicken carcass
50 grams celery
50 grams white onion
50 grams carrots
1 gram juniper berries
4 liters water

Makes 1 liter
    Wash the chicken carcass with plenty of water, drain it, and lay it out on a baking tray.
    Bake at 230°C for 15 minutes. Remove and drain excess fat. Turn the carcass over and bake it again for 30 more minutes.
    Wash and cut the vegetables into 4 pieces each. Along with the chicken carcass, transfer them to a large pot of water and cook over high heat. When it reaches the boiling point, reduce the heat to low.
    Skim the fat off the stock every 20 minutes. Let it cook for 1 hour or until it has reduced to ¼ its original volume. Remove from the heat, let sit for 30 minutes, and strain.

White butter

10 mililiters chardonnay vinegar
1 gram shallot, minced
20 grams heavy cream
1 gram ground black pepper
250 grams butter, cubed

Makes 250 grams
    Pour the white wine vinegar into a large saucepan with the shallots. Cook over high heat until the vinegar evaporates.
    Add the heavy cream and the ground pepper. Boil for 2 minutes.
    Turn off the heat, but don't remove the pan from the burner. Gradually add the butter with one hand, whisking with the other. Continue whisking until the butter is completely mixed in.
    Keep the butter in a warm place.

To Serve

4 liters water
40 grams coarse salt
480 grams tagliatelle
60 grams butter
8 grams rosemary
400 grams sausage ragù
320 milliliters white stock
40 grams Parmigiano Reggiano, grated
40 grams white butter

Heat the water in a saucepan. When it reaches a boil, add the salt. Melt the butter in a frying pan, along with the rosemary. Add the sausage ragù and the white stock.
    Add the pasta to the boiling water. Once the tagliatelle starts to float, remove it from the water and add it to the frying pan. Sauté and add the white butter and the parmesan.

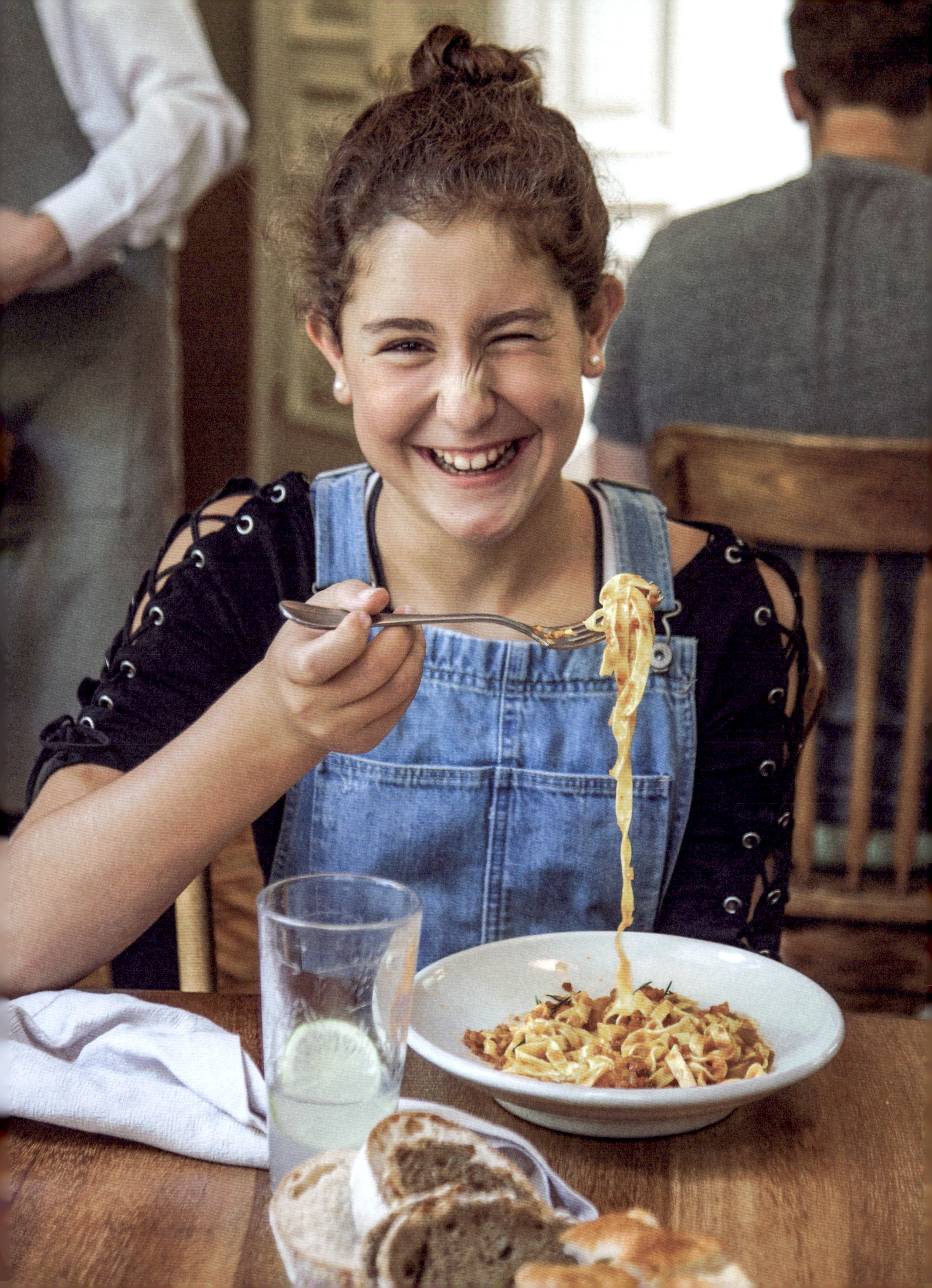

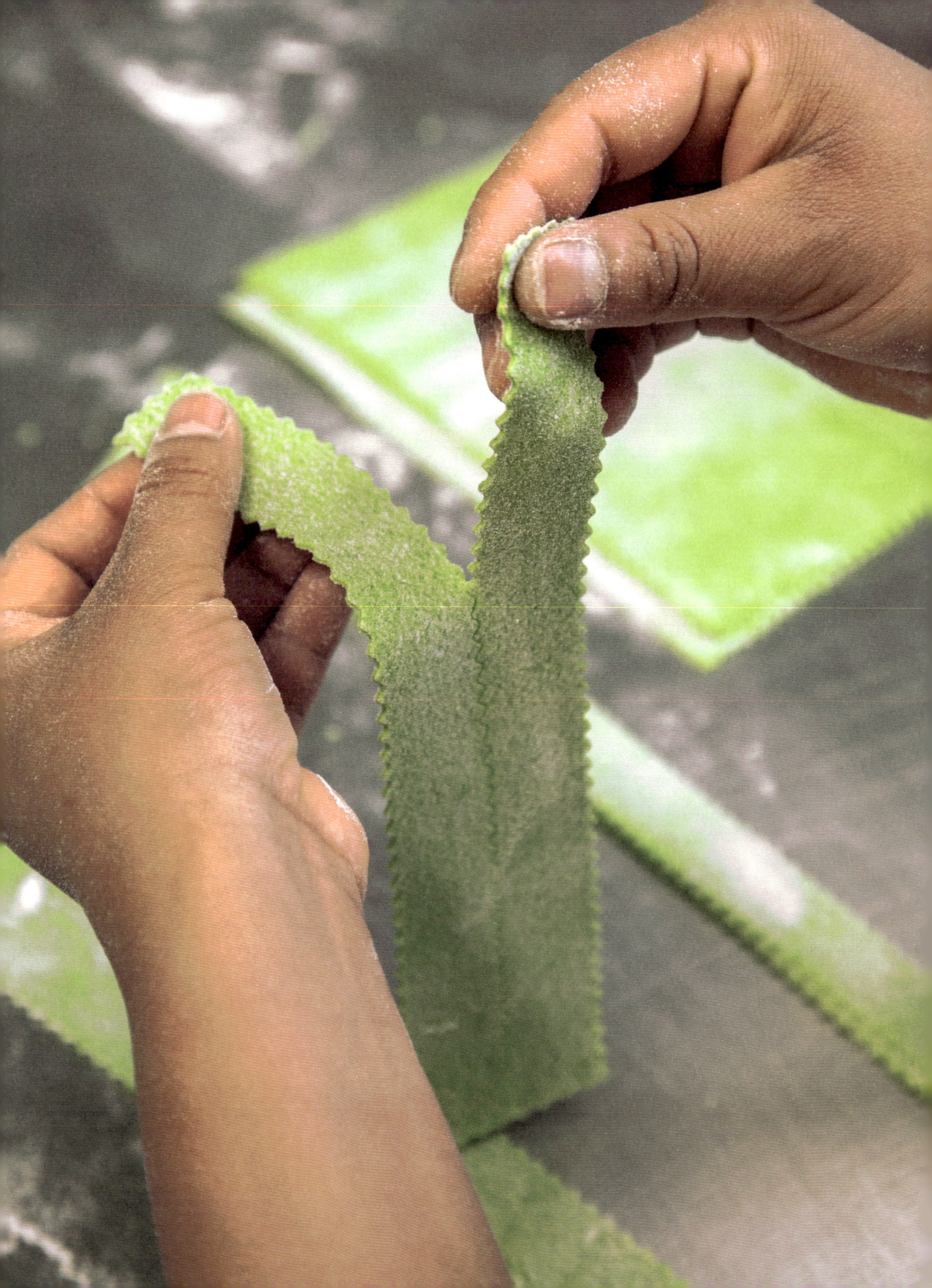

Pápalo pappardelle, duck ragù

Pappardelle is a long, flat pasta, about two centimeters wide, that's usually accompanied by a meat sauce—a ragù, as it's called in Italy. At Rosetta, we serve pappardelle with pápalo, a form of quelite or wild green. In Mexico, you'll often find pápalo in taco stands, bunched together in tin cans like flower bouquets. It's generally eaten with dishes like lamb barbacoa or cemitas, a kind of sandwich from the state of Puebla, because its powerful flavor cuts the fattiness of various meats and because it has digestive properties. However, many people dislike pápalo because its taste lingers in the mouth for several hours after consumption.

We accompany this pápalo pappardelle with a white duck ragù—an uncommon variant because it doesn't contain any tomato sauce. For the ragù, we make exclusive use of the duck legs and thighs—which have a fuller flavor and more fat than the breasts—and cook them in a broth made with their bones. As you can imagine, this is a rich ragù that tastes deeply of duck. The pápalo gives it a surprising flavor and lightens the dish.

At Rosetta, we are constantly incorporating local ingredients into our pastas. It's a way to experiment with under-used flavors and to prove that pasta, if treated as a dish and not as a mere vehicle for other dishes, is infinitely versatile.

Pápalo purée

Serves 4

100 grams pápalo
20 grams chaya
30 milliliters water
2 ice cube

Makes 100 grams
   Remove the stalks from the herbs and blanch the leaves. Then place them in a bowl of ice water to stop the cooking process.
   Drain the herbs well and blend them with an ice cube and very little water.
   Transfer the mixture to a cheesecloth to drain the liquid and extract the purée.

Pápalo pappardelle

25 grams pápalo purée

Makes 500 grams
   Follow the steps (p. 147) to make fresh pasta, substituting 25 grams of egg yolk for 25 grams of pápalo purée. Once the sheets have been formed, cut them into strips approximately 2 centimeters wide.

Duck broth

Duck broth
500 grams duck bones
80 grams white onion, quartered
20 grams garlic, unpeeled and halved
50 grams carrots, sliced
70 grams celery stalks, sliced
4 grams lightly toasted peppercorns
1 gram bay leaves
3 liters water

Makes 1 liter

Place the duck bones on a greased baking sheet and bake for 20 minutes at 235°C.

Transfer the bones to a big pot.

Add the vegetables and the pepper, the bay leaf, and the water.

Cook over medium heat. Once the water reaches a boil, reduce to low heat and cook until the contents have reduced by half. Strain and set aside the broth until ready to use.

Duck ragù
30 grams duck lard
100 grams carrots, diced into ¼-centimeter cubes
40 grams celery, diced into ¼-centimeter cubes
50 grams onion, diced into ¼-centimeter cubes
400 grams ground duck meat
4 grams salt
2 grams ground black pepper
130 milliliters white wine
2 grams rosemary
2 grams sage
400 milliliters duck broth

Duck ragù

Makes 500 grams

Place the duck lard in a saucepan with the vegetables over medium heat and cook for approximately 5 minutes. Add the meat, previously seasoned with salt and pepper, and cook for 15 minutes, stirring only occasionally. Add the white wine and let it evaporate completely. Add in the cheesecloth of herbs and the duck broth. Once the liquid reaches a boil, lower to minimum heat and cook for 40 minutes. Remove from the heat and remove the herbs from the pan.

White butter
10 milliliters white wine vinegar
1 gram shallot, minced
20 grams heavy cream
1 gram ground black pepper
250 grams butter, cubed

White butter

Makes 250 grams

Pour the white wine vinegar into a large saucepan with the shallots. Cook over high heat until the vinegar evaporates.

Add the heavy cream and the ground pepper. Boil for 2 minutes.

Turn off the heat, but don't remove the pan from the burner. Gradually add the butter with one hand, whisking with the other. Continue whisking until the butter is completely mixed in.

Keep the butter in a warm place.

To Serve

4 liters water
40 grams coarse salt
50 grams butter, cubed
20 grams pápalo
320 grams duck ragù
480 grams pápalo pappardelle
240 milliliters white stock
60 grams white butter
40 grams Parmigiano Reggiano

Heat the water in a saucepan over high heat. When it reaches a boil, add the salt.

Melt half of the butter in a frying pan and sauté the pápalo. Add the duck ragù, sauté, and then add in the white stock.

Add the pasta to the boiling water. Once it starts to float, remove it and add it to the pan. Let the pasta cook in the sauce for a few minutes.

Add the white butter and the parmesan. Toss the contents of the pan until well mixed. Top with papalo.

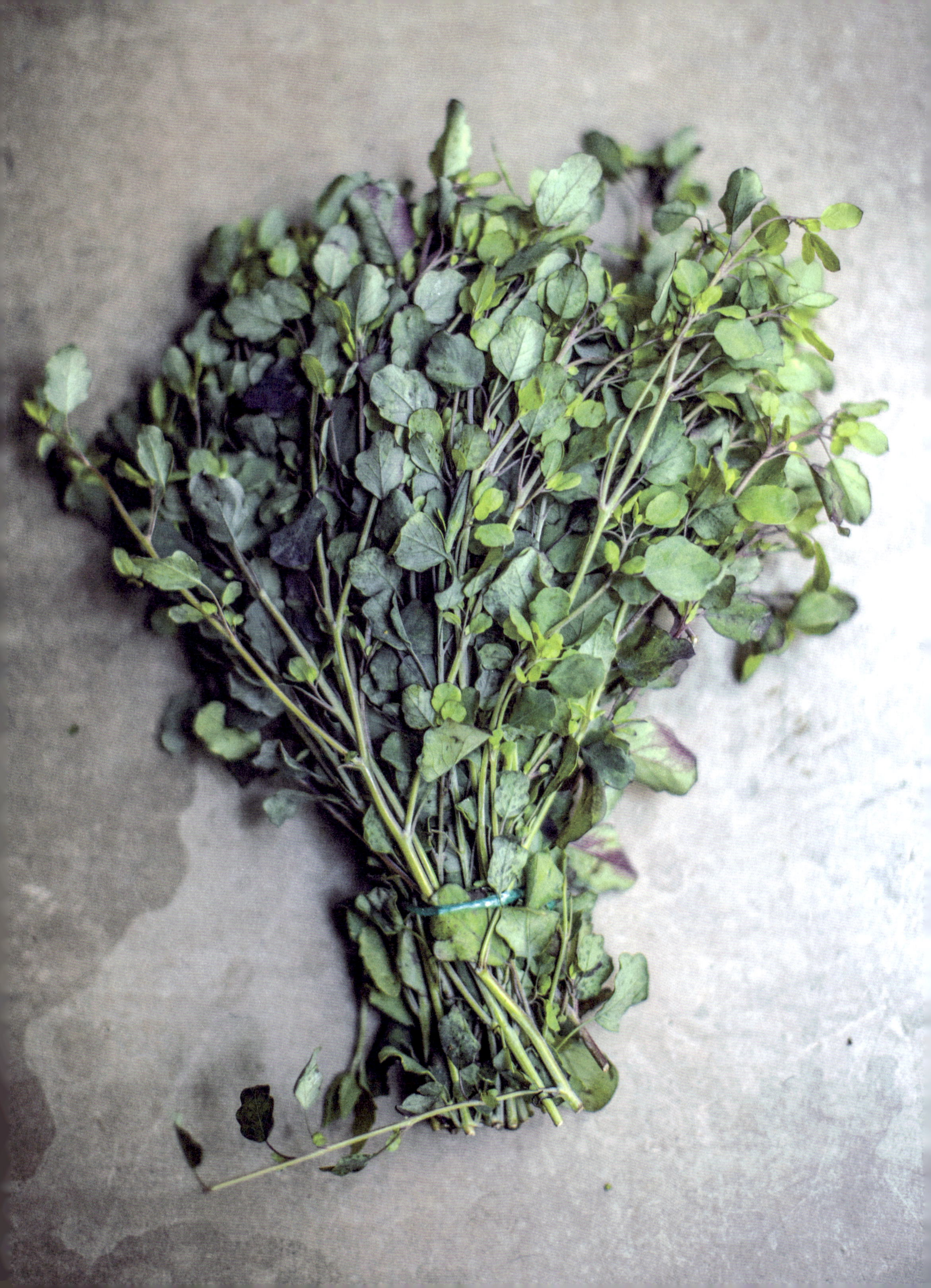

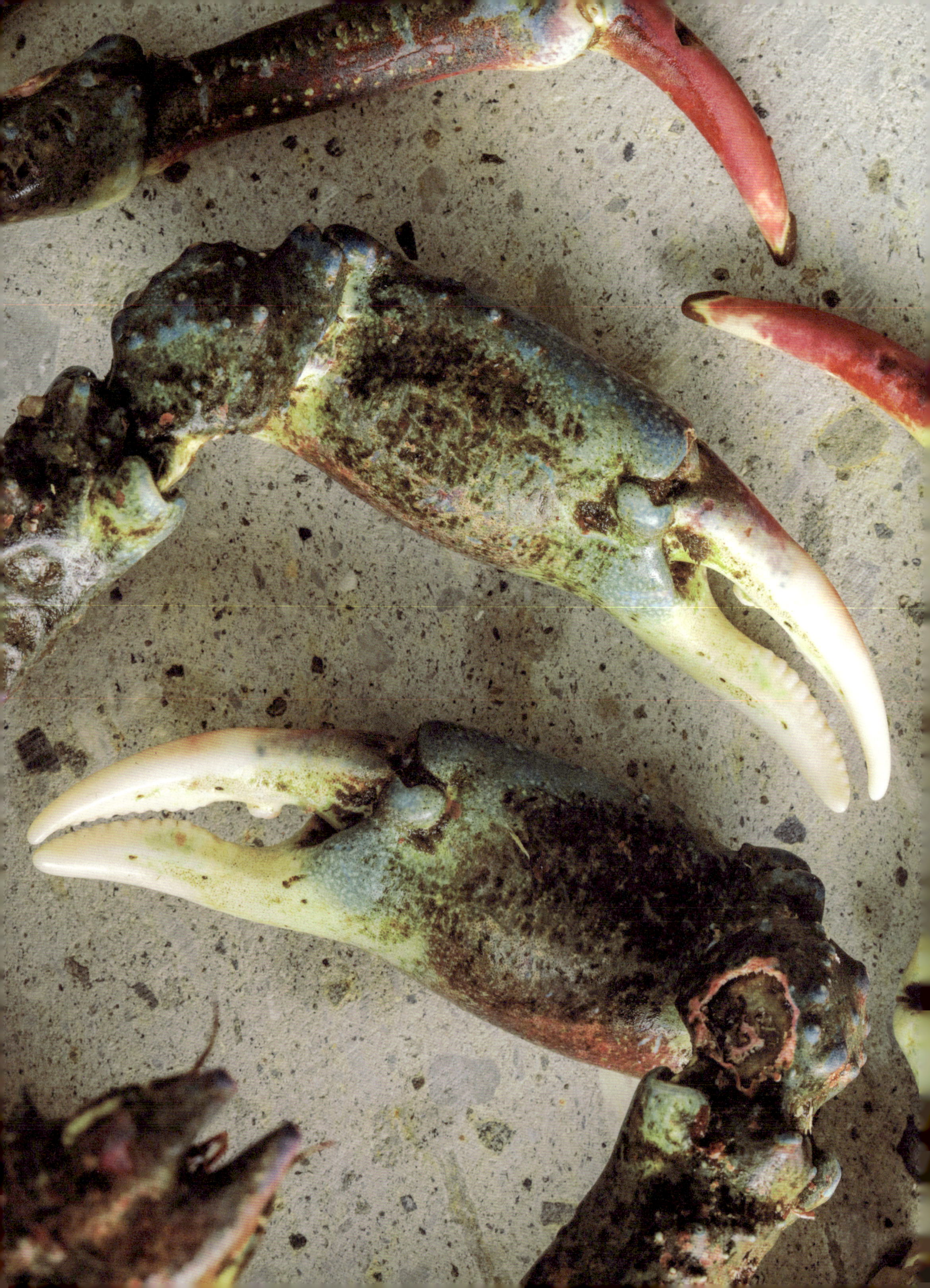

III

Animals

Mahi-mahi, lentils, carrots, parsley, and peppermint	184
Sea bass, potatoes, hoja santa, squash vine, and squash blossom	186
Beef sweetbreads, plums, yogurt, pomegranate, and zaatar	190
Our Suppliers	**197**
Wagyu beef tips, sorrel, lemon, and fennel frond	208
Black cod, endives, cauliflower, celery, golden raisins, and pine nuts	211
Suckling pig, achiote, and smoked sweet potato	213
Grouper and romesco	218
Rock cod, green romesco, bok choy, and mizuna	220
Pork neck, black romesco, and turnip flowers	222
Rabbit, carrots, and lovage	224
Scorpionfish, chorizo, and tomatoes	229
Red snapper, tamarind, and habanero	231
Quail, farro, dates, and mustard leaves	234
Cider-braised pork, apples, and elderberries	239
Chuck tail flap, avocado leaf, smoked zucchini, and chayotes	242
Striped black bass, pineapple, cascabel pepper, sorrel, tarragon, and xoconostle	244
Well-being	**249**

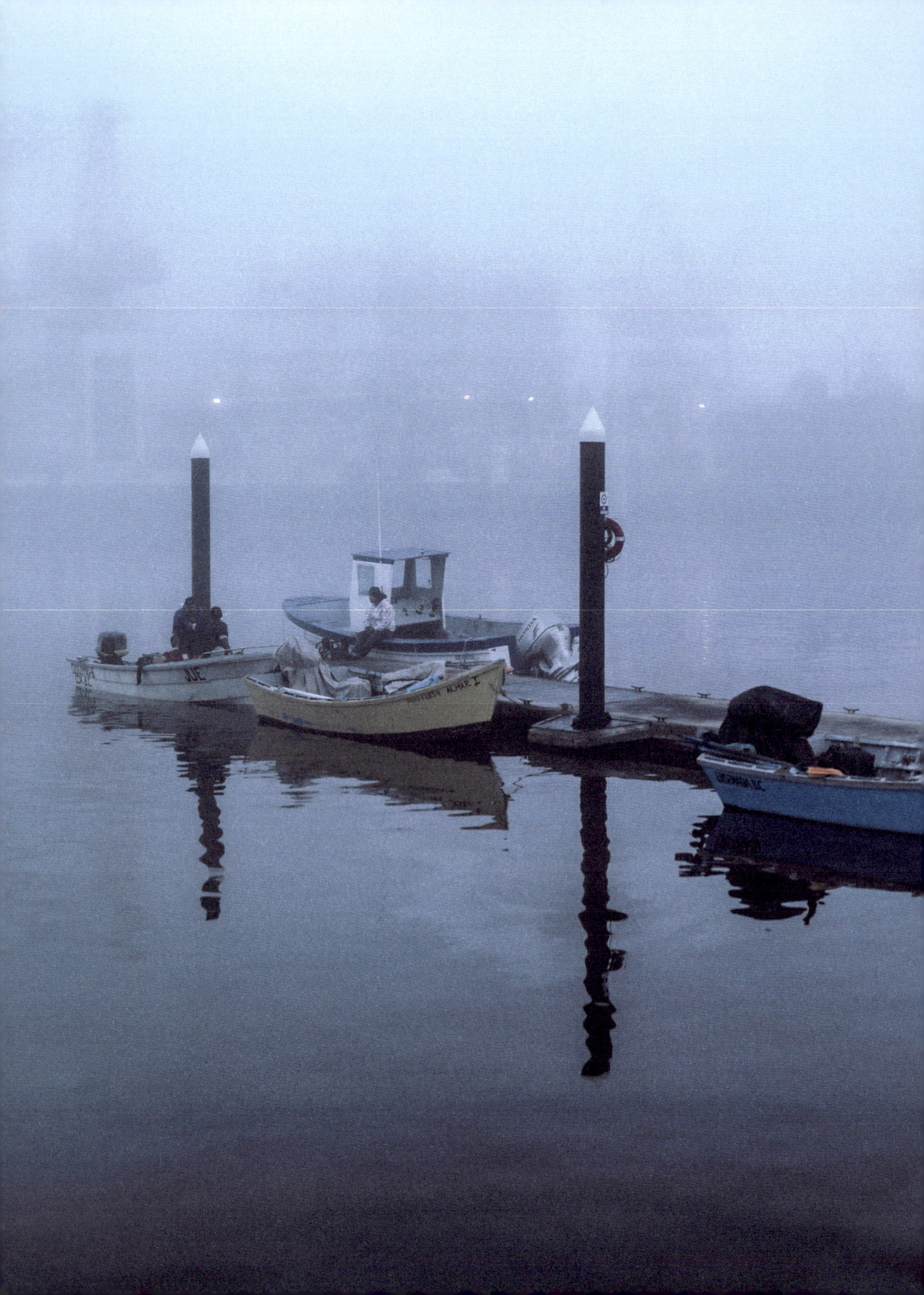

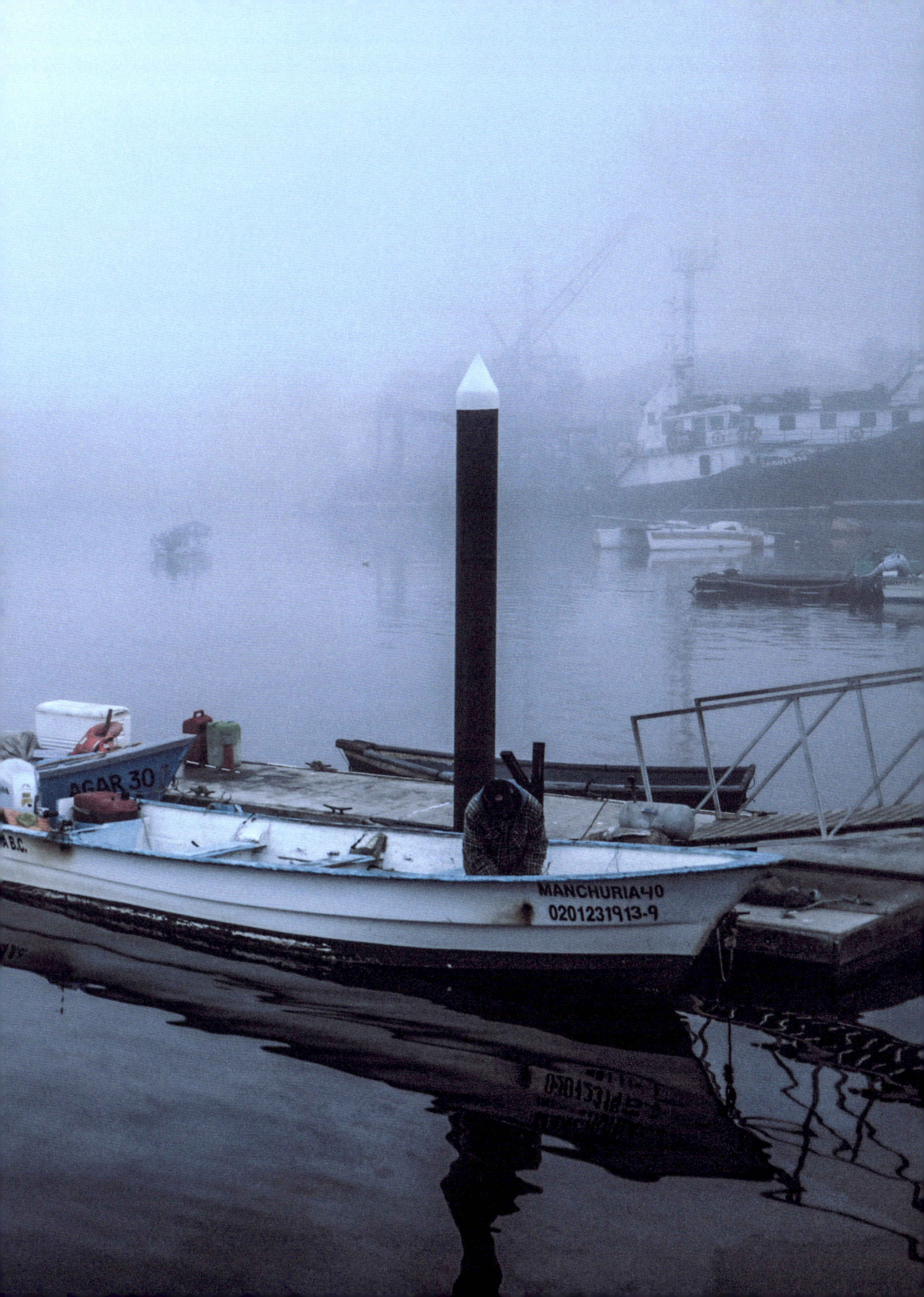
AGAR 30
MANCHURIA40
0201231913-9

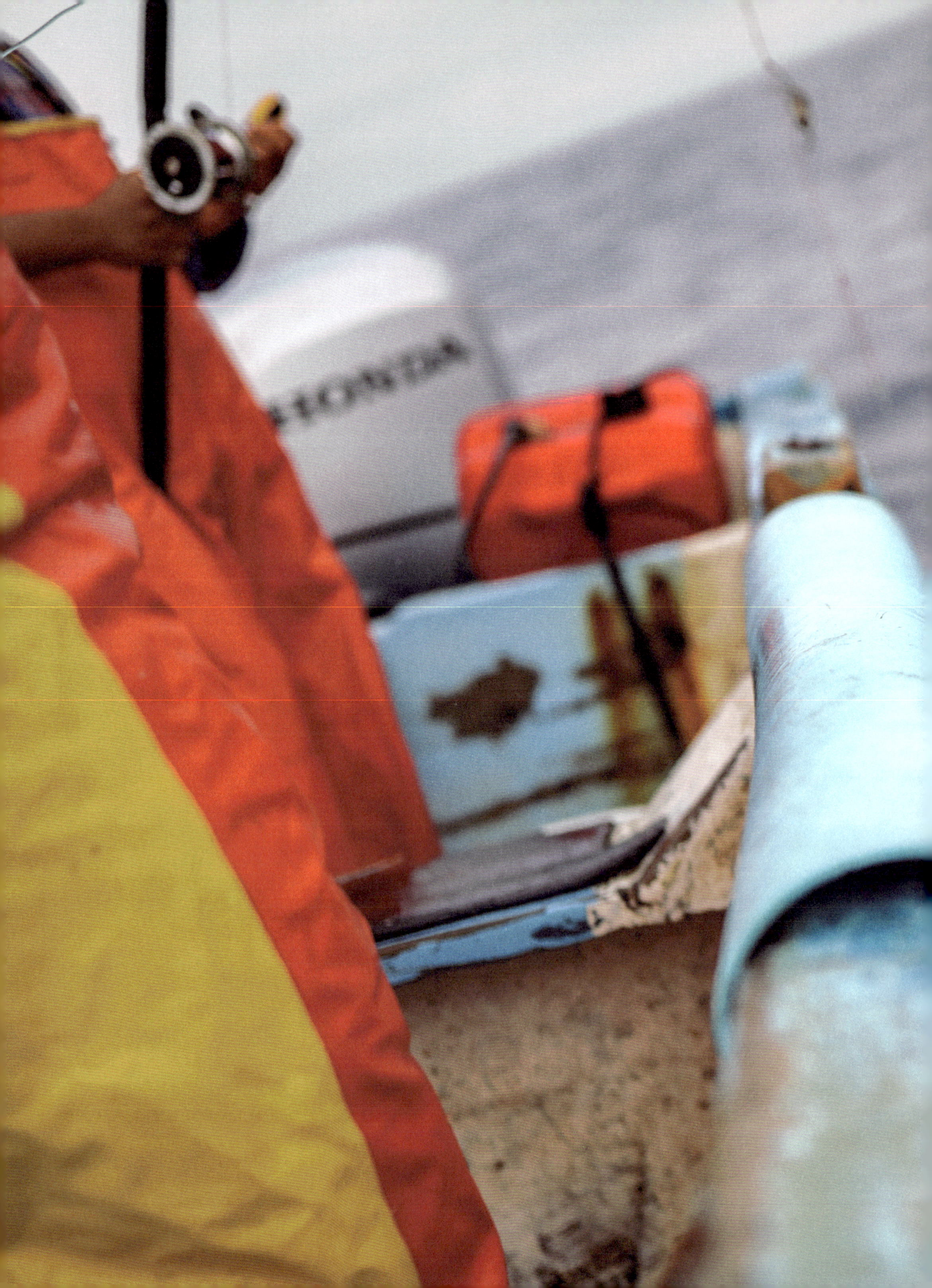

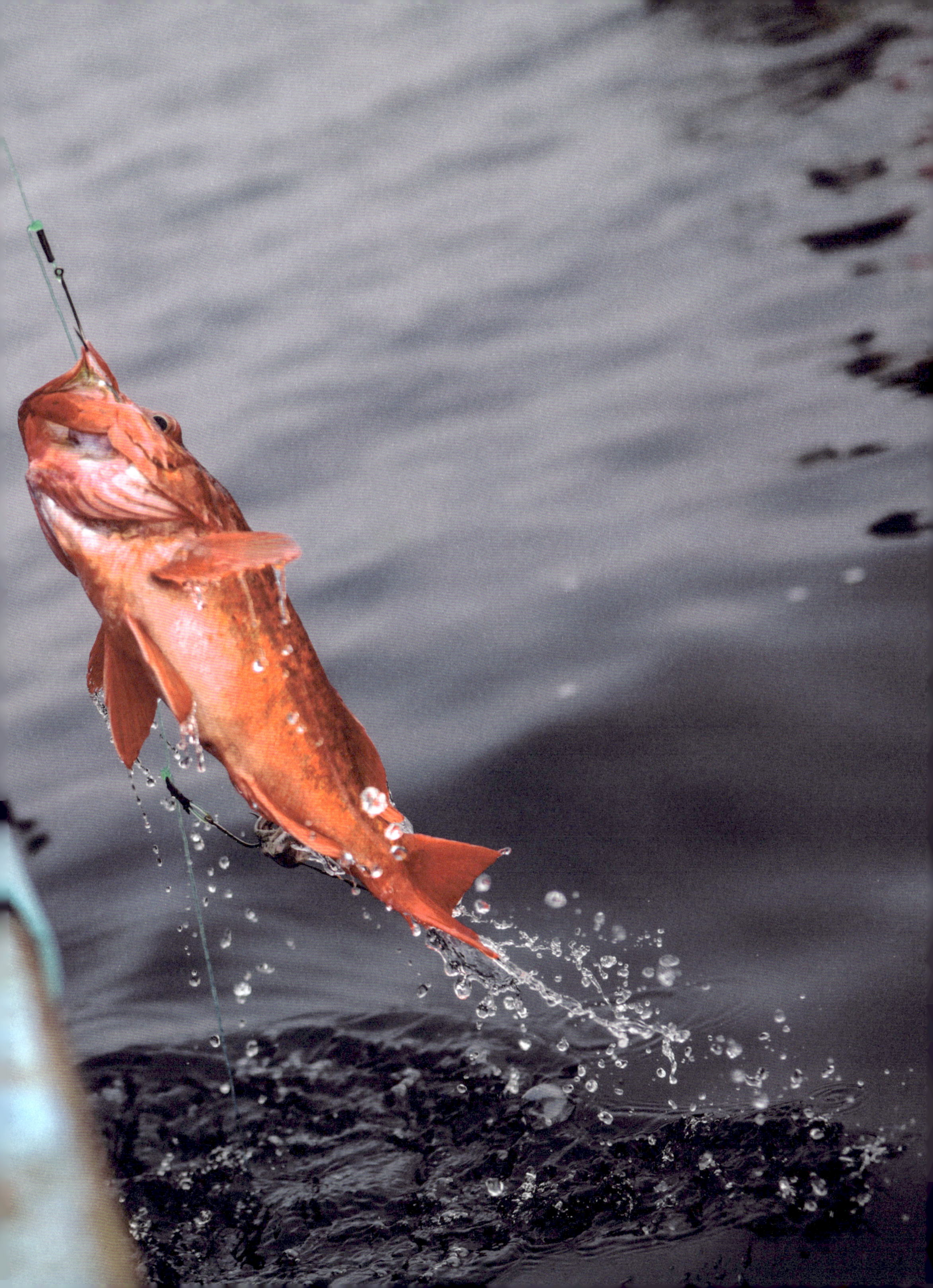

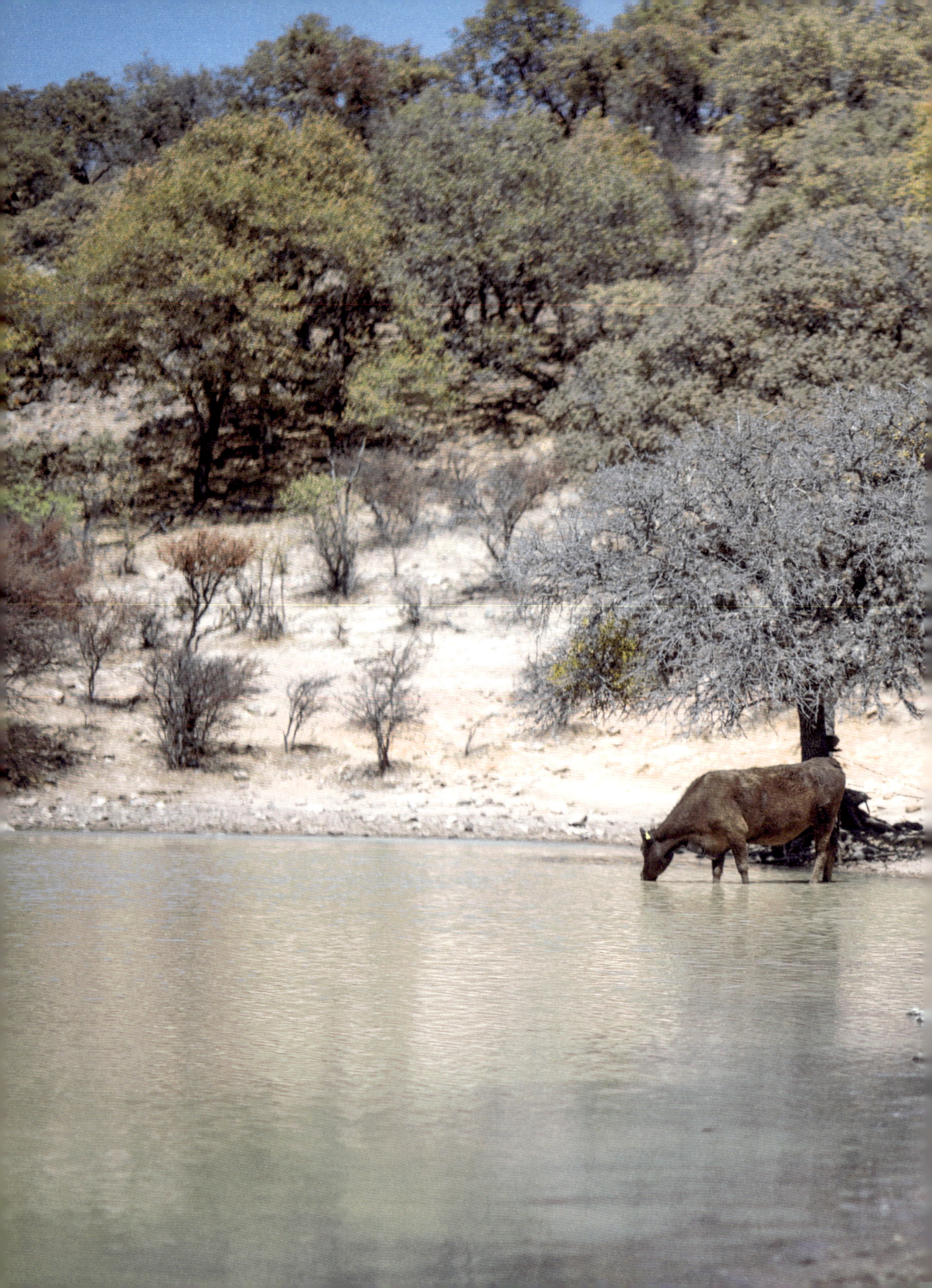

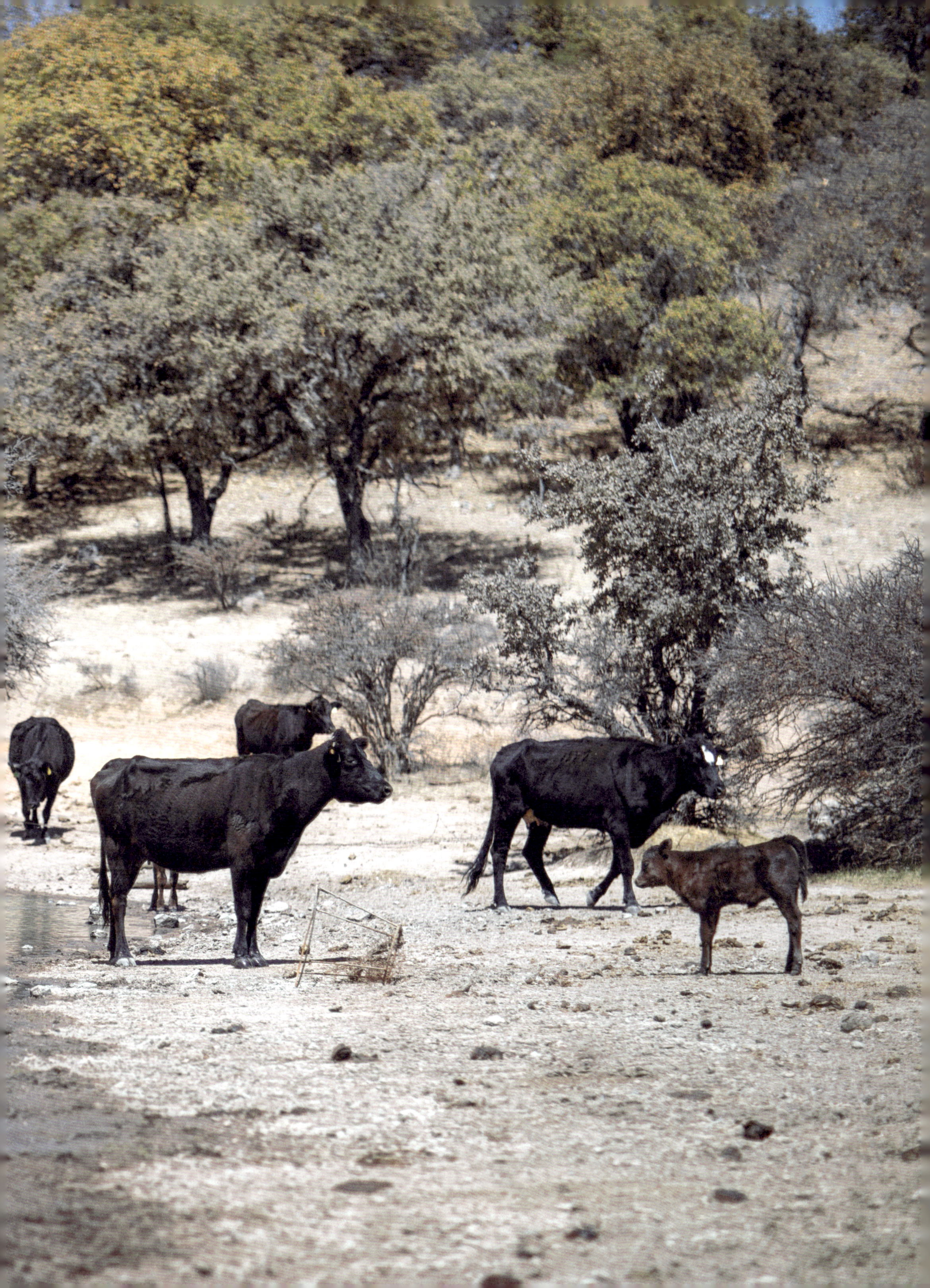

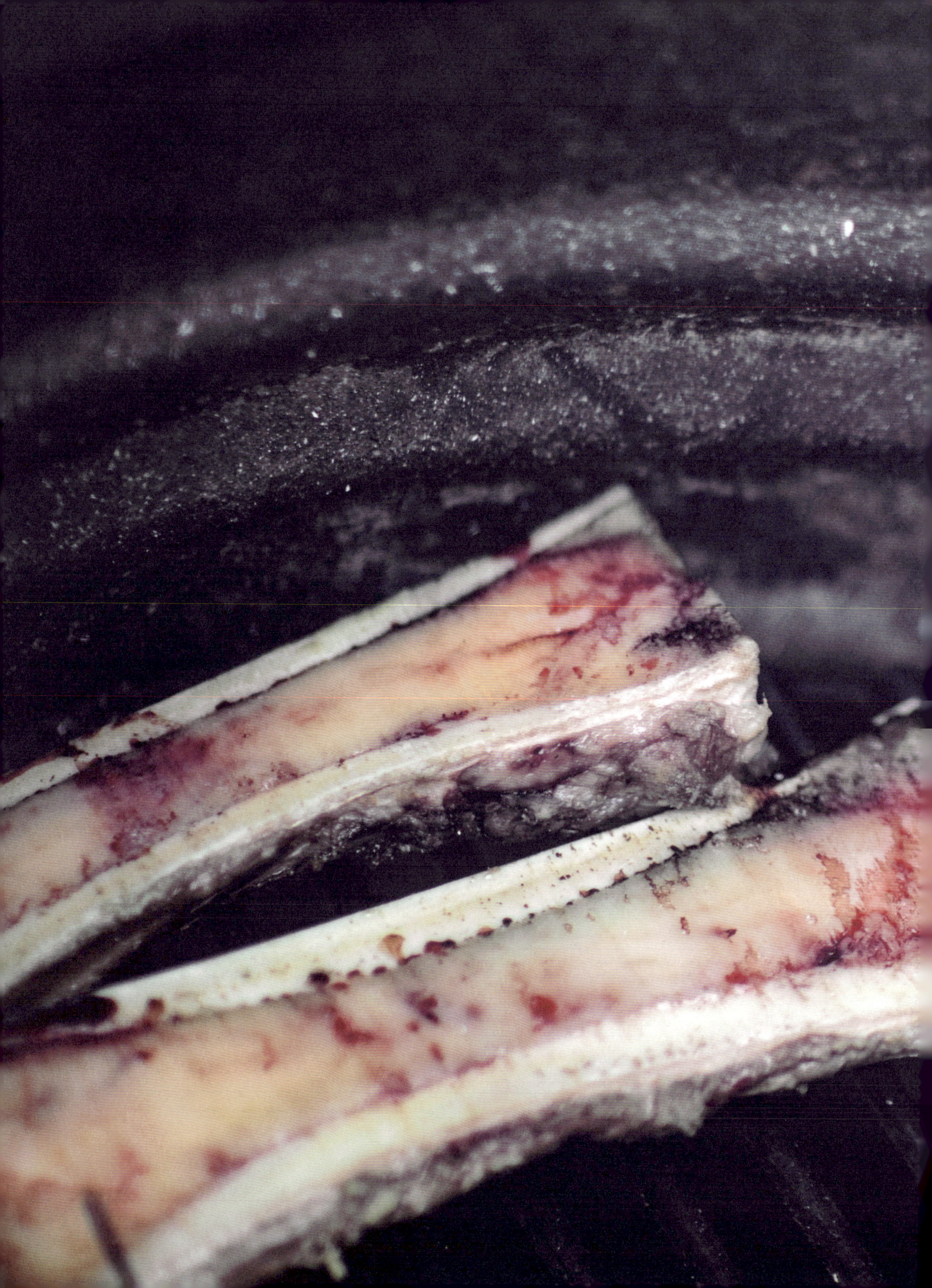

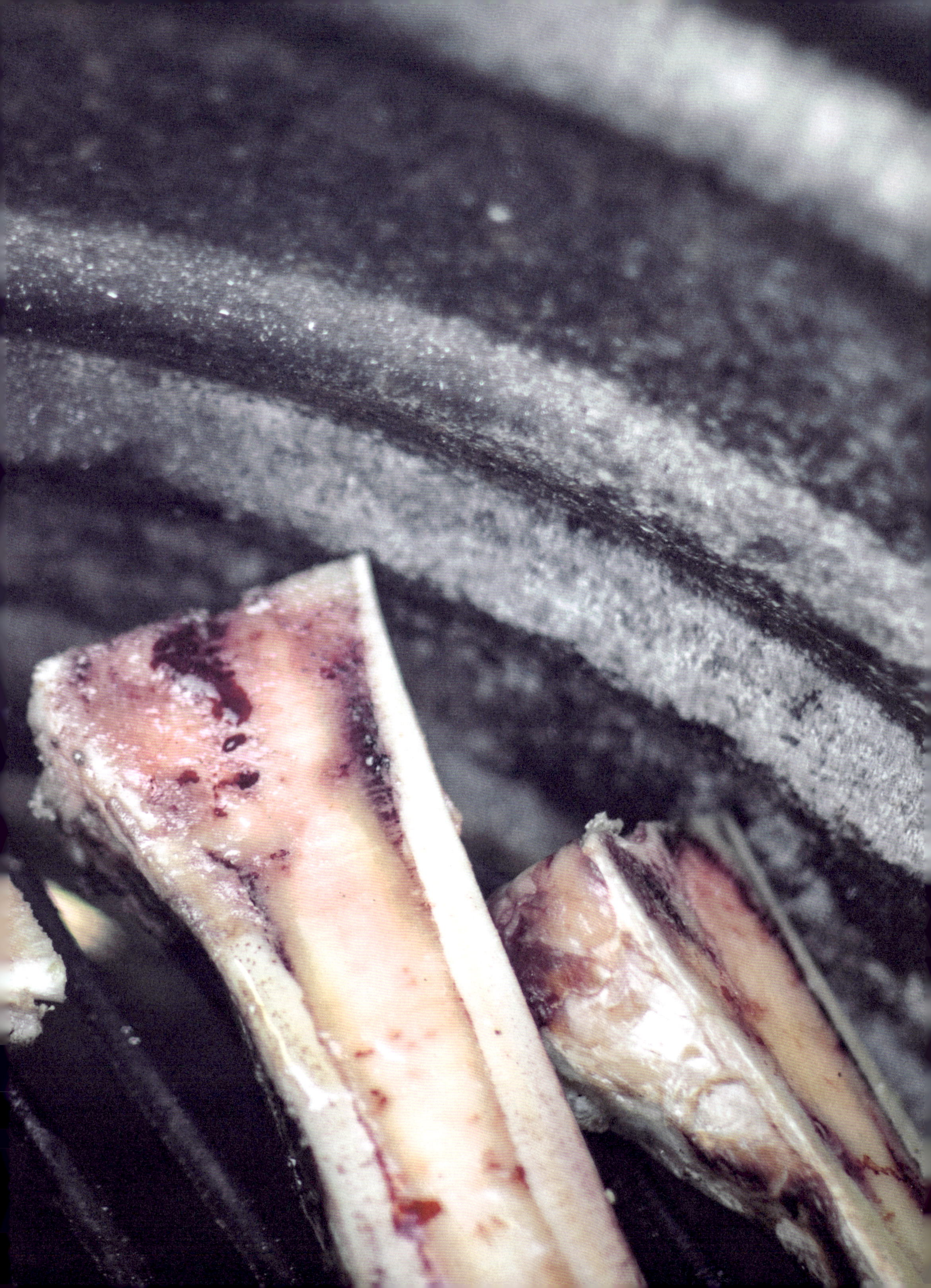

- CALDO DE AVES
- CALDO DE CORDERO
- CARNE DE AVES
- CERDO SIDRA
- CONFIT DE CONEJO
- CORDERO PORCIONADO
- CORNED BEEF
- CORDERO LIMPIO
- CABEZA DE LOMO
- FUMET
- JITOMATES HORNEADO
- JUGO DE POLLO
- JUGO DE BIRRIA
- JUGO DE CERDO
- JUGO DE CERDO/LECHE
- JUGO DE RES
- JUGO DE BETABEL
- LENGUA COCIDA /FRIA
- LENGUA COCIDA /BIRRIA
- PICKLES
- PURÉ DE APIONABO
- PURE DE CHIRIVIA
- PURE DE BETABEL
- PURE DE CALABAZA
- PARMESANO RALLADO
- RAGU CORDERO
- RAGU PATO
- RAGU SALCHICHA
- RAGU CERDO
- RECORTE DE CABEZA
- SALSA DE JITOMATE
- SHORT RIB
- MOLLEJAS

15 LTS
3 LTS
3 RECETAS.

2 Bolsas.

10 LTS
1.500 KG
8 LTS
4 LTS
6 LTS
4 LTS
6 LTS
4 LTS
8 PZAS.

5 KG.
3.500 KG

5.500 KG.
30 KG.
10.800 K.
11.200 KG
8.400 KG
42.000 KG
4 KG

45 LTS
72 ORD

Mahi-mahi, lentils, carrots, parsley, and peppermint

We make constant use of the pickling technique at Rosetta. The primary aim of pickling is to prolong the lifespan of foods by cooking them in vinegar. But it's also a good way to make our mouths water: lightly spiced vinegar piques the taste buds. It's no accident that a bowl of pickled carrots, cauliflower, peppers, and zucchini will often appear on the table of a Mexican cantina as you sip a beer.

We pickle baby rainbow carrots because we love their firm consistency and sweet flavor. We add our pickled carrots to a mound of lentils cooked al dente. While lentils are usually considered an apt ingredient for stews and other winter dishes, here—thanks to the acidity of the brine—they are revealed as a fresh ingredient, with an earthy flavor and a firm consistency somewhat like tabbouleh. To accentuate this little-known facet of lentils, we surround them with an intensely green sauce made of parsley. Finally, we add a piece of mahi-mahi, a dense fish that benefits from the fresh combination of the pickled carrots, the lentils, and the herbs.

Serves 4

Parsley sauce

40 grams parsley, with stalk
1 pinch salt
120 milliliters ice water

Makes 160 milliliters
Blend all the ingredients together.

Cooked lentils

100 grams lentils
500 milliliters water
1 pinch salt
20 milliliters chardonnay vinegar

Makes 200 grams
Cook the lentils in water over high heat for approximately 15 minutes. When they're almost completely cooked, add the salt, let them cook a couple more minutes, and remove from the burner. Strain them, lay them out on a tray, and pour the vinegar onto them.

Pickled vegetables

125 milliliters olive oil
3 grams garlic, peeled
100 grams baby rainbow carrots, finely sliced
75 grams pearl onions, finely sliced
10 grams green cuaresmeño pepper
10 grams red cuaresmeño pepper
100 milliliters white wine vinegar
2 grams black peppercorns
3 whole cloves
3 bay leaves
2 grams whole cinnamon

Makes 150 grams

Place the olive oil in a saucepan with the whole garlic. Cook over low heat until the garlic begins to brown, then remove from the burner. Once the oil has cooled, remove the garlic.

Cut the cuaresmeño peppers in half, remove the seeds, and cut into small strips.

Place the vinegar in a saucepan along with the black pepper, the cloves, the bay leaves, and the cinnamon. Begin to heat. Once the liquid starts to boil, remove. Set aside to cool, then strain.

Put the saucepan with the garlic oil back on the heat. Add the carrots. When they start to cook, add the onions and the peppers. Cook for 10 minutes over medium heat, stirring constantly. Remove the pan from the heat and add the infused vinegar.

Lemon vinaigrette

30 milliliters olive oil
10 milliliters lemon juice

Makes 40 milliliters

Put the lemon juice into a bowl, then stream in the olive oil and whisk together.

To Serve

720 grams mahi-mahi fillet
40 milliliters lemon vinaigrette
16 grams salt
200 grams cooked lentils
120 grams pickled vegetables
120 milliliters parsley sauce
8 grams peppermint
8 grams parsley
25 milliliters chardonnay vinegar
25 milliliters olive oil

Cut the fish fillet into four pieces. Place each one on a baking tray with the lemon vinaigrette and the salt. Cover with aluminum foil. Bake for 10 to 12 minutes at 250°C.

Combine the cooked lentils and the pickled vegetables without their juice. Add the chopped parsley and peppermint. Pour the vinegar and 20 milliliters of olive oil into the lentils and mix everything together.

Place parsley sauce into the center of each plate and add a few drops of olive oil. On top, place a spoonful of the lentil mixture. On top of that, place the mahi-mahi and finish off with a little more of the lentils.

Sea bass, potatoes, hoja santa, squash vine, and squash blossoms

The family of one of our servers has supplied us with fish and seafood for several years. Once, after a trip back to his hometown of Salina Cruz, Oaxaca, he returned to the restaurant with some lobsters, sea cradles, and small sea bass as a gift. I was captivated by their freshness and flavor. Since then, his mother has sent us several coolers of these fresh products every Sunday night. She isn't a fishmonger; she deals directly with the fishermen. Her business came together when we started placing regular orders with her: every Monday morning, her other children come to Rosetta with sea bass, sea cradles, freshwater shrimp, and other products from the Oaxacan coast.

Family businesses are waning in our current economic system. It's important to support them: it's a means of strengthening the small-scale economy, as well as a way to exercise solidarity among families. Besides, we're incredibly lucky to have products selected specially for our needs.

This small and tender sea bass cooks rapidly when grilled. We serve it over a sauce made with potatoes and pieces of hoja santa, sweet squash vines, and lightly cooked squash blossoms.

Serves 4

200 grams fish bones
50 grams white onions, quartered
50 grams celery, cut into chunks
50 grams fennel, cut into chunks
20 grams parsley stalks
20 grams leeks, thickly sliced
30 grams ginger, peeled and cut into large chunks
1.5 liters water

Fumet

Makes 1 liter

Wash the fish bones thoroughly.
Place all the ingredients in a large saucepan and cook over high heat.
Once the liquid starts to boil, reduce heat to low and cook for 30 minutes. Remove from the heat and strain twice.

Potato sauce

15 grams butter
20 milliliters olive oil
20 grams leeks, finely sliced
8 grams shallots, finely sliced
90 grams potatoes, peeled and finely sliced
75 milliliters fumet
1 pinch salt

Makes 160 grams

Heat the butter and the olive oil in a saucepan, adding the leeks and shallots. Sauté. Once they start to very lightly brown, add the potato and sauté for 5 more minutes.

Add the fumet and the salt. Let the potato cook until it's very soft, almost coming apart. Run the mixture through a food processor until its texture is very smooth and soft.

Potatoes and squash vine soup

20 grams squash vines
½ hoja santa leaf
40 grams potato
160 grams potato sauce
40 milliliters white wine
260 milliliters fumet
1 pinch salt

Makes 500 grams

Use a peeling knife to remove the fibers from the squash vines, then cut them into 2-centimeter diagonal logs. Blanch them in boiling water with a pinch of salt for 2 minutes, remove the water, place the vines into a bowl of ice water for 2 more minutes, and drain.

Cook the potato in a saucepan with plenty of water and a pinch of salt until you can gently insert a knife into it. Remove it from the water and transfer to a bowl of cold water. Once it's cool, cut it into small cubes.

Heat the fumet in a frying pan. Add the potato cubes, the potato sauce, the white wine, the squash vines, and the chopped hoja santa leaf. Season with salt to taste and set aside.

Lemon vinaigrette

15 milliliters olive oil
5 milliliters lemon juice

Makes 20 milliliters

Put the lemon juice into a bowl, then stream in the olive oil and whisk together.

To Serve

800 grams sea bass fillet, with skin
1 pinch salt
10 milliliters vegetable oil
500 grams potatoes, squash vines, and squash blossoms
20 milliliters lemon vinaigrette
½ hoja santa leaf
4 squash blossoms

Cut the fillet into 4 pieces and season with salt. Heat the water in a saucepan over medium heat. Cook the sea bass on the skin side for approximately 10 minutes.

Serve the potato and squash vine mixture in bowls. Dress with a few drops of lemon vinaigrette. Add chopped hoja santa. On top, place the fish fillet with the skin facing upward and add the squash blossoms.

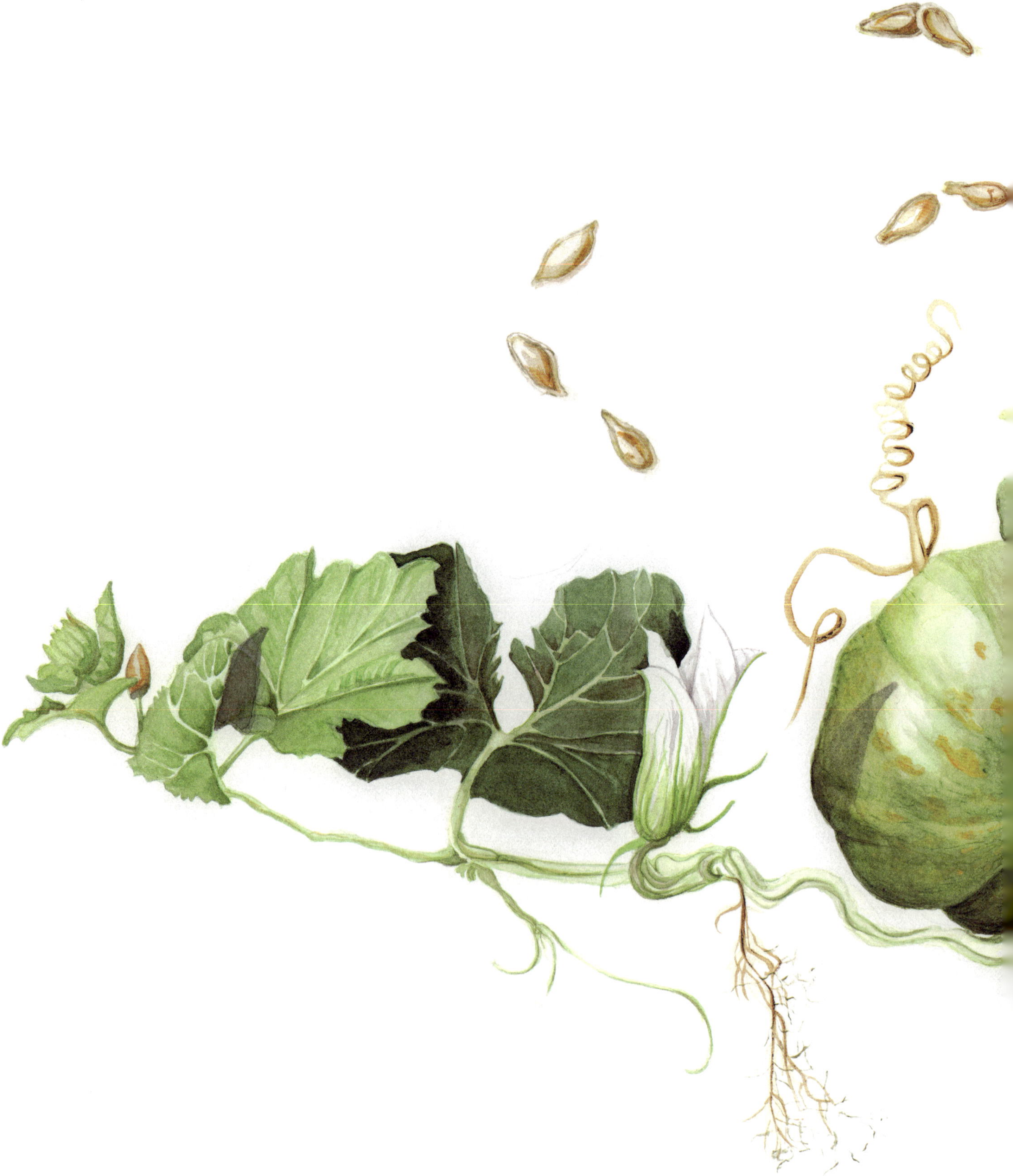

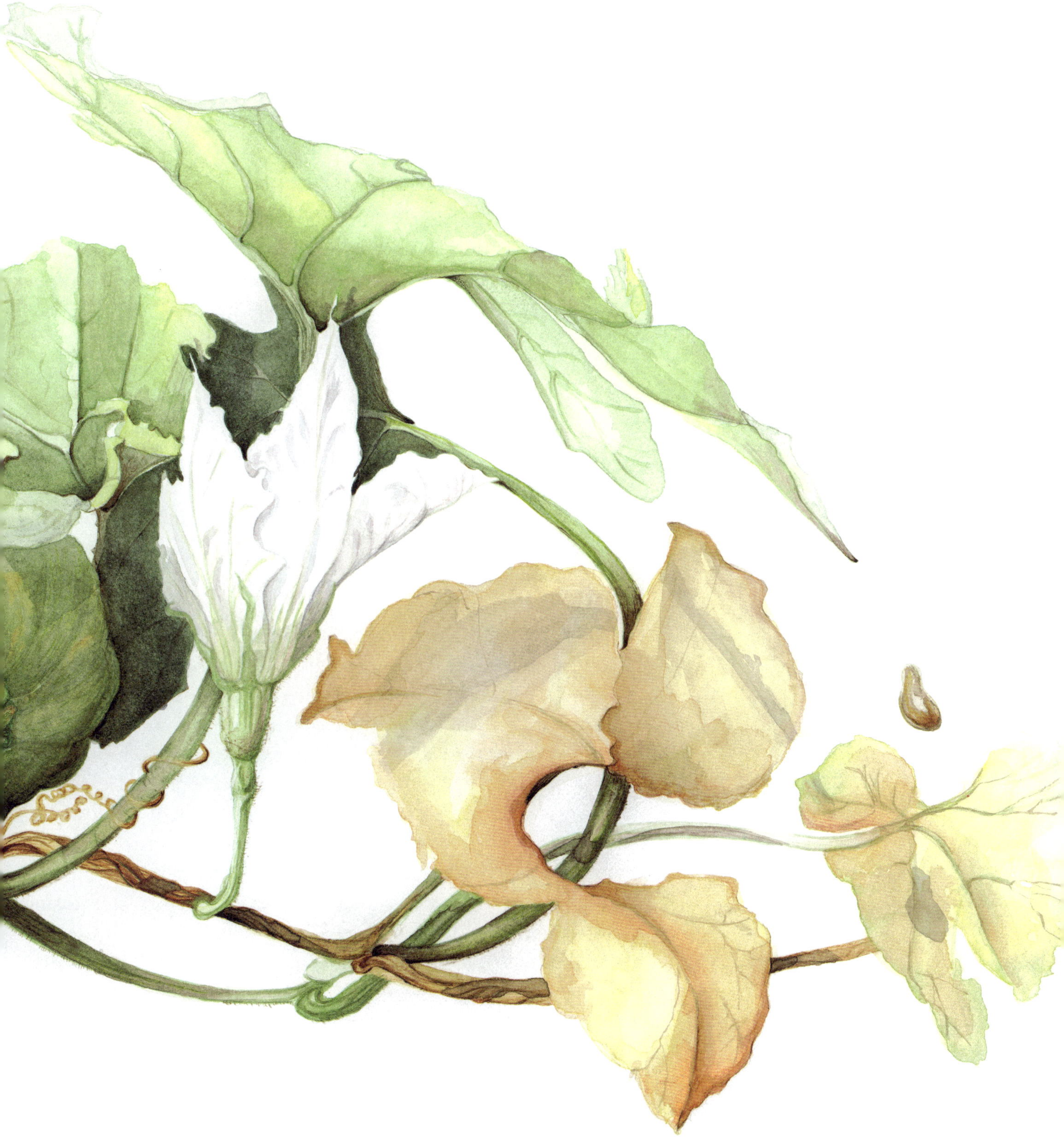

Beef sweetbreads, plums, yogurt, pomegranate, and zaatar

In recent decades, diners' taste for organ meat has diminished. The drop can be attributed in part to the high fat content of viscera, as well as because they raise cholesterol when eaten in excess. There are other reasons, too: for example, organ meat is difficult to commercialize because it's highly perishable and laborious to clean. Given how narrow a profit margin they yield, some butchers prefer not to sell them at all. None of this has prevented the inclusion of organ meat in popular Mexican dishes like menudo (pig belly soup) or hígado encebollado (liver and onions).

I like cooking with viscera because their consistency, texture, and flavors differ enormously. Each organ has something special: the creaminess of sweetbreads, the chewiness of kidneys, the fleshiness of tongue. Besides, if consumed in moderation, organ meats do contain nutritional properties, particularly protein and collagen.

Sweetbreads are cattle's thymus gland. To attain a creamy consistency, we confit them slowly. Beforehand, they spend two days covered in salt, rosemary, bay leaf, pepper, and garlic. Once cooked, we store them in their own lard. Shortly before serving, they are rejuvenated in warm water, then seared in a hot pan. This process achieves a crunchy texture on the outside without sacrificing the soft consistency on the inside. In fact, when prepared carefully, sweetbreads can reach a truly incomparable degree of softness.

Everything that nature gives us has its own virtues. It's all a matter of balance. We shouldn't overdo our consumption of high-fat foods, like viscera, but that doesn't mean we have to stop eating them altogether. With food, everything comes down to use and abuse. The most important thing is to remain aware of the quality and quantity of what we eat. No single ingredient is harmful in itself—except for industrialized foods, which are actually mixtures of processed, chemical, and even synthetic products rather than food as such.

Sweetbreads confit

Serves 4

4 pieces beef sweetbreads
44 grams salt
18 grams sugar
10 grams ground black pepper
22 grams garlic, peeled and halved
10 grams thyme
10 grams bay leaves
15 grams chopped parsley stalks
5 grams rosemary
300 grams beef lard
300 milliliters water

Makes 4 pieces

Place the sweetbreads in a bowl of water for cleaning. Rinse them, then empty the container and add fresh water. Repeat this process twice. Drain the sweetbreads thoroughly to remove the water.

Add half the salt, the sugar, and the ground black pepper. Season the sweetbreads with the mixture.

Lay out the sweetbreads in a dish. On top of them, make a layer of garlic, thyme, parsley stalks, and rosemary. Cover the dish and refrigerate for 3 days.

Transfer the sweetbreads to a saucepan, along with the herbs, the water, the rest of the salt, and the beef lard. Cook over medium heat. Once the liquid reaches a boil, reduce to low heat. Cook for 30 minutes.

Once cooked, remove from the water with tongs and set aside.

Lemon yogurt

300 milliliters yogurt
1 gram garlic oil
3 milliliters lemon juice
1 pinch salt
2 grams lime zest

Makes 300 milliliters

Combine all the ingredients together in a bowl until well mixed.

Plum sauce

225 grams plums
10 grams sugar

Makes 100 grams

Make a small cut in the upper part of each plum. Place the plums in a saucepan of boiling water for 1 minute. Remove them from the water with a spoon and place them in a bowl of ice water to stop the cooking process.

Remove the skin from the plums, cut them in half, and remove the pits.

Blend the plums with the sugar in a food processor until they have the texture of a sauce.

Pickled plums

3 plums
150 milliliters water
150 milliliters white wine vinegar

Makes 12 wedges

Make a small cut in the upper part of each plum. Place the plums in a saucepan of boiling water for 1 minute. Remove them from the water with a spoon and place them in a bowl of ice water to stop the cooking process.

Remove the skin from the plums, then the pits. Cut each plum into four wedges and mix them with the water and the white wine vinegar.

Veal broth

1.5 kilograms veal bones
50 grams butter
60 grams carrots, sliced
30 grams tomato paste
100 grams shallots, peeled and quartered
1.5 liters water

Makes 250 milliliters

Place the veal bones onto a previously greased tray and bake for 25 minutes at 200°C.

Melt the butter in a saucepan. Add the carrots and shallots and sauté. Add the tomato paste. Let the mixture cook until it starts to turn golden brown.

Add the water and the veal bones. Cook for 2 hours. Strain and return to the heat until reduced to 250 milliliters.

To Serve

4 pieces sweetbreads confit
200 milliliters lemon yogurt
100 milliliters plum sauce
12 pickled plum wedges
100 milliliters veal broth
24 peppermint leaves
4 grams zaatar
100 milliliters safflower oil

Heat a frying pan over medium heat and add the sweetbreads with their own oil. Brown for 2 minutes on each side. Lay them out on a paper towel to remove excess fat.

Spoon lemon yogurt onto long plates and add some plum sauce and pickled plums. Cut each sweetbread into three pieces and arrange them in the center of the plate. Bathe in veal broth and add the peppermint leaves around the plate. Add a pinch of zaatar.

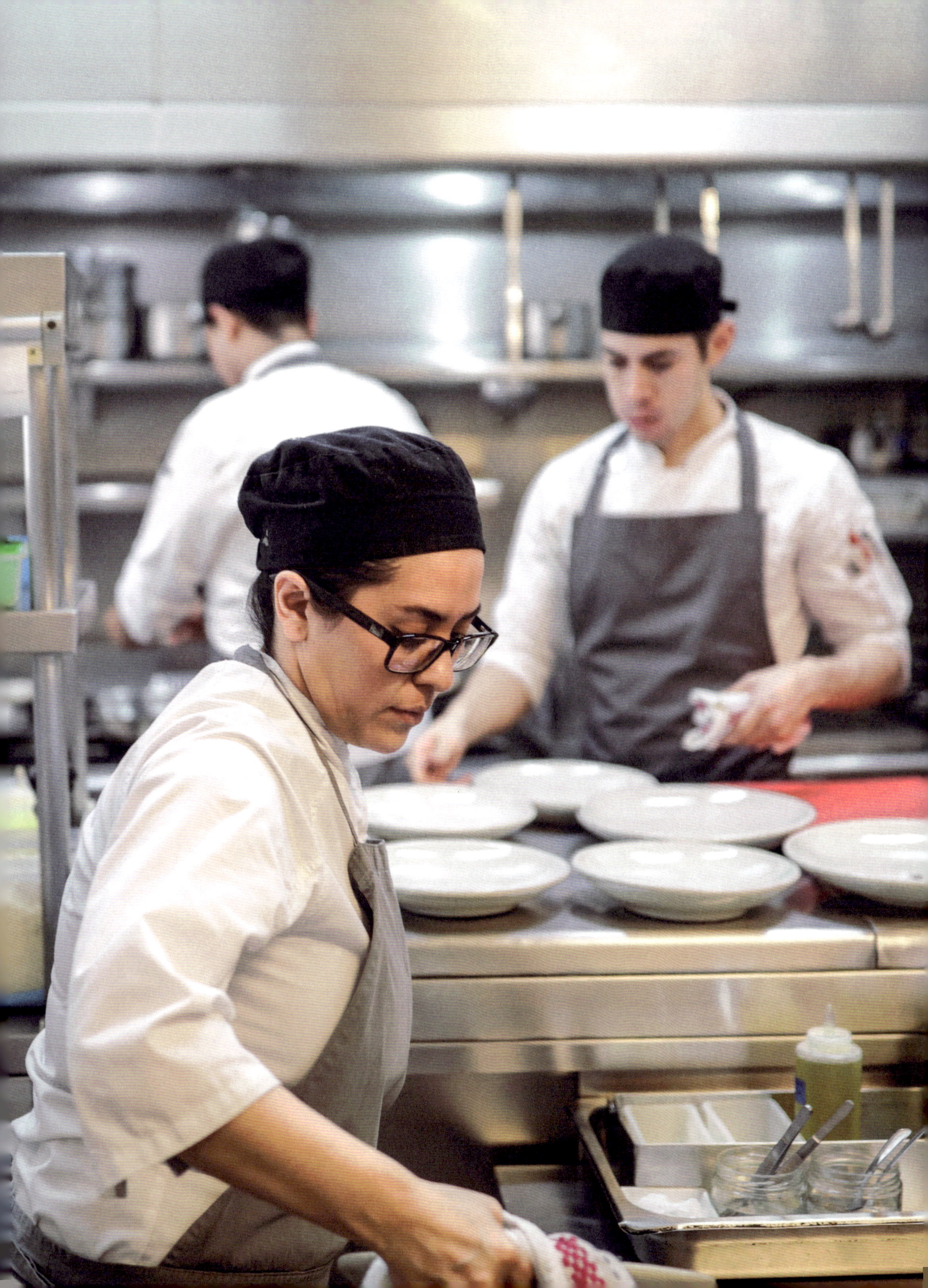

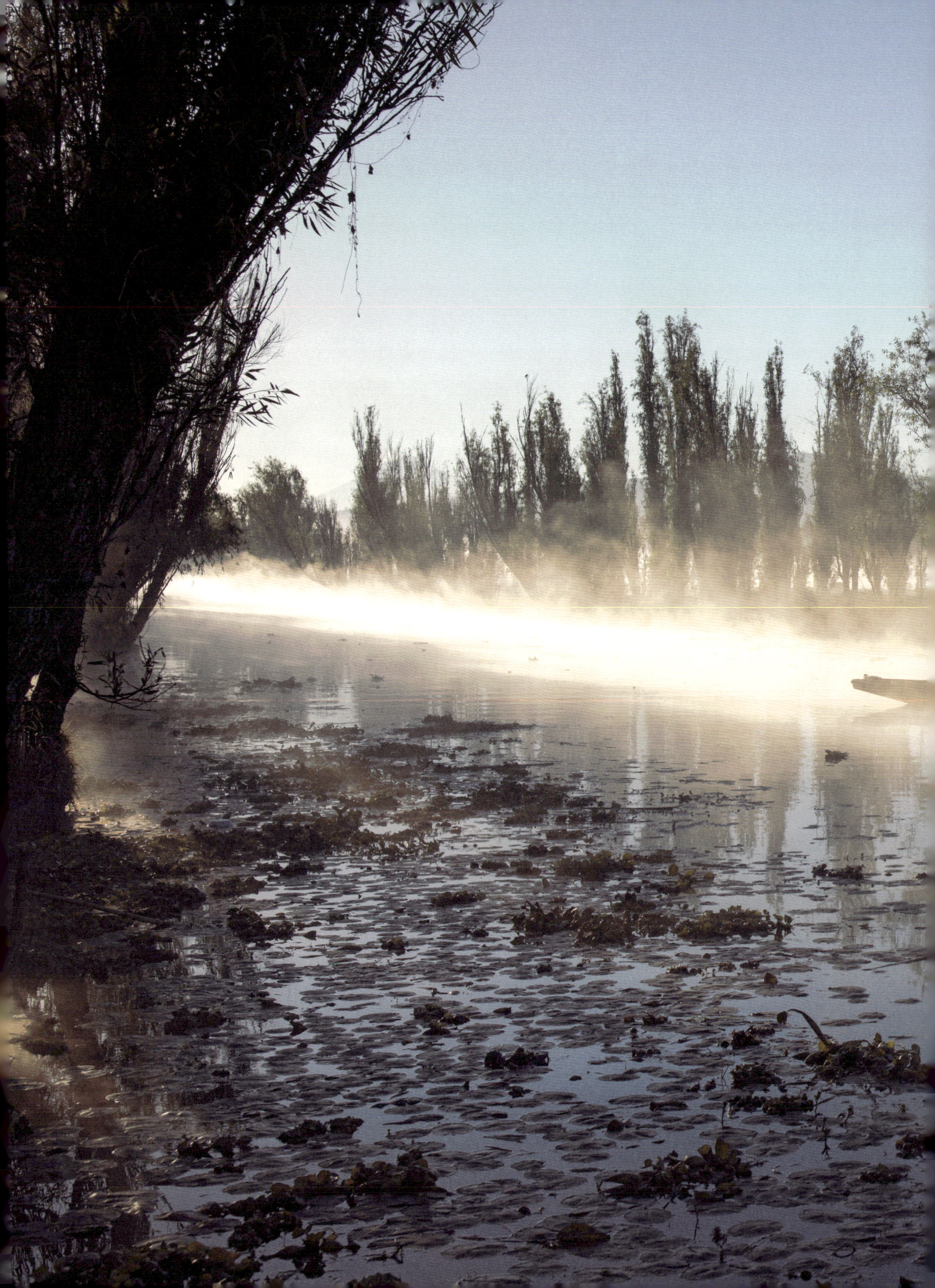

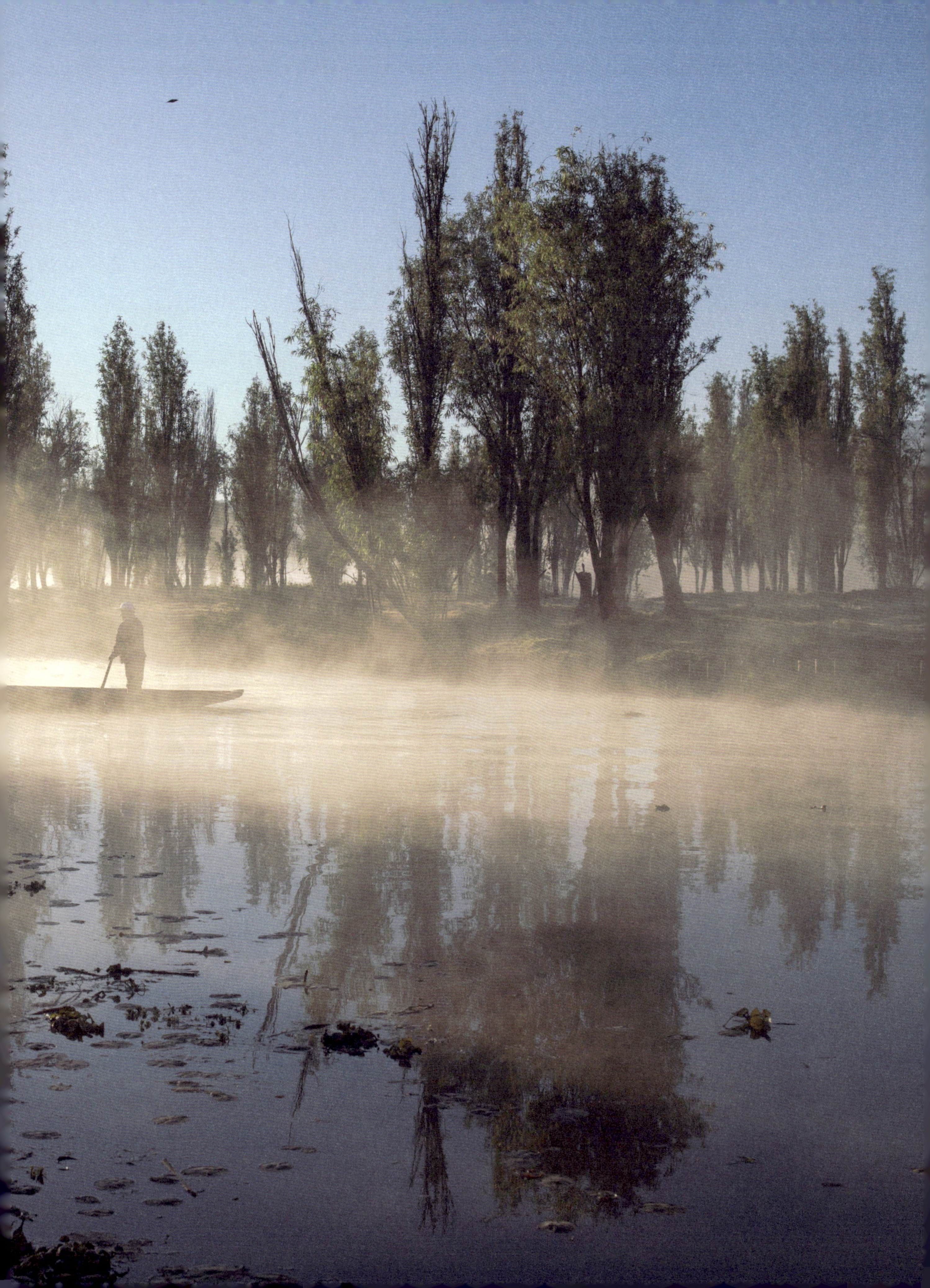

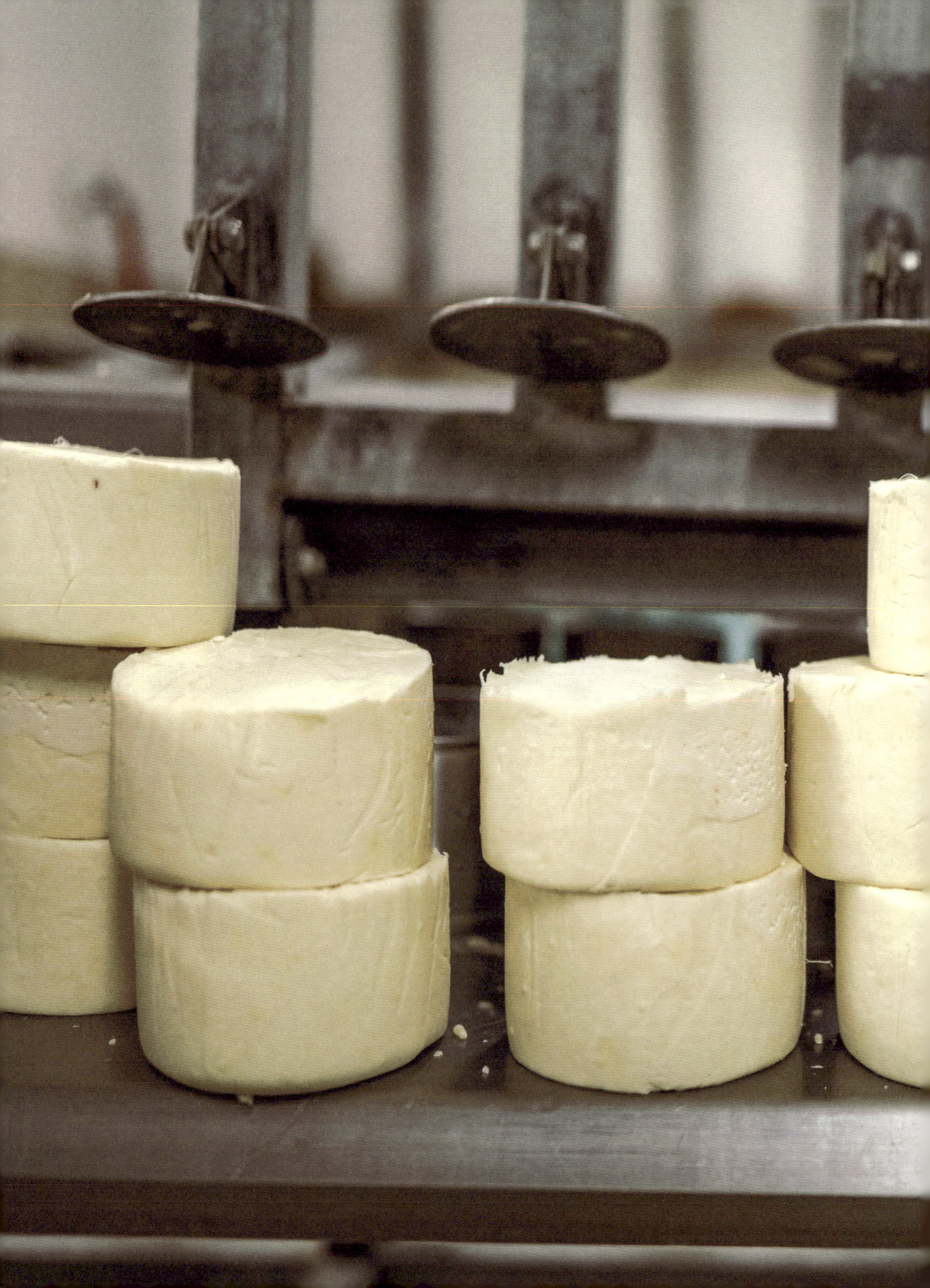

Our Suppliers

Cooks don't work alone. We work as a team in a restaurant. But we also need to work as a team with our suppliers. We must establish true, intimate alliances in which each party understands and respects the other's work. There's a constant dialogue that enriches both. Personally, I've learned about many different products, and how to use them, both from my kitchen team and from my suppliers.

At Rosetta, we seek to build these kinds of solid connections with suppliers who share our ethical principles. We like to know specifically where our ingredients come from and how they're produced, so that we can attest to their quality and be certain that they haven't been subjected to industrial or chemical processes. Whenever possible, we avoid using intermediaries. We mostly work with suppliers who are also producers. All of them are experts in the products they sell us. They maintain respectful relationships with the environment: they don't force nature to do anything; they don't use agrochemicals or genetically modified organisms (GMOs); they treat animals well. Their output is small. They're passionate people who are skilled at their jobs and who look beyond merely economic interests.

Over the years, we have constructed a broad network or chain that encompasses small producers, farmers, and fishermen located in different parts of Mexico; various community and agroecological projects; herb-growers and cattle ranchers; wine and mezcal producers; beekeepers and mushroom-pickers; cheese-makers and coffee-growers.

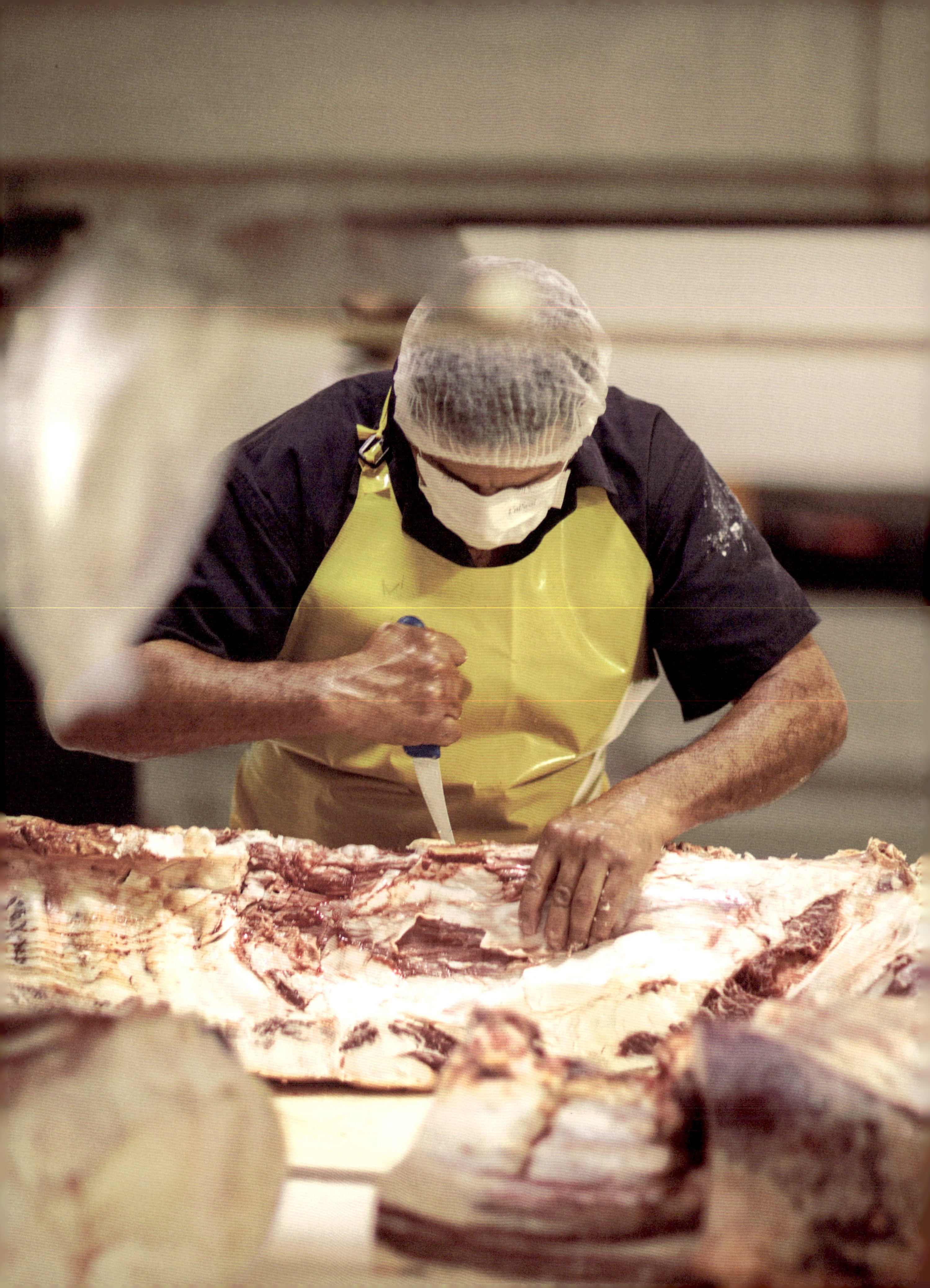

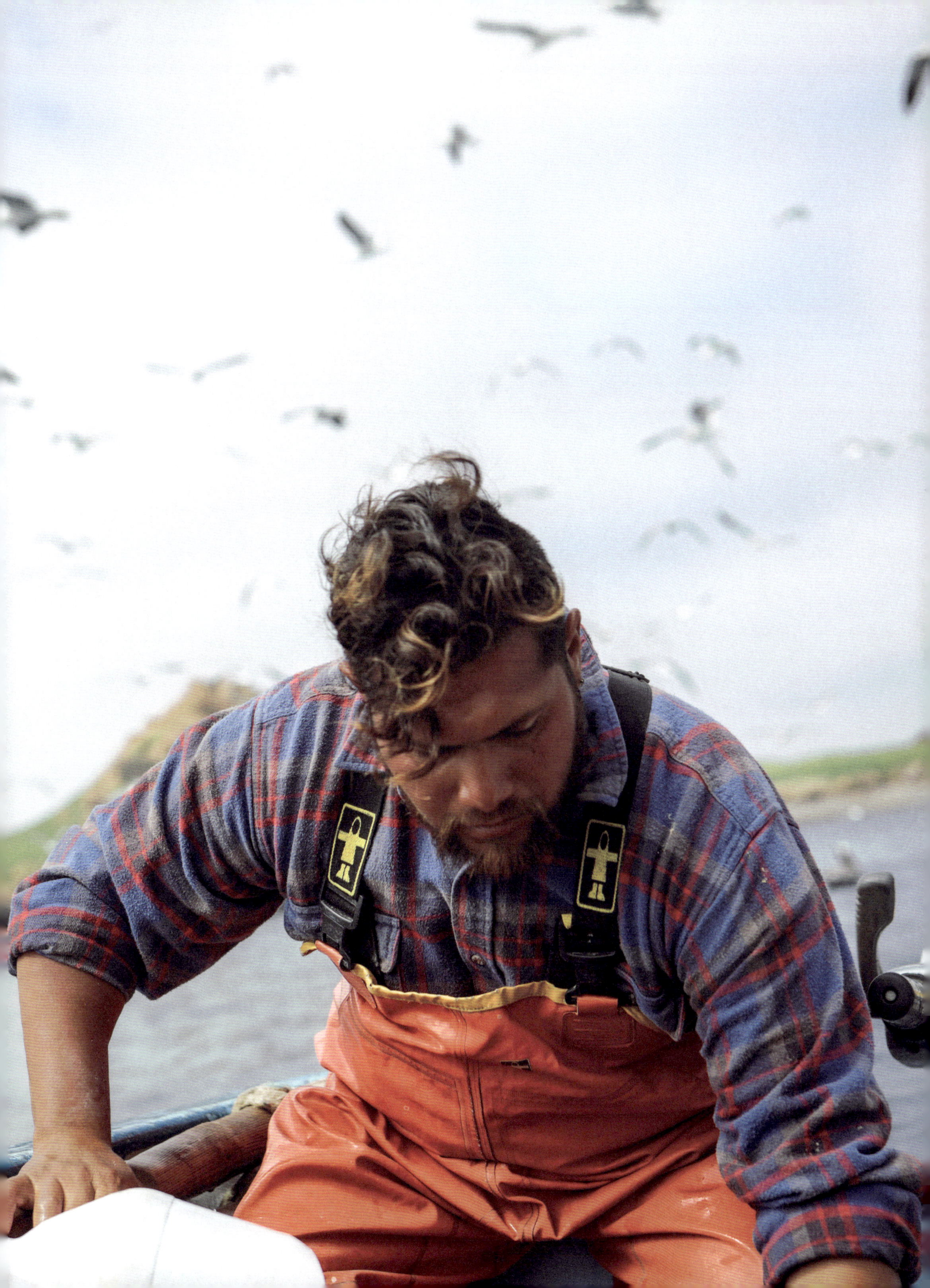

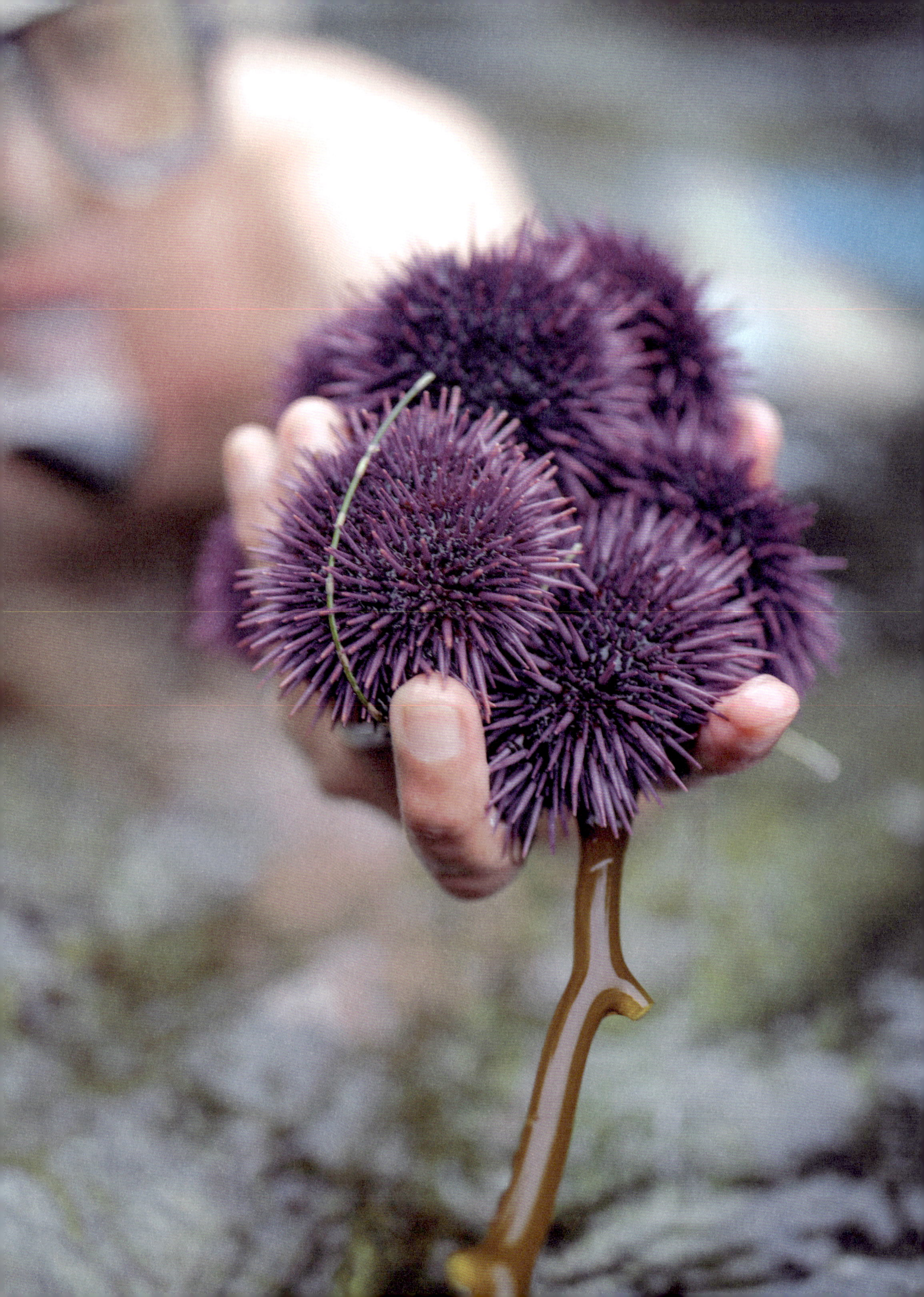

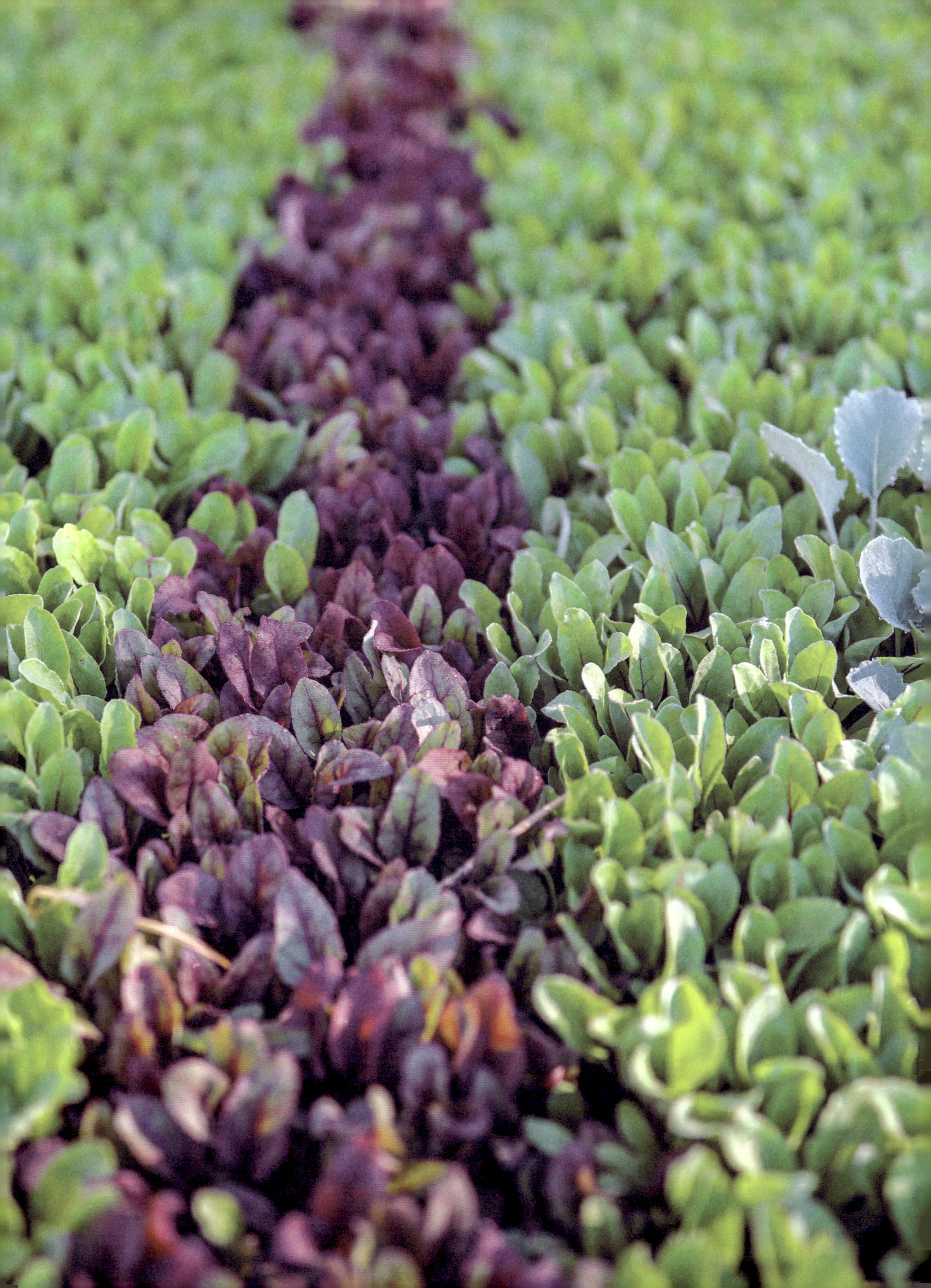

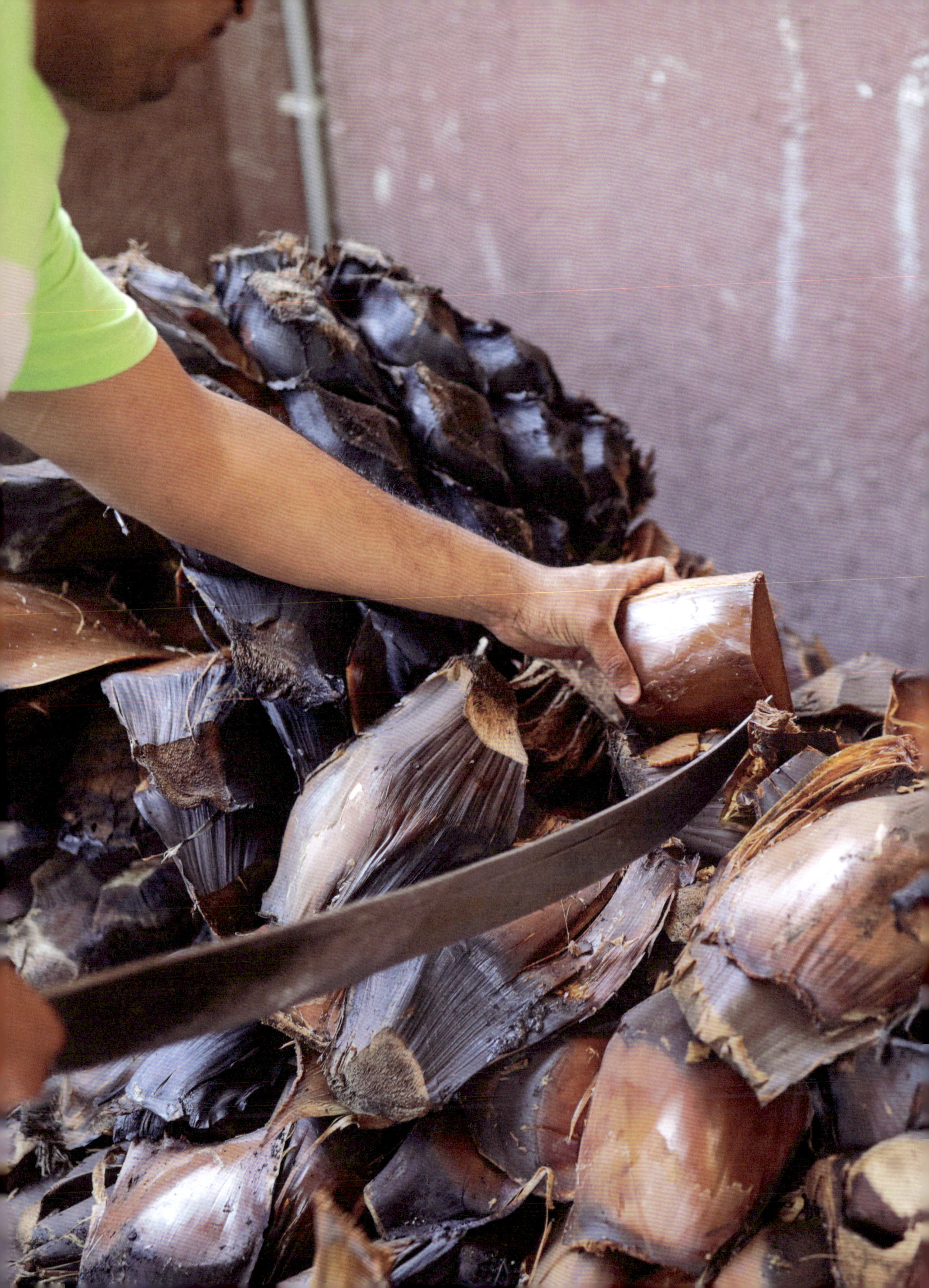

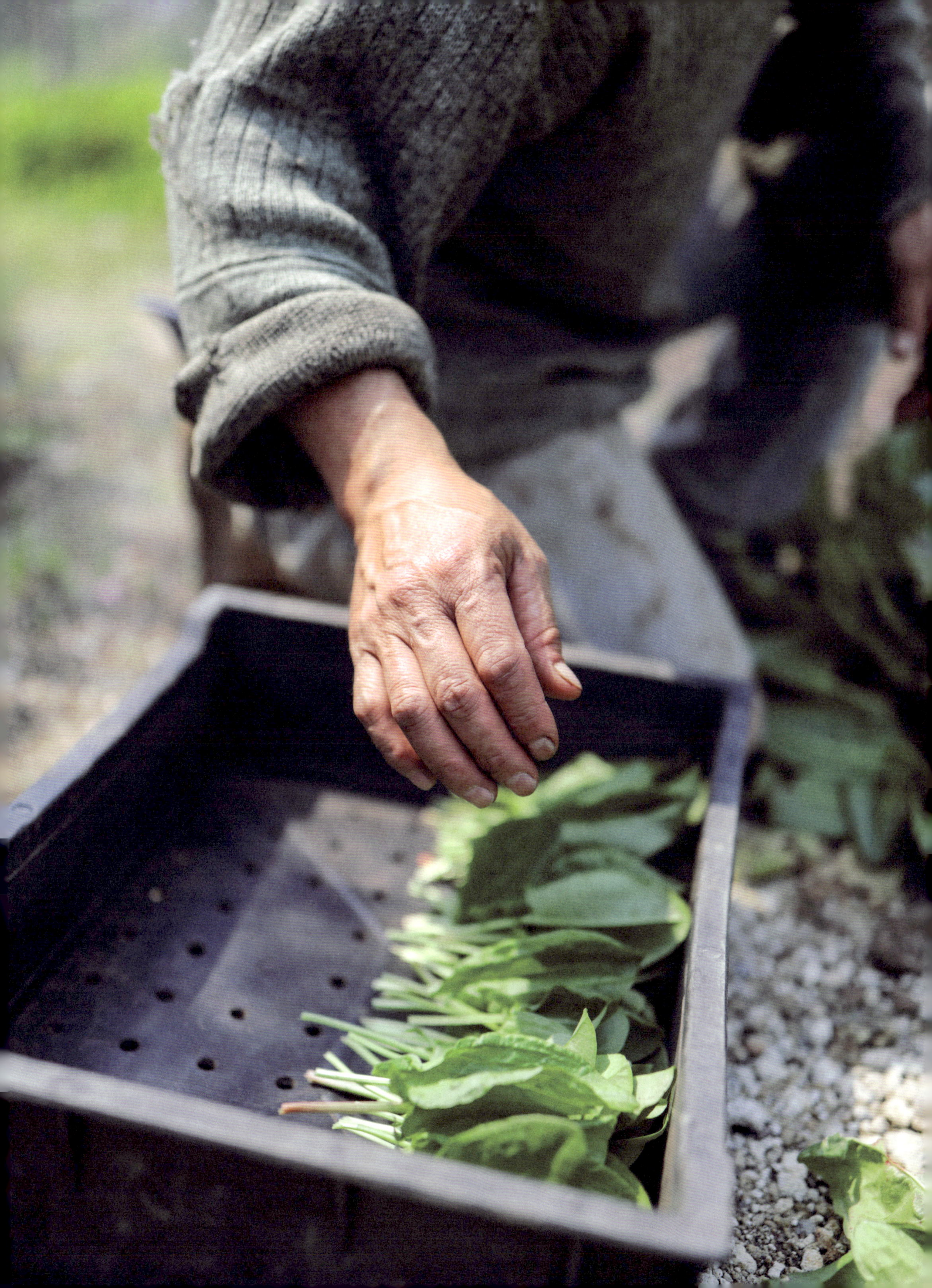

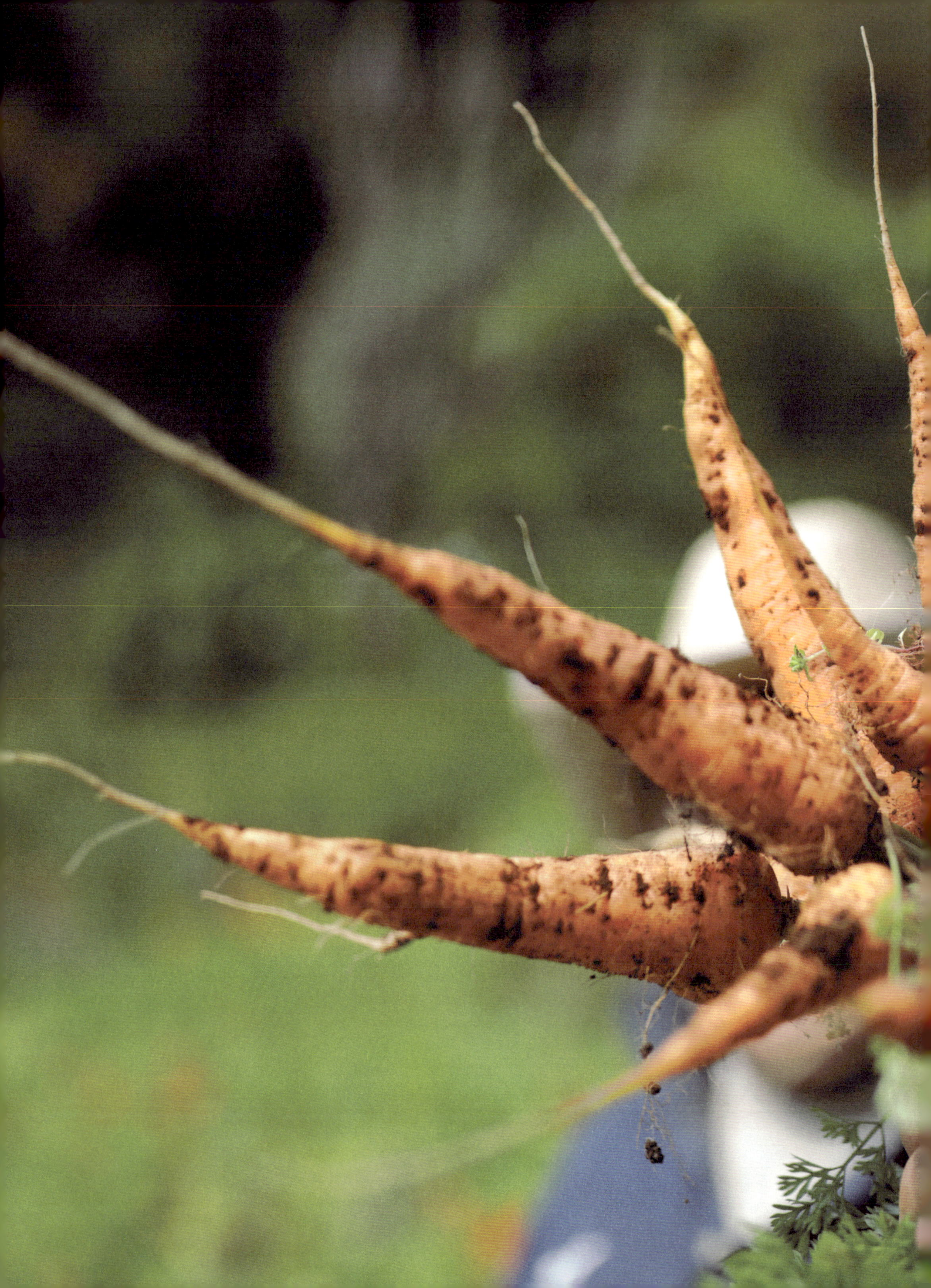

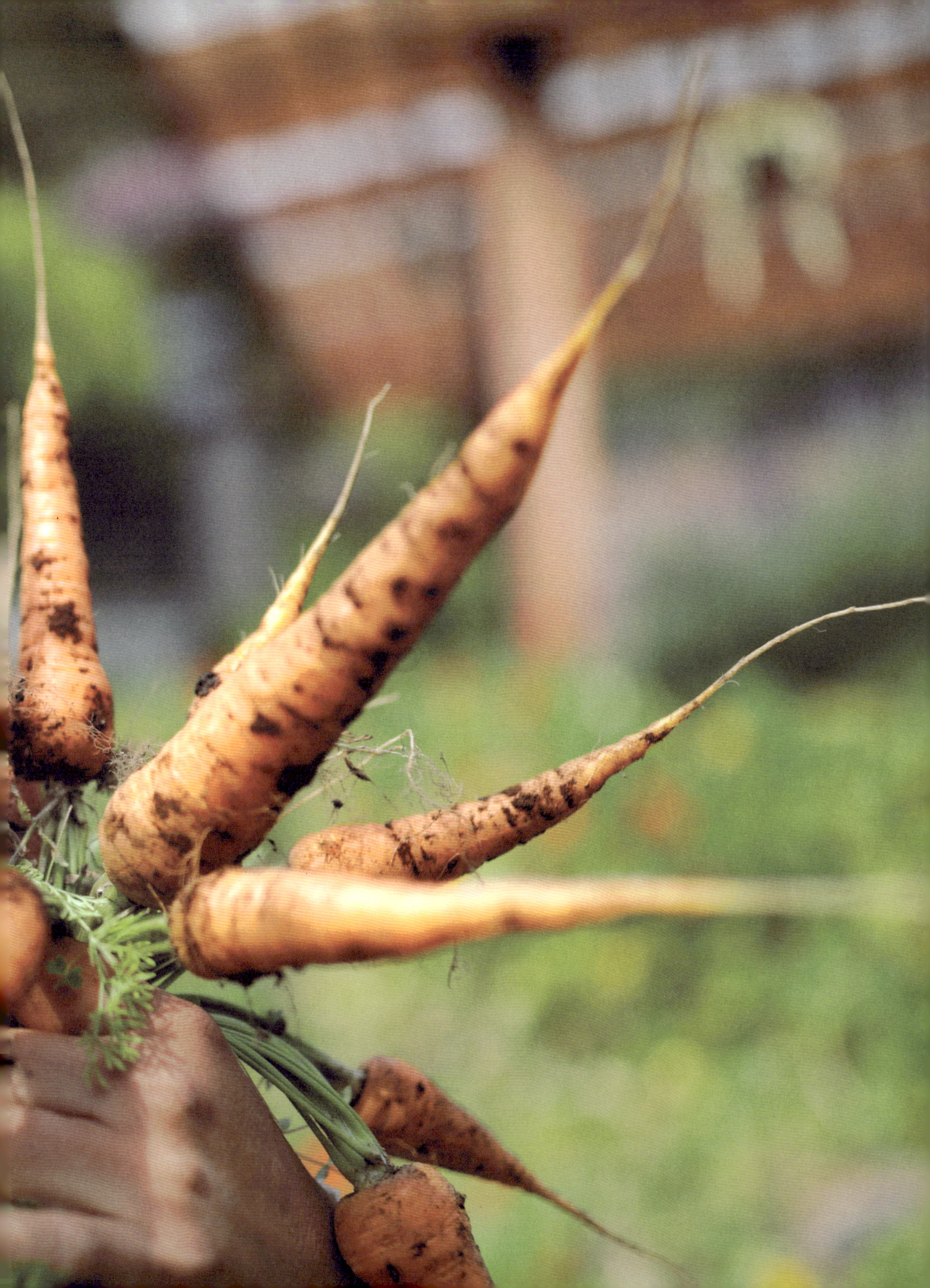

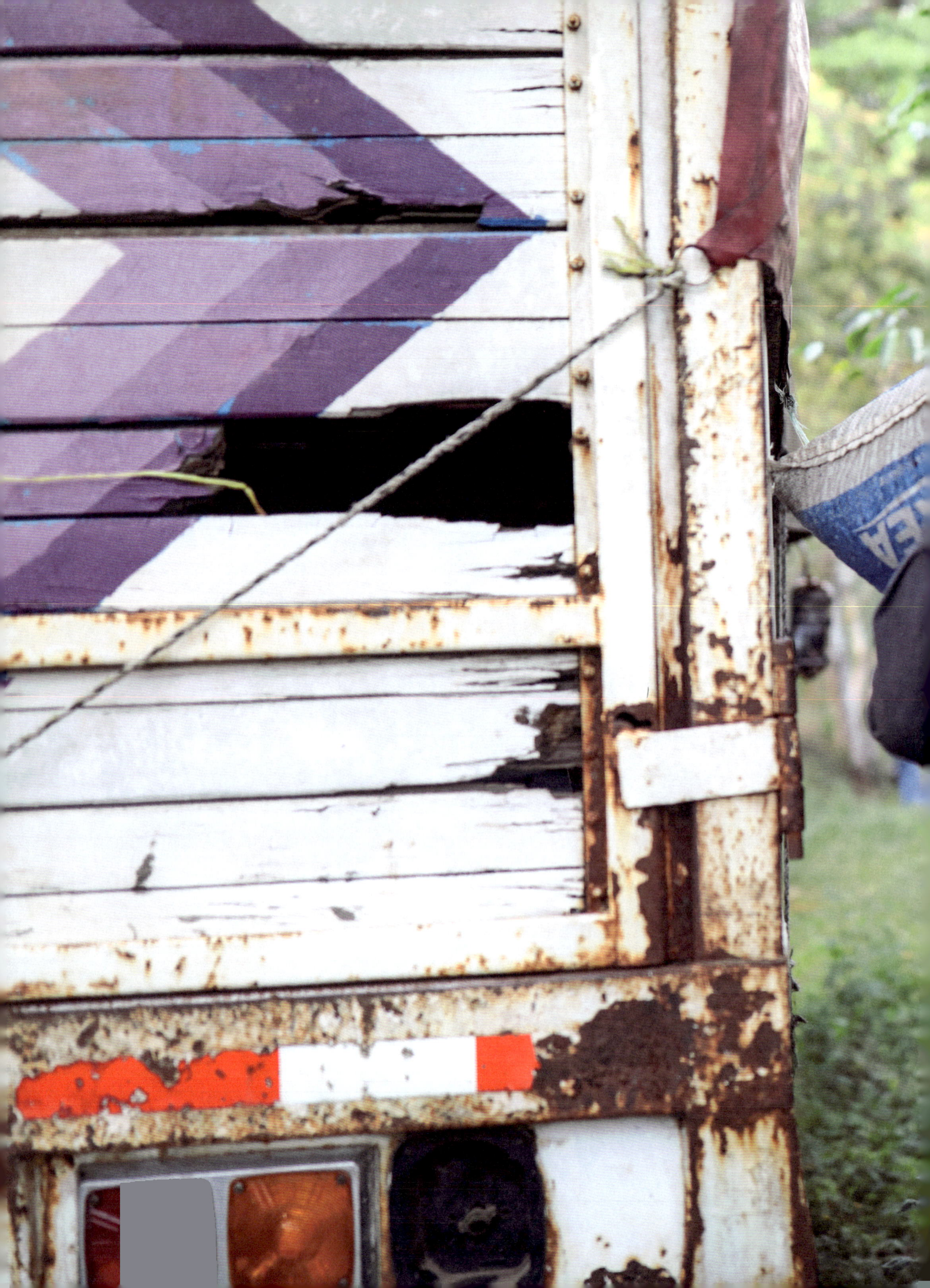

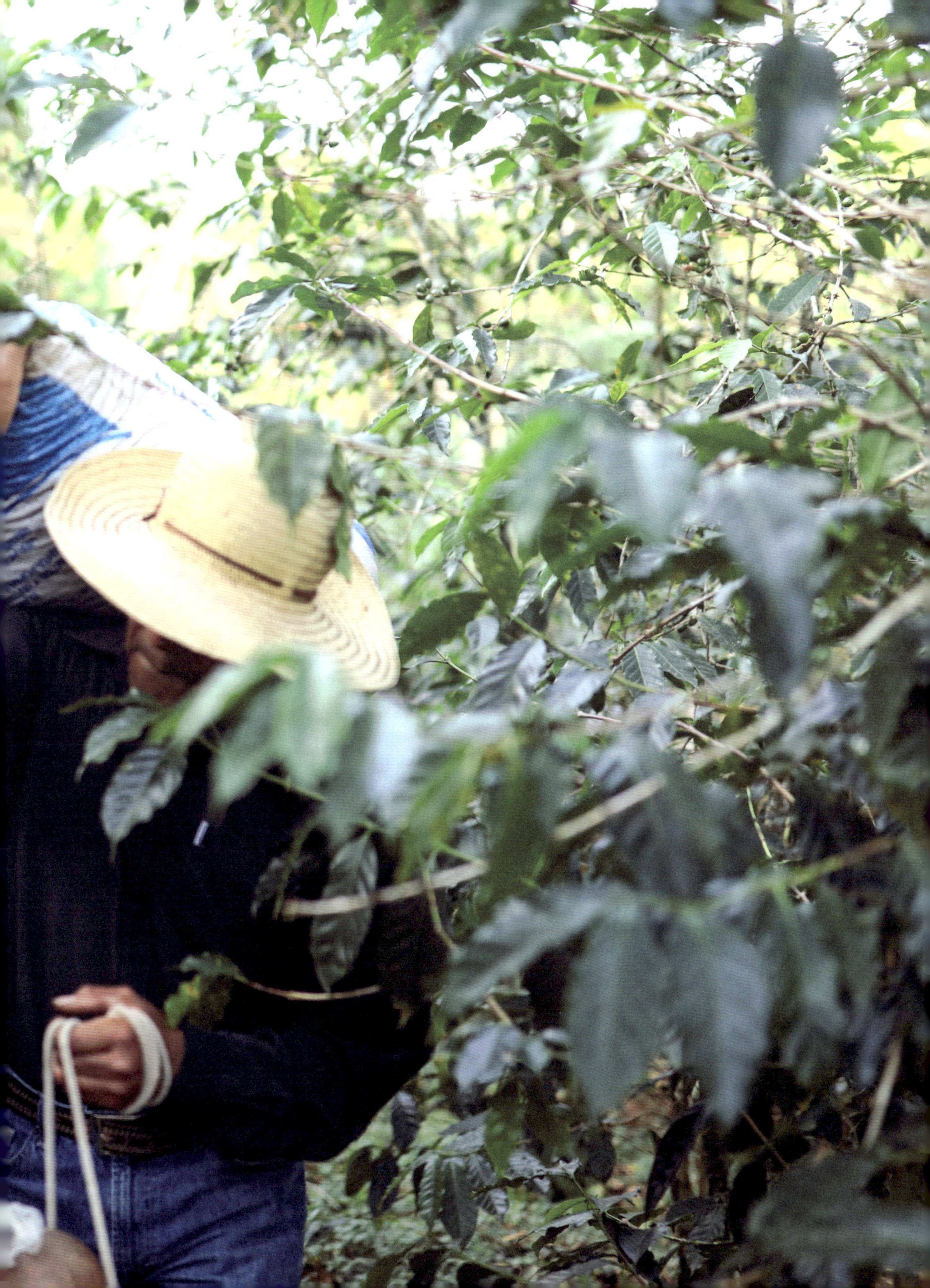

Wagyu beef tips, sorrel, lemon, and fennel frond

Wagyu beef is prized because, unlike other meats, the fat is incorporated into the muscle, not located around it. This means that the meat looks marbled when raw, and that the cooked meat is absolutely delicious. Every cut of beef boasts a balance between meat and fat. Besides, the fat melts when cooked, which moistens the meat and lends it flavor, smoothness, and a consistency that's neither too soft nor too tough.

The fat's incorporation into the meat is particular to this kind of cow, which is native to Japan. But it's also caused by certain practices used in raising these cows. Each breeding center implements them differently. I know how it's done at the ranch in northern Mexico that provides us with our Wagyu beef: the animals are allowed to graze freely, and they eat live oak leaves. The animals are also fed sesame paste and a combination of wheat, rye, and oats. They're given compacted and fermented corn called silage. Their food intake is regulated so that they eat a little bit at a time, allowing the fat to accumulate gradually rather than all at once. The process is so meticulous that it even affects their path to the slaughterhouse: the breeders take great pains to keep the animals from experiencing stress or suffering.

Wagyu beef is special for all of the reasons I've mentioned here. The conditions of an animal's life substantially affect the taste, consistency, texture, aroma, and even nutritional properties of its meat.

Pickled lemon

Serves 4

½ lemon
8 grams coarse salt
40 milliliter water
20 grams sugar
60 milliliters lemon juice
60 milliliters olive oil

Makes 10 grams

Cut the lemon into fourths and transfer to a bowl.

Add the coarse salt and mix until the lemon is entirely suffused with salt. Let it sit for 5 minutes. Place the lemon in a hermetic container, adding the lemon juice, the water, and the sugar; then seal.

Put the container in the oven for 15 minutes at 180°C.

Let the container cool at room temperature, then let it sit for 7 days so it can continue to ripen.

Once the 7 days have passed, transfer the lemon to a new container and cover it with olive oil. Keep refrigerated.

Fennel frond sauce

10 grams chaya leaves
125 grams fennel fronds
25 grams sorrel leaves
100 milliliters water
8 grams sourdough bread
20 grams anchovy fillets
5 milliliters white wine vinegar
1 pinch salt
50 milliliters olive oil

Makes 250 grams

Blanch the chaya leaves in boiling salted water, then transfer to ice water to stop the cooking process. Drain and press to remove the water.

Blend the chaya with a little water. When it turns to purée, add the rest of the herbs, the bread without the crust, the anchovies, the vinegar, and the salt. Blend and add water as needed and until the texture is smooth.

Pour into a bowl and add the olive oil.

To Serve

600 grams Wagyu beef tips
20 grams mesquite chips
8 grams salt
4 grams black pepper
20 milliliters olive oil
200 grams fennel frond sauce
1 pinch salt flakes
10 grams pickled lemon
15 grams fresh sorrel
10 grams fennel fronds

There are various techniques for smoking ingredients. Two are quite practical. The first way involves placing a tray with wood shavings into a household oven, along with the product you want to smoke. It's important to seal the oven well so that the smoke doesn't escape. The second way involves setting the product to smoke on a grill, tossing wood shavings into the coals and immediately covering the grill to keep in the smoke.

Smoke the entire cut of beef. Let it smoke for approximately 2 minutes or until the wood shavings have stopped burning and are no longer giving off smoke.

Cut the beef into 4 portions (150 grams each) and season with salt and pepper.

In a frying pan with hot oil, sear the meat for 3 to 4 minutes per side. Let it sit for 10 minutes near the heat.

Spoon the fennel frond sauce into the center of each plate. Cut the meat into patties and place each one onto the sauce. Add salt flakes and a bit of olive oil to the meat.

Add the pickled lemon, sorrel leaves, and fennel frond.

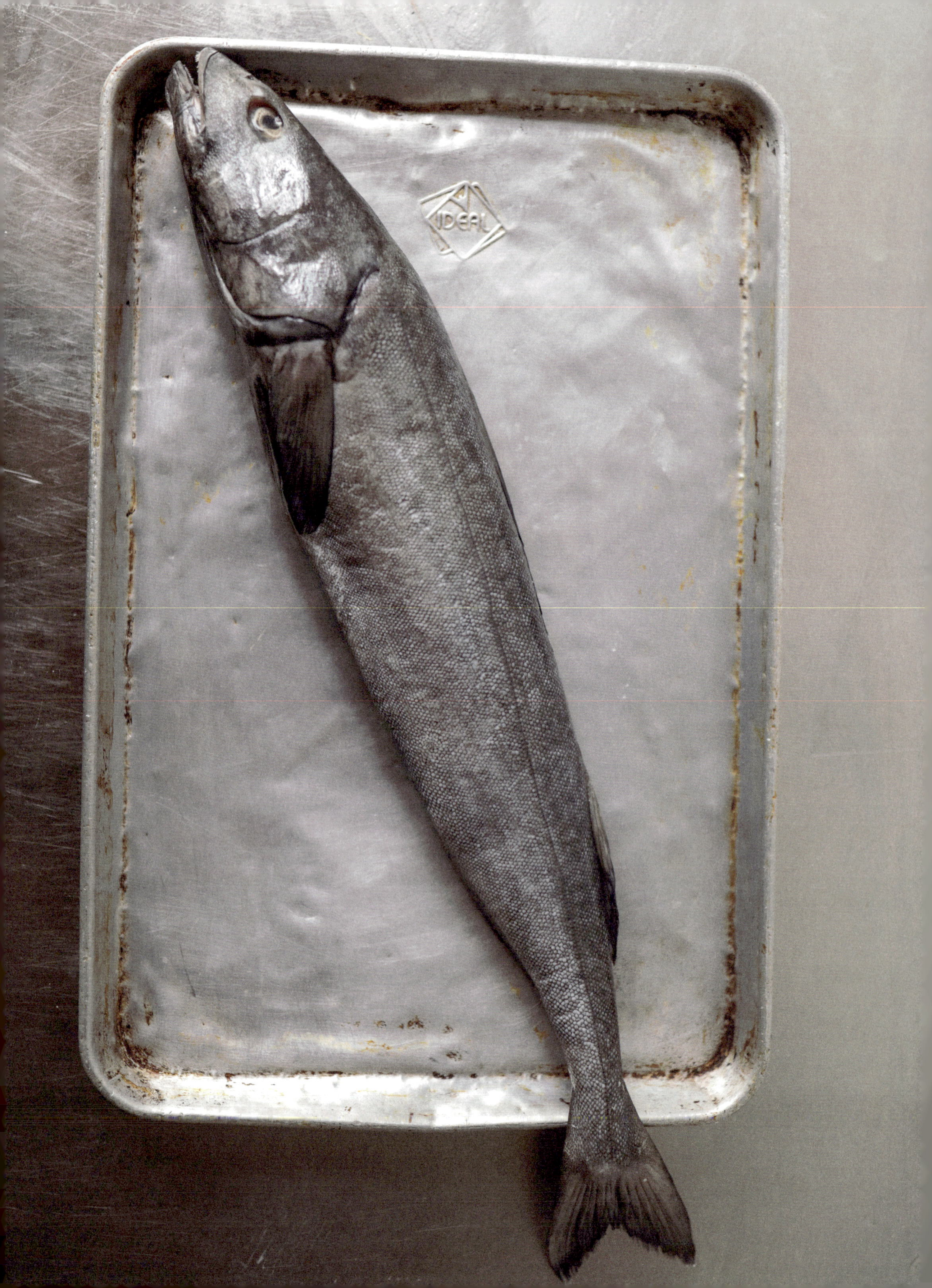
IDEAL

Black cod, endives, cauliflower, celery, golden raisins, and pine nuts

Mexico is known for its vast natural resources. But it has been dispossessed and irresponsibly exploited for hundreds of years. The country has been stripped of its most valuable raw materials—which have ended up in richer nations, where commerce permits higher sale prices. This dispossession is also evident in food. Our highest-quality vegetables, fruits, spices, grains, and fish are exported elsewhere.

Black cod, like tuna and other seafood, is an excellent example. Much of the edible marine fauna that inhabits the Mexican coasts is shipped out to places like Asia and the United States, where they are highly prized. Very little is left in Mexico. Governed by international prices, it's terribly expensive. Some of our diners assume we import our fish from Japan, though it's actually Japan that often imports seafood from Mexico. I feel strongly about serving products like this cod, not only because it demonstrates Mexican biodiversity, but also because it underscores the contemporary problems that jeopardize it.

Hydrated golden raisins

Serves 4

40 grams golden raisins
100 milliliters lemon juice
100 milliliters olive oil
40 mini capers
8 grams parsley, finely chopped

Makes 120 grams
Put the golden raisins in a bowl with the lemon juice, completely covering them.
Let them soak for at least 6 hours. Add the olive oil, the capers, and the parsley to the bowl of raisins, then set aside.

Pickled celery

100 grams celery
10 milliliters olive oil
1 pinch salt
50 milliliters white wine vinegar
50 milliliters water

Makes 100 grams
Cut the celery stalks crosswise into pieces approximately 3 centimeters thick.
Heat the olive oil in a frying pan over medium heat. Sauté the celery and add the salt, stirring until well mixed.
Once the celery starts to change color, add the vinegar and the water, then remove from the burner. Let it sit for 10 minutes and reserve.

Pickled white onion

100 grams white onions
10 milliliters olive oil
1 pinch salt
50 milliliters white wine vinegar
50 milliliters water

Makes 100 grams
 Thickly julienne the onion.
 Heat the olive oil in a frying pan over medium heat. Sauté the onion and add the salt, stirring until well mixed.
 Once the onion starts to change color, add the vinegar and the water, then remove from the burner. Let sit for 10 minutes and reserve.

Cauliflower purée

300 grams cauliflower
200 milliliters milk
40 grams butter

Makes 300 grams
 Heat all the ingredients in a saucepan over medium heat until the turnips are cooked. Remove the vegetables and blend, until the mixture has the texture of purée.

Lemon vinaigrette

15 milliliters olive oil
5 milliliters lemon juice

Makes 20 milliliters
 Put the lemon juice into a bowl, then stream in the olive oil and whisk together.

To Serve

800 grams black cod fillet, skinned
1 pinch salt
20 milliliters olive oil
40 grams cauliflower, cut into small florets
200 grams cauliflower purée
12 endive leaves
20 milliliters lemon vinaigrette
60 grams pickled celery
60 grams pickled onion
120 grams rehydrated golden onions
40 grams toasted white pine nuts

Cut the fish into four pieces and season with salt.
 Add a few drops of olive oil on a very hot frying pan and cook the fish for approximately 7 minutes.
 Sauté the cauliflower florets in a frying pan with a little olive oil.
 Heat the cauliflower purée and spoon it into the center of the plates.
 Dress the endive leaves with a bit of the lemon vinaigrette and a pinch of salt.
 Take 4 or 5 endive leaves and arrange them around the purée, lightly submerging them in it.
 Decorate the purée with the sautéed cauliflower, the pickled celery, and the pickled onion.
 Place the fish onto the purée and bathe with two spoonfuls of the rehydrated golden raisin mixture.
 Finally, add the toasted pine nuts.

Suckling pig, achiote, and smoked sweet potato

Achiote is a bush with bright orange seeds that contain red recado, also called achiote: a paste that's ultimately prepared with the crushed seeds of the same plant, along with a mixture of oregano, cumin, cloves, cinnamon, allspice, garlic, and salt.

Achiote paste is the main ingredient of cochinita pibil: a dish native to southeastern Mexico. It involves pieces of pork greased with this paste and bitter orange juice, wrapped in banana leaves, and cooked underground. Once cooked, it's always eaten with red onion and habanero pepper in vinegar.

Our dish is directly influenced by cochinita pibil: both contain pork, achiote, orange juice, vinegar, red onion, and habanero pepper. But ours is different in various ways. For one thing, we cook the pork separately, without smearing it with the achiote paste and the orange juice. The achiote, the orange juice, the vinegar, the red onion, and the habanero pepper are added all together in the form of a sauce. Finally, we add pieces of smoked sweet potato to attenuate the acidity of the sauce—and as a sort of wink to the tradition of cooking cochinita pibil underground.

What I like about this dish is that it shows how tradition can be simultaneously kept alive and reinvented in small, subtle ways.

Achiote sauce

Serves 4

35 grams red onion
1 gram habanero pepper
150 milliliters water
50 grams achiote
60 milliliters orange juice
50 milliliters white wine vinegar
10 milliliters olive oil
3.5 grams of salt

Makes 300 milliliters

Cook the onion and the habanero pepper in a very hot frying pan until they start to blacken on the outside; in other words, char them.

Blend the achiote, the onion, the salt, the habanero, and half the water.

Sauté the achiote in a pot with very hot oil and stir continuously until the mixture is quite thick.

Cook for 10 minutes or until the achiote is fully diluted. Gradually add the rest of the water until the texture is like that of a thick soup. Let it keep cooking.

Add the orange juice, then the vinegar. Bring to a boil, then remove from the heat.

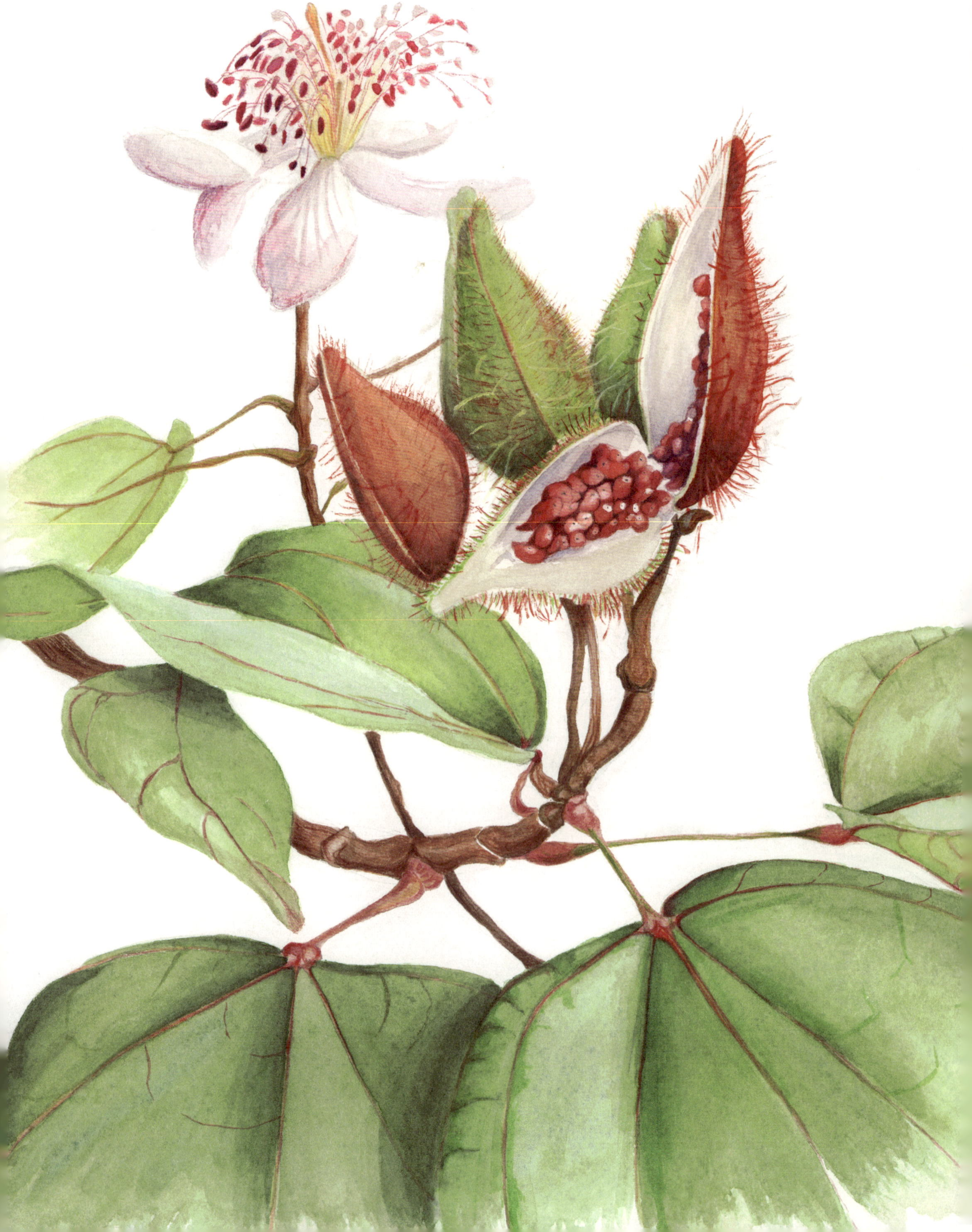

Smoked sweet potato

200 grams sweet potatoes
5 grams mesquite chips
200 grams charcoal

Makes 200 grams

Wrap the sweet potatoes in aluminum foil. Place them on a baking sheet and bake at 260°C for 35 minutes or until the sweet potatoes are soft.

Once cooked, peel the sweet potatoes and transfer them to a bowl.

Turn on the smoker with the mesquite chips and place the bowl with the sweet potatoes inside. Let it smoke for approximately 1 minute or until the shavings have stopped burning and letting off smoke.

Cut the sweet potatoes into 1-centimeter slices.

Pickled cambray onions

500 milliliters water
7.5 grams fleur de sel
2 grams black pepper
2 grams coriander seeds
90 milliliters apple vinegar
25 milliliters white wine vinegar
200 grams cambray onions
150 milliliters olive oil

Makes 200 grams

Combine all the ingredients in a pot, except the oil and the onions. Boil for 5 minutes, and then let it sit until cool. Strain.

Cut the onions un 4 or 6 pieces, depending on the size.

In another small pot heat the vinegar and the onions, until they boil. Strain and then reserve the onions in olive oil.

To Serve

110 grams sugar
135 grams salt flakes
2 juniper berries
2 whole cloves
5 grams black pepper
2 grams bay leaves
1 liter water
4 pieces suckling pig, 300 grams each
40 milliliters olive oil
200 grams baked sweet potato
260 milliliters achiote sauce
4 grams fresh marjoram

Combine the sugar, salt flakes, juniper berries, cloves, black pepper, bay leaves, and water, then transfer the mixture to a pot and bring to a boil. Set aside and let cool at room temperature.

Once the mixture has cooled off, add the meat and let it marinate for 8 hours.

Remove the meat from the brine.

Cover a tray with a grate, then place the meat on top of that. Cover with aluminum foil and bake at 180°C for 6 hours.

Place the meat on an anti-stick pan with 0.5 centimeter of pre-heated oil to brown the skin. You can cover it to protect yourself a bit.

Heat the baked sweet potatoes in a very hot pan with a little butter until they're lightly browned.

Spoon a little achiote sauce into the center of each plate. Add the sweet potato and a few fresh marjoram leaves.

Serve the suckling pig with the skin facing upward and add more marjoram leaves and picked cambray onions.

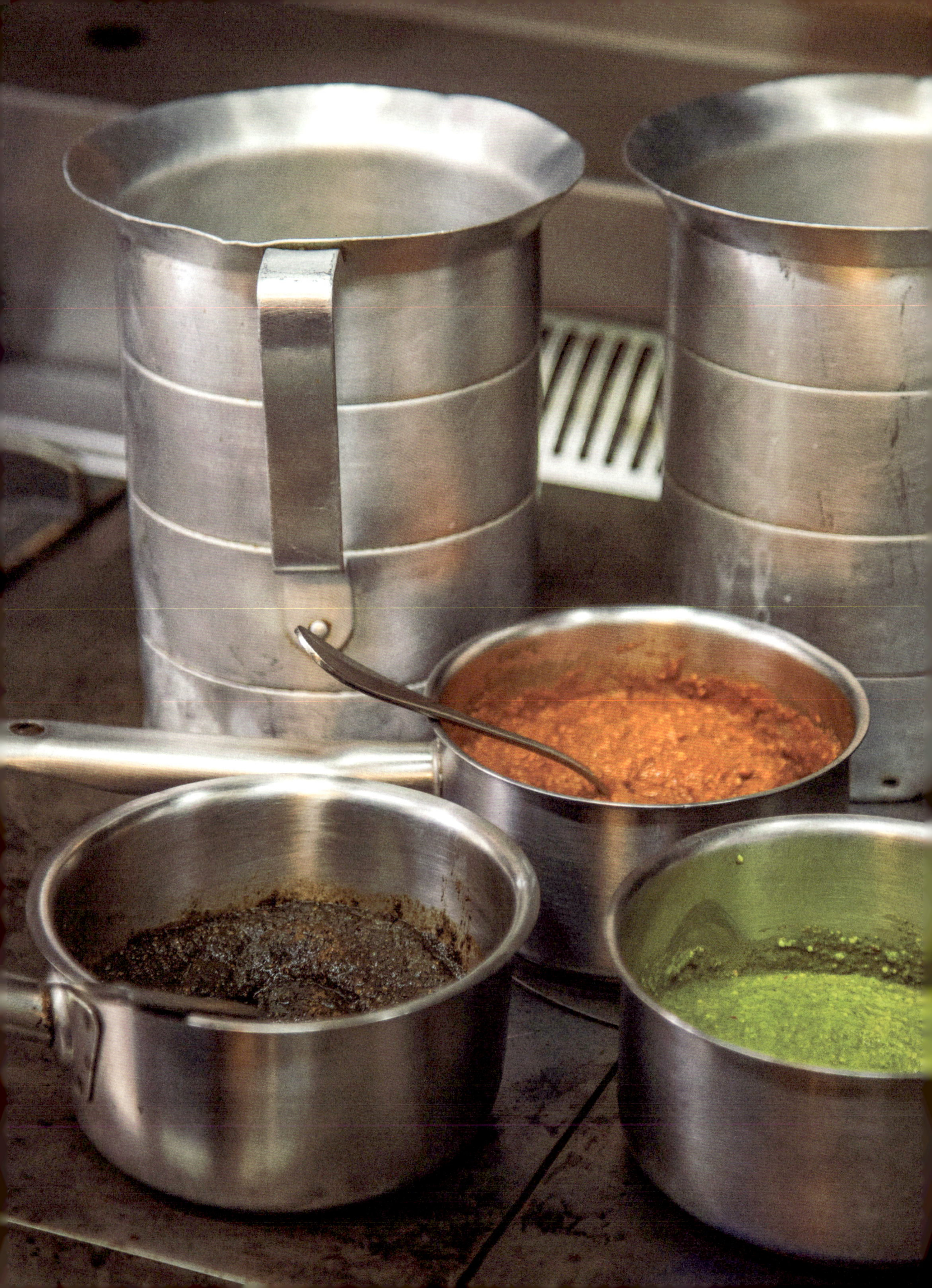

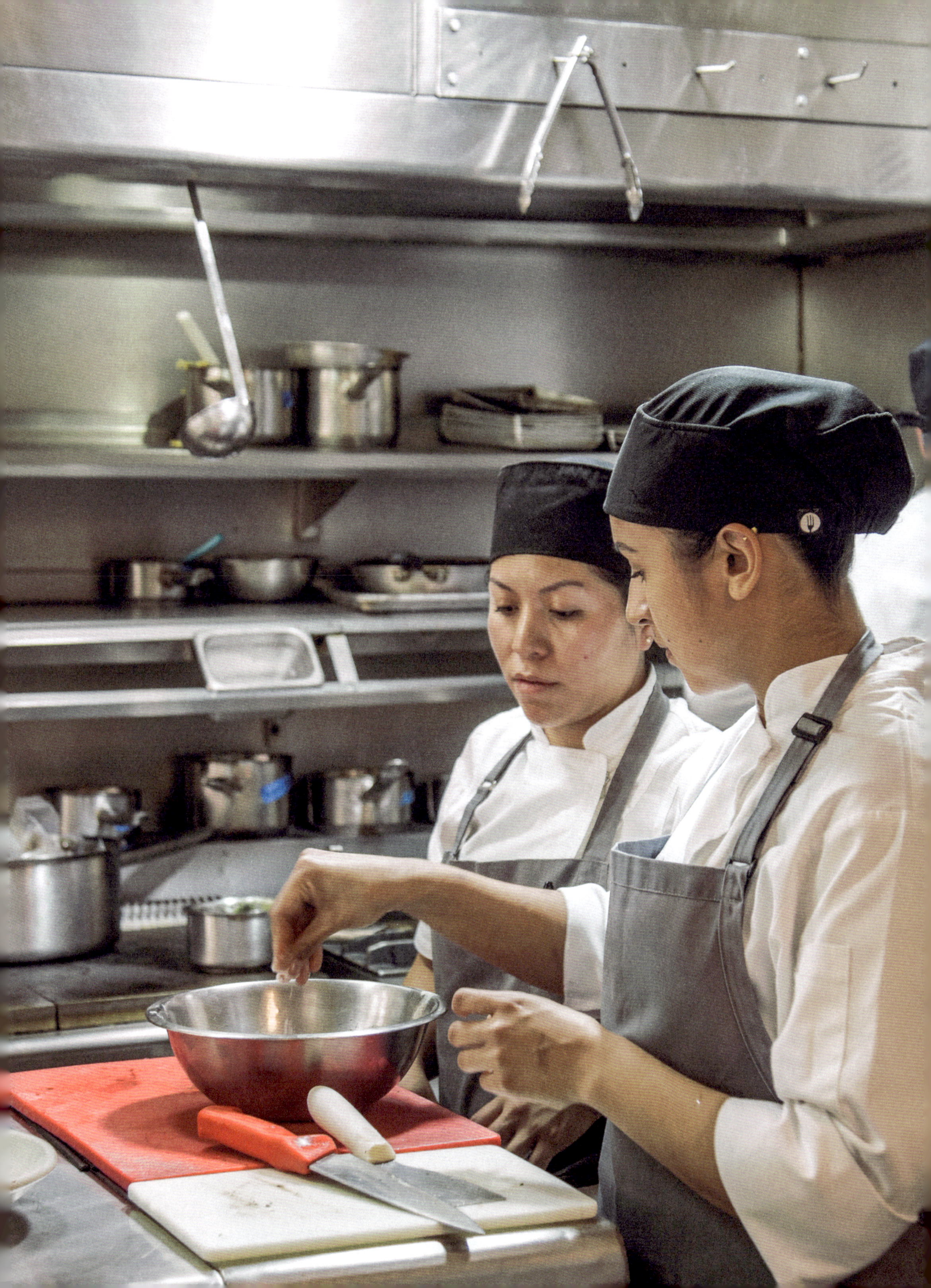

Grouper and romesco

Romesco is a traditional Catalan sauce. It's made from tomatoes, peppers, garlic, bread, almonds, oil, and vinegar. The peppers in question are called ñora peppers; without them, according to the Catalans, it's impossible to make an authentic romesco. As it turns out, the famous ñora peppers are actually fresh cascabel peppers, as we call them in Mexico, but they aren't hot at all. This often happens with peppers: the intensity of the heat changes depending on the soil where they grow.

At Rosetta, following this principle, we've adapted the traditional romesco recipe by substituting dried peppers for ñora peppers. We tested it several times. First, we prepared romesco with cascabel peppers, but the result wasn't our favorite, even though it's the kind of pepper that most resembles the ñora. We ended up opting for ancho and chipotle peppers. Their smoky flavor evoked calçots, a kind of scallion that's char-grilled to accompany the romesco in Catalonia.

Our romesco isn't really a romesco; it's an adapted sauce, derived from the memory of a classic. At Rosetta, we're enormously influenced by what moves us, touches us, and fascinates us. When we adapt a recipe, there are changes, ideas, and interventions; an adaptation always ends up being something more. This is the wonder of cooking. Influences, memories, and desires all materialize in a single dish.

Romesco

Serves 4

400 grams ripe tomatoes
1 gram thyme
35 grams garlic
65 grams almond
35 grams sourdough bread, sliced
2 grams chipotle
10 grams ancho pepper
110 grams red bell pepper
17 milliliters chardonnay vinegar
40 milliliters olive oil
9 grams salt

Makes 400 grams

Cut the tomatoes in half, place them on a previously greased baking tray, and scatter them with thyme.

Bake for 35 minutes at 200°C, remove from the oven, and set aside.

Cut the garlic cloves in half and wrap them in aluminum foil. Bake them for 20 minutes at 200°C or until soft.

Cook the almonds in a saucepan of boiling water for 3 minutes, drain them, and skin them. Heat a frying pan and toast them lightly.

Cut the slices of bread into 2-centimeter cubes. Heat olive oil in a frying pan and toast the cubes.

Hydrate the dried peppers with hot water, de-vein them, and seed them.

Char the bell peppers directly on the fire and remove the skin.

Run the almonds and the bread through a food processor until they form a powder and set aside.

Blend the bell peppers together with the tomatoes, the hot peppers, and the garlic, gradually adding the vinegar and the olive oil until completely mixed together. Mix with the almonds and bread. Finally, add the salt.

Guajillo pepper escabeche

5 grams garlic, peeled
10 grams guajillo pepper, seeded and de-veined
120 milliliters white wine vinegar
120 milliliters olive oil

Makes 250 milliliters

Heat olive oil in a saucepan with all of the garlic and chile guajillo. Let simmer for 20 minutes, remove the saucepan from the heat and remove the garlic from the oil.

Let the oil cool for 10 minutes. Add the vinegar and reserve.

Anchovy bread

100 grams sourdough bread, sliced
15 milliliters olive oil
10 gram anchovies in olive oil

Makes 100 grams

Cut the bread into small pieces, lay them out on a baking sheet, sprinkle them with olive oil, and toast for 5 minutes at 200°C.

In a double boiler, heat the anchovies with their own oil for 10 minutes or until they dissolve. Remove them from the heat and mix them with the toasted bread pieces until they also dissolve.

Lemon vinaigrette

105 milliliters olive oil
35 milliliters lemon juice

Makes 140 milliliters

Put the lemon juice into a bowl, then stream in the olive oil and whisk together.

To Serve

800 grams grouper fillet, skinned
1 pinch salt
140 milliliters lemon vinaigrette
360 grams romesco
60 milliliters guajillo pepper vinaigrette
20 grams anchovy bread
8 grams lemon zest

Cut the fish fillet into four pieces and season with salt. Place the fillets in an oven-proof dish, add the lemon vinaigrette, and cover tightly with aluminum foil so that the steam won't escape.

Cook the fish in the oven at 250°C for 15 minutes, depending on the thickness of the fillets.

Spoon the romesco into deep dishes. Place the fish fillets on top. Bathe the grouper with a spoonful of guajillo pepper escabeche, add the anchovy bread, and finally sprinkle with a bit of lemon zest.

Rock cod, green romesco, bok choy, and mizuna

Green romesco is a variant of the romesco. The idea was to use green peppers, dried peppers, and tomatillos instead of red tomatoes. When roasted, the tomatillos and the green peppers become less astringent, but no less herbal. This variant does use cascabel peppers, but they're joined by chipotle, too, which lends a smoky flavor to the dish. Even with these substantial changes—and with the new herbal quality coming through—the green sauce wasn't much different than the original red kind. So we decided to add a concentrated herb purée (hoja santa, parsley, and chaya). The result was a kind of hybrid between romesco and pesto. Fresh and herbal, it paired well with the marine flavor of the rock cod, a firm-textured fish found in the cold waters of Ensenada, Baja California. This is how we always work to create a dish: gradually modifying a flavor, a classic sauce, or an idea until we craft it into something new.

I love working with ingredients in a single color. It's something I've done intuitively in the past, and now, as I write this book, I realize that I do it often. Could it be that the color palette is connected somehow to the flavor palate? I don't know, but I like to imagine that it is. Some colors are intimately associated with the seasons, with different moods and feelings, and with particular sensations. I don't know anything about the theoretical reasons behind it, but in the practice of cooking, I think it's clear that there's something powerful at work.

Green romesco

Serves 4

300 grams tomatillos
1 gram fresh thyme
80 grams green bell pepper
25 grams garlic
½ dried chipotle pepper
1 cascabel peppers
50 grams whole almonds
25 grams sourdough bread
12.5 milliliters chardonnay vinegar
100 milliliters olive oil
6 grams salt
40 grams chaya leaves
30 grams parsley
30 grams hoja santa leaves

Makes 400 grams

Cut the tomatoes in half, place them on a previously greased baking tray, and scatter them with thyme.

Bake for 35 minutes at 200°C, remove from the oven, and set aside.

Cut the garlic cloves in half and wrap them in aluminum foil. Bake them for 20 minutes at 200°C or until soft.

Cook the almonds in a saucepan of boiling water for 3 minutes, drain them, and skin them. Heat a frying pan and toast them lightly.

Cut the slices of bread into 2-centimeter cubes. Heat olive oil in a frying pan and toast the cubes.

Hydrate the dried peppers with hot water, de-vein them, and seed them.

Char the bell peppers directly on the fire and remove the skin.

Run the almonds and the bread through a food processor until they form a powder and set aside.

Blend the bell peppers together with the tomatoes, the hot peppers, and the garlic, gradually adding in the vinegar and half the olive oil until completely mixed together. Mix with the almonds and bread. Finally, add the salt.

Blanch the chaya leaves and transfer them to a bowl of ice water to stop the cooking process. Do the same with the hoja santa leaves and the parsley. Drain and press the herbs. Put the remaining olive oil in the blender, add the herbs, and blend until it forms the texture of a purée.

Combine the herb purée with the previous mixture in a bowl and whisk together.

Lemon vinaigrette

105 milliliters olive oil
35 milliliters lemon juice

Makes 140 milliliters

Put the lemon juice into a bowl, then stream in the olive oil and whisk together.

To Serve

10 grams dried cascabel pepper
25 grams dry bread
800 grams rock cod fillet
200 grams green romesco
140 milliliters lemon vinaigrette
8 grams salt
60 grams bok choy
20 grams mizuna
20 grams arugula

Crush the cascabel pepper until it turns into a powder, then strain.

Cut the dry bread into ½-centimeber cubes. Sprinkle the pepper powder onto the bread so that it sticks to the cubes.

Cut the fish fillet into four pieces and season with salt. Place the fillets in an oven-proof dish, add 130 milliliters of the lemon vinaigrette, and cover tightly with aluminum foil so that the steam won't escape.

Cook the fish in the oven at 250°C for 15 or 20 minutes, depending on the thickness of the fillets.

Add ¼ of the liquid from the cooked fish to the green romesco, mixing together with a spoon.

Blanch the bok choy for 1 minute and mix with the 10 remaining milliliters of the lemon vinaigrette.

Place a spoonful of green romesco in the center of each plate, add the bok choy, and place the fish fillet on top. Add the spiced bread, then the mizuna and the arugula.

Pork neck, black romesco, and turnip flowers

Black romesco is another variant of romesco. Some traditional Mexican dishes contain the ash of vegetables, peppers, and spices; this inspired our black romesco. We wanted the lightly smoky taste of our romesco to become more intensely charred.

For this dish, we roast the tomatoes and the peppers, just as in a romesco. This time, though, we don't peel the peppers, so that their charred skin adds more flavor. We use morita and pasilla peppers, adding in charred onion and recado negro, a paste made from peppers, spices, and burnt tortillas that comes from the Yucatan Peninsula.

This is a spicier, earthier romesco than the original. The morita pepper is very hot, and the recado negro accentuates it. The fact that the sauce contains ash means that it has to be accompanied by something intense: that's what prompted us to choose top pork loin, which is the neck of the pig. This under-explored pork cut is appealing because it has equal parts fat and meat. Which is why, when cooked, the flesh moistens from the fat and doesn't feel dry. We receive the entire pig neck at the restaurant, skin and all. We let it mature for at least a week. As a result, the flesh dries out a bit, its flavor intensifies, its fibers loosen, and the meat gets softer.

Black romesco

Serves 4

300 grams tomatoes
25 grams garlic
80 grams red bell pepper
½ morita pepper
1 pasilla pepper
1 gram thyme
50 grams whole almonds
25 grams white sourdough bread
125 milliliters red wine vinegar
30 milliliters olive oil
100 grams white onion
6 grams salt
50 grams recado negro
100 milliliters water

Makes 500 grams

Cut the tomatoes in half, place them on a previously greased baking tray, and scatter with thyme.

Bake for 35 minutes at 200°C, remove from the oven, and set aside.

Cut the onion into fourths, place it on a baking pan, and bake for 20 minutes at 200°C or until charred on the outside.

Cut the garlic cloves in half and wrap them in aluminum foil. Bake them for 20 minutes at 200°C or until soft.

Cook the almonds in a saucepan of boiling water for 3 minutes, drain them, and skin them. Heat a frying pan and toast them lightly.

Cut the slices of bread into 2-centimeter cubes. Heat the olive oil in a frying pan and toast the cubes.

Hydrate the dried peppers in hot water, de-vein them, and remove the seeds.

Char the bell peppers directly on the fire, de-vein them, and remove the seeds without removing the charred skin.

Run the almonds and the bread through a food processor until they form a powder and set aside.

Blend the bell peppers together with the tomatoes, the hot peppers, and the garlic, gradually adding in the vinegar and the olive oil until completely mixed together. Mix with the almonds and bread. Finally, add the salt.

Dilute the recado negro in a saucepan of water. Heat until it thickens. Add the liquid to the previous mixture and whisk together.

To Serve

1 kilogram pork neck
5 grams salt
8 grams black pepper
40 milliliters safflower oil
240 grams black romesco
80 grams turnip flowers
20 milliliters chardonnay vinegar
20 milliliters olive oil
4 grams salt flakes

Wash the pork neck, removing all excess fat. Cut into 4 pieces and season with salt and pepper. Heat a little oil in a frying pan and cook the meat for approximately 5 to 7 minutes on each side without moving it. Let it sit near the heat for 10 minutes.

Re-heat the black romesco until warm and spoon into the center of the plates. Cut the pork neck into patties and place on top of the romesco.

Blanch the turnip flowers, drain, and dress with the vinegar, olive oil and salt flakes. Place the romesco in the middle of a plate, top with the meat and finish with salt and oil.

Rabbit, carrots, and lovage

Rabbit stands out among all animal proteins for its lack of fat; in other words, it's a lean meat. This quality also means that it has to be cooked with highly specific methods. Otherwise, the meat ends up being very dry. We choose to prepare it as a confit: we cook it slowly in lard and spices so that it moistens and softens.

This dish also calls for carrots, served in two different ways. First, as a purée. Second, pickled in vinegar. The former emphasizes the carrots' sweetness; the latter stresses their acidity and crunchiness.

The rabbit confit and the carrots come together with the help of a lovage juice that we pour around both ingredients. Lovage is an herb that tastes like celery, though its flavor is more concentrated. It pairs very well with sweeter vegetables like carrots, peas, and beets.

This dish inspired the creation of lovage ice cream. Today, we serve it alongside a carrot mille feuille at Lardo, my casual restaurant, which opened in 2015. I often do this: I take an element from one dish and use it as the basis for a completely new one.

Carrot purée

Serves 4

½ lemon
2 grams dried thyme
50 milliliters water
250 grams carrots, sliced
50 grams butter, cut into small cubes

Makes 250 grams
  Zest the lemon and put the zest into a tea strainer, along with the thyme.
  Put the water, the tea strainer, the carrots, and the cubed butter into a saucepan. Cover the pan and cook for 25 minutes. Remove the strainer and blend until the mixture has the texture of a purée.

Lovage juice

15 grams lovage, with stalk
1 pinch salt
25 milliliters ice water

Makes 60 milliliters
  Blend all the ingredients until well mixed and liquid in consistency. Refrigerate in a covered bowl.

Pickled carrots

120 grams small carrots
1 liter water
15 grams salt

Makes 120 grams

Blanch the carrots, placing them in a saucepan of boiling water with salt for 3 minutes. Remove from the heat and place them in a container of ice water. Peel them by hand and set aside.

Rabbit confit

20 grams salt
15 grams sugar
7 grams ground black pepper
1 piece of rabbit meat (2 kilograms)
5 grams thyme
5 grams bay leaves
20 grams garlic, peeled and halved
850 milliliters water
375 grams pork lard
30 grams salt flakes

Makes 680 grams

Mix the salt, the sugar, and the pepper; season the rabbit with the mixture. Combine with the herbs and the garlic and marinate for 24 hours in the refrigerator.

Transfer the rabbit, herbs, garlic, water, lard and salt flakes to a large saucepan. Cook over medium heat. As soon as it starts to boil, lower the heat and cook for 2 hours.

Remove the pan from the heat and the rabbit from the broth. Remove the excess of bones, divide into portions and reserve in a little of the confit's fat.

To Serve

680 grams rabbit confit
240 grams carrot purée
60 milliliters lovage juice
120 grams pickled carrots
6 grams carrot leaves

Transfer the rabbit meat to a very hot frying pan and sauté until golden brown.

Heat the carrot purée and place a spoonful into the center of each plate. Beside it, add the lovage broth and the sauteed carrots. Place the rabbit meat on top of it, adding the carrot leaves.

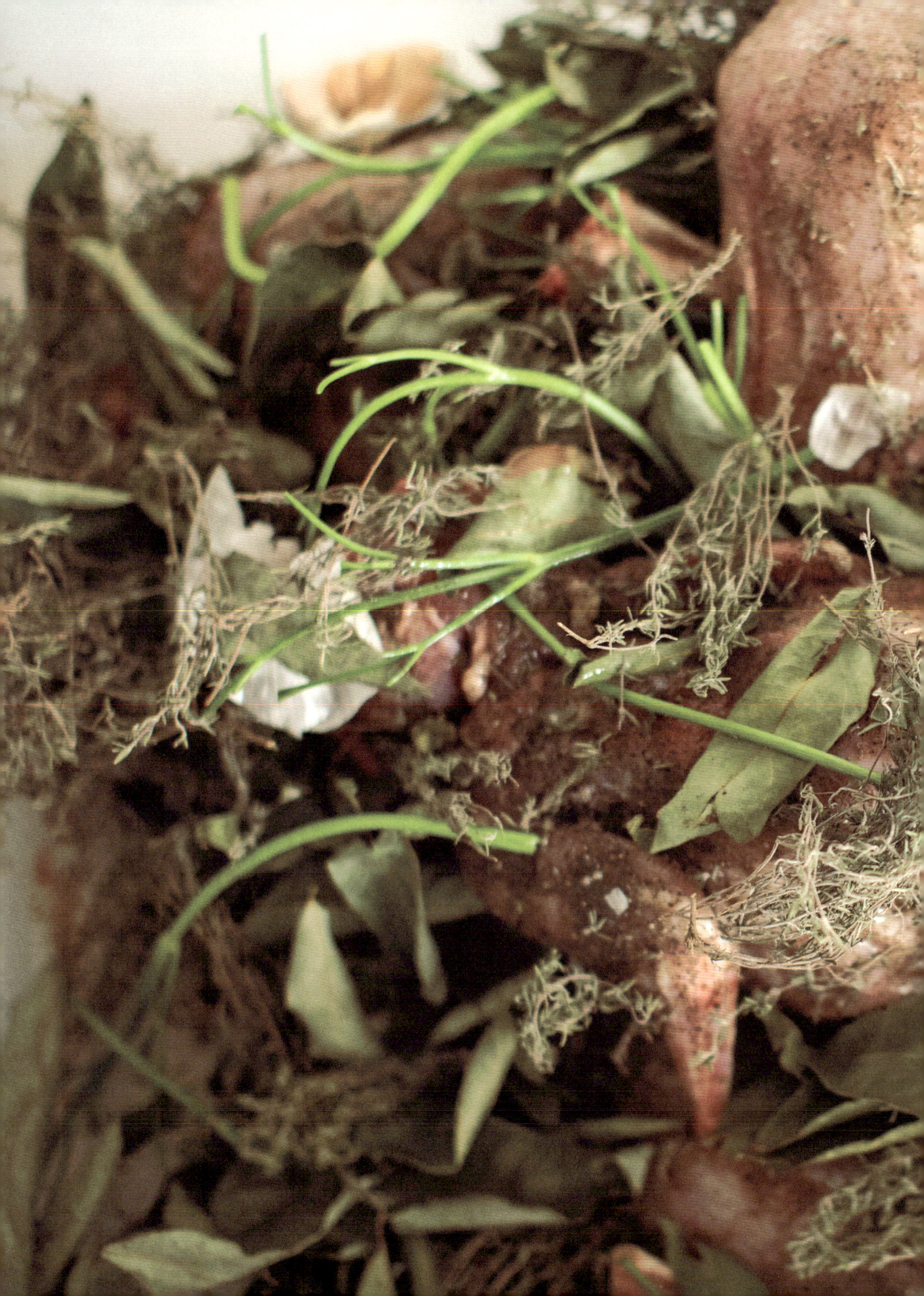

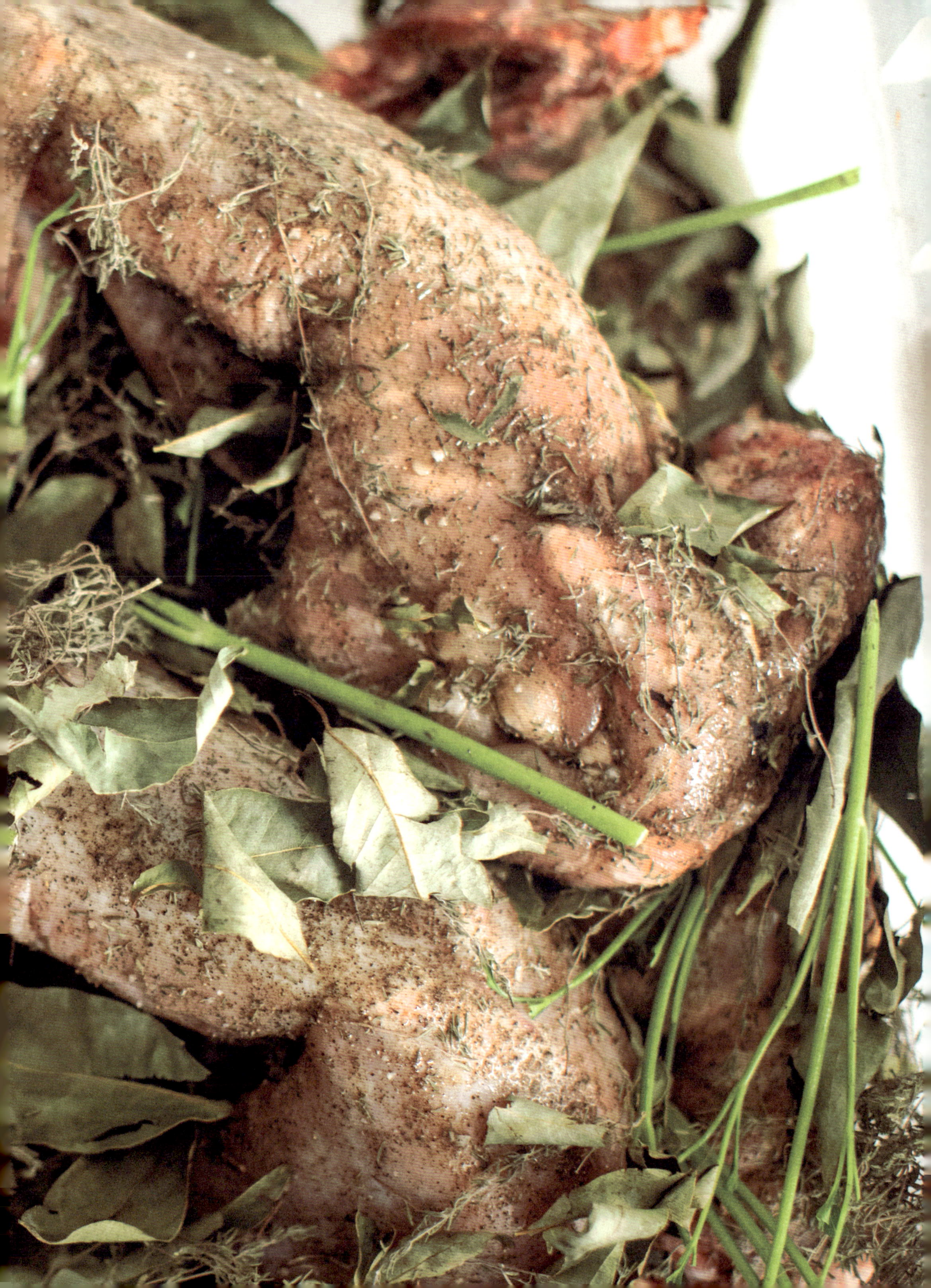

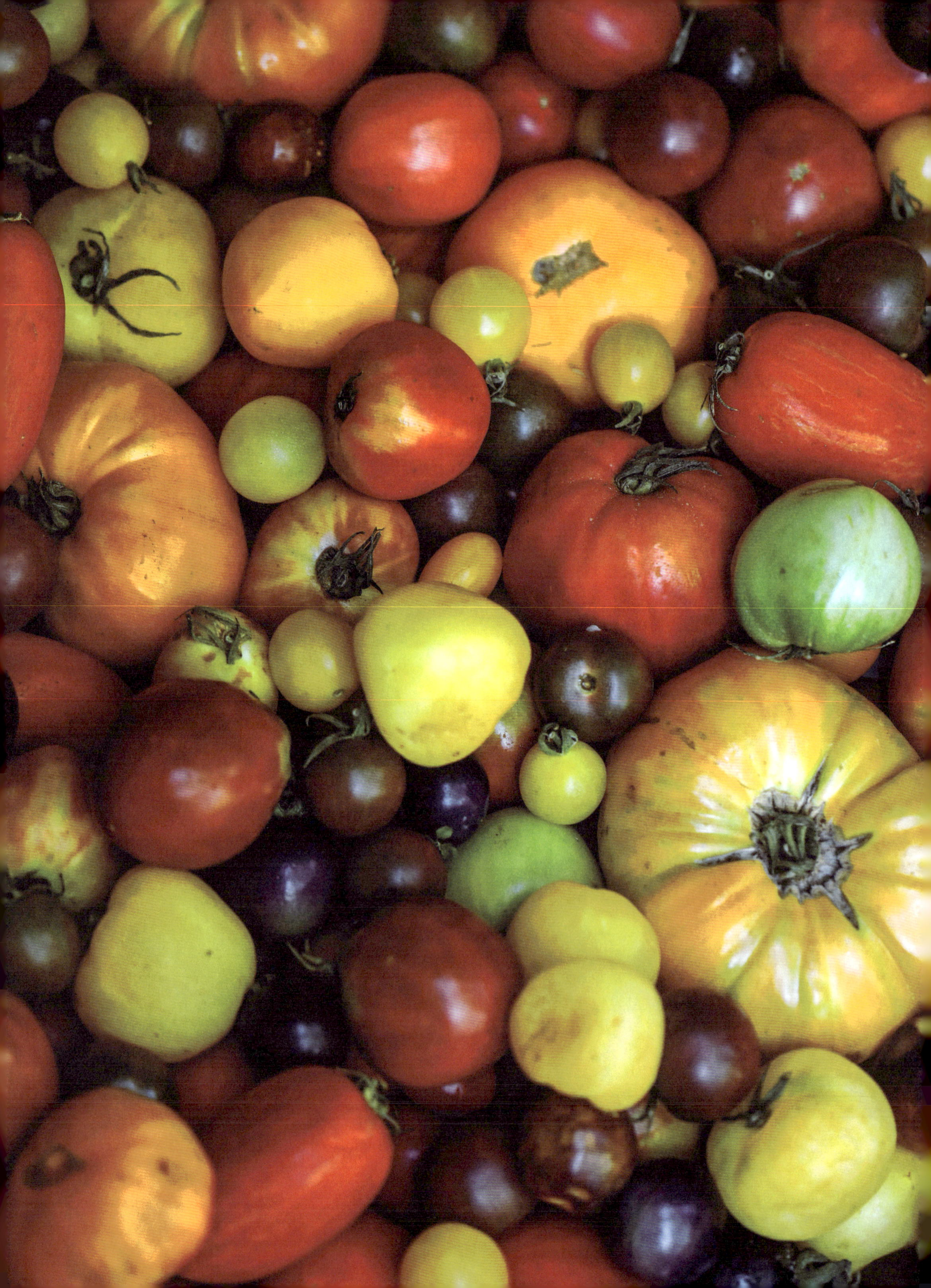

Scorpionfish, chorizo, and tomatoes

A classic is something that can be interpreted in infinite ways and endures over time. This applies both to literature and to cooking. I enjoy returning to classic dishes, even if they're out of fashion for some reason or other. I like revisiting them, appropriating them, adapting them, playing with them. I like to think that new flavors can also emerge from a return to the classics.

Raw tomato sauce

Serves 4

100 grams tomatoes
10 milliliters lemon juice
1 pinch salt
15 milliliters olive oil

Makes 100 milliliters
  Cut the tomatoes in half and grate them to get out all the pulp, discarding the skin.
  Strain the pulp and mix it with the lemon juice and salt. Gradually add the oil, emulsifying with a whisk.

Smoked chorizo

160 grams chorizo
10 grams mesquite chips
200 grams charcoal

Makes 150 grams
  There are various techniques for smoking ingredients. Two are quite practical. The first way involves placing a tray with wood shavings into a household oven, along with the product you want to smoke. It's important to seal the oven well so that the smoke doesn't escape. The second way involves setting the product to smoke on a grill, tossing wood shavings into the coals and immediately covering the grill to keep in the smoke.
  Smoke the chorizo. Let it sit for approximately 2 minutes or until the wood shavings have stopped burning and are no longer giving off smoke.

To Serve

720 grams scorpionfish fillet, with skin
20 grams salt
40 milliliters olive oil
80 grams baguette, sliced
½ garlic clove
300 grams heirloom tomatoes
8 grams chives, minced
10 milliliters red wine vinegar
160 grams smoked chorizo, sliced
80 milliliters raw tomato sauce
3 grams red onion

Cut the fish into 4 pieces, season with salt, and place in a frying pan with a bit of hot olive oil.

Cook for 7 minutes on the skin-side, turn over, and cook for approximately 3 more minutes.

Toast the baguette slices in the oven for 3 minutes at 180°C.

Once toasted, rub the garlic onto the bread, add a little olive oil, and chop it up.

Cut the tomatoes in half. Mix them together with the chopped bread, the garlic, the chives, the red wine vinegar, and a little olive oil.

Place the chorizo slices in a hot frying pan and brown on both sides.

Once browned, cut each slice into fourths and add them to the prior mixture, along with the oil from the chorizo.

Place the mixture in the middle of each plate, followed by the fish on top of it, and finally by the tomato sauce around the fish.

Red snapper, tamarind, and habanero

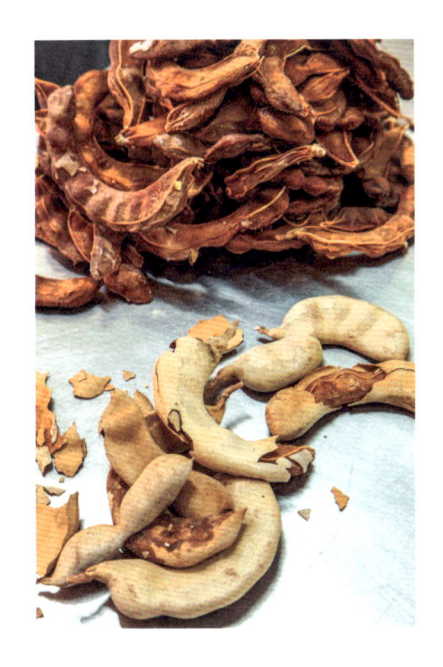

In Mexico, we consume tamarind in aguas frescas (fruit-infused waters), popsicles, and sweets from childhood onward. A sizable dose of sugar is added to all of these products, hiding the fruit's real flavor. Tamarind, for instance, is truly acidic. It's surprising how the excessive use of sugar keeps us from experiencing the real flavor of certain ingredients. This happens not only with tamarind, but also with hibiscus, to give another example.

It's often thought that the intense acidity of certain ingredients is a negative thing, which is why people add sugar. For me, though, strong acidity has wonderful qualities: it refreshes the palate, whets the appetite, and keeps flavors from getting bland. That's why I like tamarind.

We cook tamarind as a purée, and then we add melted coconut fat infused with habanero. The combination of tamarind and hot pepper is a common one. In fact, many tamarind candies are spicy in Mexico. There is a time-honored Mexican tradition of eating fruit with hot pepper.

This dish has a central duality: it expresses a lesser-known side of tamarind, and at the same time, in pairing tamarind with pepper, it respects the traditional use of its flavor.

Tamarind purée

Serves 4

125 grams tamarind pulp
75 grams butter
2.5 grams ginger
2.5 milliliters orange juice

Makes 200 grams

Heat the tamarind and ginger in a frying pan until warm. Add the butter, stirring constantly with a whisk, until well mixed. Then add the orange juice and remove from the heat.

Coconut and habanero emulsion

90 grams coconut oil
110 milliliters water
2 grams habanero pepper

Makes 200 milliliters

Heat the water in a saucepan along with the habanero. Crush the pepper a bit to release its spiciness. When the water reaches a boil, remove from the heat. When the water is lukewarm, add the coconut oil and remove the habanero.

Lemon vinaigrette

15 milliliters olive oil
5 milliliters lemon juice

Makes 20 milliliters

Put the lemon juice into a bowl, then stream in the olive oil and whisk together.

To Serve

800 grams red snapper fillet, with skin
6 grams salt
200 grams tamarind purée
8 grams parsley leaves
4 grams lemon balm leaves
10 grams peppermint leaves
20 grams cucumber, peeled
20 grams pearl onions, sliced
4 gram red cuaresmeño pepper, cut into half-moon slices
20 grams cashews, toasted and salted
20 milliliters lemon vinaigrette
200 grams coconut and habanero emulsion

Cut the fish into 4 pieces and season with salt. Cook the fish on the skin-side in a hot frying pan.

Heat the tamarind purée in a frying pan, stirring constantly to keep the butter from separating.

Spoon purée into the center of the plates.

Make a salad, mixing the herb leaves, the cucumbers (sliced in half and seeded), the pearl onions, the cuaresmeño pepper, the cashews, the vinaigrette, and a pinch of salt. Place a bit of this salad onto the purée, followed by the skinned red snapper fillet. Bathe with the coconut and habanero emulsion, finishing off with a little more of the salad on top of the fish.

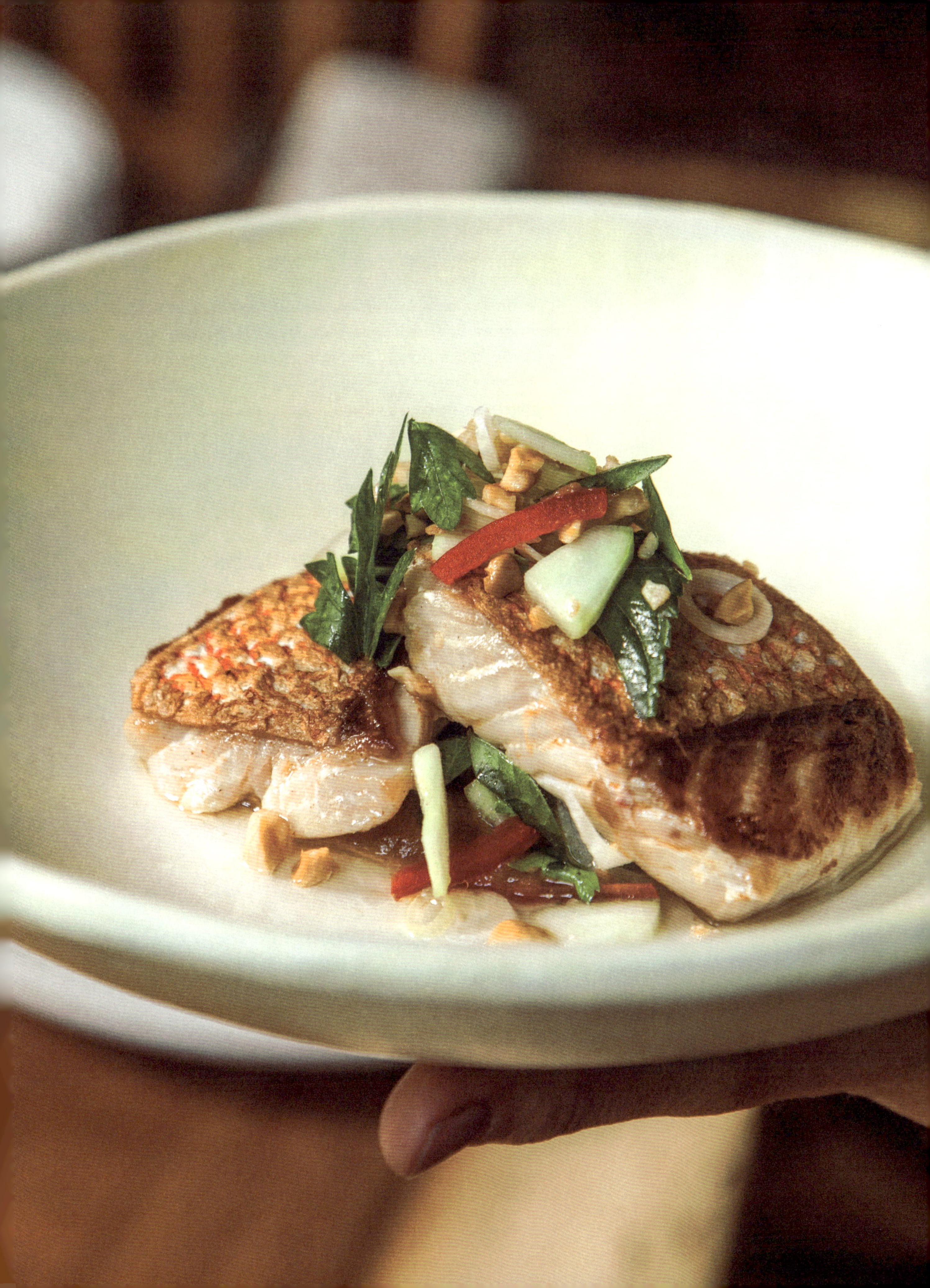

Quail, farro, dates, and mustard leaves

Small animals, given that their bones are tiny and difficult to remove, demand more time and patience than a cut of beef. They make for laborious consumption: you need to use your hands to extract the little bits of meat. Which is some people's nightmare, even when they know how delicious they are. This is why we serve quails with the bones already removed. You could say that we invert the effort: we transfer the tedious work from the table to the kitchen. But we also gain something. Once boneless, the small amount of meat in this animal is consolidated and thus easier to enjoy.

For this recipe, we make a duck broth and add farro, a grain we use often at Rosetta. In this dish, we turn to farro not only for its unique nutty flavor, but also because its starch serves to absorb and concentrate the liquids. In this way, the taste of the quail can come forth in all its fullness.

Serves 4

150 grams farro
750 milliliters water
1 pinch salt

Cooked farro

Makes 300 grams

Put the farro in a pot of boiling water with the salt and cook over medium heat until soft. Add more water if necessary. Once it's done, drain the excess water and set aside until use. Cover it with parchment paper or plastic wrap to keep it from drying out.

200 grams dried dates, pitted
160 milliliters milk
2 grams whole cinnamon

Date purée

Makes 250 grams

In a pot add the milk and the cinnamon until boil.
Soak the dates in the milk mix and refrigerate it for 12 hours
Remove the cinnamon stick and blend the mixture until it has the consistency of a puree.

Smoked dates

4 dates soaked in water the night before
10 grams mesquite chips
200 grams charcoal

Makes 4 pieces

Remove the dates from the milk and transfer them to a bowl.

There are various techniques for smoking ingredients. Two are quite practical. The first way involves placing a tray with wood shavings into a household oven, along with the product you want to smoke. It's important to seal the oven well so that the smoke doesn't escape. The second way involves setting the product to smoke on a grill, tossing wood shavings into the coals and immediately covering the grill to keep in the smoke.

Smoke the dates. Let them sit for approximately 2 minutes or until the wood shavings have stopped burning and are no longer giving off smoke.

White stock

500 grams chicken carcass
50 grams celery
50 grams white onion
50 grams carrots
1 gram juniper berries
4 liters water

Makes 1 liter

Wash the chicken carcass with plenty of water, drain it, and lay it out on a baking tray.

Bake at 230°C for 15 minutes. Remove and drain excess fat. Turn the carcass over and bake it again for 30 more minutes.

Wash and cut the vegetables into 4 pieces each. Along with the chicken carcass, transfer them to a large pot of water and cook over high heat. When it reaches the boiling point, reduce the heat to low.

Skim the fat off the stock every 20 minutes. Let it cook for an hour, or until it has reduced to ¼ its original volume. Remove from the heat, let sit for 30 minutes, and strain.

Duck broth

500 grams duck bones
80 grams white onion, quartered
20 grams garlic, unpeeled and halved
50 grams carrots, sliced
70 grams celery stalks, sliced
4 grams lightly toasted peppercorns
1 gram bay leaves
3 liters water

Makes 1 liter

Place the duck bones on a greased baking sheet and bake for 20 minutes at 235°C.

Transfer the bones to a saucepan.

Lower the temperature of the oven to 180°C. Arrange the vegetables on the same baking sheet and bake for 30 minutes, shifting them around every 10 minutes.

Add the vegetables and the fat on the tray to the duck bones. Add the peppercorns, the bay leaves, and the water.

Cook over medium heat. Once the water reaches a boil, reduce to low heat and cook until the contents have reduced by half. Strain and set aside the broth until ready to use.

Garlic oil

150 milliliters extra-virgin olive oil
50 grams garlic, finely minced

Makes 200 milliliters

Add the garlic to the oil and let it infuse for at least 6 hours before use. Refrigerate or keep in a cool place.

Animals

300 grams seedless tomatoes, quartered
30 grams basil
50 grams salted capers
3 grams sugar
3 grams salt
150 grams olive oil
100 grams dried chile de árbol, seeded

5 milliliters garlic oil
5 grams chile de árbol sauce
150 milliliters duck broth
300 grams farro
250 grams date purée
50 milliliters white stock
8 pieces quail meat, bones removed
1 pinch salt
1 pinch ground black pepper
20 milliliters olive oil
12 mustard leaves, stalk removed

Chile de árbol sauce

Makes 550 grams

Strip the leaves off the basil.
Mix all the ingredients together in a bowl and refrigerate overnight.
Blend the mixture until the texture is thick.

To Serve

In a pot, cook the garlic oil and the chile de árbol sauce over medium heat. Brown for 2 minutes, then add the duck broth. Once it starts to boil, add the salt and remove the pan from the heat. Set aside near heat.

Mix the farro, the date purée, and the white broth together in a pot. Cook over medium heat. Season with pepper. Set aside near heat.

Season the quail with salt. Warm olive oil in a pan over high heat, then cook the quail pieces on the breast-side for 5 minutes. Turn them over and cook on the other side for 3 more minutes. Set aside near heat.

Place some farro in the center of each deep dish. On top of it, arrange 5 cubes of smoked dates. Pour in the duck broth around the farro and arrange the quails on top of it, breast-side up, leaning one gently against the other. Add mustard leaves around them.

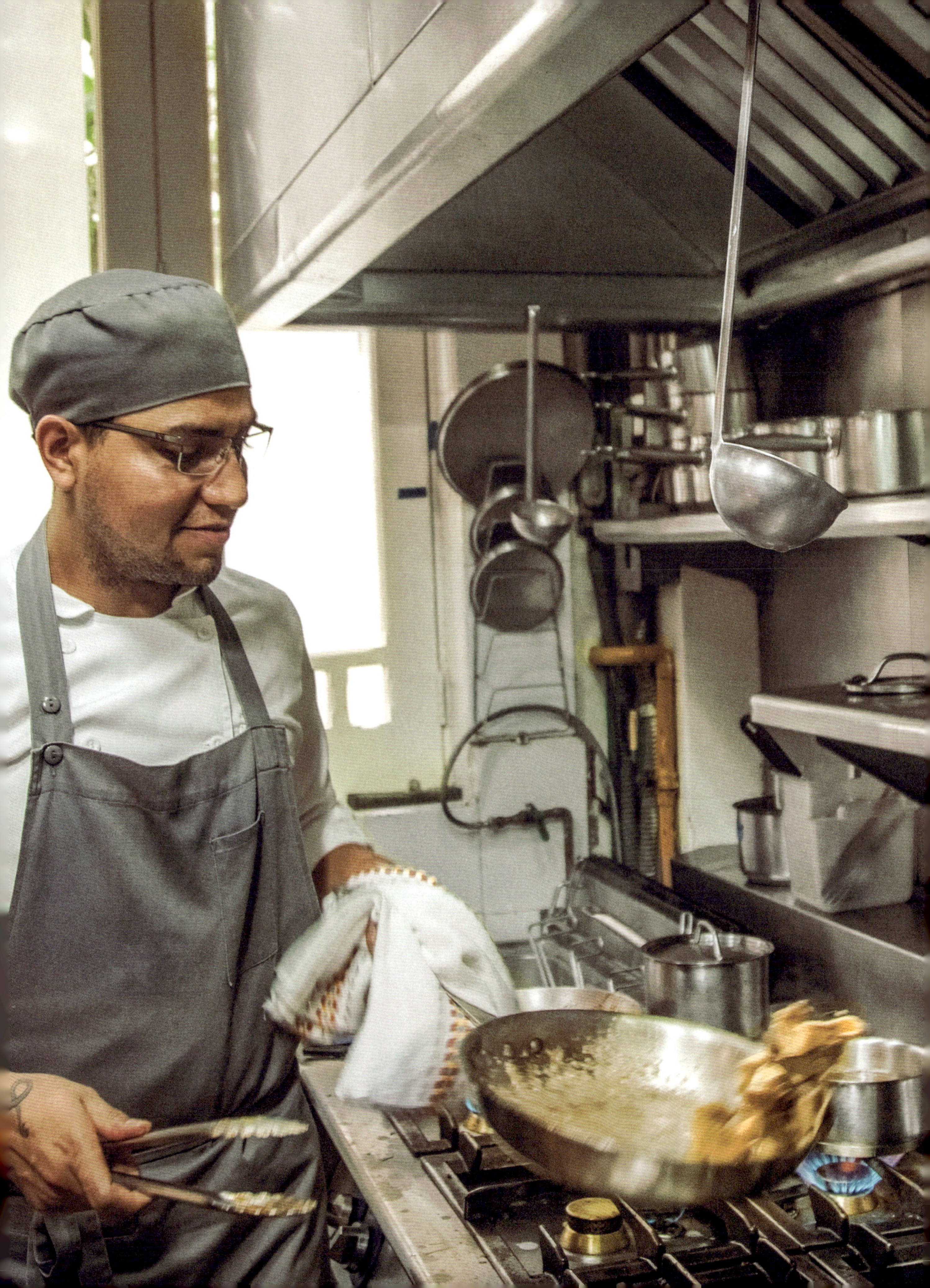

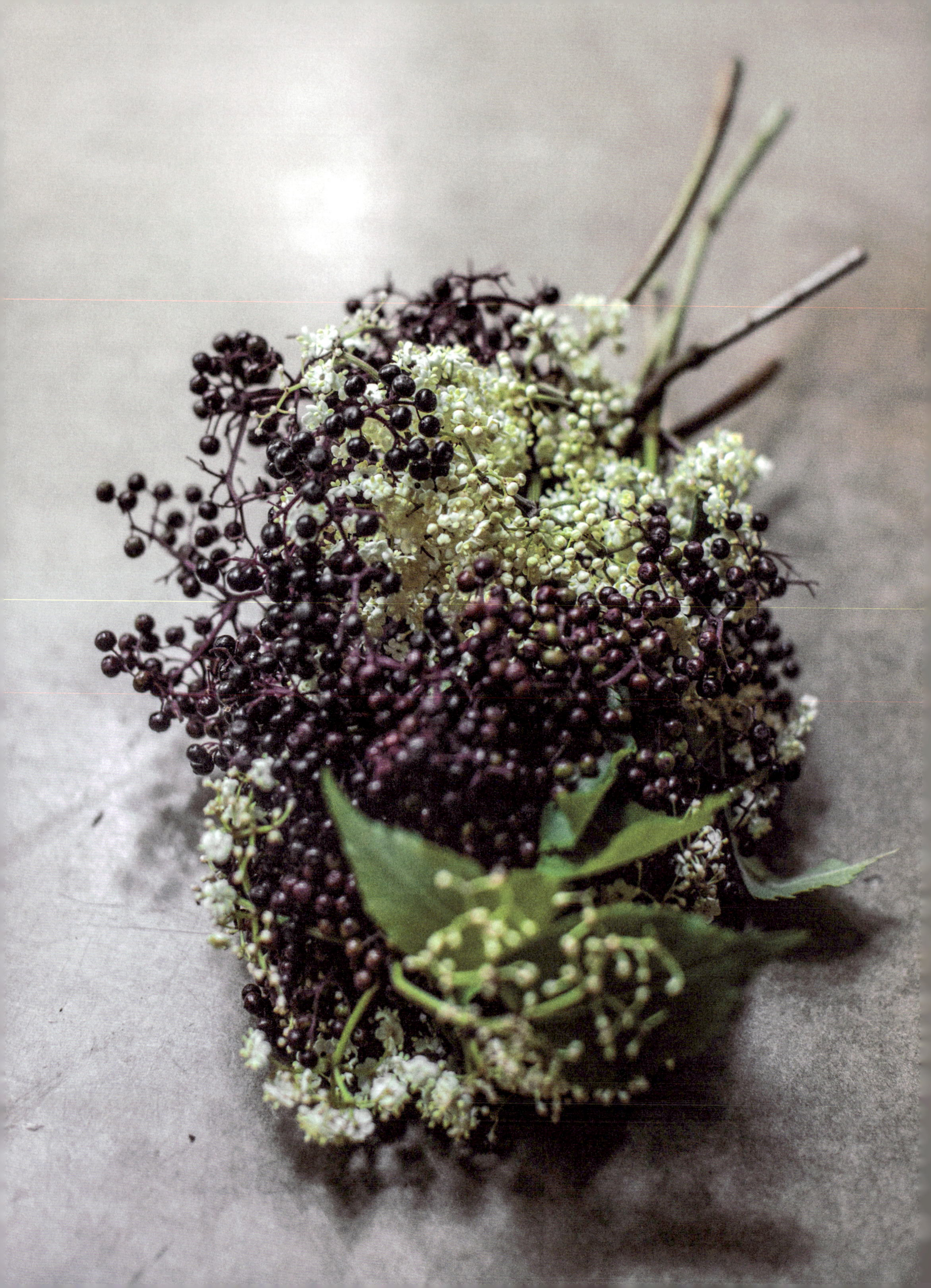

Cider-braised pork, apples, and elderberries

I wouldn't have created this dish if we hadn't had access to such high-quality pigs. These are a cross between two different breeds: Mangalica and Cuino. They have a concentrated flavor and at least twice as much fat as other pigs. We receive whole pigs at the restaurant, sent to us by a small breeder in the mountains of Oaxaca. There, the animals are fed corn, alfafa, acorns, chilacayotas, and bitter berries. Once they come to us, we hang up the meat for two weeks, which means it becomes concentrated and its fibers soften.

Each part of an animal calls for a specific preparation method. And every cook becomes a kind of medium who has to listen to the product. Legs, for instance, are among the toughest parts of an animal, which means they need to be braised: slowly cooked in liquid for several hours.

For this dish, we opted for cider. Cider is light, its acidity is discrete, and it's less invasive than wine (which is often used for braising). The sauce yielded by the caramelization of the juices from the meat and the reduced cider after braising is golden, aromatic, and slightly bittersweet. To reinforce the flavor of the cider, we make an apple purée, spiced with ginger. Most apples grown in Mexico are sweet, and the ginger intensifies them.

Elderberries come from the elder tree. This tree has clusters of white flowers and other clusters of small, very dark berries. Their flavor is tart, astringent, like grapes. We add these berries precisely because they contribute tannic touches that balance out the sweetness of the apple and the oiliness of the pork juice.

Pork stock

Serves 4

500 grams pork bones
50 grams celery
50 grams white onion
50 grams carrots
4 liters water

Makes 1 liter

Wash the pork bones with plenty of water.

Drain the bones and lay them out on a baking sheet.

Bake at 230° C for 15 minutes, remove, drain the excess fat, turn over the bones, and bake again for 20 more minutes or until they start to lightly brown.

Wash and cut each vegetable into 4 pieces.

Transfer the bones and the vegetables to a large pot of cold water. Cook over high heat until the water reaches a boil; at that point, reduce to the lowest possible heat.

Skim the fat off the stock every 20 minutes to remove impurities.

Cook for 1 hour or until reduced to ¼ its original volume. Turn off the burner, let it sit for 30 minutes, and strain.

Cider-braised pork

1.2 kilograms pork leg
35 grams salt
50 milliliters olive oil
270 grams turnips, cubed
400 grams carrots, quartered
140 grams leeks, quartered
20 grams garlic, lightly smashed and peeled
220 grams celery stalks, quartered
110 grams shallots, peeled and halved
10 grams bay leaves
260 milliliters cider
1 liter pork broth

Makes 800 grams

Season the pork leg with salt.

Heat the olive oil in a saucepan over medium heat. Sear the meat on all sides and set aside.

In the same saucepan, sauté the vegetables until they start to brown, then add 50 milliliters of cider.

Place the meat and the vegetables in a deep baking pan. Add the bay leaves on top of them, as well as the rest of the cider and the pork stock. Cover and bake for 3.5 hours at 180°C.

Apple purée

510 grams heirloom apples

Makes 120 grams

    Core the apples and cut them into wedges. Transfer them to a pot of boiling water and cook until soft. Remove the apples from the water and blend them until you have a purée.

Poached apples

350 grams heirloom apples
10 grams orange juice
50 grams sugar
250 grams white wine vinegar
45 milliliters water
45 milliliters lemon juice

Makes 100 grams

    Place all ingredients in a container and let infuse for 12 hours. Pour the contents into a saucepan and heat. Once it reaches a boil, remove from the heat, strain, and set aside.

Picked ginger

10 milliliters ginger juice
20 grams clean ginger
21 milliliters white wine vinegar
20 grams sugar

Makes 20 grams

    Place all the ingredients in a container and let it sit for 3 days.

Pickled elderberries

100 grams elderberries
100 milliliters red wine vinegar
100 milliliters water

Makes 100 grams

    Heat the water and the vinegar until they reach 37°C, then remove from the heat. Add the elderberries to the still-hot water. Let sit for 4 hours.

To Serve

120 grams apple purée
80 grams poached apples
20 grams butter
12 grams fresh thyme
1 pinch salt
100 grams pickled elderberries
4 green shisho leaves
10 grams picked ginger

In a frying pan, heat the cider-braised pork leg until the juice has thickened and reduced by half. Remove from the burner and set aside near the heat.

    Put the butter in another frying pan and brown the poached apples with a pinch of salt and the fresh thyme.

    Serve some hot apple purée on each plate. On top, arrange the pork leg and the poached apples, then add the pickled elderberries, some finely sliced picked ginger and the shisho leaves.

Chuck tail flap, avocado leaf, smoked zucchini, and chayotes

The notion of the entrée or the main course implies that a meal occurs in stages: that it starts with less substantial dishes until culminating in something more sizeable, a dish generally featuring animal protein. Vegetables and herbs tend to play a supporting role in such a system: they're the accompaniment, a garnish. This hierarchy unsettles me for several reasons. First and foremost, because I believe that the flavor range of vegetables and herbs is genuinely delicious—perhaps even more so than that of the animal world. In addition, vegetables and herbs take on different flavors according to the soil they're grown in: they have an intimate relationship with the earth. By contrast, livestock almost always eat prepared foods rather than grazing. As a result, all industrially raised meat tastes the same, no matter where it comes from.

While the chuck tail flap may seem like the star of this dish, it's actually dominated by herbs and vegetables. The most intense flavor is that of the avocado leaf: aromatic and anise-flavored, it tastes very different than the avocado fruit. Besides, it has wonderful digestive properties, which is why it's often used to make beans in traditional Mexican cooking. Chayote, served raw, contributes the crunchy texture that defines this dish. Finally, smoked zucchini complements the avocado leaf with its vegetal tone.

Smoked zucchini purée

Serves 4

600 grams zucchini
30 grams chaya leaves
10 grams mesquite chips
5 grams avocado leaves, dried and toasted
50 milliliters olive oil
7 grams salt
200 grams charcoal

Makes 500 grams

Cut the zucchini in half, peel, and set aside the middle part. Blanch the zucchini skin in salted boiling water for 2 minutes, remove, and transfer to a bowl of ice water. In that same water, blanch the chaya leaves for 30 seconds, remove, and transfer to ice water to stop the cooking process. Drain and put in a bowl.

There are various techniques for smoking ingredients. Two are quite practical. The first way involves placing a tray with wood shavings into a household oven, along with the product you want to smoke. It's important to seal the oven well so that the smoke doesn't escape. The second way involves setting the product to smoke on a grill, tossing wood shavings into the coals and immediately covering the grill to keep in the smoke.

Smoke the middle part of the zucchini for approximately 2 minutes or until the wood shavings have stopped burning and are no longer giving off smoke.

If they seem undercooked, bake them at 200° C for approximately 8 minutes or until tender.

Blend the chaya leaves with the zucchini skin and smoked middle parts. Add the avocado leaves, the olive oil, and the salt, processing until completely mixed and smooth in texture.

To Serve

100 milliliters lime juice
2 grams habanero pepper
680 grams chuck tail flap
1 pinch salt
1 pinch ground black pepper
10 milliliters olive oil
80 grams chayote, julienned
10 grams red onion, feather-cut
10 grams cilantro shoots

Place the lime juice in a bowl and add the habanero pepper, halved and seeded. Let it infuse. Once the juice is as spicy as you like, remove the pepper and refrigerate.

Season the chuck tail flap with salt and pepper. Let it sit at room temperature so it won't be cold when you cook it.

Heat the olive oil in a frying pan over high heat. Sear the meat for 3 minutes on each side. Let it sit near the heat for 10 more minutes.

Add the lime juice, the chayote, the red onion, and a pinch of salt, then set aside.

Heat the purée in a frying pan over medium heat. Once hot, spoon it into the center of each plate.

Serve the meat alongside the purée and the dressed chayote. Add the cilantro shoots.

Striped black bass, pineapple, cascabel pepper, sorrel, tarragon, and xoconostle

The xoconostle is a kind of cactus fruit. It's similar in appearance to the prickly pear, though the xoconostle is smaller. Pale green when cut, it slowly turns pink as it ripens. Unlike the prickly pear, which is very sweet, the xoconostle is intensely acidic (its name comes from the Náhuatl xococ, which means bitter, and nochtl, cactus). It also differs from the prickly pear in that its seeds accumulate in the center of the fruit, which makes it easier to remove them, and its skin is thicker. This fruit is often used in the so-called salsa borracha, or "drunk sauce": a sauce that accompanies barbacoa meat and is made with pasilla peppers and pulque. (The xoconostle is generally associated with pulque because both come from the same region, central Mexico, where nopales and maguey plants grow.)

At Rosetta, we use xoconostle when we want to give a dish a jolt of acidity. We use it raw, whether cubed or in a juice, which makes its acidity even more intense. In this dish, the xoconostle cubes mitigate the fattiness of the sea bass and refresh both the pineapple purée and the cascabel pepper sauce with peanuts.

Xoconostle escabeche

166 milliliters water
100 grams xoconostle
8 grams cascabel chilli
200 milliliters oil

Makes 400 milliliters

Blend the water and the xoconostle (with seeds) to make a juice, and then strain.

In a pot heat the oil and the cascabel chilli, let it sit over low heat for 15 minutes, or until the oil is impregnated with the chilli, strain and let it cool.

Mix the xoconostle juice and the infused oil. Let it sit

Tarragon vinegar

Serves 4

200 milliliters white wine vinegar
10 grams tarragon

Makes 200 milliliters

Combine in a glass bowl and let infuse for at least 12 hours before use.

Cascabel pepper sauce

15 grams white onion, cubed
1.5 grams garlic
35 milliliters olive oil
3.5 grams cascabel pepper, de-veined
1.5 grams morita pepper
40 grams peanuts
25 grams almonds, slivered
1 pinch salt

Makes 120 grams

In a frying pan, fry the onion and the garlic in a bit of olive oil for 5 minutes over medium heat.

Add the peanuts to the frying pan and cook until they start to brown.

Add the almonds, cook until they start to brown, and remove from the heat.

Remove all contents from the frying pan. In the same oil, fry the peppers for 5 minutes. Remove them from the heat and crush them with the oil. Add the peanut and almond mixture to the food processor and season with salt. If it's very thick, add a bit of olive oil to lighten it.

Pineapple purée

2.3 kilograms peeled honey queen pineapple
185 grams butter

Makes 600 grams

Cut the pineapple into fourths, remove the center, and slice thin. Cook the slices in a pot over low heat until they have completely disintegrated and dried out; their weight must be reduced to 500 grams.

Crush the pineapple along with the butter until the mixture forms a smooth purée. Strain and set aside until you're ready to use.

To Serve

900 grams striped black bass fillet, with skin
1 pinch salt
200 milliliters olive oil
200 grams pineapple purée
120 grams cascabel pepper sauce
32 grams sorrel, chopped
4 grams tarragon leaves
20 milliliters tarragon vinegar
1 xoconostle, chopped into very small cubes
400 milliliters xoconostle escabeche

Divide the fish into 4 pieces and season with salt.

Place them in a frying pan on the skin-side with a little olive oil. Cook for 8 to 10 minutes over medium heat. Turn over the fish and cook for 2 more minutes.

Turn over the fish and cook for 2 more minutes.

Serve the fish with the hot pineapple purée and the cascabel pepper sauce and the xoconostle escabeche.

Combine the sorrel, the tarragon, and the xoconostle. Dress with the tarragon vinegar, a bit of olive oil, and the salt. Sprinkle some of this mixture onto the fish.

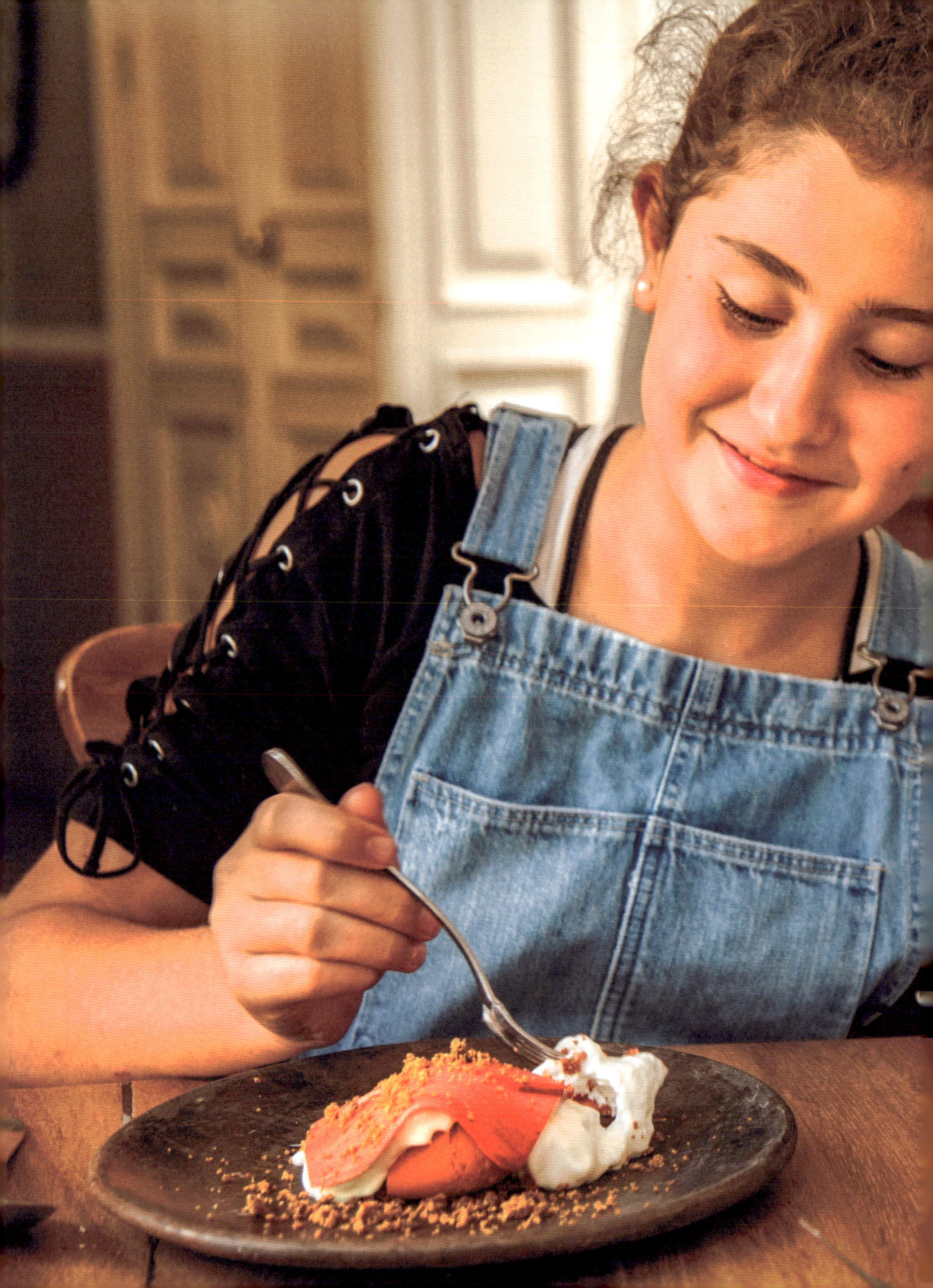

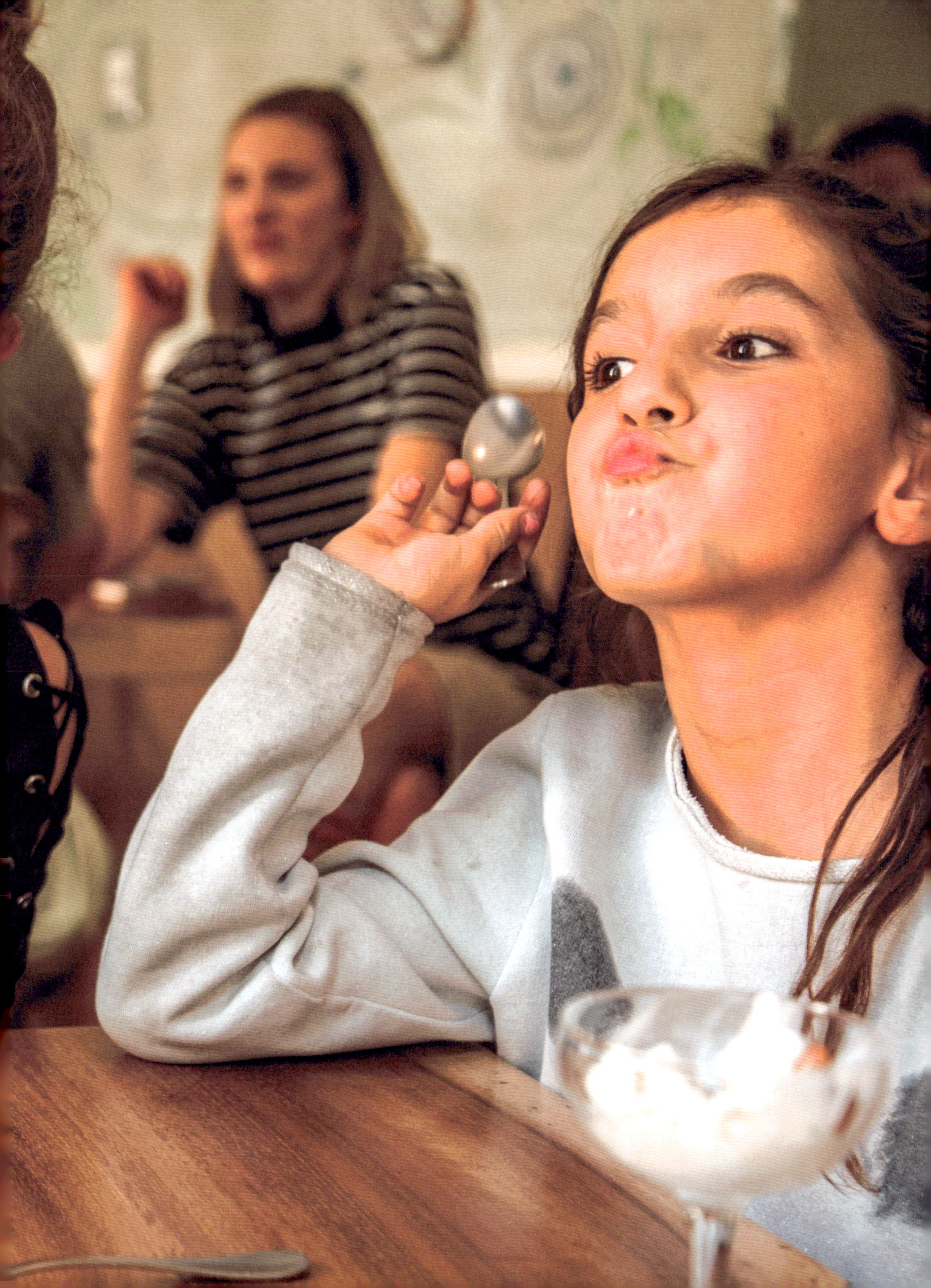

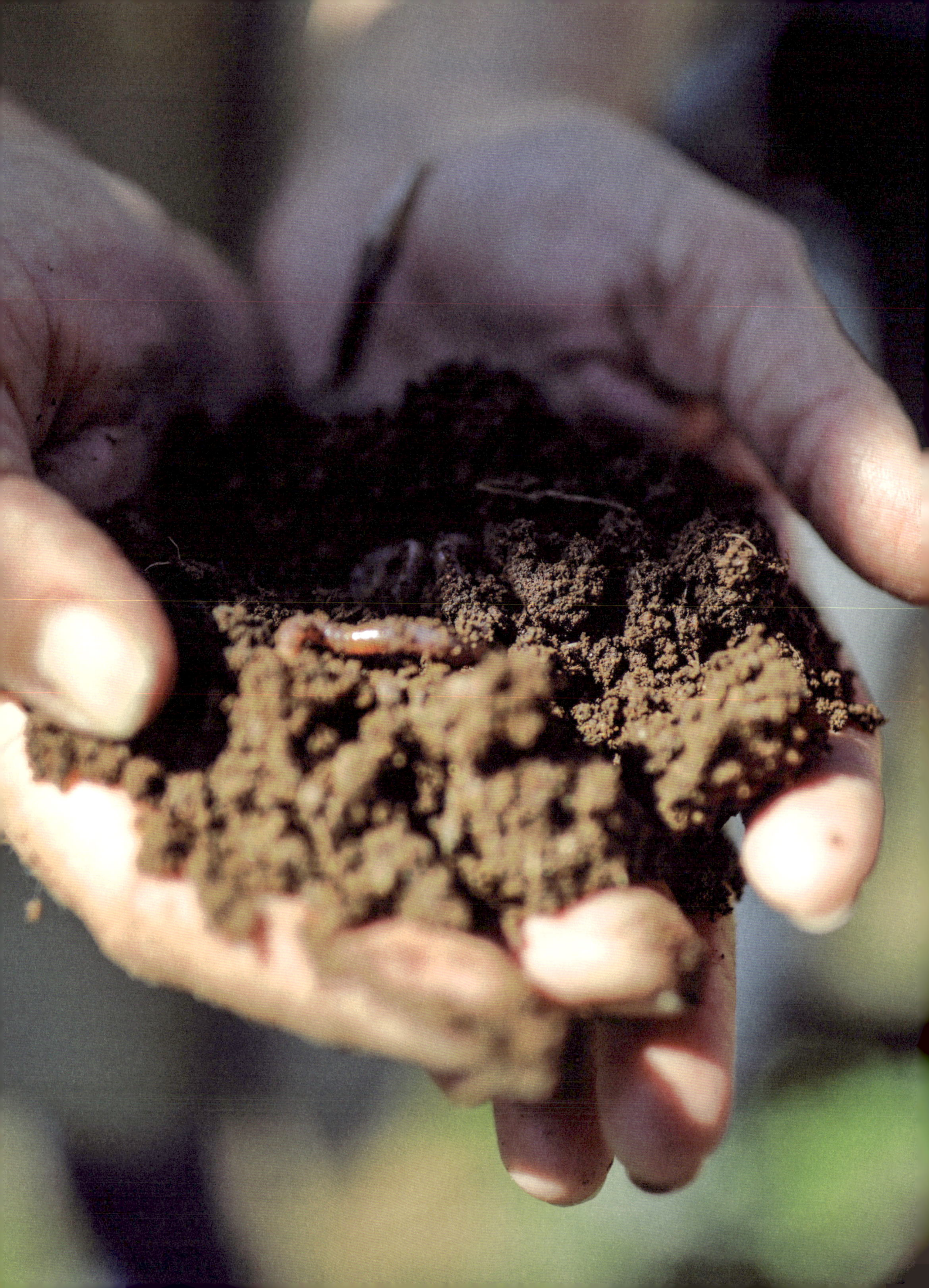

Well-being

My favorite restaurants are the ones I leave feeling light and full of energy. I dislike feeling stuffed and sleepy after a meal. Which is why, when I get ready to prepare a dish, I don't only take flavors into account; I also consider how the food will affect the people who eat it. I worry about how they'll feel when they finish. I want to foster a sense of physical, sensorial, and even mental well-being. At Rosetta, we do several things to achieve this goal. Portions are never excessive. Our menu favors plants, vegetables, seeds, grains, and legumes. We don't rule out using any ingredients, but we always make sure they're of the highest possible quality. Our ingredients are local, grown sustainably and without chemicals; they're fresh and don't contain preservatives. We avoid using fat in abundance. Our desserts are low in sugar and we design them to be light and easy to digest. Most of our beverages are artisanally produced.

Actually, though, we're talking about a more general issue here: the close connection between food and our physical, emotional, and mental health. I'm convinced that what we consume has a direct effect on our bodies and our minds. Today, it's understood that many illnesses and health problems are caused by poor nutritional habits. The growing consumption of low-nutrient processed foods and sugary drinks has yielded a tragic paradox in many countries, including Mexico: on the one hand, high rates of malnutrition; at the same time, high rates of obesity. These simultaneous realities emerge from the imposition of an economic system that controls people's diets from production to consumption. It foments intensive or industrial agriculture based on monoculture, using agrochemicals like fertilizers and insecticides, and on genetically modified organisms (GMOs). Moreover, it promotes the consumption of processed foods and strengthens the domain of supermarkets and convenience stores.

Of course, we cooks can't single-handedly change this complex situation. That said, I do believe we can contribute in our own small way. For one thing, we can raise awareness about such problems. But we must also encourage the consumption of high-quality products; support farmers and agroecological production; champion projects associated with sustainable growing techniques like the chinampa (small artificial islands built on freshwater lakes for agricultural use) and the milpa (an intercropping system of regional vegetables); promote a balanced diet that respects nature; and fight for biodiversity and food sovereignty.

In short, we cooks must care about the effects of food in the very broadest sense: on the environment, on our health, and on the well-being of society.

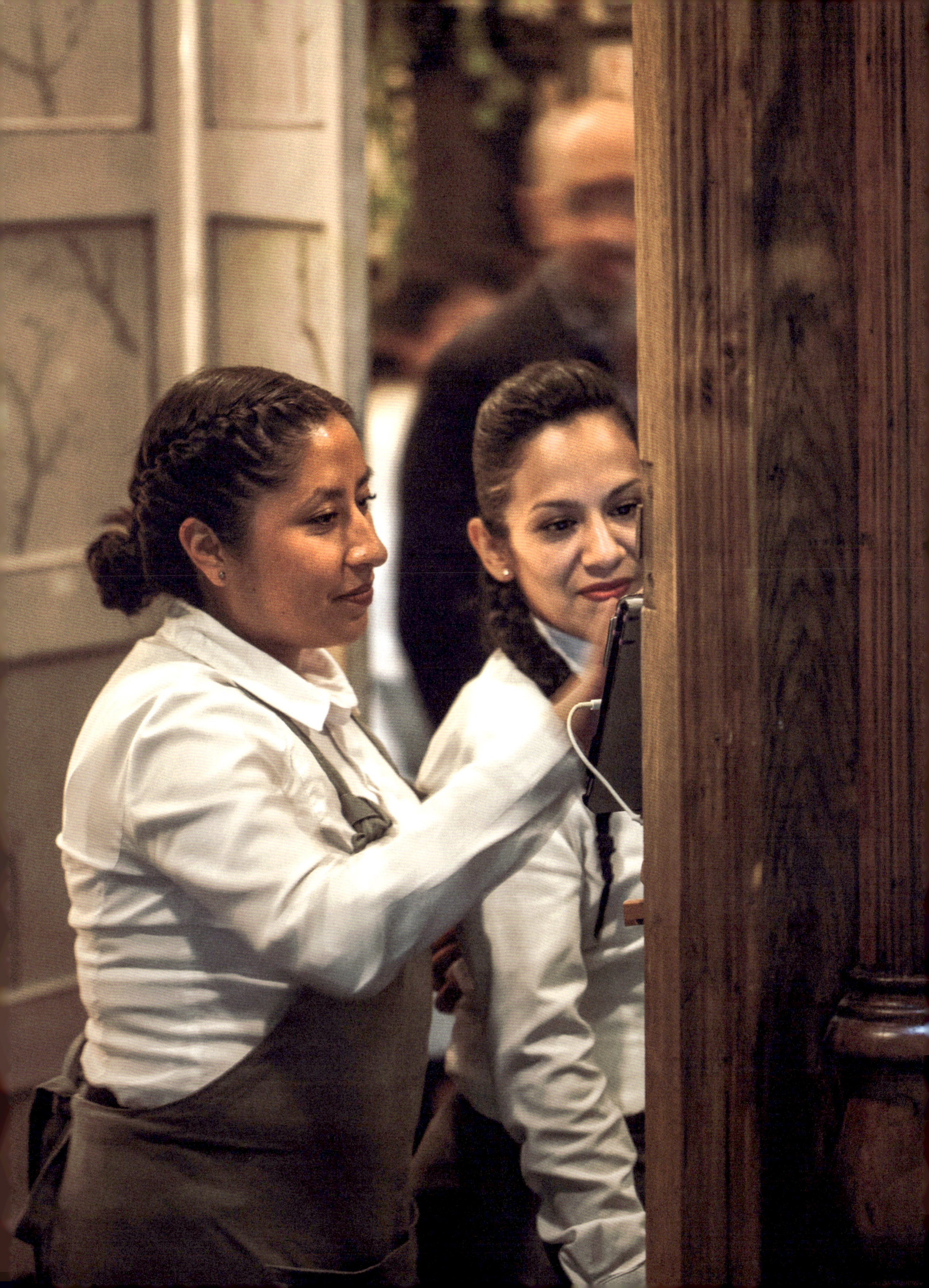

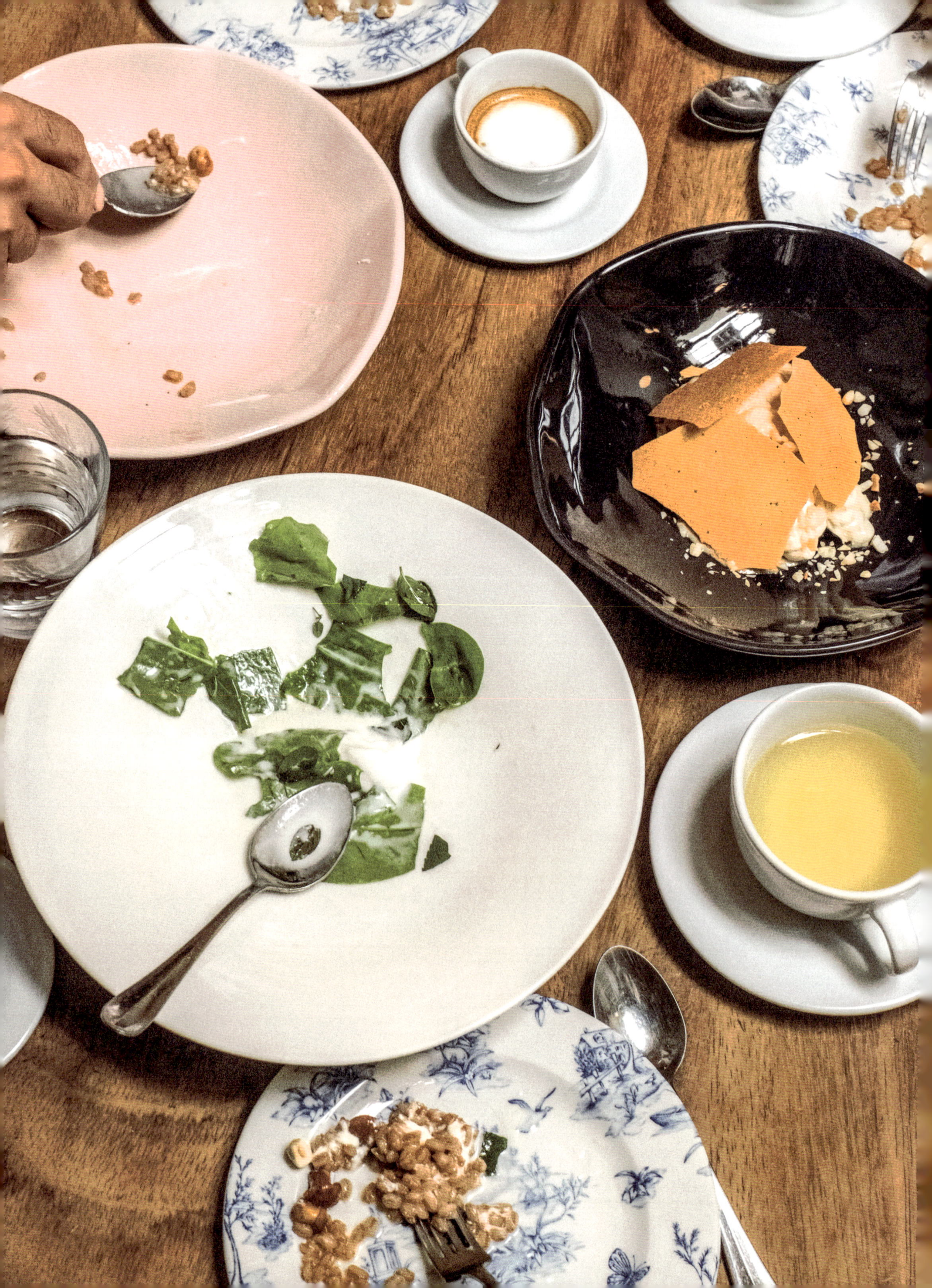

IV
Endings

Bread and cheese	259
Amaranth bread	260
Walnut raisin bread	262
Smoked meringue, sour cream, pulque, and vanilla	267
Pink mole, strawberries, raspberries, hibiscus flowers, and yogurt foam	269
Farro, Tzalancab honey, chantarelles, and mascarpone	273
Nanches, yucca flowers, sour cream, and lemon	275
Pulque, prickly pear, xoconostle, and dragon fruit	280
Chocolate and hazelnut mousse	282
Licorice ice cream, banana, and macadamia nuts	284
Barley, olive oil, and lavender	286
Fresh herbs, olive oil and rosemary ice cream	289
Nicuatole, sweet lime, and macadamia	291
Melipona honey, pollen, and chamomile	294
Mamey, pixtle, and taxcalate	297
Ice creams and sorbets	301
Coffee	**307**
Amaretti	315

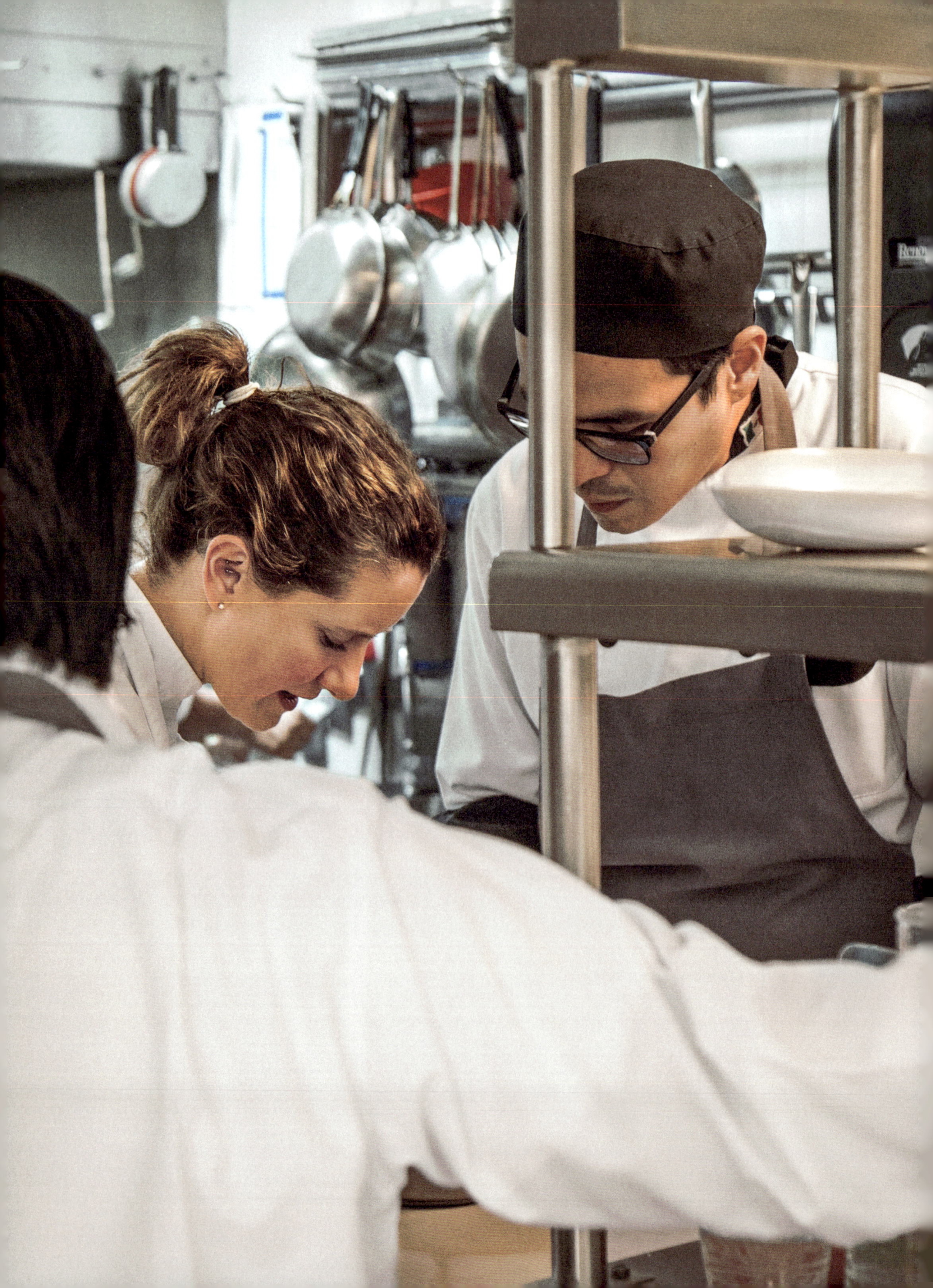

Comanda de cocina
Mesa   # 9
Mesero   : Alberto Alvarez
Día   : 07/09/17
Folio   : 13-57
13-1-18

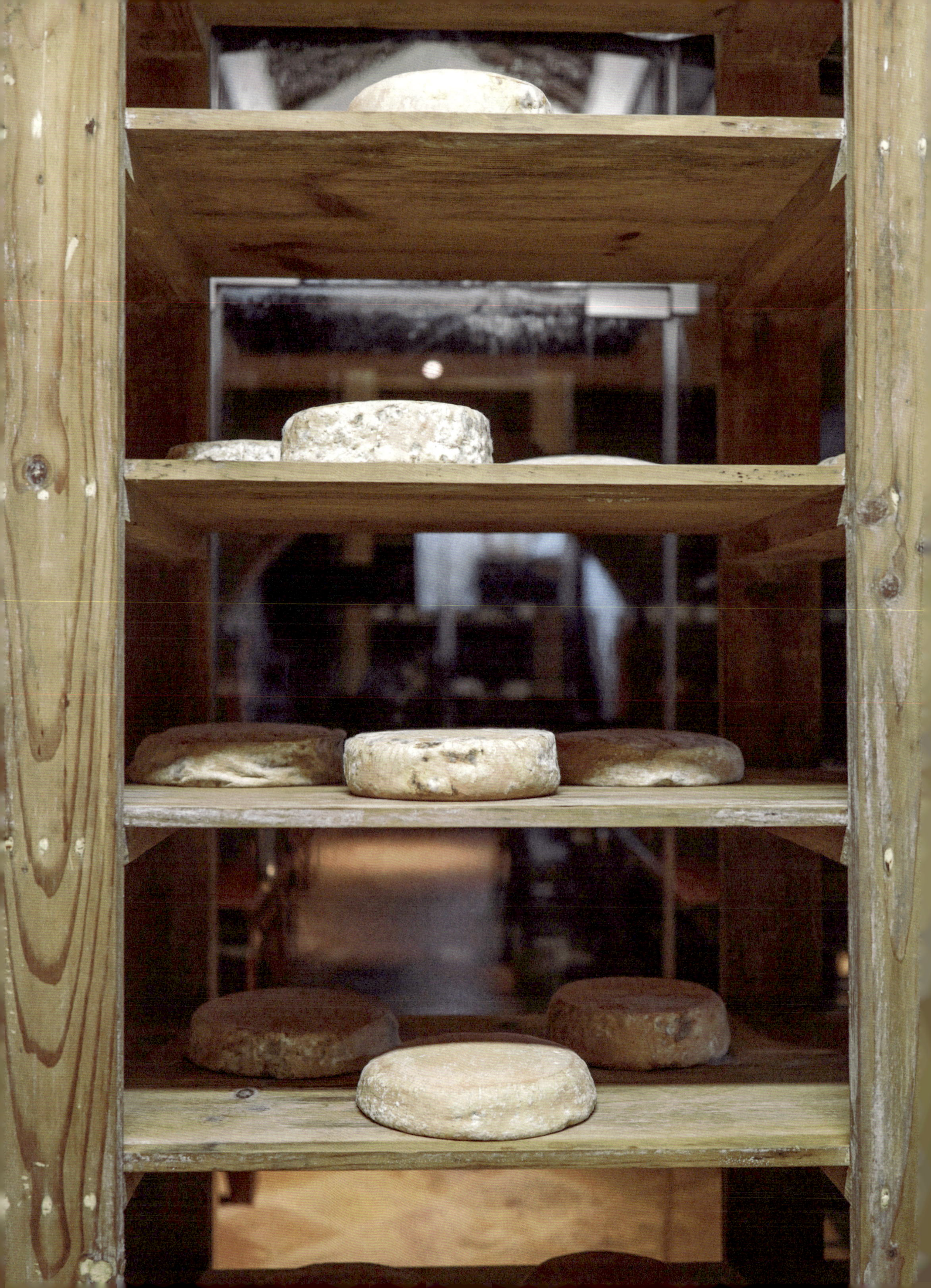

Bread and cheese

Many people enjoy finishing a meal with some good cheese and a piece of bread. At Rosetta, we make very different kinds of bread to pair with cheese. But all of them emerge from the same intention: we think of bread as a dish in itself.

We generally make bread with a little sweetness in it to accompany our cheeses. Sometimes it contains nuts or dried fruit; sometimes we use a sweet-tasting grain like amaranth or oats. Over the years, we've served hazelnut and fig bread, chestnut bread, sourdough, mesquite bread, oat bread, walnut raisin bread, and many other varieties as a counterpart to our cheeses. We choose the kind of bread depending on the cheeses we have on hand at the time. It's important to cultivate this connection: the taste of the cheese changes according to the bread it's eaten with.

We exclusively serve Mexican-made cheeses because we're committed to supporting the people who produce them: this is the only way to guarantee access to excellent, locally made cheeses in Mexico. We cooks need to support small-scale producers who know their trade inside out and oversee the entire process, from milking to maturing. Thanks to them, we can offer cheeses made with high-quality dairy at Rosetta: free of chemicals and additives and often unpasteurized. We feel strongly about respecting their flavor and structure, and so we serve these cheeses without manipulating them in any way.

Amaranth bread

Amaranth is a pseudo-grain. It's actually a very beautiful quelite, green or bougainvillea-pink in color, high in protein. It has an earthy flavor that sweetens slightly when toasted. Amaranth is an ancient food source that has gained more recognition in Mexico in recent years, mainly in the form of alegrías: compact bars, solidified with honey, made of toasted and puffed amaranth.

To make this bread, we toast previously inflated amaranth and then grind it. We add water and sourdough starter to this dust, forming a natural yeast that we set aside for 72 hours. After this long period of rest, we add more water and amaranth to the mixture, in addition to wheat and salt. We don't use synthetic yeast, and the entire fermentation process is thanks to the sourdough starter and the long wait.

This process yields bread with a strong crust and springy inner dough. It stays fresh for quite some time. Its flavor is unique, something between sweet and earthy with an acidic note. This flavor combination, as well as the consistency of the center, makes it an ideal bread to pair with cheese at the end of a meal.

Amaranth starter

Makes 4 loaves

190 milliliters water
200 grams sourdough starter
300 grams amaranth, crushed and ground
100 grams creamed honey

Makes 800 grams

Place 140 milliliters of water, 50 grams of sourdough starter, and 70 grams of amaranth in a medium-sized bowl and mix them thoroughly with your hands. Set aside for 3 hours at room temperature, then refrigerate for 24 hours.

Add 150 grams of amaranth and 50 more grams of sourdough starter to the previous mixture. Set aside again for 3 hours and refrigerate for 24 more hours.

Finally, add 80 more grams of amaranth, 100 grams of sourdough starter, 50 milliliters of water, and the creamed honey. Set aside for 3 hours and refrigerate for 24 hours.

To Serve

475 milliliters water
16 grams salt
750 grams wheat flour
200 grams sourdough starter
800 grams amaranth starter
30 grams amaranth, crushed and ground

Combine all the ingredients in a large bowl. Mix with your hands, making circular motions. Once everything is mixed together, place the dough on a surface and start to knead it, striking it lightly until the texture is even and stretchy.

Place the dough in a bowl and let it sit at room temperature for 1 hour. Fold the dough in half, then in half again, and let it sit again for 40 minutes. Fold the dough again and let it sit for 30 more minutes.

Divide the dough into 4 equal parts and shape each one into a ball. Place each piece in a basket with a floured cloth, the smooth surface of the bread facing downward, and cover it with the cloth. Set them aside at room temperature for 2 hours, then refrigerate for 12 to 15 hours.

Carefully transfer the loaves to a baking sheet with the smooth surface of the bread facing upward.

Bake with steam at 260°C for approximately 25 minutes.

Endings

Walnut raisin bread

The combination of bread and nuts has existed for hundreds of years, and in Europe it remains one of the most-consumed kinds of bread. In my opinion, a good nut bread needs to use the highest-quality nuts possible, and they need to be fresh. When you add raisins to the mix, the bread gets moister, sweeter, and more acidic. At Rosetta, we make a dense, compact bread with lots of walnuts and raisins. We like to pair this bread with creamy, minimally acidic, cow-milk cheeses like Ramonetti, which is produced in the Ojos Negros valley in Baja California. I especially enjoy this bread when cut into thick slices and lightly toasted, which brings out the oil from the nuts and intensifies its aroma. Something I've noticed about all bread, but even more strikingly with this kind, is that the flavor changes depending on the thickness of the slice. It's hard to describe these differences in words. But you can see it—and taste it—for yourself.

Overnight starter

Makes 3 loaves

Makes 335 grams

190 grams wheat flour
50 grams sourdough starter
95 milliliters water

Place all the ingredients in a bowl and mix them together until smooth and even. Cover the bowl with plastic wrap, making sure the plastic doesn't touch the mixture. Let it sit in a warm place for 12 to 24 hours.

To Serve

525 grams high-protein wheat flour
150 grams rye flour
15 grams salt
7.5 grams ground cinnamon
3 grams dry yeast
440 milliliters water
150 grams sourdough starter
335 grams overnight starter
340 grams raisins
260 grams walnuts, chopped

Place the flours, the salt, and the cinnamon into a large bowl.

Dissolve the yeast in a little water. Make a hollow in the middle of the dry ingredients and pour in the dissolved yeast.

Gradually pour the rest of the water into the center, followed by the sourdough starter and the overnight starter. Mix with your fingers in a circular motion from the center outward.

Once everything is mixed together, place the dough on a wooden surface, then add the raisins and chopped walnuts to the center of the dough. Fold the ends of the dough toward the middle until completely covered. Knead, striking the dough lightly against the surface until the texture is even and stretchy.

Place the dough on a clean, floured surface and divide it into 3 equal parts. First, shape each piece into a rectangle, then roll it up to form an oval-shaped loaf.

Place each piece into a basket with a floured cloth and cover it with the cloth. Let sit for 2 hours at room temperature.

Transfer the loaves to a baking sheet, leaving a good amount of space between them.

Bake with steam 250°C for 30 minutes. Rotate the baking sheet after 15 minutes for even browning.

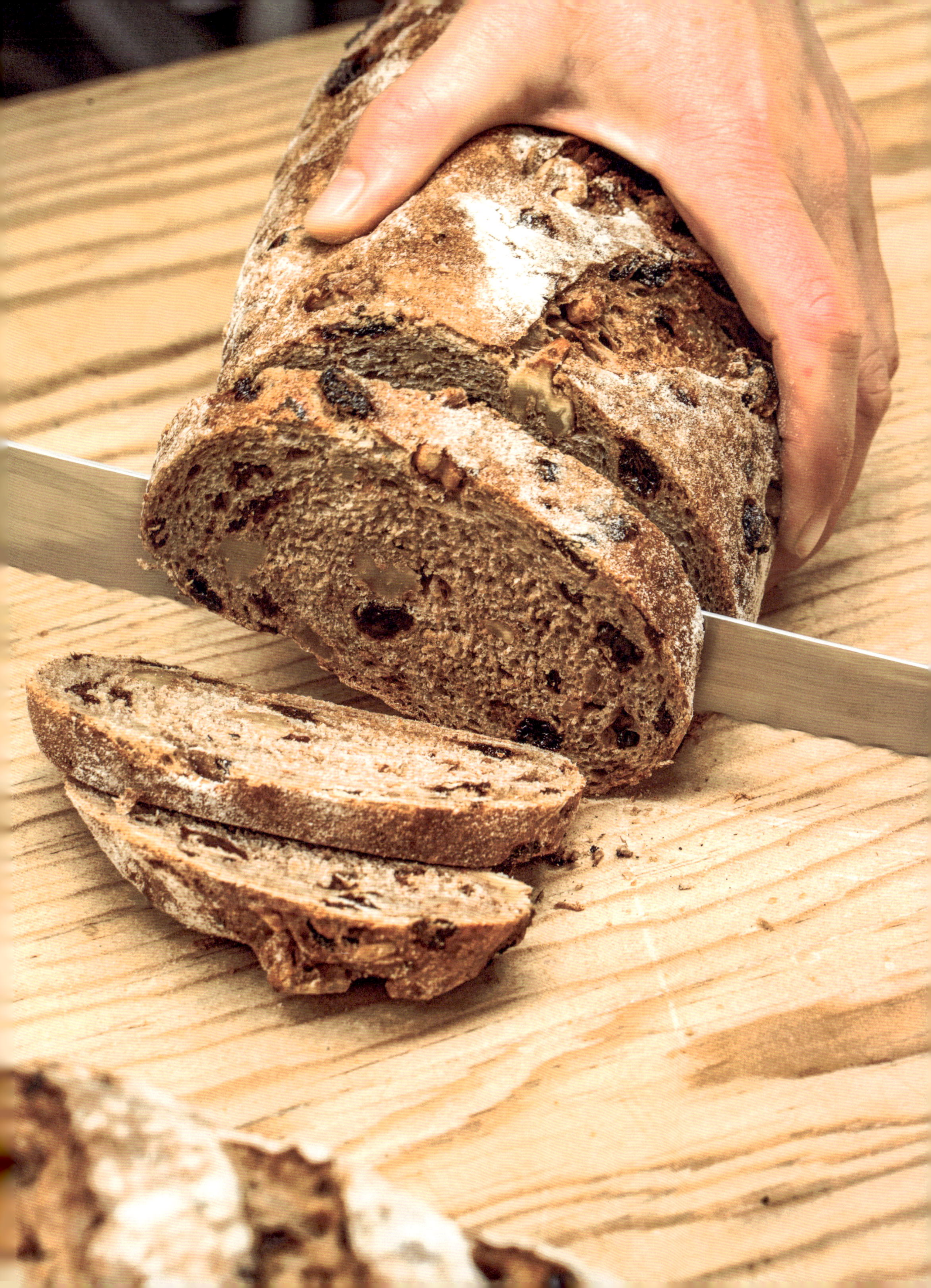

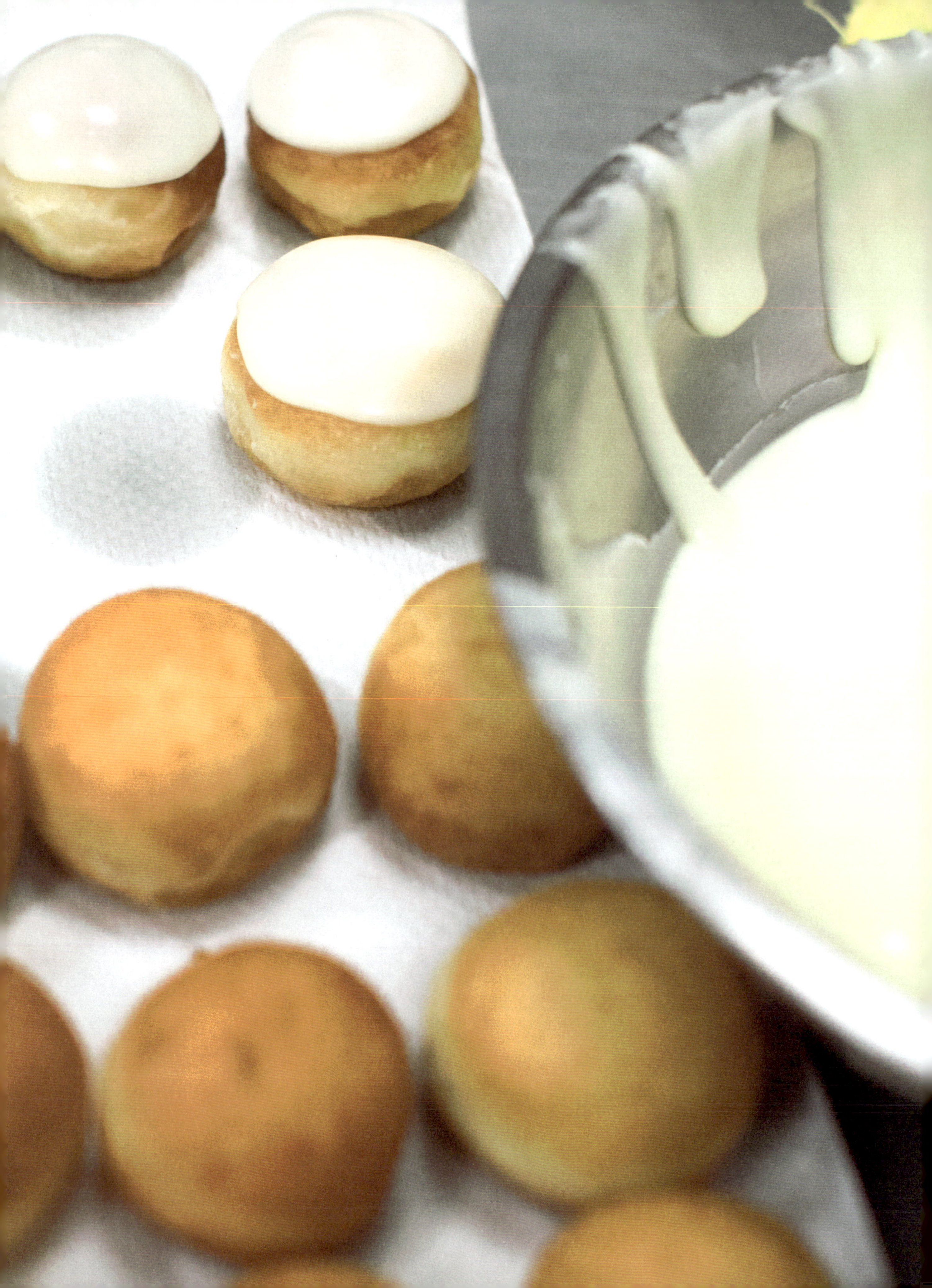

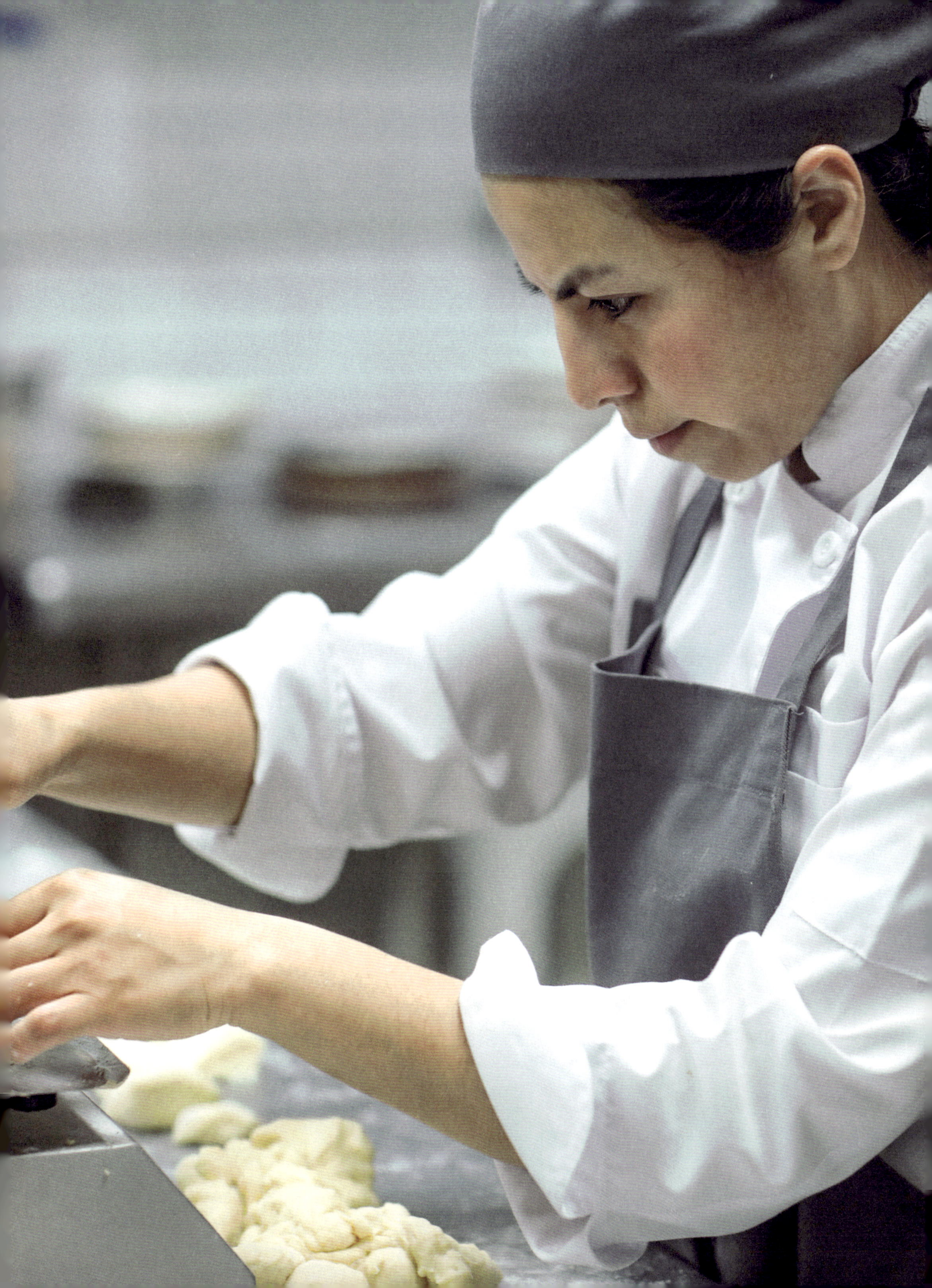

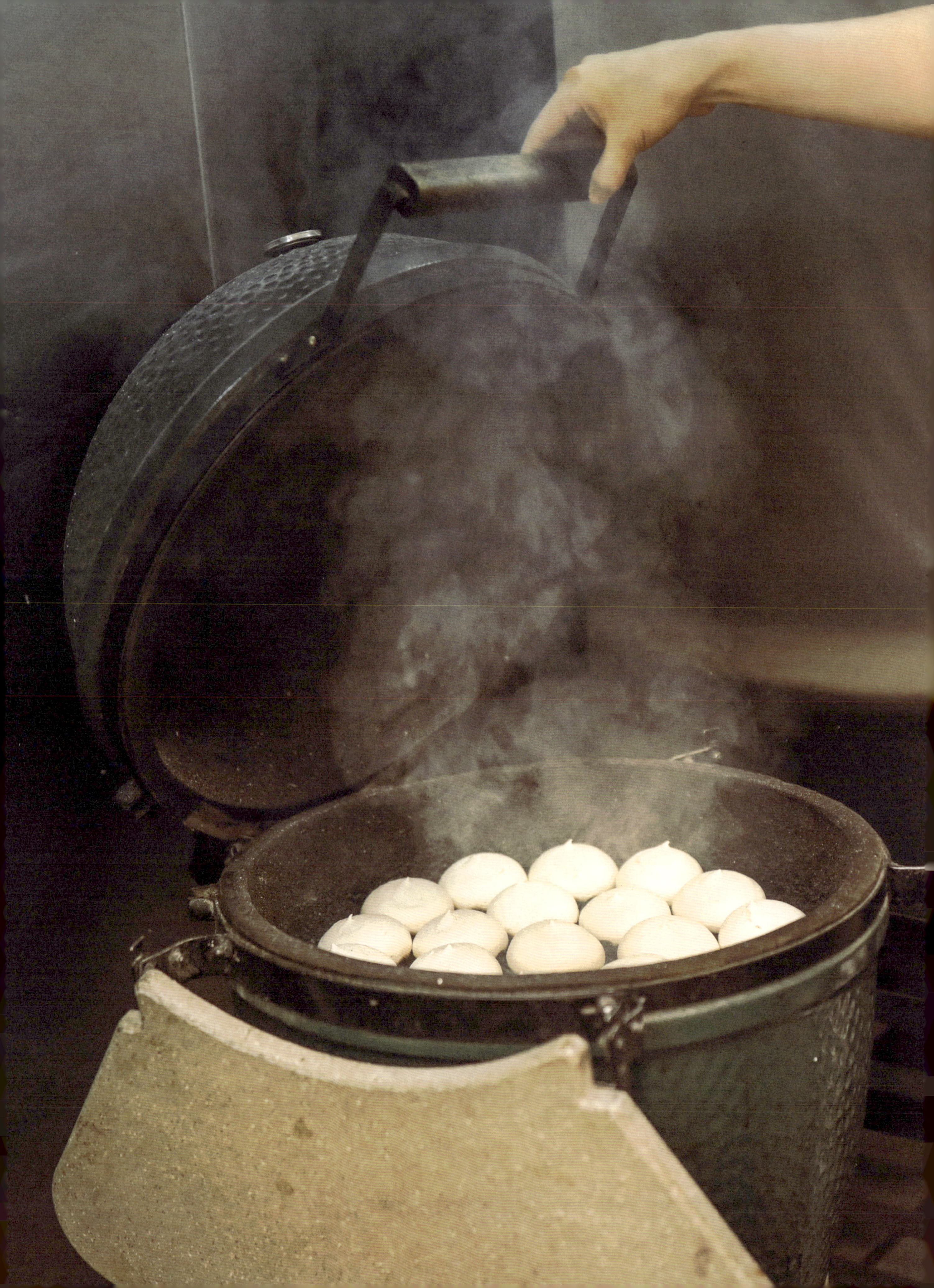

Smoked meringue, sour cream, pulque, and vanilla

Meringues are still cooked on wood-burning stoves in many Mexican villages. And in the central region of Mexico, meringues are made with pulque, an alcoholic beverage made from fermented aguamiel, which is the sap of the maguey. This gives the meringues a delicate but nor rubbery texture. The classic combination of meringues with cream and vanilla ice cream has been altered here: we add pulque to the ice cream and the cream and we smoke the pulque meringue. The changes are subtle, but the result is radically different from the desserts found in traditional Mexican bakeries.

Smoked meringues

Serves 4

105 milliliters egg whites
200 grams sugar
20 milliliters pulque
15 grams mesquite chips

Makes 12 meringues

Beat the egg whites. When they start to foam a bit on the sides, gradually add the sugar. Once soft peaks form, stream in the pulque.

Transfer the mixture to a pastry sleeve and shape meringues measuring 7 centimeters in diameter on a baking sheet.

Bake at 140°C for 40 minutes.

Let cool at room temperature.

Turn on the smoker with the mesquite chips and let the meringues smoke for 5 minutes or until no more smoke is being produced.

Pulque foam

1.5 grams gelatin sheets
33 milliliters milk
100 milliliters pulque
50 grams plain organic yogurt
1 siphon

Makes 180 grams

Hydrate the gelatin in ice water.

Heat the milk to 50°C, then remove from the heat and add the previously drained gelatin.

Add the pulque and the yogurt all at once. Mix with a hand blender.

Strain and transfer the mixture to the siphon. Charge it, shake, and refrigerate for 2 hours before use.

Sour cream panna cottas

3 grams gelatin sheets
180 milliliters milk
20 grams sugar
115 milliliters sour cream

Makes 4 panna cottas
 Hydrate the gelatin in ice water.
 Heat the milk to 50°C, then remove from the heat and add the previously drained gelatin.
 Mix with a hand blender. Strain and add the sour cream.
 Mix well.
 Pour into rings, measuring 8 centimeters in diameter, previously wrapped with a layer of aluminum foil so the liquid won't escape. Refrigerate for at least 2 hours.

Pulque ice cream with vanilla

100 milliliters milk
330 milliliters heavy cream
80 grams fat-free powdered milk
160 grams dextrose
15 grams stabilizer
220 grams sugar
2 vanilla pods
160 grams pulque

Makes 1 liter
 Place the milk, the heavy cream, the powdered milk, and the dextrose in a saucepan. Mix with a hand blender to remove all lumps. Heat to 40°C, then add the stabilizer, the sugar, and the previously halved vanilla pods. Heat to 85°C, then remove from the stove.
 Cool on top of a bowl of ice until the temperature drops to 4°C. Transfer the mixture to another bowl and refrigerate for 6 to 12 hours.
 Add the pulque and immediately run the mixture through an ice cream machine until it's as smooth as you like.

To Serve

4 sour cream panna cottas
200 grams pulque ice cream with vanilla
180 grams pulque foam
4 smoked meringues

Place each panna cotta in the middle of a deep dish. Add the ice cream on top, then the pulque foam.
 Finally, add the smoked meringue in pieces.

Pink mole, strawberries, raspberries, hibiscus flowers, and yogurt foam

This dessert is a derivation of the pink mole we originally served with suckling pig. Mole sauces contain so many seeds and spices that it's easy to imagine them as desserts—especially this one, which includes beets and pink pepper for an added kick.

For one thing, we increased the amount of white chocolate in the mole. And unlike in the savory version of the dish, we used yogurt instead of pulque, and we added hibiscus flowers, strawberries, raspberries, and a bit of sugar. We rarely use strawberries or raspberries at Rosetta. Their flavor has been corrupted by the food industry, which has flattened them into homogeneity by using their artificial variants. In this dish, though, they add sweetness and texture to the buttery, complexly spiced mole.

This dessert blurs the line between sweet and savory. And it reminds us that the pre-established ideas about how to use raw materials are completely arbitrary.

Pink mole

Serves 4

35 grams butter
12 grams safflower seed butter
25 grams almonds, peeled
25 grams pink pine nuts
25 grams sesame seeds
5 grams pink pepper
1 whole clove
4 leaves dried thyme
330 milliliters milk
35 grams sugar
50 grams beet, peeled and cubed
1.5 grams chipotle peppers, de-veined
20 grams dried hibiscus flowers
70 grams yogurt
160 grams white chocolate

Makes 500 grams

Melt the butter and the oil in a frying pan, then add the almonds. When they start to toast, add the pink pine nuts and the sesame seeds. Let them brown and remove from the heat.

In a pot, combine the pink pepper, the clove, the thyme, the milk, the sugar, the beets, the chipotle pepper, and the hibiscus flowers, first wrapping the hibiscus flowers in a piece of cheesecloth so you can remove them easily when they're done infusing.

Heat the pot, bringing the liquid to a boil. Lower the heat and let it simmer for 5 minutes. Remove from the heat and extract the hibiscus flowers.

Run the mixture through a food processor until everything is fully ground.

Add the previously toasted almonds, pine nuts, and sesame seeds, then grind again until it has the texture of mole.

Transfer the mixture to a bowl, then add the yogurt and the melted white chocolate.

Mix well.

Refrigerate for 2 hours, or until just before use.

Yogurt foam

2 grams gelatin sheets
60 grams heavy cream
25 grams sugar
230 grams yogurt
1 siphon

Makes 300 grams

Hydrate the gelatin with ice.

Heat half the cream and add the sugar. When it dissolves, remove from the heat.

Mix the hot cream with the cold cream. Add the previously hydrated gelatin. Mix well and add the yogurt.

Strain and transfer to the siphon, then close and charge it.

Shake the siphon and refrigerate for at least 2 hours before use.

Caramelized pink pine nuts

70 grams pink pine nuts
30 grams powdered sugar
2 grams cocoa butter

Makes 70 grams

Put the pine nuts and the sugar in a frying pan over medium heat. Cook until the sugar has caramelized and takes on the color of pale caramel.

Pour the mixture into a bowl and add the cocoa butter. Mix well and spread out the mixture on parchment paper.

Hibiscus flower powder

40 grams hibiscus flowers

Makes 20 grams

Dehydrate the flowers in the oven at 40°C.

Crush the flowers in a food processor until they turn to powder.

To Serve

200 grams pink mole
100 grams strawberries
100 grams raspberries
70 grams caramelized pink pine nuts
100 grams yogurt foam
10 grams hibiscus flower powder

Serve the pink mole on half the plate. Arrange the strawberries and raspberries on top of the mole.

Add the caramelized pine nuts on top of the fruit and cover with the yogurt foam.

Sprinkle a little hibiscus powder over the plate.

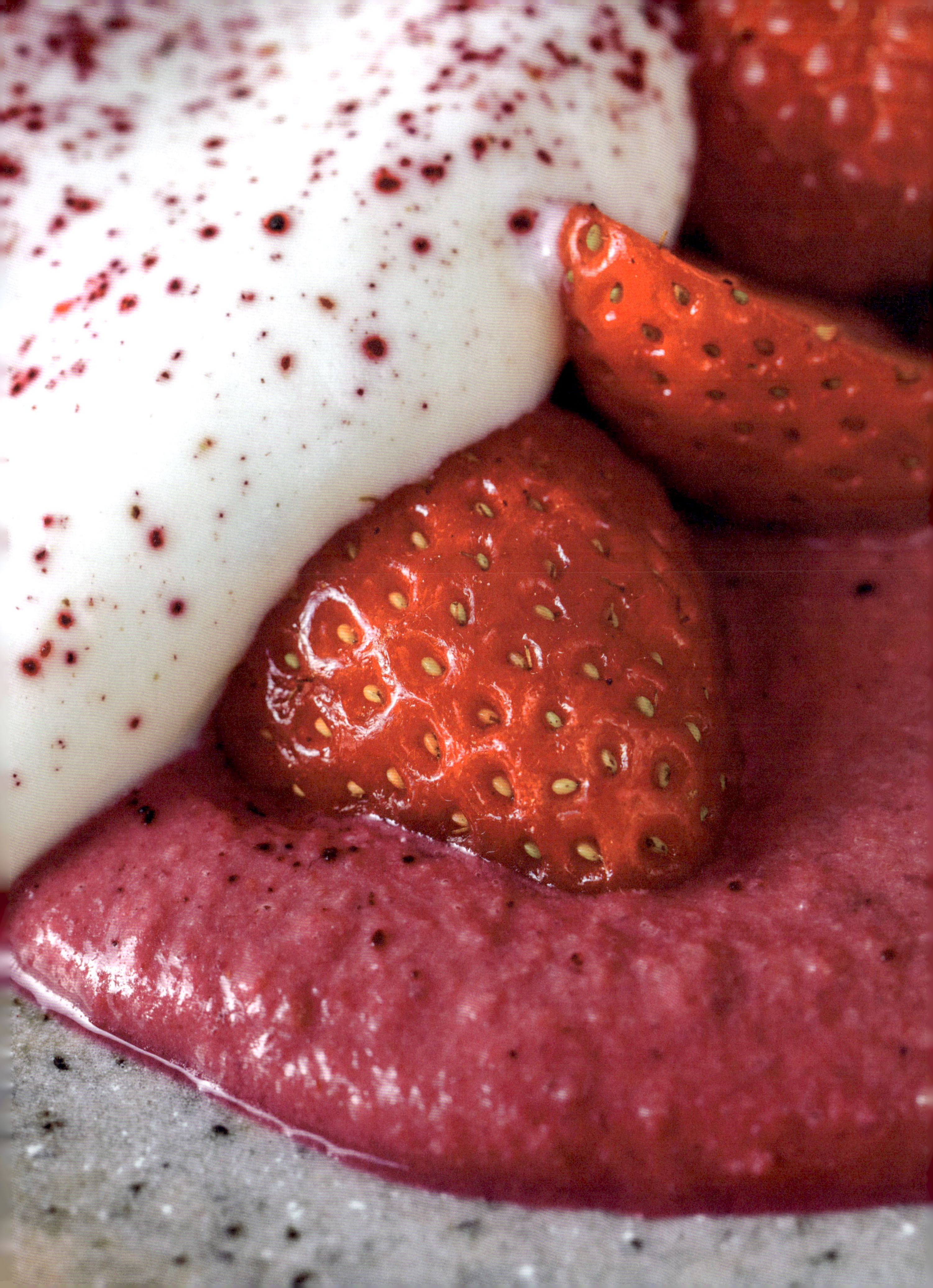

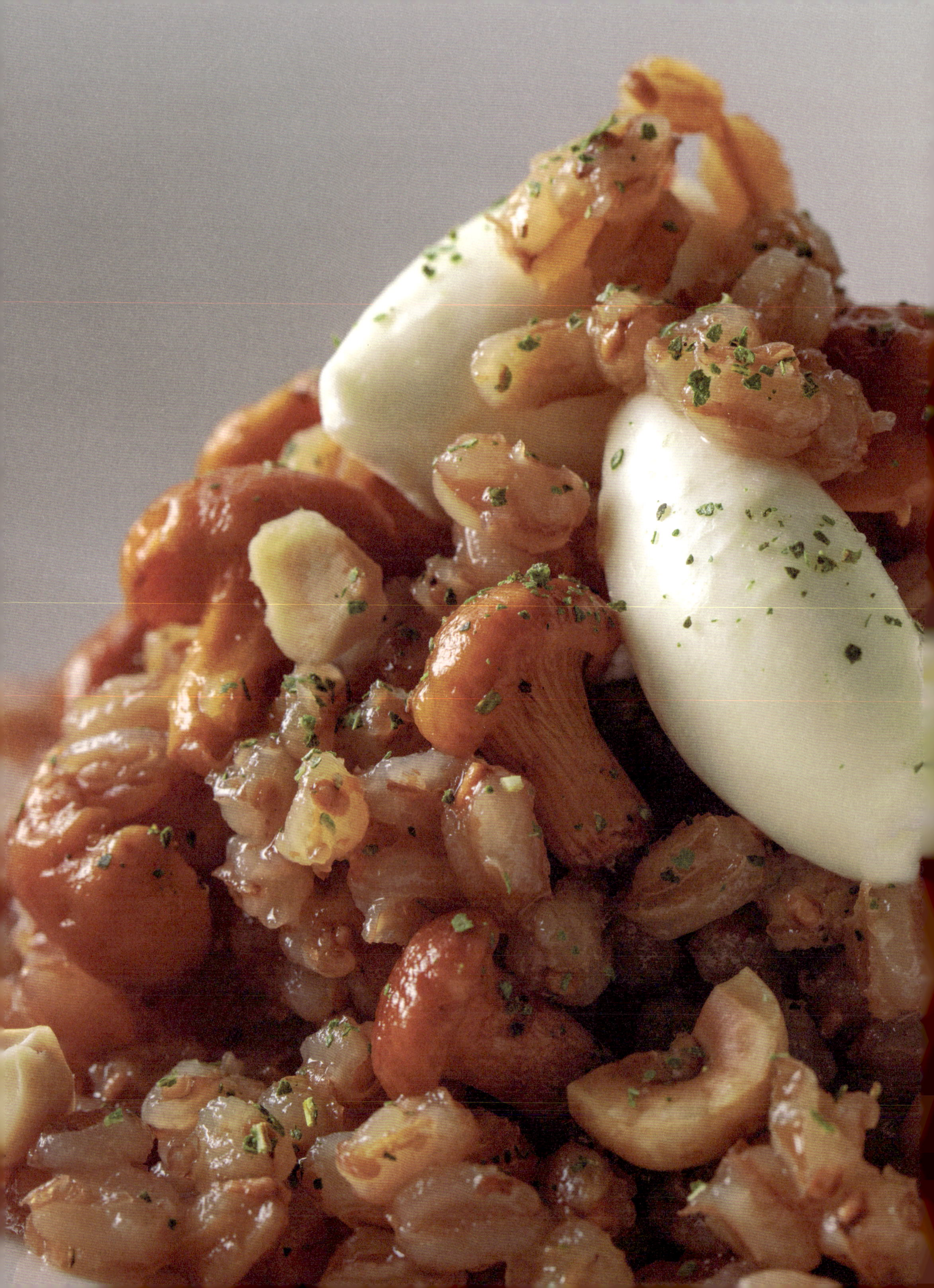

Farro, Tzalancab honey, chantarelles, and goat cheese

In Mexico, hallucinogenic mushrooms are typically preserved in honey so they can be consumed in the off-season. In Italy, white truffles are conserved in acacia honey, which absorbs the scent of the truffle and makes the honey taste exquisite. Inspired by these examples—and because I wanted to preserve some of the wild mushrooms that abound in Mexico during the rainy season—this dessert was born.

The chanterelle mushroom has sweet notes and is firm enough to cook in water and honey without disintegrating. It's a beautiful synergy: the mushroom is suffused with the aroma of the honey and the honey with the aroma of the mushroom. At Rosetta, we use an aromatic honey from the jabín, chaká, and kitinché flowers; it comes from Tzalancab, on the Yucatán Peninsula. This honey is what moistens the farro, one of the longest-cultivated grains, which has a nutty flavor and a solid consistency that isn't easily altered.

Once we have this grain, mushroom, and honey combination, we add mascarpone to balance out the sweetness. We also add hazelnuts, which remind me of the damp areas where mushrooms grow.

Farro with honey

Serves 4

100 grams farro
2.3 liters water
200 grams Tzalancab honey
1 gram salt

Makes 200 grams

Soak the farro in plenty of cold water.

In a pot, heat 300 milliliters of water, the honey, the salt, and the farro, letting it cook until all the water has evaporated and the honey sticks to the farro.

Then add 2 liters of water to finish cooking the farro, pouring in half a liter at a time and waiting for it to be absorbed, until the farro is completely cooked.

Strain and cool by spreading the farro onto a baking sheet.

Chanterelles with honey

250 grams chanterelles
200 grams Tzalancab honey
300 milliliters water

Makes 250 grams

Clean the chanterelles with a damp cloth, removing all dirt and impurities. Trim each stalk, leaving the head and half the stalk.

Combine the water, the honey and the chanterelles in a bowl.

Place this mixture in a pot and cook over low heat for 20 minutes.

Cool in a bowl of ice water to stop the cooking process.

Creamy goat cheese

10 grams Tzalancab honey
20 mililitres water
125 grams goat cheese

Makes 150 grams

Dissolve the honey in water. Add it to the cheese and store in a pastry bag for at least two hours in refrigeration.

Toasted hazelnuts

60 grams hazelnuts

Makes 60 grams

Place the hazelnuts on a baking sheet and bake at 180°C for 8 minutes or until browned.

Let the hazelnuts cool a bit, then peel them with a tea towel, cut them in half, and set aside.

Fig leaf salt

50 grams salt flakes
1 fig leaf

Makes 50 grams

Run the leaf and the salt through a blender until they make a powder.
Lay out the powder on a baking sheet and bake at 40°C until dry.

To Serve

200 grams farro with honey
150 grams creamy goat cheese
200 grams chanterelles with honey
60 grams toasted hazelnuts
8 grams fig leaf salt

Mix the farro with the chanterelles and the hazelnuts. Distribute the mascarpone across the farro. Sprinkle a bit of the fig leaf salt on top.

Nanches, yucca flowers, sour cream, and lemon

The nanche is a fruit I wasn't familiar with until a few years ago. It's used to make popsicles, jams, liqueurs, and not much else. It's the size of a cherry and has a large pit. Little-known and underexplored, it has a lactic flavor I haven't experienced in any other fruit. That's exactly what inspired me to use it. The most demanding and least complacent ingredients are the ones I find most satisfying when we manage to make them shine, for at least two reasons: a neglected product gets recognized and it takes on a new use when mixed with atypical flavors.

Another neglected ingredient, generally unfamiliar to the residents of Mexico's major cities—even though it's been used for hundreds of years—is the yucca flower. Its season is short: it appears in the spring and vanishes with the summer rains. We pickle the flowers in mild vinegar and lemon to prolong their lifespan, remove their bitterness, and preserve their fleshy texture.

These two special ingredients are united by the fattiness of the cream and the lemon's aroma, which act as bridges between the sweetness of the nanche in syrup and the acidity of the pickled yucca flowers.

Serves 4

100 milliliters white wine vinegar
100 milliliters water
4 grams lemon zest
4 yucca flowers

3 grams gelatin sheets
265 milliliters milk
20 grams sugar
2 grams lemon zest
175 milliliters sour cream

Pickled yucca flowers

Makes 4 pieces

Mix the water and the vinegar with the lemon zest. Transfer the mixture to a bowl, along with the yucca flowers. Cover and refrigerate for 12 hours.

Panna cottas

Makes 4 pieces

Hydrate the gelatin in ice water for 10 minutes.

Heat the milk, the sugar, and the lemon zest in a pot to 60°C and remove from the heat.

Make sure the sugar is completely incorporated, then add the previously hydrated and drained gelatin. Mix until the gelatin dissolves.

Add the sour cream and mix until uniform.

Divide the mixture into 4 molds measuring 6.5 centimeters wide by 4 centimeters long.

Cool for 2 hours or until they set.

Endings

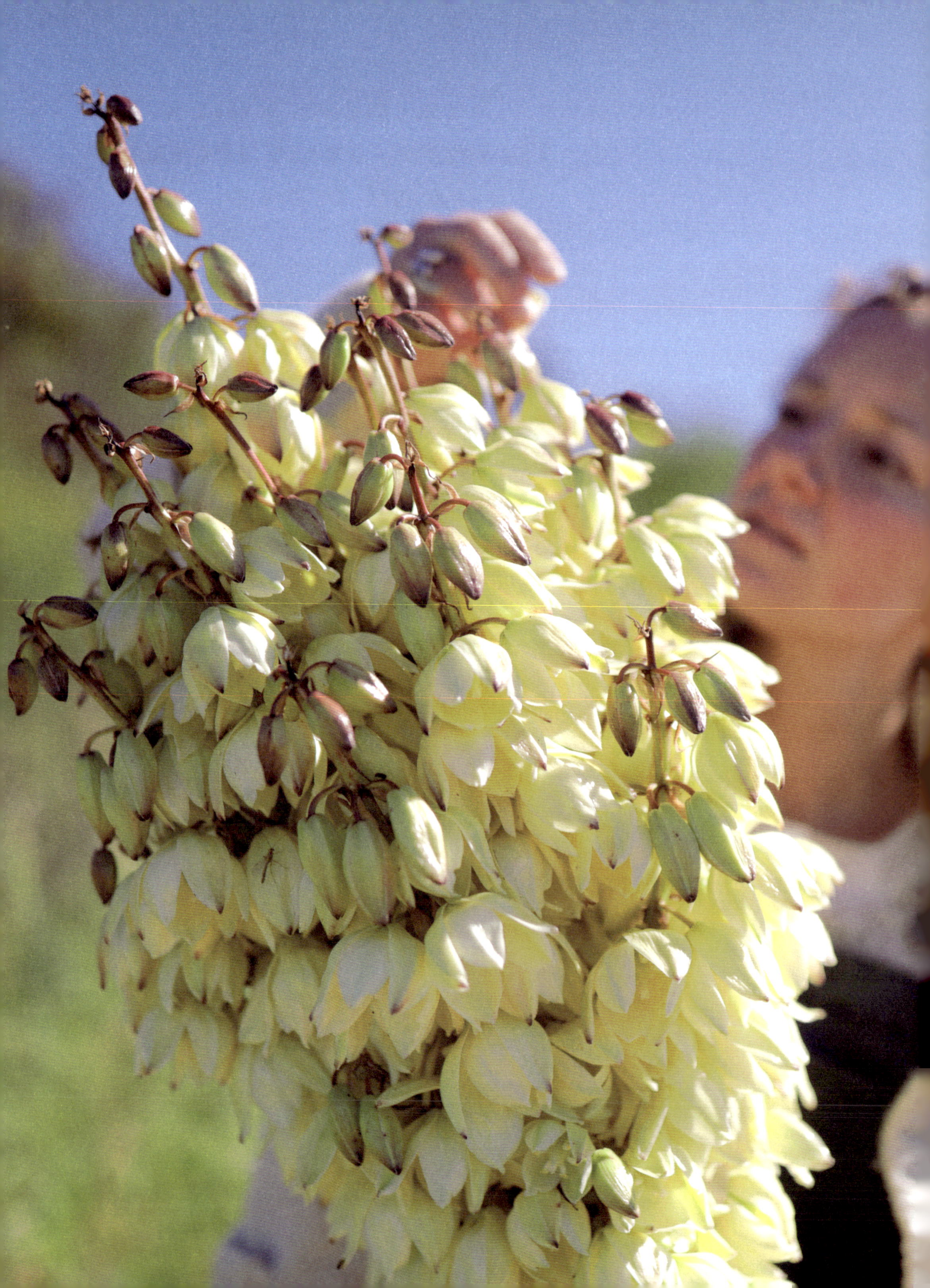

Nanches in syrup

250 milliliters water
30 grams sugar
28 nanches

Makes 28 pieces
　Pit the nanches with a cherry pitter.
　Heat the water and the sugar together to 60°C, remove from the heat, and add the nanches.
　Let sit at room temperature until completely cool.

Lemon ice cream

60 grams fat-free powdered milk
390 milliliters milk
75 grams heavy cream
5 grams lemon zest
145 grams inverted sugar
70 grams sugar
10 grams stabilizer
240 milliliters lemon juice

Makes 1 liter
　Combine the powdered milk with the milk and the cream. Crush with a hand blender, add the lemon zest, and heat to 40°C.
　Mix the inverted sugar and the sugar with the stabilizer and add to the milk. Heat to 85°C, then cool quickly.
　Refrigerate for 6 to 8 hours.
　Add the lemon juice and immediately run the mixture through the ice cream machine until it's as smooth as you like.

Nanche sorbet

500 grams nanche pulp
205 milliliters water
130 grams sugar
2 grams stabilizer
131 grams inverted sugar
30 milliliters lemon juice

Makes 1 liter
　Crush the nanche pulp with the hand blender until you have a light, smooth purée.
　Place the water, the sugar, and the inverted sugar in a saucepan. Heat to 40°C. Then add the stabilizer and heat to 85°C.
　Mix in a bowl all the dry ingredients.
　Put the water in a pot and heat until 40°c. Remove from fire and mix with the dry ingredients with a hand blender. Return to the fire and heat until 85°C.
　Refrigerate for 6 to 12 hours. Crush the mixture with a hand blender and run it through the ice cream machine until it's as smooth as you like.

To Serve

4 panna cottas
28 nanches in syrup
4 infused yucca flowers
120 grams lemon ice cream
120 grams nanche sorbet
4 grams lemon zest

Remove the panna cottas from the molds and place one in the middle of each plate. Around it, serve a spoonful of the nanche syrup.
　Place 3 nanches in syrup on top of the cream and 4 others around it.
　Strip the petals from the flowers and arrange them on top of and around the panna cottas. Add a bit of the ice cream and sorbet on top.
　Add a bit of lemon zest.

Endings

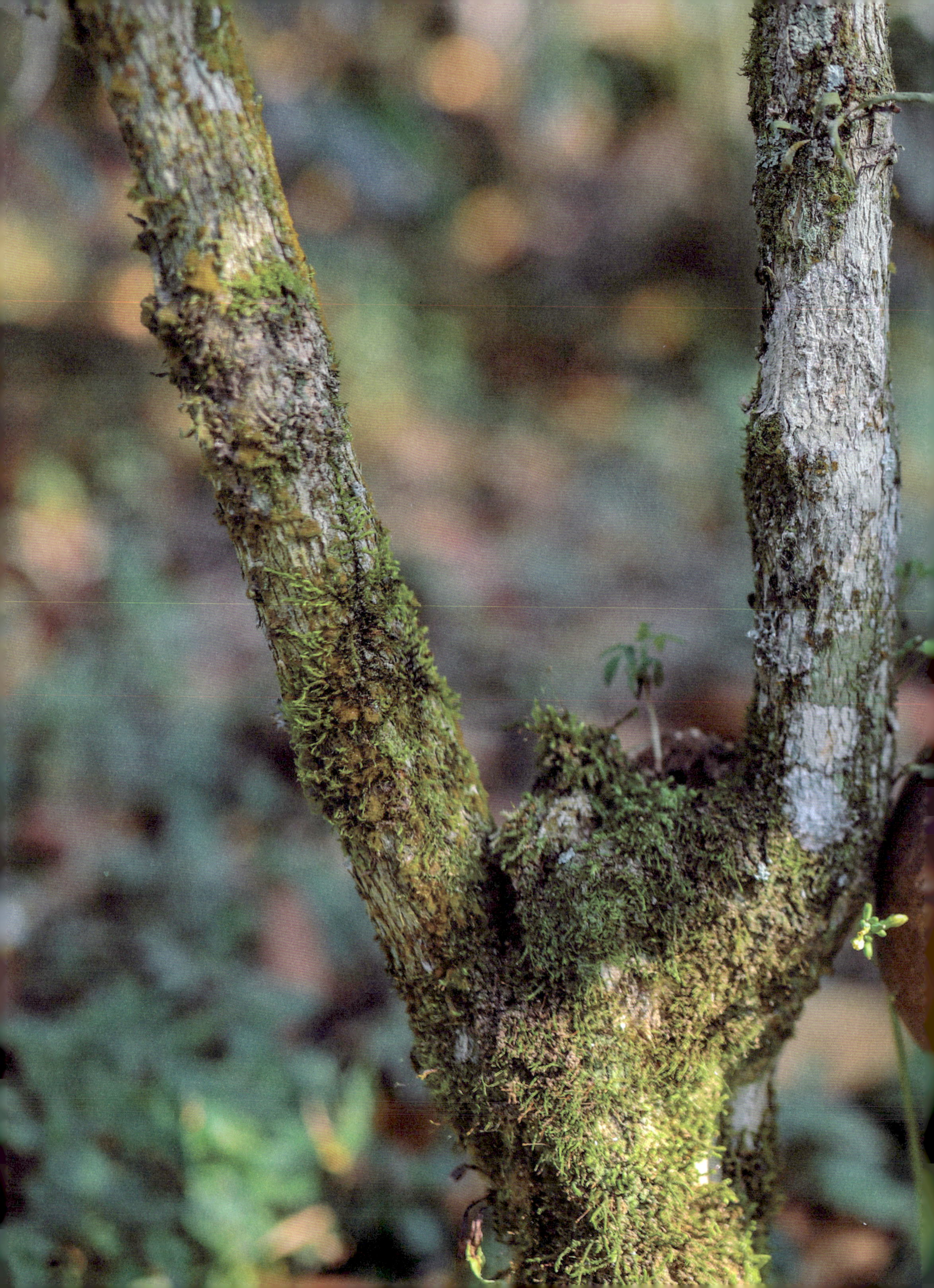

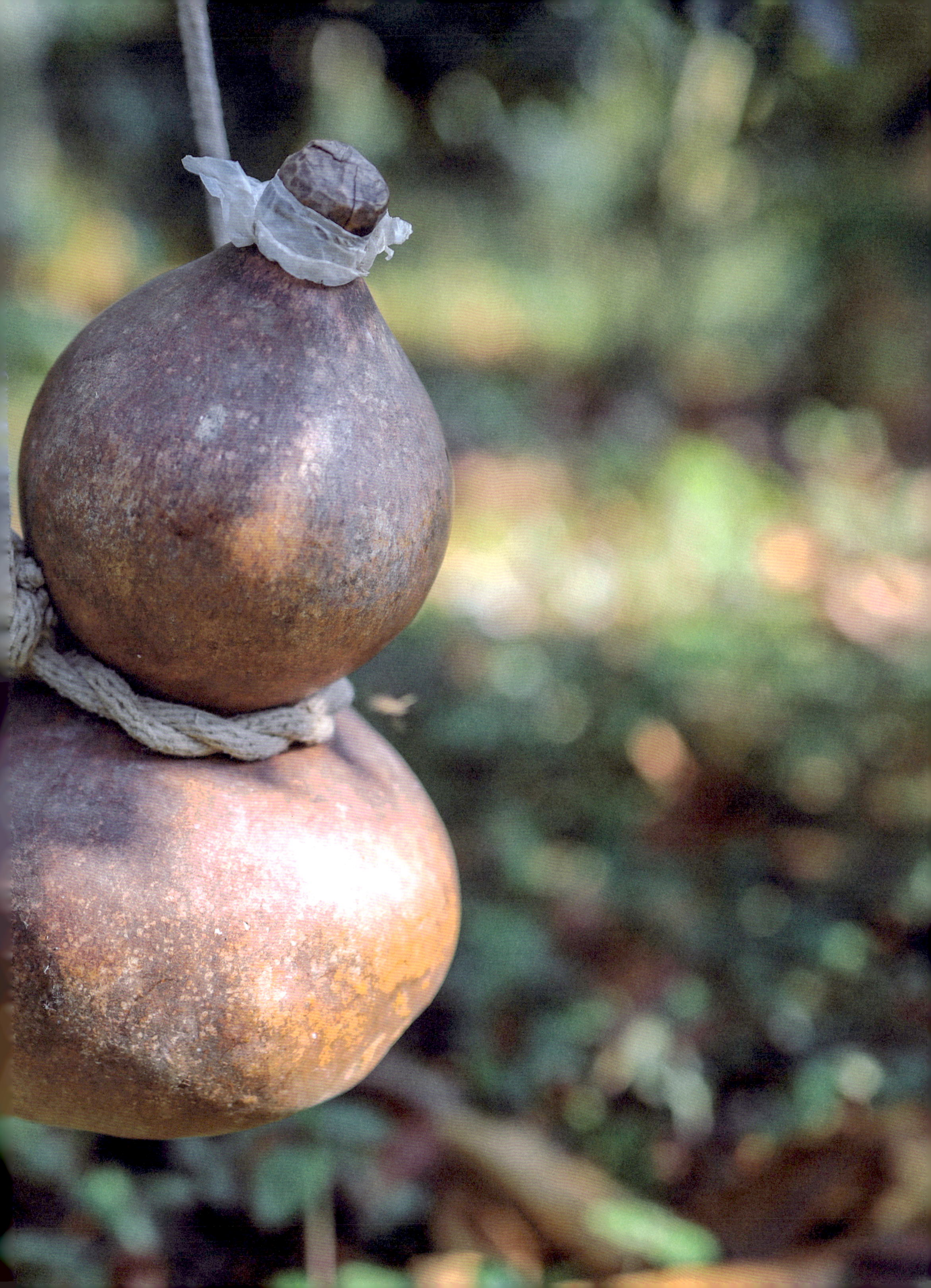

Pulque, prickly pear, xoconostle, and dragon fruit

During my childhood and teenage years, I spent weekends in Velasco, a little town past Real del Monte in the state of Hidalgo. In this village, which didn't have paved roads at the time, was a soccer field surrounded by small convenience stores selling various basic products, as well as pan dulce made in the town bakery's wood-fired oven. At the far end of the village was a garden, a beautiful space full of old trees; the English, who came to the area to mine for silver in the late nineteenth century, had planted this garden. That's where we'd gather with my mother's side of the family.

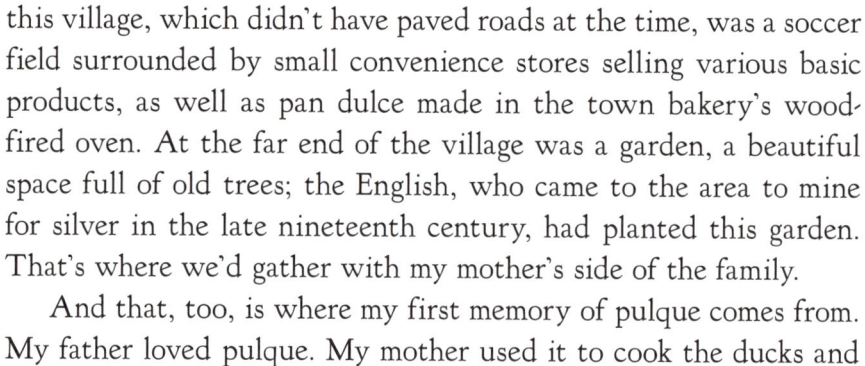

And that, too, is where my first memory of pulque comes from. My father loved pulque. My mother used it to cook the ducks and pigeons my father and brothers hunted in the area. I was a little girl when I tried it for the first time. We were at the tinacal, a place in the fields by the pulque-producing agaves that houses the enormous wooden tubs used to ferment the aguamiel and turn it into pulque. We'd gone there on horseback to buy pulque for the adults. Its viscous consistency surprised me.

Later, I spent a summer in the Metztitlán ravine, doing the catering for Japón, my brother Carlos's first film. There I'd see men and women sitting down beneath the walnut trees for their midday meal. They'd hang their flasks of pulque from the branches of those enormous trees to keep it cool. This drink quenched their thirst and gave them energy to carry on with their workday. It was during those weeks that I started drinking pulque—sometimes plain, sometimes cured with local fruits, sometimes mixed with oatmeal or nuts like a smoothie. Its fermented flavor and its thick, treacly texture reminded me of yogurt and other fermented dairy drinks. I've been a fan ever since.

I thought about serving pulque when I opened Rosetta. It's a tricky drink to stock: it spoils quickly, since it's not pasteurized, and its consistency can be unsettling to a first-time drinker. I discarded the idea. A few years later, at a dinner in Oaxaca, I made this dessert after a visit to the Tlaxiaco market. There I'd found both pulque and multiple varieties of dragon fruit and prickly pears, including jiotillas, a kind of sweet red cactus fruit with tiny seeds

Endings

and delicate skin. When pulque is made into a foam, it loses its viscosity; once red fruits are added, it becomes truly seductive. After that dinner, we started serving this dessert at Rosetta with red prickly pear and xoconostle, which has an acidity that balances out the sweetness of the prickly pear.

Xoconostle sorbet

Serves 4

4 grams gelatin sheets
900 grams xoconostle juice
150 grams sugar
7.5 grams glycerin
22.5 grams inverted sugar
4 grams stabilizer

Makes 1 liter
Hydrate the gelatin sheets in cold water.
Place half the xoconostle juice, the sugar, the glycerin, and the inverted sugar in a saucepan. Mix with a hand blender and heat to 40°C, then add the stabilizer and heat to 85°C. Let cool to 60°C, drain, and add the previously hydrated gelatin to the mixture.
Cool the syrup on top of a bowl of ice to 4°C. Add the rest of the juice.
Let sit for 6 to 12 hours. Crush the mixture with the hand blender and put it through the ice cream machine until it's as smooth as you like.

Pulque foam

75 grams white chocolate
75 grams yogurt at room temperature
90 milliliters pulque
1 siphon

Makes 240 grams
Melt the white chocolate in a double boiler.
Mix and emulsify the chocolate with the yogurt, then add the pulque. Use the hand blender until the mixture is uniform.
Strain, put the mixture into the ½ liter siphon, charge it, shake it, and refrigerate for 2 hours.

Prickly pear ice

50 milliliters water
35 grams sugar
5 milliliters lemon juice
125 grams red prickly pear juice
0.5 grams salt

Makes 200 grams
Heat the water and the sugar to 60°C, remove from the heat, and cool at room temperature. Then add the lemon juice, along with the prickly pear juice and the salt, and freeze the mixture. Mix every 20 minutes until ice flakes appear.

To Serve

2 dragon fruits
120 grams prickly pear ice
180 grams pulque foam
200 grams xoconostle sorbet

Cut one of the dragon fruits into small cubes; slice the other.
Place a dragon fruit slice in the middle of each plate and add two spoonfuls of shaved ice on top. Cover with pulque foam and the cubes of fresh dragon fruit. Place a spoonful of xoconostle sorbet onto each plate.

Chocolate and hazelnut mousse

This crumble is a mousse made with gianduja, which is a chocolate-hazelnut mixture from northern Italy. It was one of the first desserts we served at Rosetta. In those early days, we tended to offer more classic European-style dishes, things that were easy to serve and didn't call for much additional exploration. Little by little, we got more creative and adventurous, and we started coming up with bolder options. Still, this dessert continued to dominate the menu. Even though it was our bestselling dessert, we eventually decided to stop serving it; otherwise, other desserts wouldn't have gotten to make their way into the world.

Hazelnut base

Serves 8

90 grams pailleté feuilletine
58 grams chocolate, 54% cacao
124 grams hazelnut praline

Makes 270 grams

Melt the chocolate in a double boiler, taking care not to heat over 45°C. Temper the praline in a separate double boiler for a couple minutes. Combine the chocolate and the praline, emulsifying with a spatula, then add the pailleté feuilletine.

Transfer the mixture into a stainless steel ring, measuring 24 centimeters in diameter, and cover with acetate paper.

Vanilla pastry cream

300 milliliters heavy cream
300 milliliters milk
1 vanilla pod
70 grams egg yolks
70 grams sugar
30 grams cornstarch

Makes 600 grams

Heat the cream, the milk, and the vanilla. When it reaches a boil, remove from the heat and let infuse for 20 minutes.

Mix the yolks with the sugar, the cornstarch, and a bit of the milk from the infusion. Whisk until it whitens.

Add the egg yolk mixture to the milk and return the milk to the burner.

Heat to 85°C or until the first bubble appears, whisking constantly. Make sure to whisk every part of the surface to prevent lumps from forming.

Transfer the cream to a bowl and cool on top of a bowl of ice as quickly as possible.

Refrigerate until use.

150 grams gianduja
110 grams vanilla pastry cream
150 grams heavy cream
20 grams powdered raw cacao
Hazelnut base

To Serve

Heat the gianduja until it melts at 40°C. Add the pastry cream to the gianduja and emulsify with a hand blender.

Semi-whip the cream. Once the gianduja has cooled to under 15°C, add it to the cream.

Transfer the mixture to a ring, on top of the hazelnut base.

Place the ring in the freezer and store there until the mixture is completely frozen.

Remove the ring. Refrigerate the mousse so that it starts to defrost and soften.

Before serving, sprinkle with raw cacao.

Licorice ice cream, banana, and macadamia nuts

An Italian friend, a woman I worked with in London, was crazy about licorice ice cream. At night, after long and intense shifts at the restaurant, she'd ask the pastry chef for a scoop. I was always surprised by how much she loved the flavor, how it re-energized her somehow. The first time I tried licorice, I honestly wasn't sure whether I liked it or not. It was a completely new flavor to me; there was something fascinating and intriguing about it. It was very sweet, but it wasn't simplistic. Its sweetness was powerful, anise-y, dominant. I forced myself to keep trying it until I was entirely captivated by it.

The strong, sweet flavor of licorice makes it difficult to combine with other ingredients. It goes well with coffee: they're both torrefied and they're equally potent. In fact, at Café Nin—the café we opened in 2015—we use licorice ice cream in our affogato, which is a scoop of ice cream drowned in espresso. The intensity of the licorice is diluted when paired with milk and turned into ice cream, and the bitterness of the coffee goes well with the sweetness of the licorice.

The traditional link between licorice and coffee inspired me to combine it with macadamia nuts and bananas, two ingredients that grow in the same kind of soil and environment as coffee does and which also accompany it nicely. I often make these kinds of flavor associations: one taste leads us to another, forming an endless chain of kindred flavors.

Bananas and macadamia nuts work well in this dessert because the creaminess of both ingredients neutralizes the intensity of the licorice. Seen from another angle, the licorice intensifies the subtle flavors of the bananas and macadamia nuts.

Licorice ice cream

Serves 4

170 grams heavy cream
575 milliliters milk
44 grams fat-free powdered milk
135 grams dextrose
23 grams powdered licorice
6 grams stabilizer
25 grams trimoline

Makes 1 liter

Heat the heavy cream and the milk in a saucepan to 85°C.

Combine the powders in a bowl and add the previous mixture, now hot, along with the trimoline. Mix with a hand blender.

Let the mixture cool, then refrigerate for 4 hours.

Run the mixture through an ice cream machine until it's as smooth as you like.

Macadamia cream

120 grams macadamia nuts
200 milliliters milk
5 grams cornstarch
10 grams egg yolks

Makes 200 grams

Toast the macadamia nuts in the oven for 6 minutes at 180°C.

Heat the milk in a pot to 60°C, then remove from the heat, add the macadamias to the milk, and let sit until completely cool.

Crush the macadamias with a hand blender until completely ground up, then strain and set aside 200 milliliters of the milk.

Mix the cornstarch and the yolks with half of that milk.

Heat the other half of the milk to 50°C, then add the half with the cornstarch and the yolks, whisking constantly.

Cook until the mixture has the consistency of pastry cream. Remove from the heat and cool, placing it on top of a bowl of ice.

Plantain paper

200 grams plantains, peeled
10 grams sugar
15 grams egg whites

Makes 150 grams

Using a hand blender, crush the bananas with the sugar.

Cook in a frying pan, mixing constantly, until the excess water has reduced and you're left with 170 grams of pulp.

Cool to room temperature and add the egg whites, mixing with a spatula. Lay out the mixture as finely as possible onto anti-stick paper.

Bake at 160°C for 4 minutes or until done.

To Serve

2 bananas
200 grams macadamia cream
60 grams toasted macadamias
400 grams licorice ice cream
150 grams plantain paper

Cut the bananas into ½-centimeter slices and place 1 slice on each plate.

With the help of a pastry bag, add the macadamia cream on top of the banana, followed by the toasted macadamia nuts and two spoonfuls of licorice ice cream. Cover with plantain paper.

Barley, olive oil, and lavender

When I was a little girl, my father would drink a hot milk, he'd make with a powder he bought in the United States, which he said was the kind used to make malts there. In those days, in the 1980s, before the North American Free Trade Agreement, you couldn't find US products in Mexico. As a child, I was intensely curious about these mysterious foreign goods.

I'd forgotten that drink my father so enjoyed until a few years ago. Visiting a friend's brewery, I was met with the scent of barley as it cooked. I tasted the broth that gave off that aroma—the liquid that would later become beer—and it tasted like a sweet liquid cereal. Then I asked him if I could try the different kinds of grains he had in his storeroom. In fact, those grains were all the same kind of barley with different degrees of toastedness. There was, I felt, a lot I could explore in the kitchen. This dessert expresses how a grain—barley, in this case—can yield distinct flavor tones depending on how much it's toasted. Every ingredient contains an infinite spectrum of flavors.

This dessert consists of an ice cream made from the very sweetest (or least toasted) barley, and three barley sablés with a range of toastedness. Once cooked, the sablés break apart and are mixed together, which guarantees that no level of toasting predominates. We place the ice cream on top of the sablé bits, drizzling it with a bit of olive oil for a dash of bitterness. Finally, we add a few grains of salt to stress the sweetness of the barley and the caramel taste of the ice cream. And we add a few fresh lavender petals, which break with the sugariness of the barley and that prevent monotony.

Serves 4

Light barley sablés
125 grams light barley
10 grams flax seeds
55 grams brown sugar
1 gram salt flakes
1.5 grams baking powder
1 gram baking soda
50 milliliters water
3 milliliters vanilla extract
50 grams cocoa butter

Two-barley sablés
100 grams light barley
25 grams dark barley
10 grams flax seeds
55 grams brown sugar
1 gram salt flakes
1.5 grams baking powder
1 gram baking soda
50 milliliters water
3 milliliters vanilla extract
50 grams cocoa butter

Dark barley sablés
125 grams dark barley
10 grams flax seeds
55 grams brown sugar
1 gram salt flakes
1.5 grams baking powder
1 gram baking soda
50 milliliters water
3 milliliters vanilla extract
50 grams cocoa butter

Barley ice cream
740 milliliters milk
220 grams light barley
36 grams inverted sugar
80 grams sugar
40 grams fat-free powdered milk
8 grams stabilizer

To Serve
2 light barley sablés
1 two-barley sablé
½ dark barley sablé
200 grams barley ice cream
80 milliliters olive oil
4 grams fresh lavender flowers
1 pinch salt flakes

Light barley sablés

Makes 4 sablés

Run the barley through a food processor until it has the texture of flour.
Repeat the process with the flax.
Combine all the dry ingredients, then do the same with the wet ones.
Heat the cocoa butter a little to soften it and mix it with all the ingredients. Work the mixture with your hands until well combined.
Make 4 balls weighing 70 grams each and place them on a baking sheet. Then press them with your hands to form cookie-shapes, measuring 6 centimeters wide by 1.5 centimeters tall, and freeze them for 20 minutes.
Once cold, bake for 12 minutes at 190°C.
Let cool at room temperature.

Two-barley sablés

Makes 4 sablés
Repeat the steps you followed for the previous sablés.

Dark barley sablés

Makes 4 sablés
Repeat the steps you followed for the light barley sablés.

Barley ice cream

Makes 1 liter
Place the milk in a bowl with the barley and let infuse, refrigerating for 12 hours.
Blend and strain the mixture. Gradually add the inverted sugar, the sugar, the powdered milk, and the stabilizer to the milk, using a hand blender.
Transfer to a saucepan and heat to 85°C, then lower the temperature to 4°C, moving it to a cold container on top of a bowl of ice.
Run the mixture through the ice cream machine until it's as smooth as you like.

To Serve

Each portion of dessert will have ½ light barley sablé, ¼ two-barley sablé, and one-eighth dark barley sablé.
Break all the sablés into uneven pieces, set some to the side. Place the rest in the center of the plate.
Place 50 grams of ice cream on top of them, then add more sablé bits on top of the ice cream.
Use a dessert spoon to make a hollow in the center of the ice cream and pour the olive oil in there. Add the lavender petals and the salt flakes.

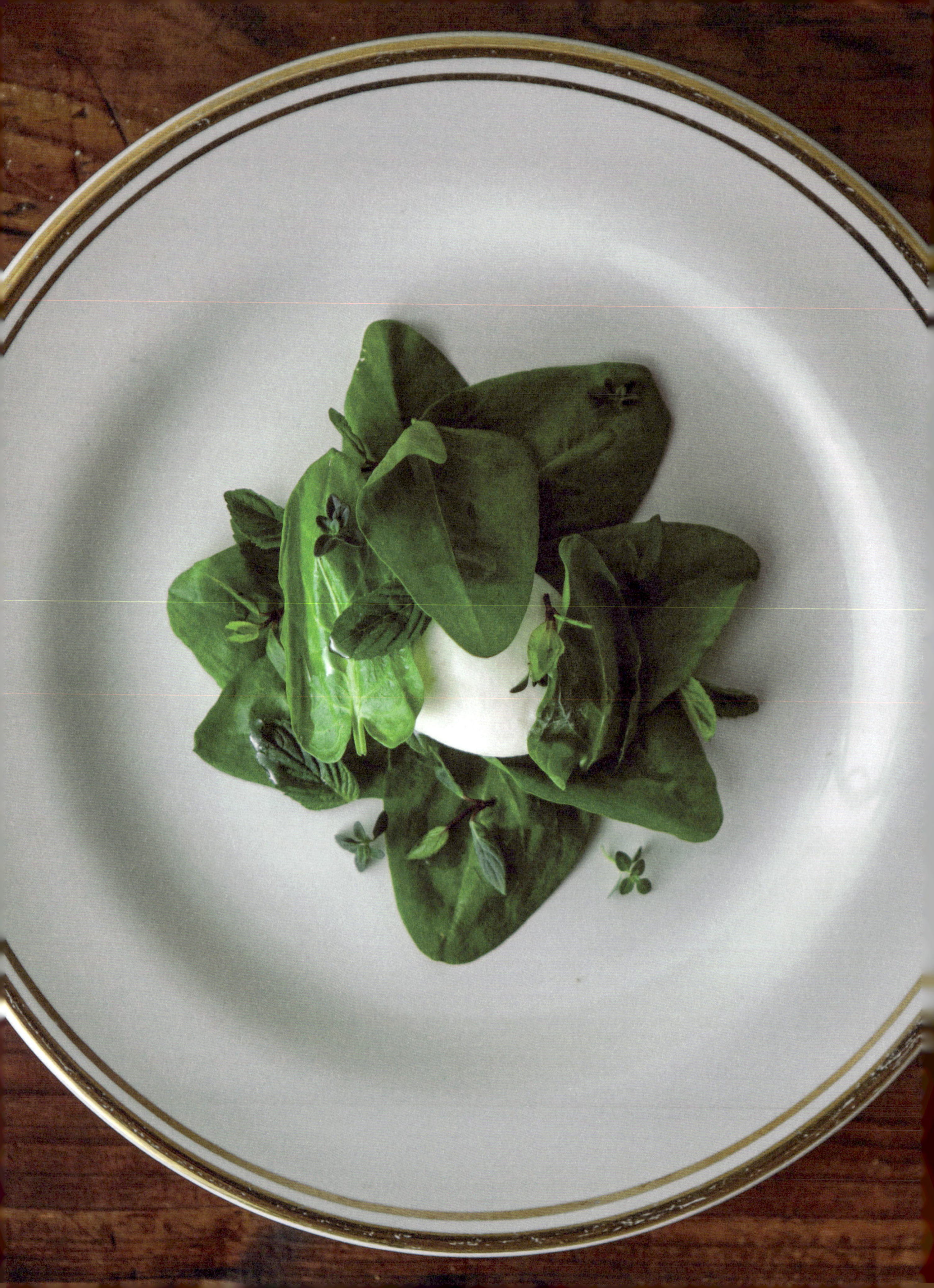

Fresh herbs, olive oil and rosemary ice cream

This dessert was a creative trigger: once we made it, we started delving into light, low-sugar dishes—something many people don't associate with the world of desserts. My dad still insists that I don't actually make desserts; he thinks true desserts have egg yolks and sugar. As for me, I think it's appealing to finish a meal with something that cleanses the palate and is easy to digest. This dessert is exactly that: an ice cream made with a slow rosemary infusion, served on a bed of fresh herbs and dressed with a light syrup (more rosemary and olive oil to tie the herbs and the ice cream together). At first, there wasn't much demand for the rosemary ice cream, but over time it's become one of our most popular desserts.

Rosemary ice cream

Serves 4

110 milliliters milk
100 grams rosemary
340 grams heavy cream
80 grams fat-free powdered milk
300 grams dextrose
140 grams sugar
15 grams stabilizer

Makes 1 liter

Heat the milk to 60°C, remove from the heat, and add the rosemary. Let it infuse, refrigerated, for 24 hours.

Strain the milk, then add the cream, the powdered milk, and the dextrose. Crush to remove all lumps.

Heat the mixture to 40°C. Combine the sugar and the stabilizer, then add them to the milk. Heat again to 85°C. Cool as quickly as possible.

Set aside for 6 to 12 hours so the food stabilizer becomes well hydrated.

Run through an ice cream machine and freeze until use.

Rosemary syrup

170 milliliters water
100 grams sugar
17 grams rosemary
33 grams olive oil

Makes 200 milliliters

Put the water, the sugar, and the rosemary in a pot. Heat over medium heat. When the temperature reaches 98°C, remove it and strain immediately so that the rosemary won't give off a bitter taste.

Stream in the oil while mixing with a hand blender. Set aside until use.

To Serve

20 grams sorrel
6 grams mint
6 grams peppermint
2 grams lemon thyme
10 milliliters olive oil
20 grams rosemary syrup
200 grams rosemary ice cream

Combine the sorrel, the mint, and the peppermint, then arrange this mixture in the center of the plates.

Add the lemon thyme leaves. Dress with the oil and the rosemary syrup. Add rosemary ice cream to each plate, adding a few more drops of olive oil.

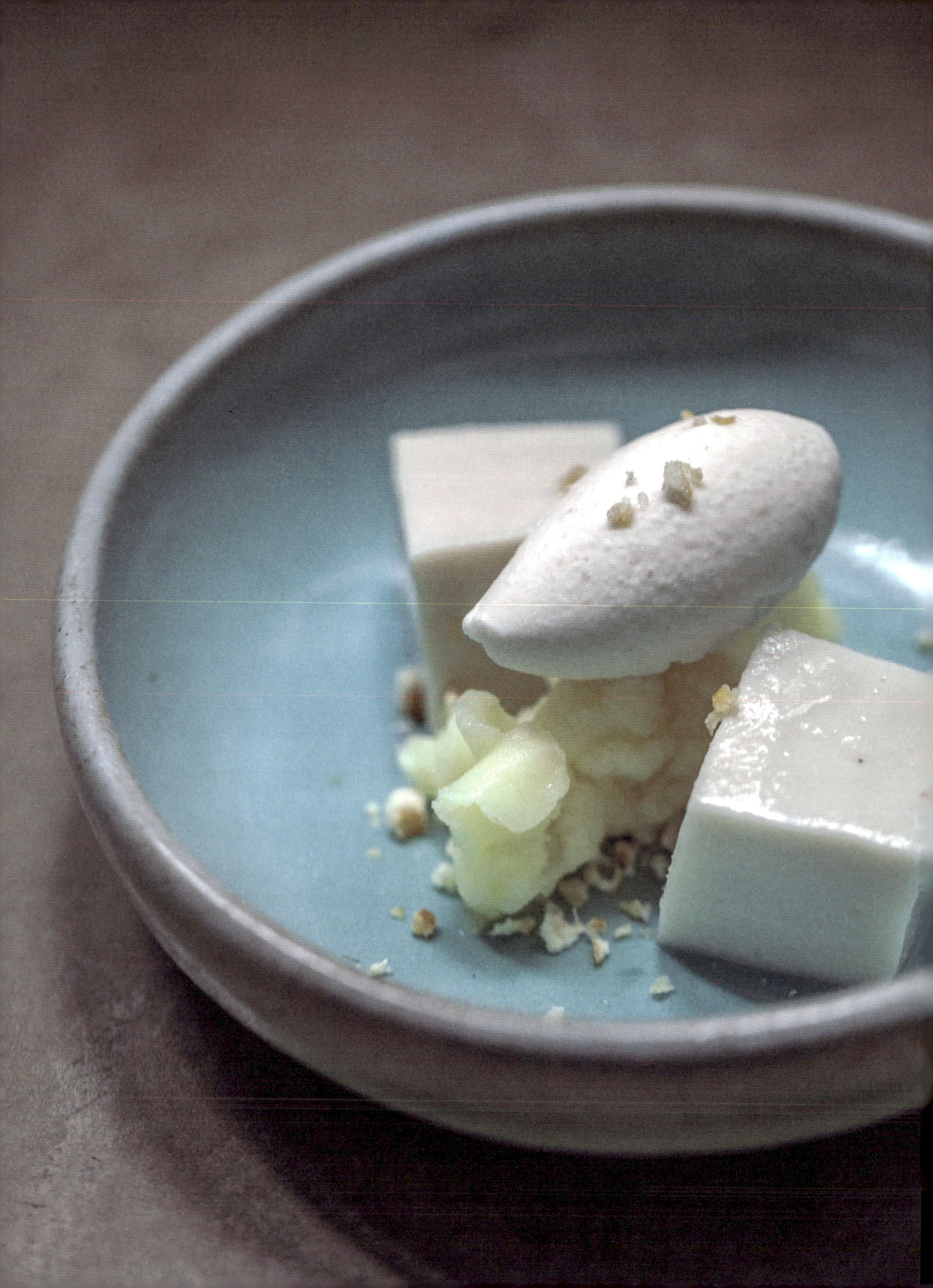

Nicuatole, sweet lime, and macadamia

More and more people are deciding to stop consuming dairy and other animal products. This can be a problem for pastry chefs, but it can also be a compelling challenge. How can we make a dessert that feels creamy without using dairy, egg, or any other animal product, when the dessert world is typically based on those very ingredients?

Nuts and certain grains are good substitutes for the pleasing richness of dairy—which, according to recent recommendations, should not be consumed in excess, as many people struggle to digest it. Using so-called nut "milks," which have a high fat content, is an ideal way to add dairy-free creaminess. The macadamia is among the fattiest nuts. It's also tropical; unlike other nuts, it grows in hot, humid climates.

For this dessert, we lightly toast the macadamia nuts, just enough for their color to change from pale to light-hued. We don't want them to really taste like toasted nuts. But when they start to brown, their oils begin to emerge and their flavor intensifies. Later, we soak them in water for some time to soften them, and then we blend them to make a "milk." We use this macadamia milk both for the sorbet and for the nicuatole.

Nicuatole is a dessert from Oaxaca. Many mistake it for jello because it's made with fruit and because they're similar in consistency. However, there's no gelatin in nicuatole, just corn. Not only does this make it a vegan dessert; it also grants it unique characteristics. It's gelatinous, but not slippery. It's compact, dense, and lumpy like atole, the traditional Mexican corn-based drink.

To make our nicuatole, we use macadamia milk instead of fruit. Macadamia makes the already dense nicuatole even denser. We add sweet lime, which is the subtlest citrus fruit in terms of acidity but the most intense in terms of aroma, to attenuate the oiliness of the macadamia and the density of the corn. What's more, its muted, gentle bitterness emphasizes the flavor of the macadamia.

Macadamia milk

Serves 4

400 milliliters water
170 grams macadamia nuts

Makes 500 grams

Lay out the macadamia nuts on a baking sheet and toast them in the oven at 160°C for approximately 7 minutes.

Add the water to a large saucepan and heat. Once it reaches 60°C, remove from the heat, add the toasted macadamia nuts, and let sit overnight.

Crush in a food processer and strain.

Macadamia nicuatoles

20 grams cornstarch
100 milliliters water
400 milliliters macadamia milk
20 grams sugar

Dissolve the cornstarch in the water and then put it in a pot with the macadamia milk and the sugar. Cook over medium heat, whisking constantly. Once its volume has reduced by half, remove from the heat. Pour the mix into four individual rectangular molds. If you have acetate paper, use it to line the molds, so you'll be able to remove the contents more easily.

Refrigerate for at least 2 hours before serving.

Candied sweet lime

1 sweet lime
150 grams sugar

Makes 20 grams

Peel the sweet lime with a sharp knife and cut the peel into approximately ½-centimeter juliennes. Place the peel in a pot with plenty of water until perfectly covered. Once it reaches a boil, drain the water and repeat this process twice more.

Drain well and add the sugar. Return to heat until the syrup formed reaches 100°C. Remove from the heat, drain, and let cool. Toss the juliennes in sugar and let them dry overnight on a perforated tray.

Sweet lime sorbet

5 grams gelatin sheets
1.2 kilograms sweet lime juice
75 grams sweet lime zest
200 grams sugar
10 grams glycerin
30 grams powdered glucose
5 grams stabilizer

Makes 1 liter

Hydrate the gelatin sheets in cold water.

Place half the sweet lime juice, the sweet lime zest, the sugar, the glycerin, and the glucose in a saucepan; heat to 40°C, then add the stabilizer and heat to 85°C. Let cool to 60°C, drain, and add the gelatin sheets.

Cool the mixture over a bowl of ice. When it reaches 4°C, add the rest of the sweet lime juice.

Let sit for 6 to 12 hours. Crush the mixture with the hand blender and put it through the ice cream machine until it's as smooth as you like.

Macadamia sorbet

2.5 grams gelatin sheets
835 grams macadamia milk
110 grams sugar
10 grams glycerin
25 grams inverted sugar
5 grams stabilizer

Makes 1 liter

Hydrate the gelatin sheets in cold water.

Place half the macadamia milk, the sugar, the glycerin, and the inverted sugar in a saucepan; heat to 40°C, then add the stabilizer and heat to 85°C. Let cool to 60°C, drain, and add the gelatin sheets.

Place the mixture on a bowl of ice to cool quickly. When it reaches 4°C, add the rest of the macadamia milk.

Let sit for 6 to 12 hours. Crush the mixture with the hand blender and put it through the ice cream machine until it's as smooth as you like.

To Serve

4 macadamia nicuatoles
200 grams sweet lime sorbet
120 grams macadamia sorbet
12 grams candied sweet lime

Remove each nicuatole from its mold and cut in half to obtain 2 cubes.

Serve the sweet lime sorbet and the nicuatole beside it. On top, serve the macadamia sorbet and the candied sweet lime.

Melipona honey, pollen, and chamomile

Unlike European bees, Melipona or Scaptotrigona mexicana bees—which are stingless—produce a liquid honey with a fresh, bittersweet, and mentholated flavor. Most Melipona bees are found on the Yucatán Peninsula. The Maya domesticated them in the pre-Columbian era and have used them ever since in their communities, not only as a food source but also for medicinal purposes.

Melipona bees produce very little honey. As a result, this honey has been pushed into the background in recent years; today, this species is in danger of extinction.

With its lightly acidic flavor, the Melipona honey in this dish contrasts with the sweetness of the pollen. The chamomile adds a floral note to the dessert. What I like about this combination, besides the taste, is that it fosters a sense of well-being. It's a light dessert, but it's still pleasingly sweet.

Serves 4

Chamomile apples

125 milliliters water
3 grams chamomile
100 grams green apples, peeled

Makes 100 grams

Heat the water to 80°C, remove from the heat, and add the chamomile. Let infuse for 15 minutes. Strain and let cool.

Dice the apple into small cubes and submerge them in the chamomile infusion for 24 hours.

Melipona honey jello

1.5 grams gelatin sheets
65 grams Melipona honey
65 milliliters water

Makes 130 grams

Hydrate the gelatin sheets in cold water.

Heat the water to 60°C, remove from the heat, and add the previously drained gelatin.

Mix well until dissolved, then add the honey all at once.

Pour into a bowl and refrigerate until it sets.

Melipona honey foam

1.5 grams gelatin sheets
130 milliliters water
70 grams Melipona honey
50 milliliters heavy cream
1 siphon

Makes 120 grams

Hydrate the gelatin sheets in ice water.
Heat the water to 60°C, remove from the heat, and add the previously drained gelatin.
Mix well until dissolved, add the honey all at once, and mix again. Then add the cream, strain, and pour into a siphon.
Close it, charge, shake, and refrigerate for at least 2 hours before use.

Pollen ice cream

190 milliliters milk
40 grams heavy cream
75 grams sugar
50 grams dextrose
35 grams fat-free powdered milk
8 grams stabilizer
20 grams pollen
500 grams yogurt

Makes 1 liter

Place the milk, the cream, the sugar, the dextrose, and the powdered milk in a saucepan. Heat to 40°C, then add the stabilizer and the pollen and heat to 85°C.
Cool by placing the mixture on a bowl of ice until the temperature drops to 4°C, then mix with the yogurt.
Crush the mixture with a hand blender, strain, and run through the ice cream machine until it's as smooth as you like.

To Serve

100 grams chamomile apples
80 grams Melipona honey jello
200 grams pollen ice cream
100 grams Melipona honey foam
3 grams powdered chamomile
3 grams powdered pollen

Drain the apples and divide them into 4 deep dishes.
Use a coffee spoon to distribute pieces of honey jello around the apple.
Serve 50 grams of pollen ice cream over the apple on each plate. Cover the ice cream with honey foam.
Scatter the chamomile and the pollen over the honey foam.

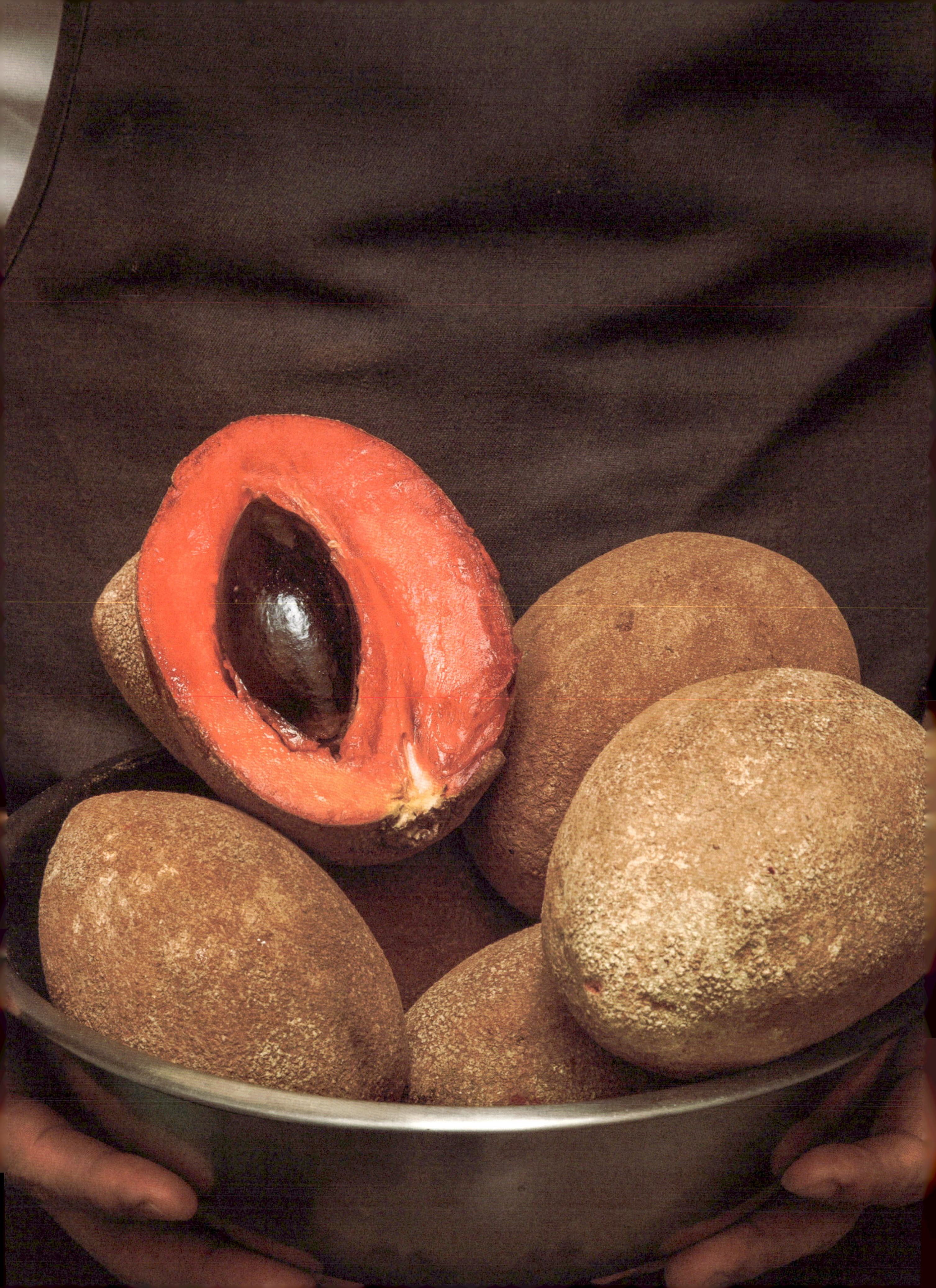

Mamey, pixtle, and taxcalate

The mamey is a generous fruit: its orange pulp is sweet and creamy, and its large pit tastes like bitter almond. This pit is known as pixtle. It's often used in beauty products, although it appears in cooking, too. Once, eating in a Oaxacan market, I realized it was the ingredient that perfumes and creates the foam in tejate, a refreshing corn- and cacao-based drink consumed in the middle of the day.

We use pixtle to infuse the cream accompanying the mamey. (The infusion process must be brief; otherwise the pit's bitter taste overpowers the liquid.) The mamey pulp is made into shavings. We use what couldn't be shaved to make a vibrant sorbet. This way, we make use of the entire fruit, wasting nothing. In addition, we make a crumble out of taxcalate, another corn and cacao drink that resembles tejate. Taxcalate is from Chiapas, and it also contains achiote and cinnamon.

This dessert emerged, then, from tejate and taxcalate, two drinks that have existed in Mexico since pre-Hispanic times. Culinary tradition isn't a thing of the past. It lives among us, which means it's also constantly changing. This is especially evident in countries like Mexico, where the past is always present.

Serves 4

1 mamey

Mamey shavings

Makes 160 grams
Cut the mamey in the finest sheets you possibly can.
Refrigerate between sheets of plastic until use.

Taxcalate crumbs

20 grams flour
30 grams taxcalate
14 grams brown sugar
1 pinch salt
1 pinch powdered cinnamon
38.5 grams butter at room temperature

Makes 100 grams
Combine all dry ingredients in a bowl. Add the butter to the dry ingredients and mix with your hands. Once everything is mixed together, place pieces of the mixture on a baking sheet covered with anti-stick paper and freeze for 2 hours or until hardened.
Bake at 180°C for 24 minutes, until the color of the dough starts to take on a toasted hue. Move them around with a spatula every 6 minutes so that the pieces start to break apart into crumbs and can cook uniformly.
Remove from the oven and let cool at room temperature.

Endings

Pixtle foam

2 grams gelatin sheets
75 milliliters milk
180 grams heavy cream
26.5 grams pixtle, grated
12 grams sugar
7.5 grams inverted sugar
1 siphon

Makes 300 grams

Hydrate the gelatin in ice water.

Place the milk and the cream in a saucepan with the pixtle and heat at 60°C. Remove from heat and let infuse for 15 minutes.

Using a hand blender, crush the mixture so that the pixtle lets off more flavor.

Strain and return the milk to the saucepan on the burner. Add the sugar and the inverted sugar. Re-heat to 60°C again and remove from the heat.

Add the previously hydrated gelatin, strain, and transfer the liquid to the siphon.

Close and charge the siphon. Shake and refrigerate for a couple hours before use.

Mamey sorbet

390 grams mamey pulp
240 milliliters water
100 grams sugar
65 grams inverted sugar
3 grams stabilizer

Makes 1 liter

Mix the mamey pulp with 140 grams of water and crush with the hand blender until you obtain a light, smooth purée.

Put the rest of the water into a saucepan, then add the sugar and the inverted sugar. Heat to 40°C, add the stabilizer, and heat to 85°C.

Cool by placing the mixture onto a bowl of ice until it reaches 4°C, then mix it with the mamey.

Let sit for 6 to 12 hours. Crush the mixture with the hand blender and put it through the ice cream machine until it's as smooth as you like.

To Serve

60 grams taxcalate crumbs
160 grams mamey shavings
200 grams mamey sorbet
250 grams pixtle foam

Place some crumbs in the center of each plate. On top, serve 50 grams of mamey sorbet and cover it with pixtle foam.

Add the mamey shavings on top of the foam. Sprinkle with more crumbs.

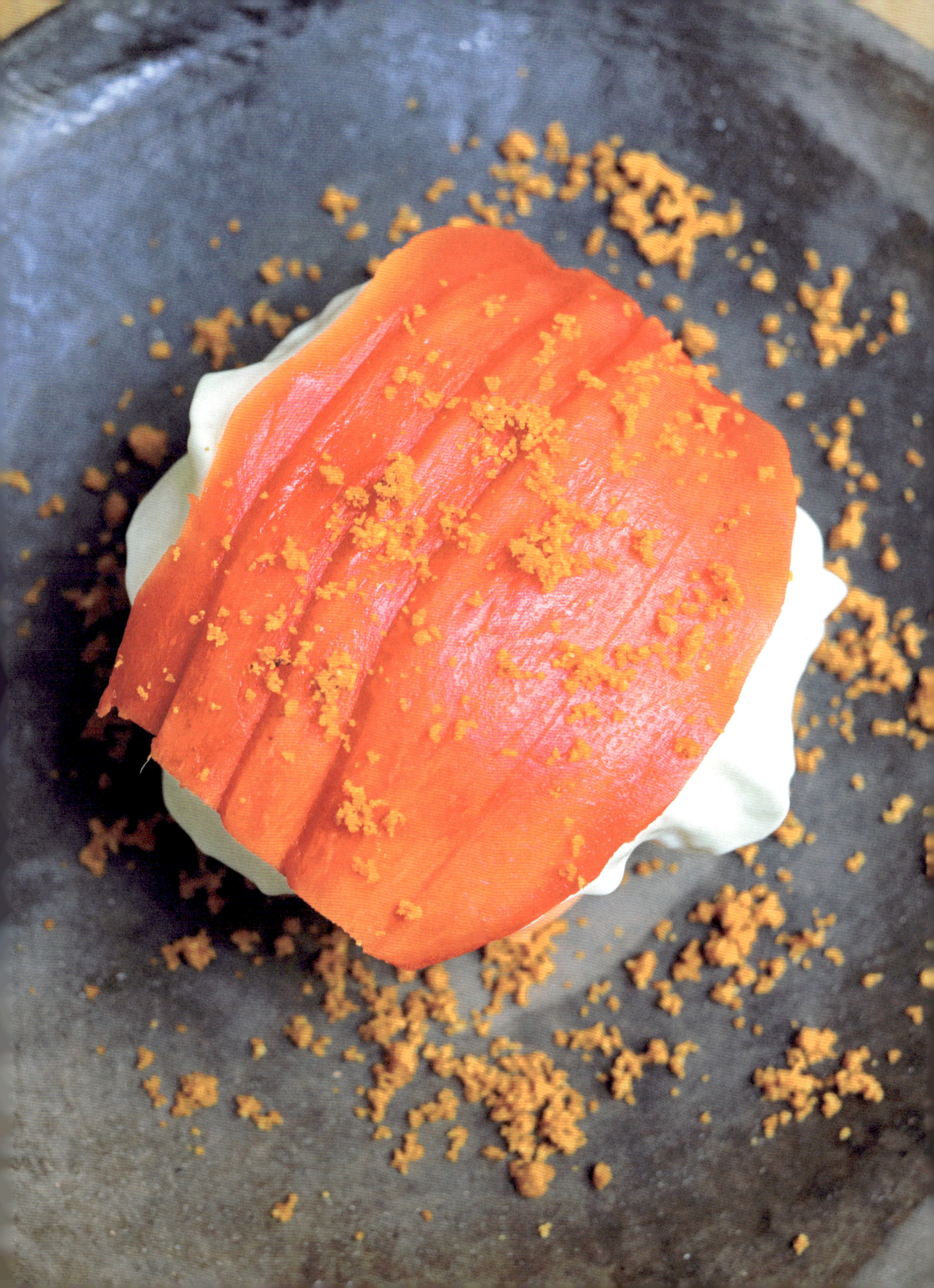

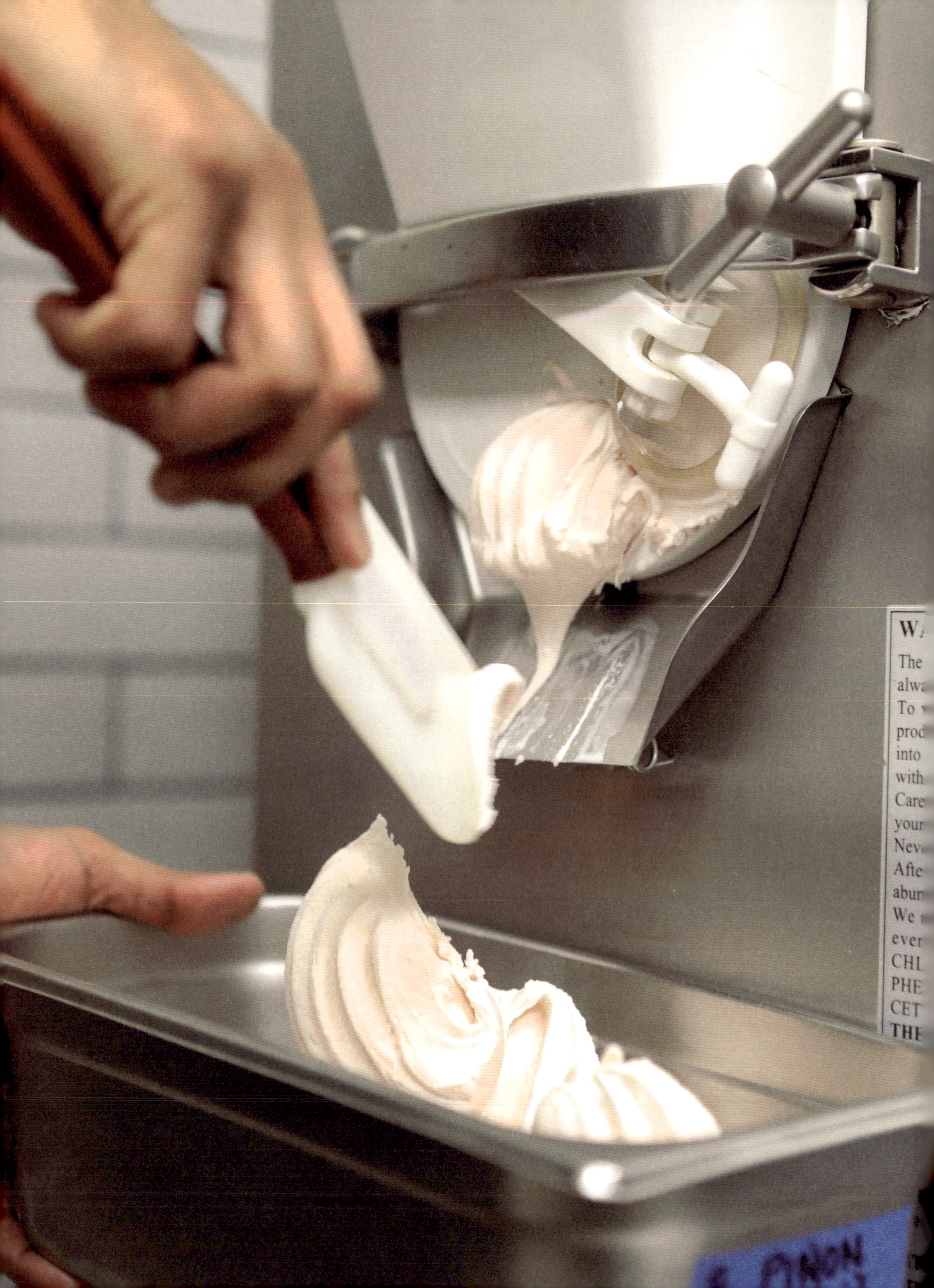

Ice creams and sorbets

At Rosetta, we often use ice creams and sorbets in desserts and certain dishes as a way to refresh them and temper their sweetness. We also like to serve them separately, because they offer a light way to end a meal and cleanse the palate. While we prepare them with many different ingredients (fruits, nuts, spices), I think the herb-based ones are the most special of all—precisely because, in addition to being cold, they're refreshing and they aid digestion.

We generally avoid making high-sugar ice creams and sorbets. The minimal sugar we do add helps achieve a creamy texture and avoid crystallization. Besides the health benefits of consuming less sugar, it's easier to distinguish among the flavors of different ingredients when the sugar content is low.

PIÑON
7.09.17

Sorbet
3.0

S. Piñon
28/09/17

S. Piñon
4.09.17

Sorbete Cocoa
05/09/19

H. Cacahuate
7.09.17

H. CARDAMOMO
6.09.17

Lemon verbena ice cream

555 milliliters milk
170 milliliters heavy cream
40 grams fat-free powdered milk
35 grams sugar
155 grams dextrose
7 grams stabilizer
205 grams yogurt
65 grams fresh lemon verbena

Makes 1 liter

Combine the milk, the heavy cream, the powdered milk, and the dextrose in a bowl. Whip with a hand blender until completely mixed.

Transfer the mixture to a saucepan over medium heat. Once it reaches 40°C, add the sugar and the stabilizer and mix continuously with a hand blender. Once it reaches 85°C, remove from the heat and lower the temperature to 4°C, then place it on a bowl of ice.

Add the yogurt and mix with the hand blender until uniform.

Transfer the mixture to a bowl, cover with plastic wrap (the plastic should touch the surface), and refrigerate for at least 8 hours.

Add the fresh lemon verbena to the mixture and crush with the electric blender.

Strain and run the mixture through an ice cream machine until it's as smooth as you like.

Lovage ice cream

580 milliliters milk
50 grams lovage
70 grams inverted sugar
105 grams sugar
7 grams stabilizer
210 grams yogurt

Makes 1 liter

Place the milk and the lovage in a bowl and let infuse, refrigerating for 12 hours.

Blend and strain the mixture. Add the milk, the inverted sugar, the sugar, and the stabilizer, then mix with a hand blender to remove all the lumps.

Transfer the mixture to a saucepan and heat to 85°C. Cool it off by placing it on top of a bowl of ice until the temperature drops to 4°C.
Add the yogurt and mix with the hand blender until uniform.

Run the mixture through an ice cream machine until it's as smooth as you like.

Avocado leaf ice cream

555 milliliters milk
40 grams avocado leaves
100 grams inverted sugar
100 grams sugar
6.5 grams stabilizer
200 grams yogurt

Makes 1 liter

Place the milk and the avocado leaves in a bowl and let infuse, refrigerating for 12 hours.

Blend and strain the mixture. Add the milk, the inverted sugar, the sugar, and the stabilizer, then mix with a hand blender to remove all the lumps.

Transfer the mixture to a saucepan and heat to 85°C. Cool it off by placing it on top of a bowl of ice until the temperature drops to 4°C.
Add the yogurt and mix with the hand blender until uniform.

Run the mixture through an ice cream machine until it's as smooth as you like.

Fig leaf ice cream

555 milliliters milk
70 grams fig leaves
171 grams heavy cream
40 grams fat-free powdered milk
70 grams sugar
155 grams dextrose
7 grams stabilizer

Makes 1 liter

Place the milk and the fig leaves in a bowl and let infuse, refrigerating for 12 hours.

Blend and strain the mixture. Add the milk, the heavy cream, the powdered milk, the sugar, the dextrose, and the stabilizer, then mix with a hand blender to remove all the lumps.

Transfer the mixture to a saucepan and heat to 85°C. Cool it off by placing it on top of a bowl of ice until the temperature drops to 4°C. Add the yogurt and mix with the hand blender until uniform.

Run the mixture through an ice cream machine until it's as smooth as you like.

Ginger ice cream

565 milliliters milk
175 grams heavy cream
70 grams sugar
65 grams inverted sugar
50 grams fat-free powdered milk
5 grams stabilizer
25 grams fresh ginger
80 grams candied ginger

Makes 1 liter

Put the milk, the cream, the sugar, the inverted sugar, and the powdered milk in a saucepan. Heat to 40°C and add the stabilizer. When the temperature rises to 85°C, remove from the heat.

Peel and cube the fresh ginger, then poach it in hot water.

Cube the candied ginger in the same way.

Add both gingers to the previous mixture and refrigerate for 6 to 12 hours.

Strain the mixture and set aside the ginger in a bowl. Using a hand blender, crush the ginger with a bit of the liquid mixture. Add it to the rest of the mixture and strain.

Run the mixture through an ice cream machine until it's as smooth as you like.

Pink pine nut sorbet

200 grams pink pine nuts
800 milliliters water
5 grams gelatin sheets
135 grams sugar
5 grams stabilizer
20 grams inverted sugar

Makes 1 liter

Toast the pine nuts in the oven for 5 minutes at 180°C and heat the water. Once toasted, add the pine nuts to the hot water and let sit for 30 minutes.

Blend the previous mixture for 10 seconds and strain.

Hydrate the gelatin sheets in cold water.

Combine half the pine nut water, the sugar, and the inverted sugar in a saucepan. Heat to 40°C, add the stabilizer, and heat to 85°C. Let cool to 60°C, drain, and add the previously hydrated gelatin.

Cool on top of a bowl of ice until the temperature drops to 4°C. Add the rest of the pine nut water to the previous mixture.

Let sit for 6 to 12 hours. Mix with a hand blender, then run the mixture through an ice cream machine until it's as smooth as you like.

Endings

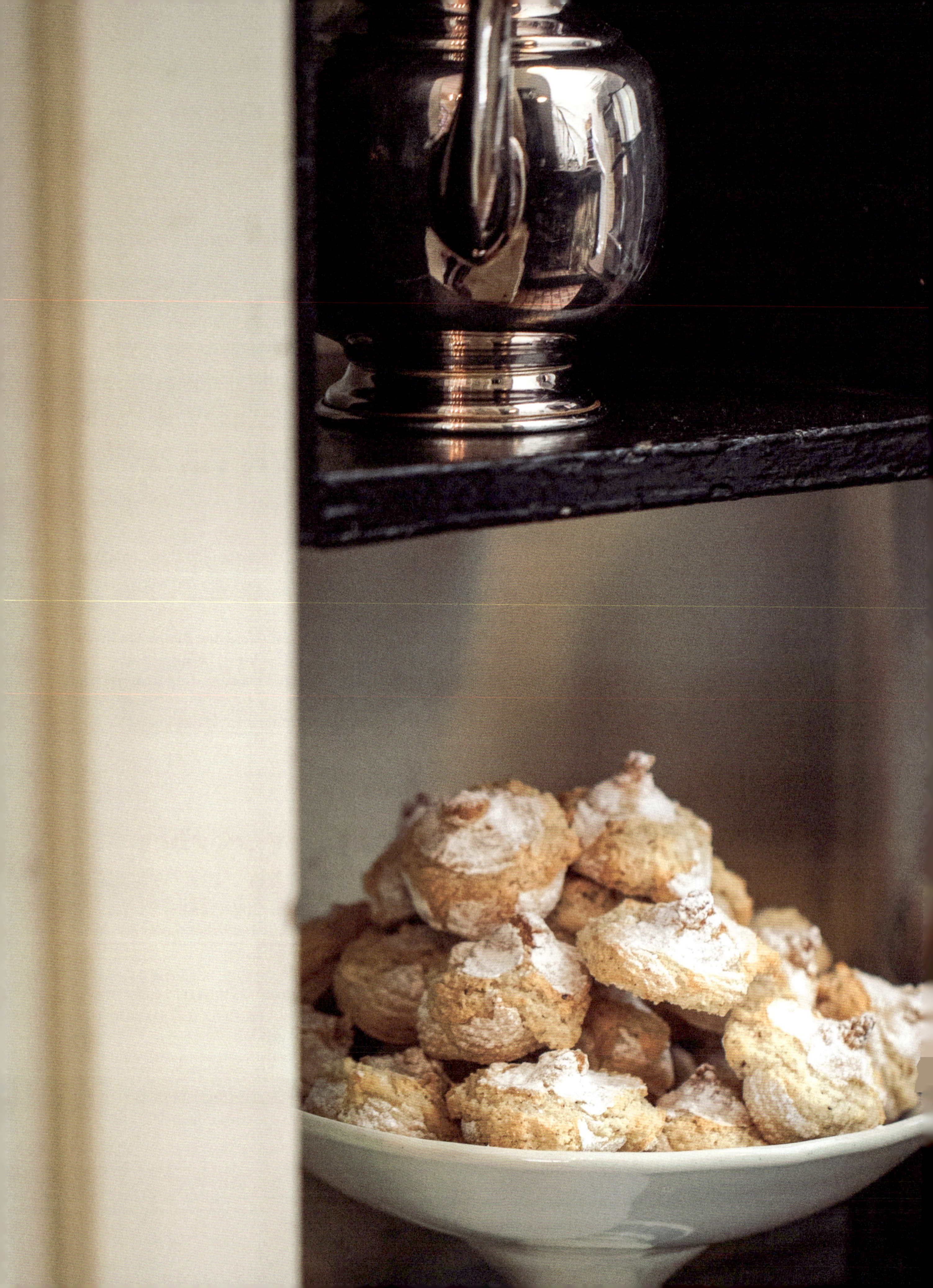

Coffee

Coffee is an example of the tragedy faced by so many Mexican products. Mexico is a country with a long coffee-growing tradition, diverse and enormous regions suitable for its cultivation, and vastly knowledgeable farmers who specialize in the process. Nonetheless, for both economic and cultural reasons, it's sometimes difficult to find good coffee in Mexican restaurants. We cooks can foster the consumption of local, high-quality coffee, sustainably grown by small-scale producers who are paid fairly for their work. At Rosetta (and at our bakery, La Panadería), we serve Mexican coffee from the coffee plantations in Pacho Viejo, a small town in the state of Veracruz, which is about 1,200 meters above sea level and has a warm, humid climate. We buy it from Artemio Zapata and his family, who carry out the entire process without the use of machinery: from growing the coffee to harvesting, selecting, cleaning, and drying the beans. They toast the beans every two weeks to maintain their freshness and flavor. And we grind them just before preparing a cup of coffee.

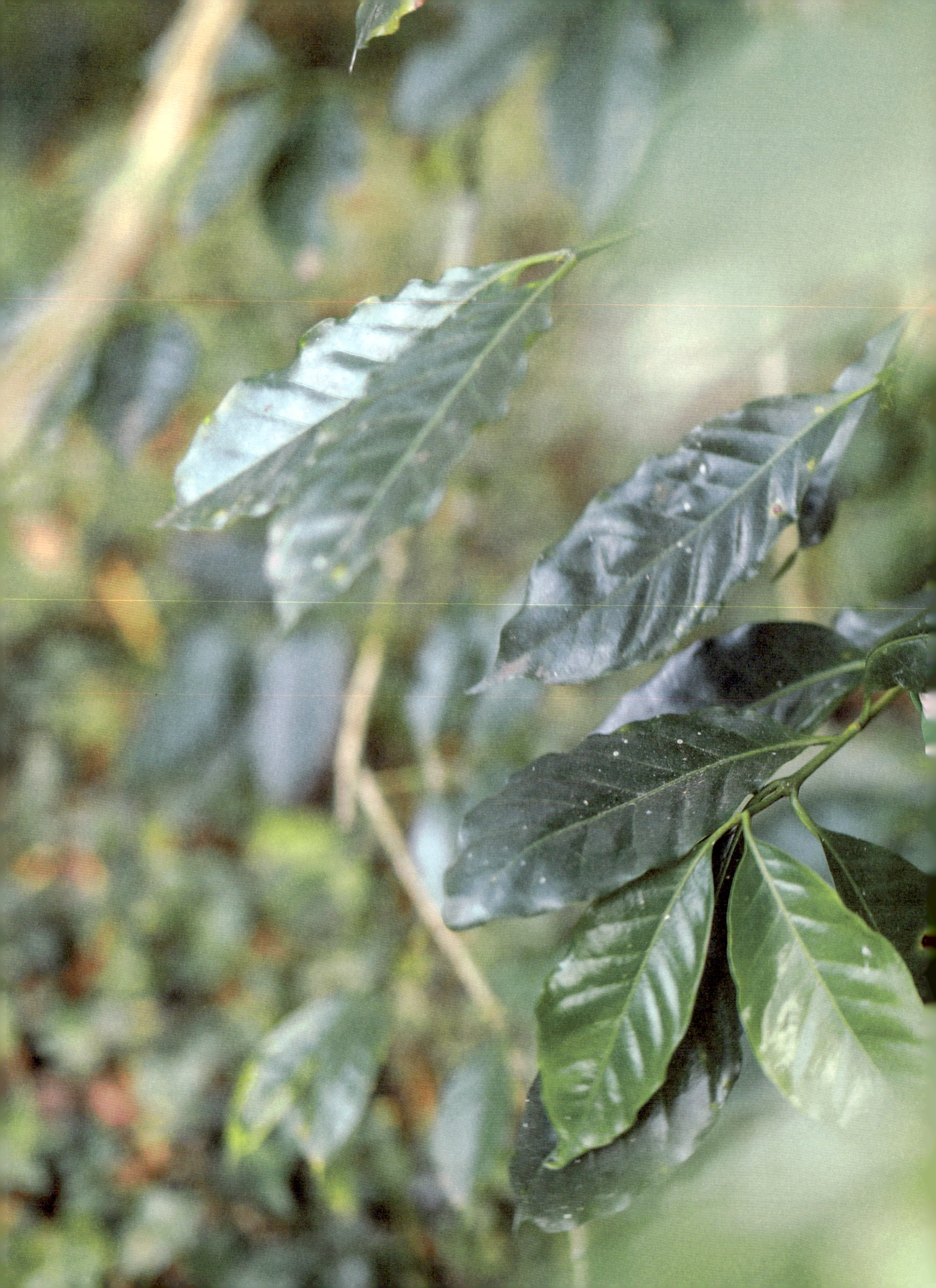

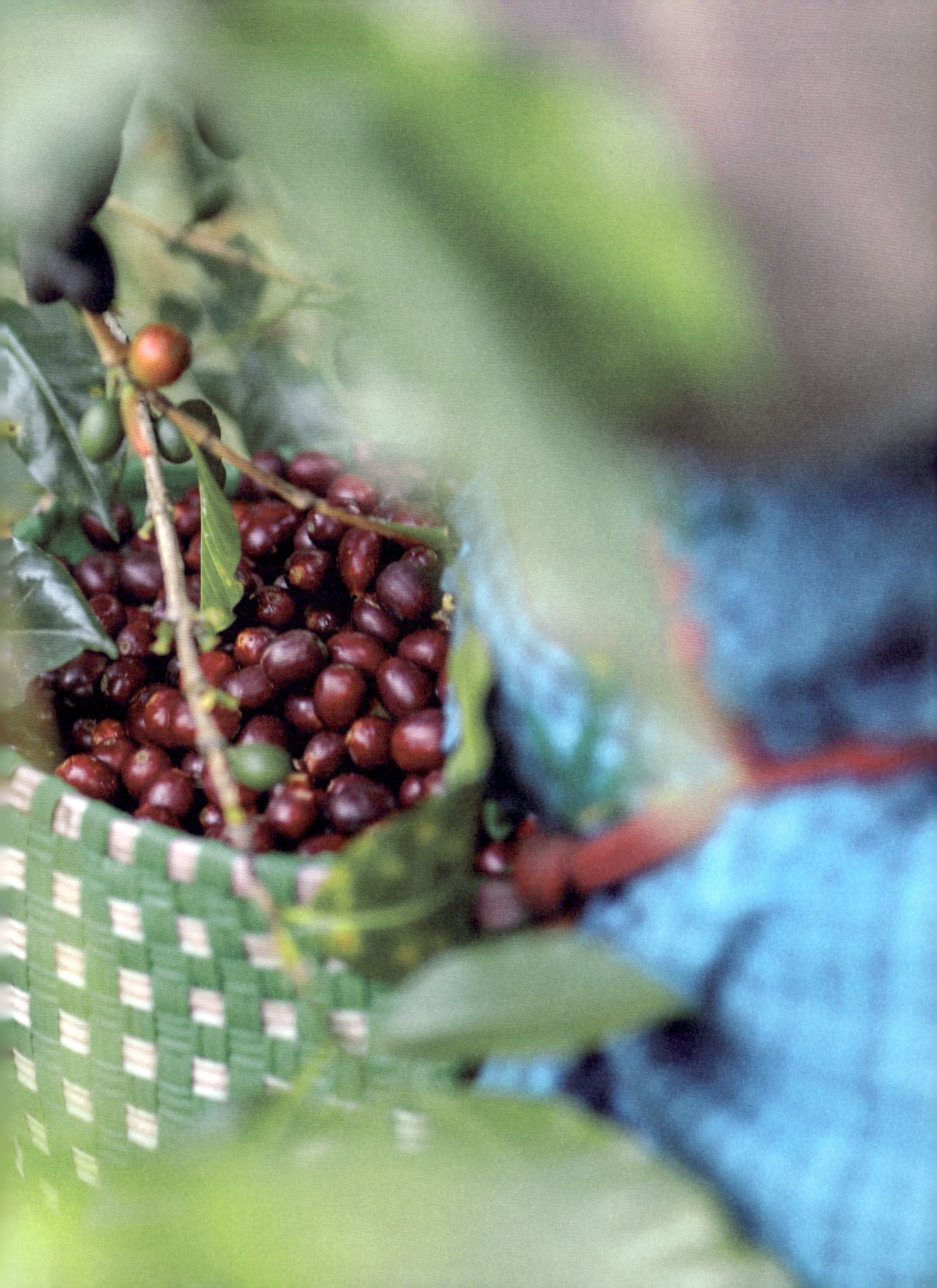

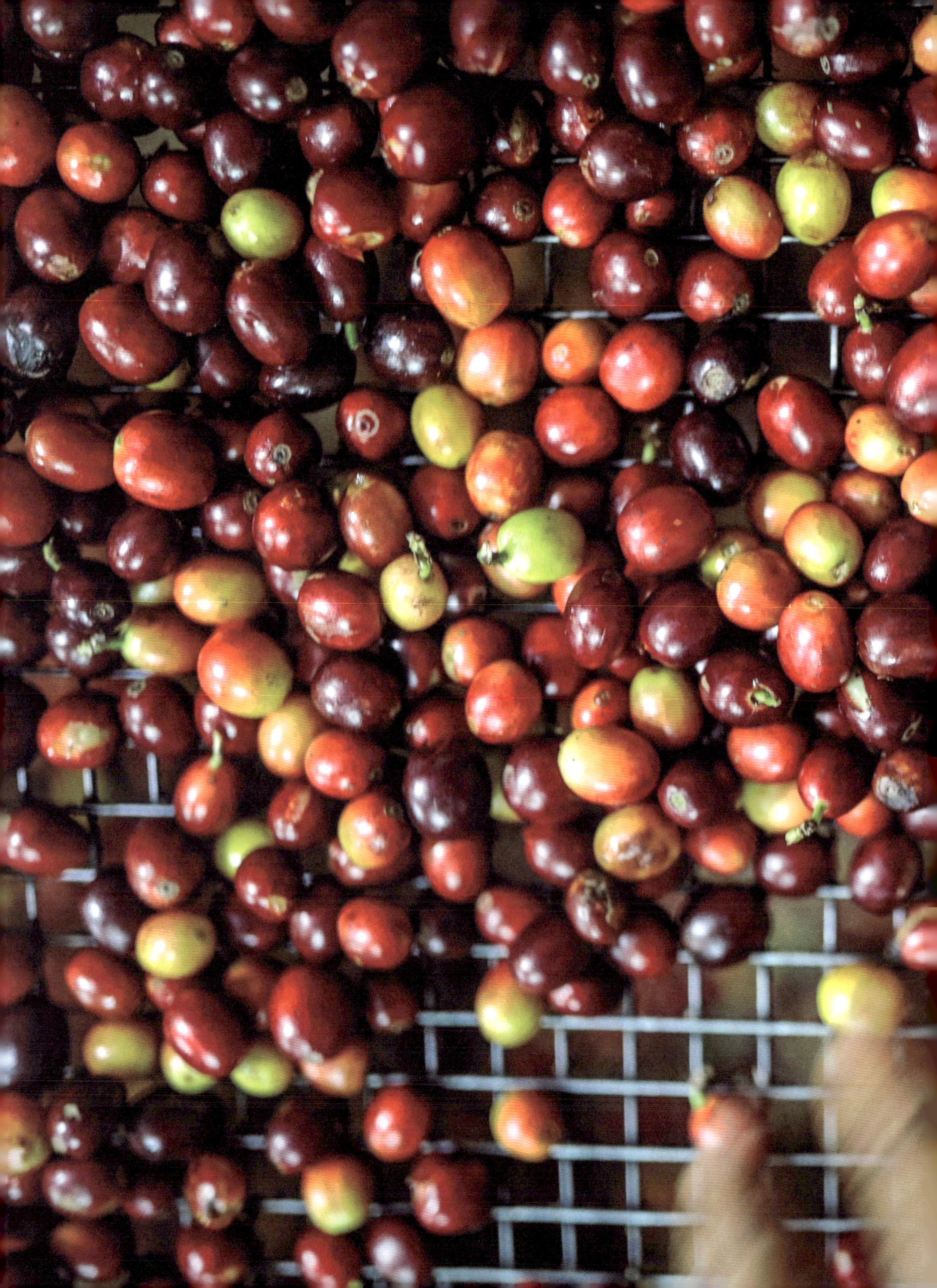

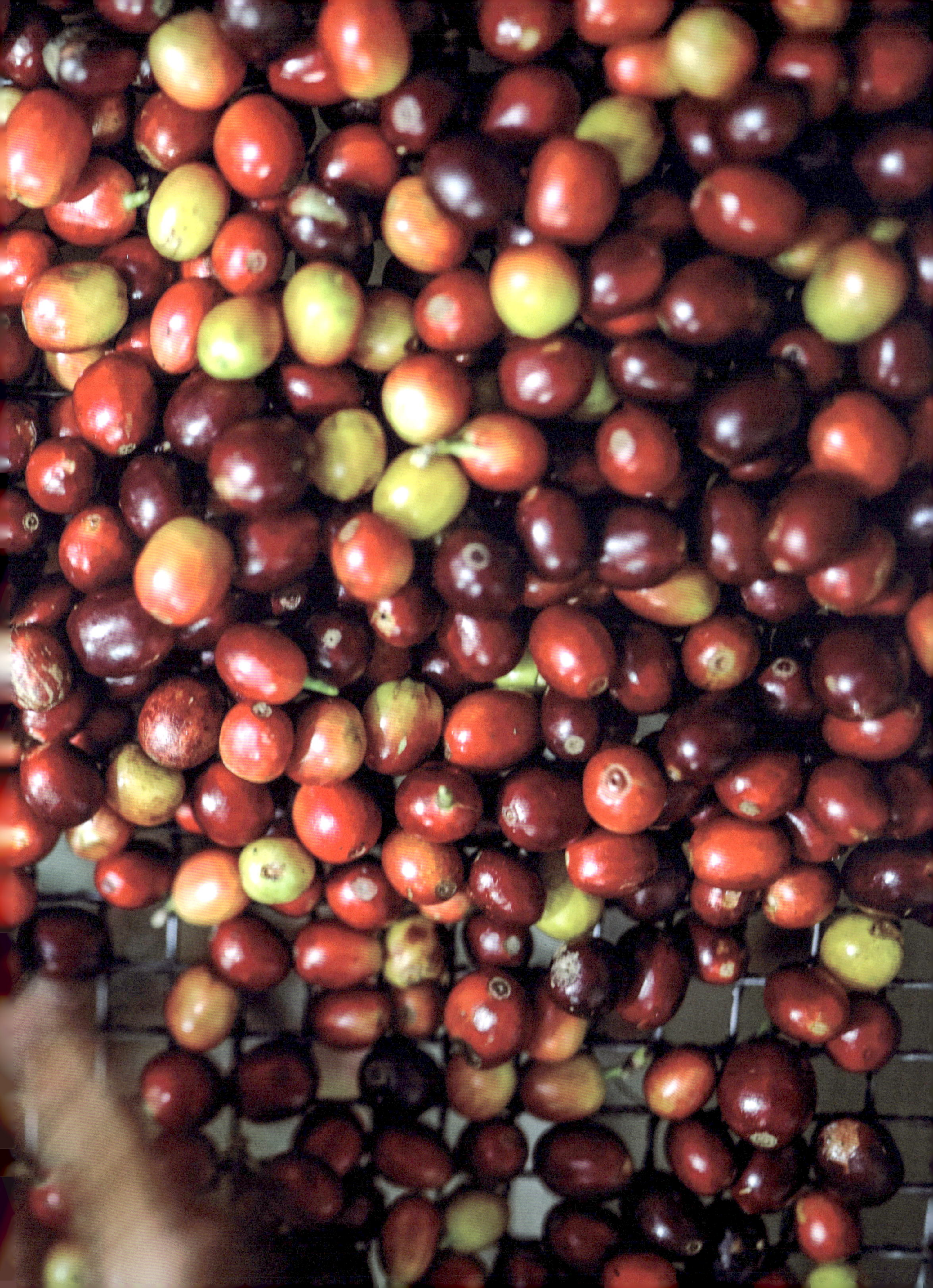

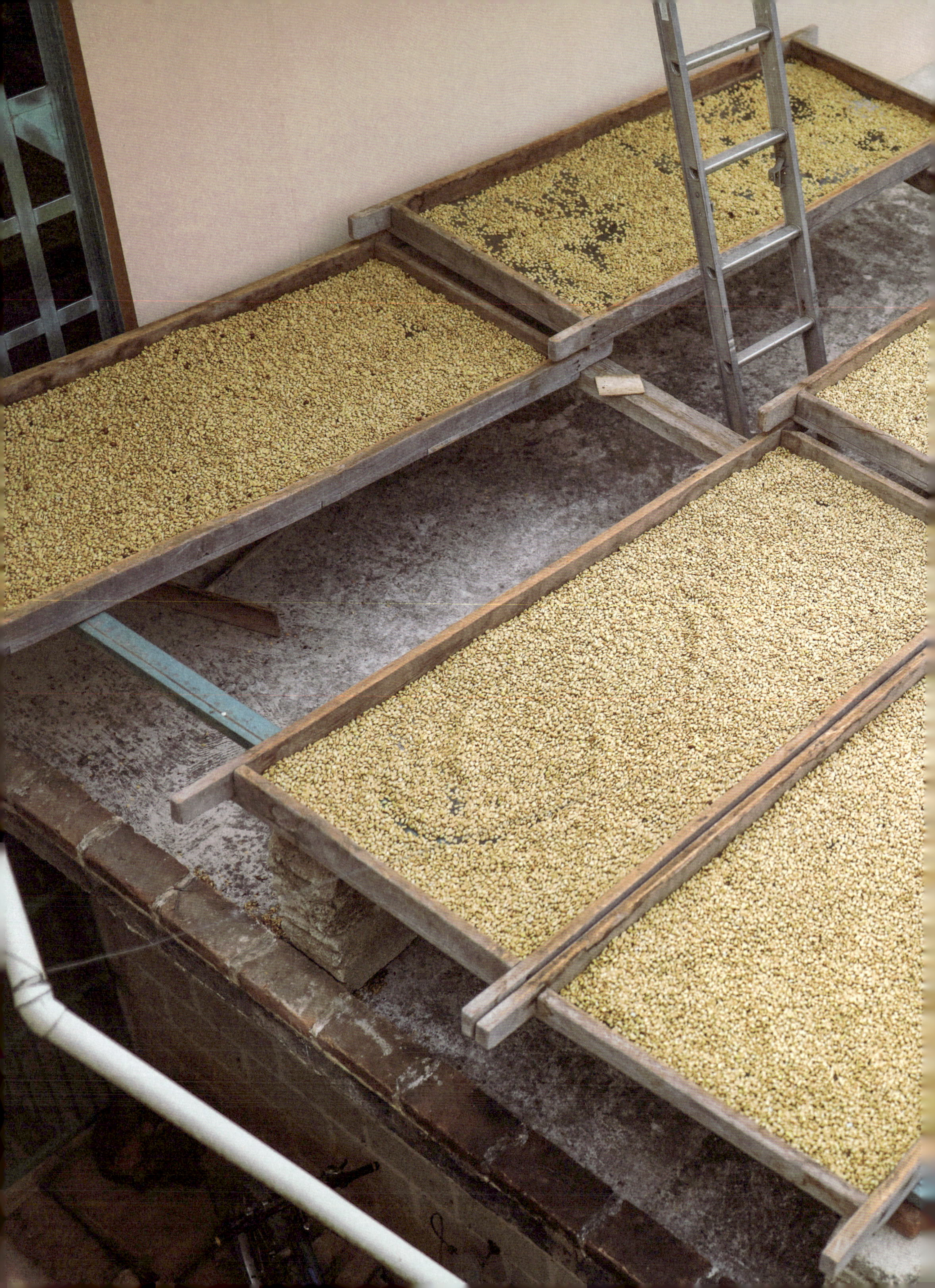

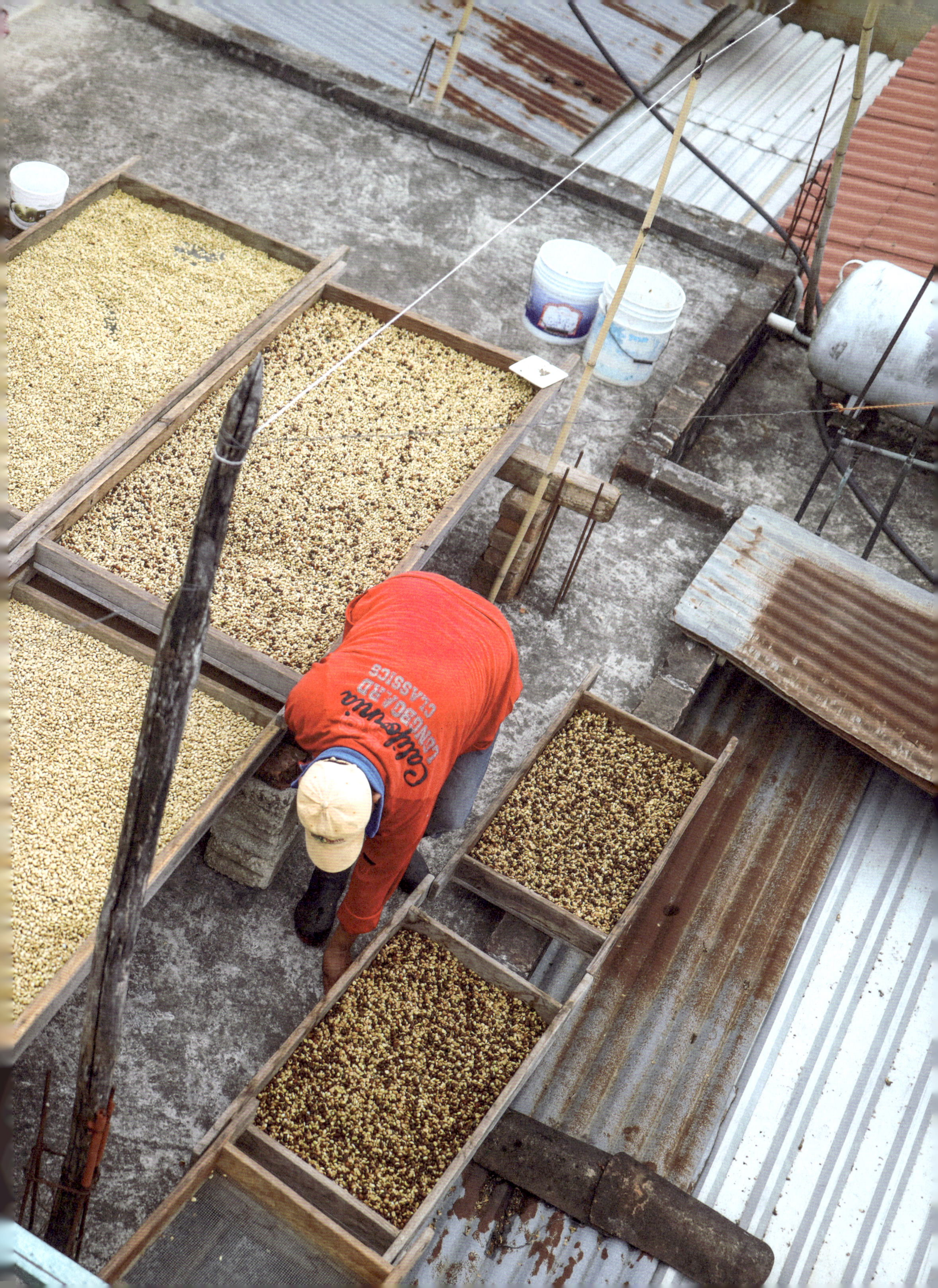
CLASSICS

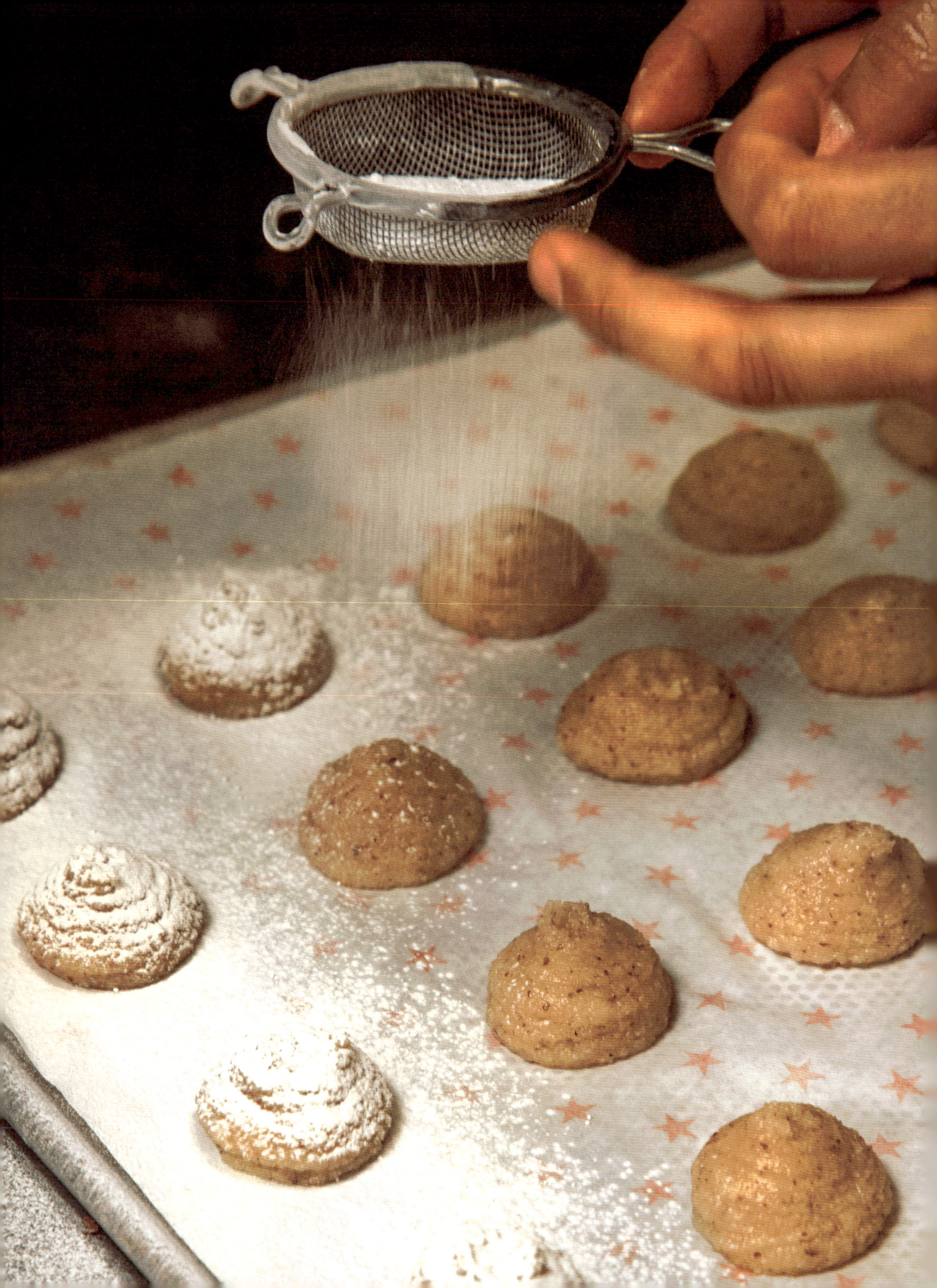

Amaretti

Italians generally eat cookies with their coffee after a meal. One variety of these cookies is amaretti, a kind of compact almond-based meringue from northern Italy. Its name means "bitter" because one of its ingredients is the bitter almond. This almond, which is also the kind used to make the liqueur called amaretto, is profoundly aromatic. And when combined with the better-known sweet almonds, its flavor intensifies. In addition, its bitter flavor cuts the sweetness of the cookie, which makes it an ideal companion to coffee.

I learned to make these cookies when I worked at the London restaurant Locanda Locatelli. During the first years of Rosetta, we'd make them without bitter almonds because they're impossible to find in Mexico (their importation is restricted in various countries because they're toxic if eaten in excess). Some years later, we realized that the mamey pit, known as pixtle, is almost identical in flavor. We've made amaretti with pixtle instead of bitter almonds ever since. It's amazing to find the same flavors in ingredients that come from such wildly different contexts: the fruit of a tree that's native to Asia and now grown in Europe; the pit of a tropical fruit that's native to the Americas.

Makes 24 pieces

80 grams almonds, blanched
20 grams pixtle (mamey pit)
12 grams hazelnuts, toasted and blanched
250 grams sugar
60 grams egg whites

Put the almonds, the pixtle, and the toasted hazelnuts in a food processor. Blend at medium speed for 4 minutes or until the mixture starts to release its oils and stick to the container of the processor.

Add the sugar and keep blending for 90 seconds, pausing and stirring every 30 seconds.

Add the egg whites to the mixture and keep blending at medium speed for 30 seconds.

Transfer the mixture to a pastry bag.

On a silicone baking mat, shape the amaretto biscuits into balls that are 3 centimeters in diameter, leaving 2 centimeters of space between them.

Sprinkle evenly with powdered sugar and let sit for 12 hours at room temperature.

Bake at 180°C for 9 minutes.

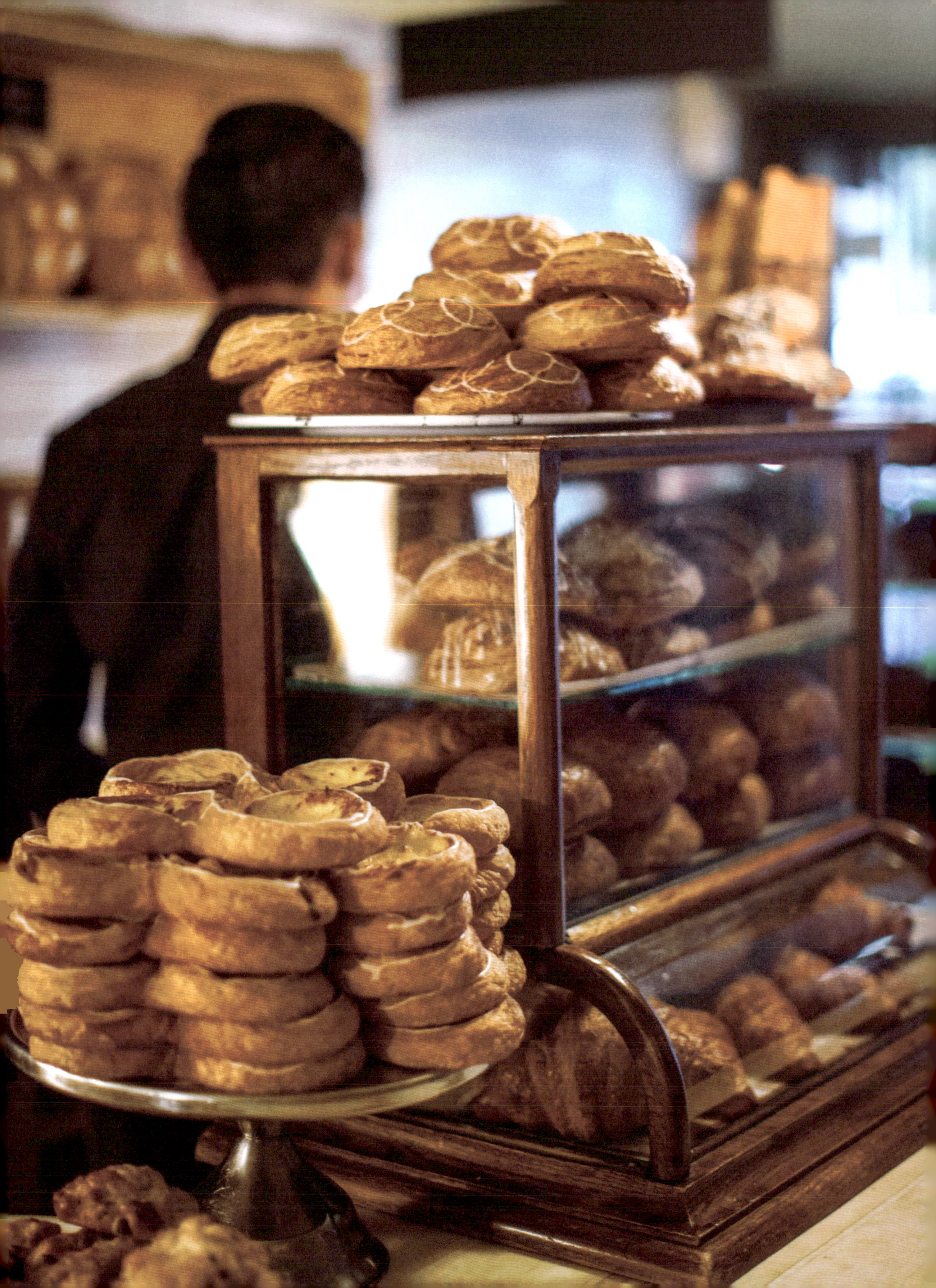

V
La Panadería

La Panadería	**325**
Berry mille feuille	328
Rosemary bun	332
Concha	336
Guava roll	338

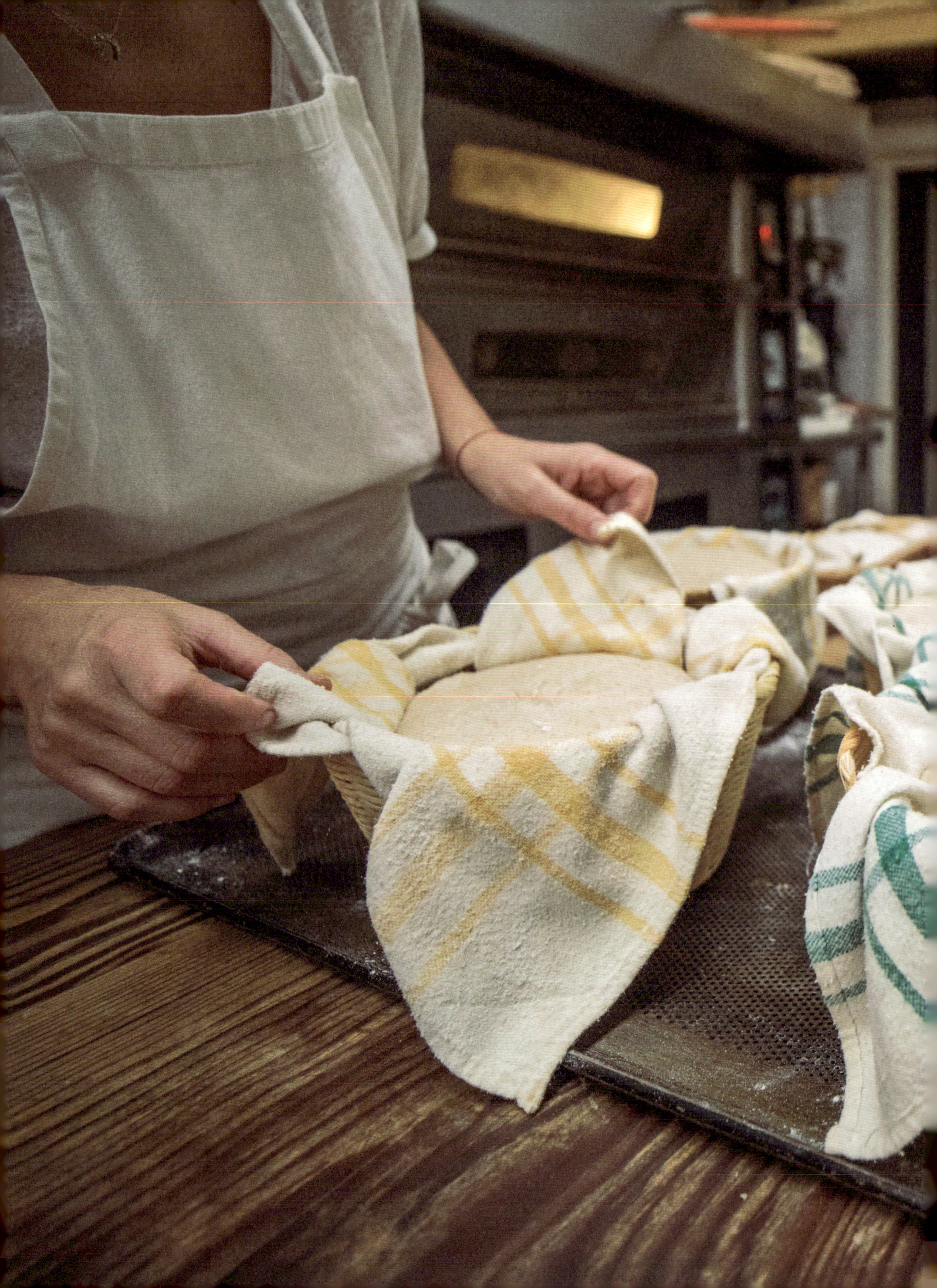

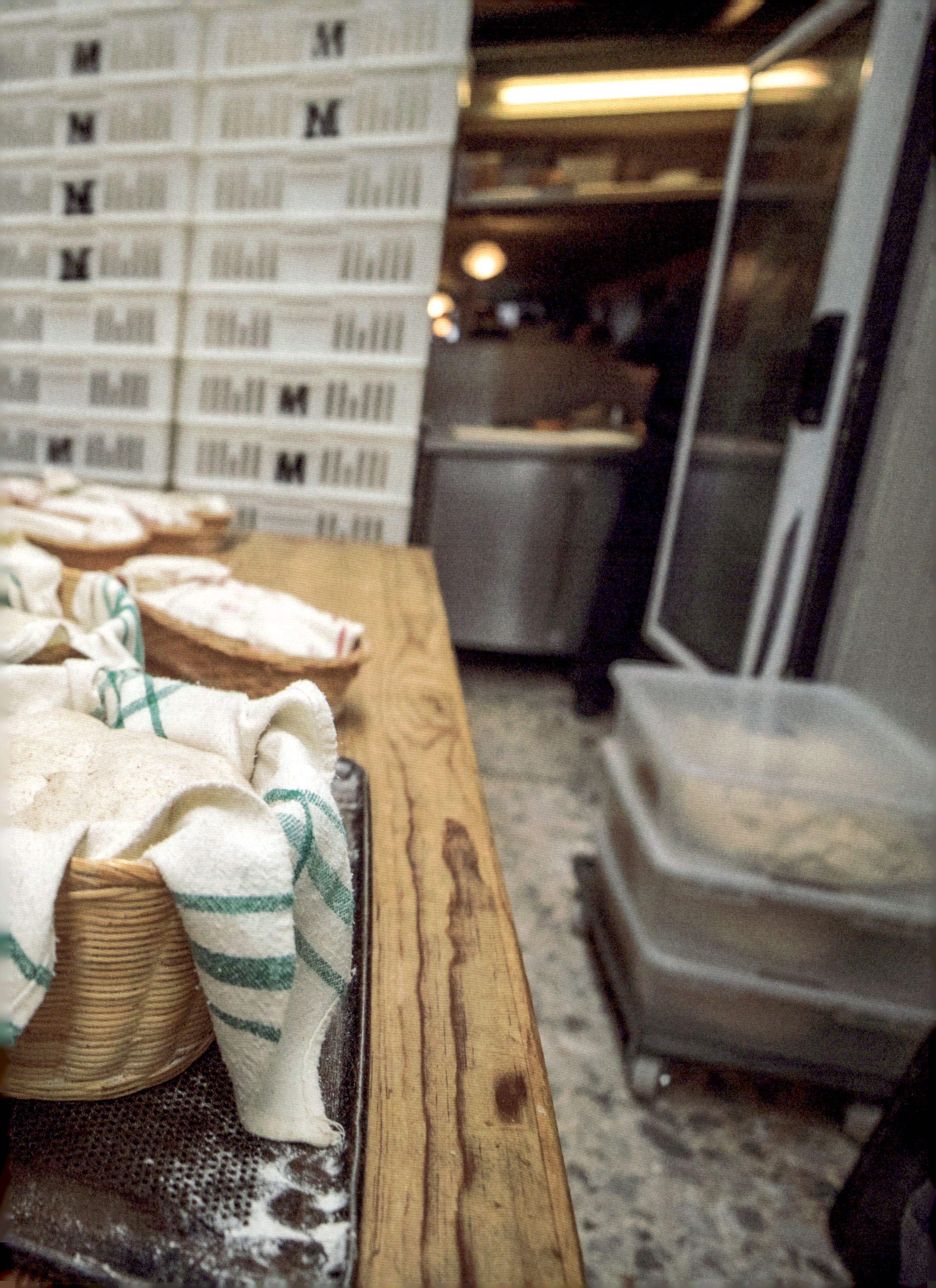

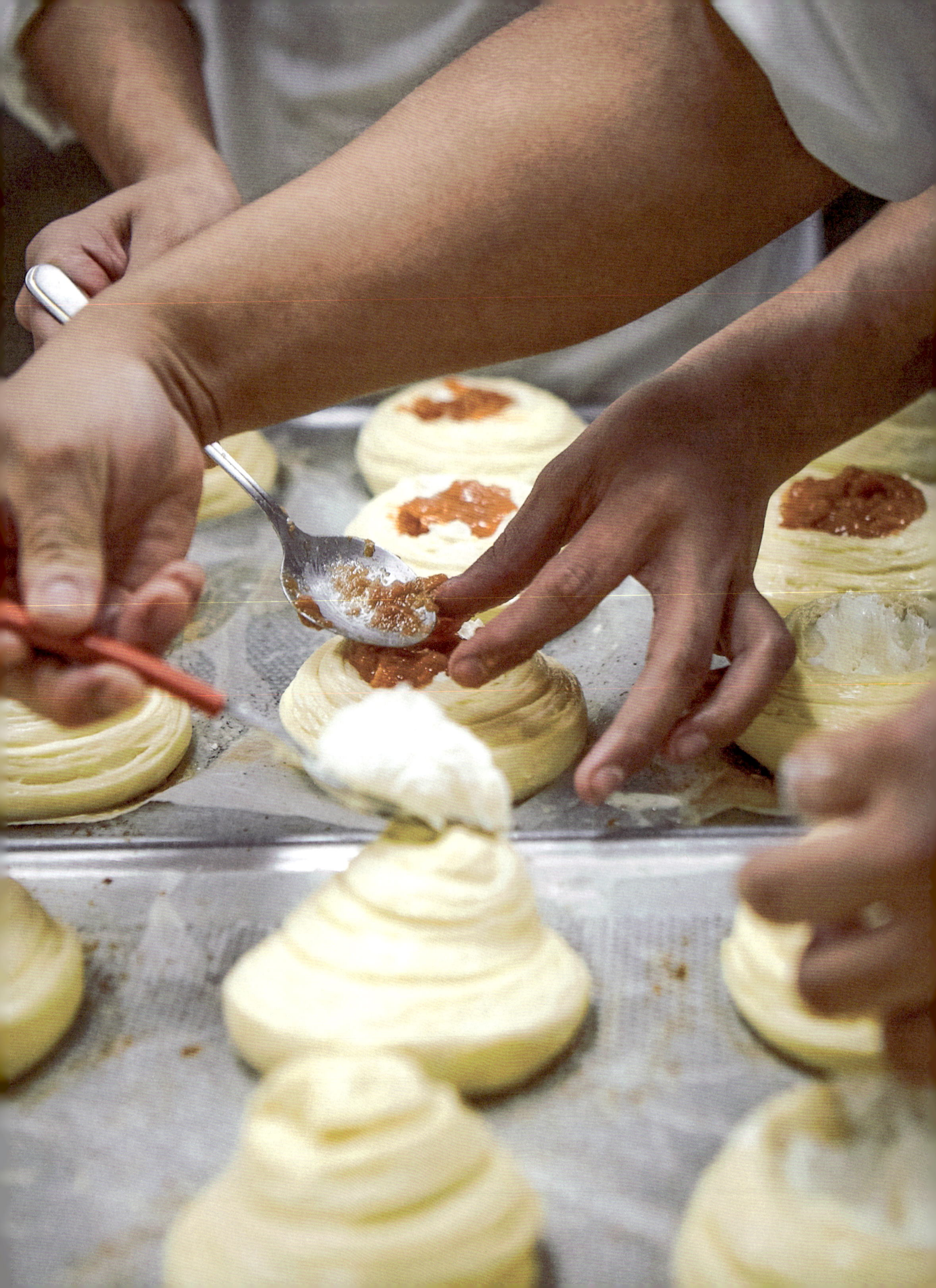

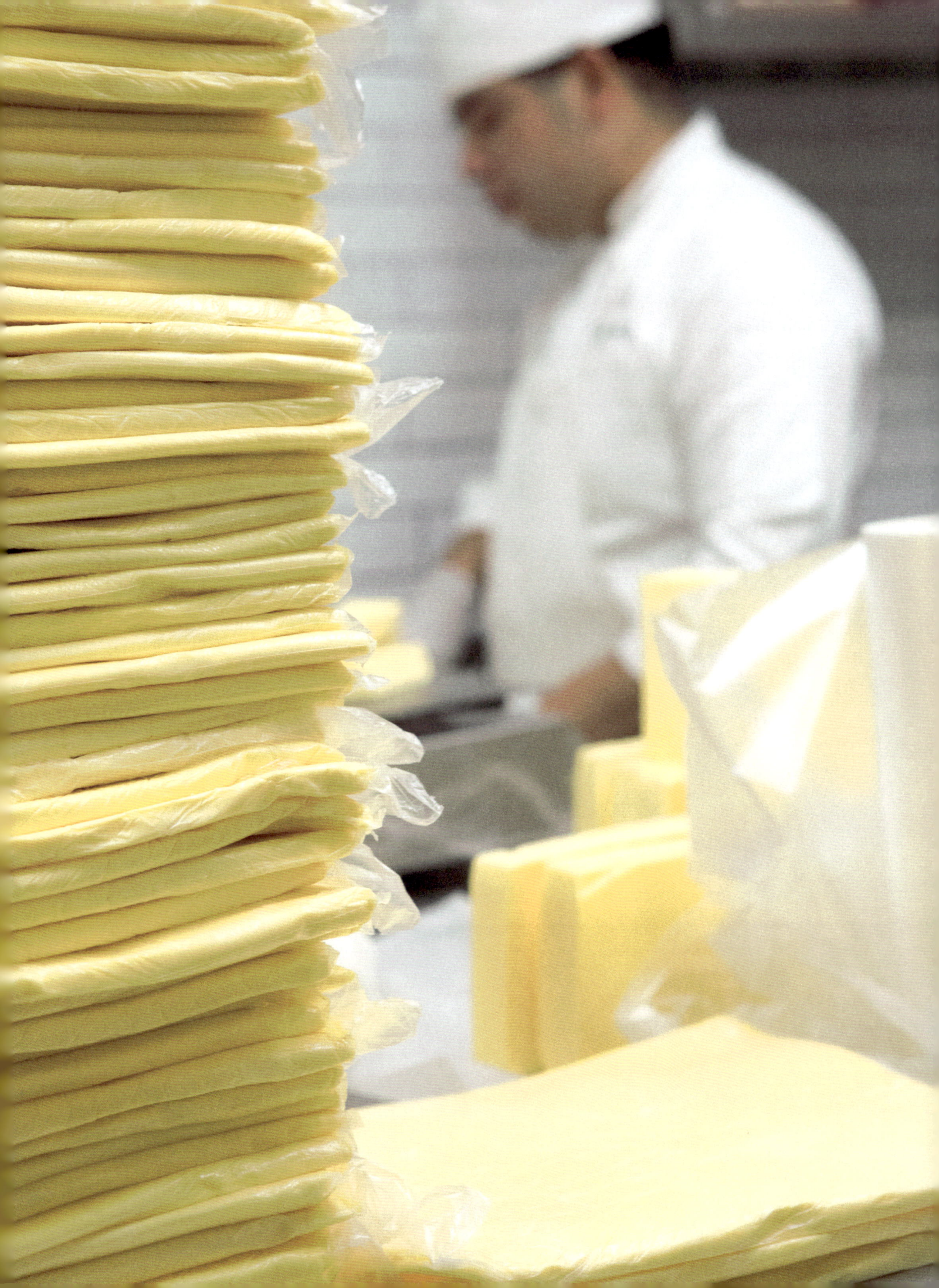

PANADERIA
179a

La Panadería

Bread is among my favorite kinds of food to eat and to make. I always dreamed that, if I had a restaurant someday, it would offer exceptionally good bread. When I opened Rosetta, I thought it would be best if we made the bread ourselves, so we could ensure that it was high-quality. And we did; even at the very beginning, we dedicated a lot of effort to our bread. We made sourdough, focaccia, nut and raisin bread, whole wheat. Our neighbors started coming by early in the morning, before we opened for meals, in hopes of buying our bread. Its popularity led us to move the bakery to a different location, albeit to a storefront just a few dozen meters away from the restaurant. That's how the Panadería was born.

Little by little, we started to make other things besides the bread we needed for the restaurant. First, classic European-style bread and pastries like croissants, pain au chocolat, baguettes, scones, and ciabatta. Then traditional Mexican pan dulce like the concha, the pan de muerto, the chilindrina, and the rosca de reyes. We also began to explore certain Mexican recipes that are lesser known in urban areas, like pulque bread and cemitas. We came up with our own recipes, too. The most famous one may be the guava roll. But there's also the rosemary bun, the tarragon roll, and the honey whole-grain croissant. No less importantly, we also began to explore other grains and products beyond wheat. Today, we use flours made from mesquite, buckwheat, amaranth, ramón, rye, quinoa, corn, spelt, and oats.

Although it runs on its own rhythm, La Panadería remains inextricably linked to Rosetta, the restaurant. They share knowledge and tasks. Products come and go between the two. They feed each other. They're part of the same universe.

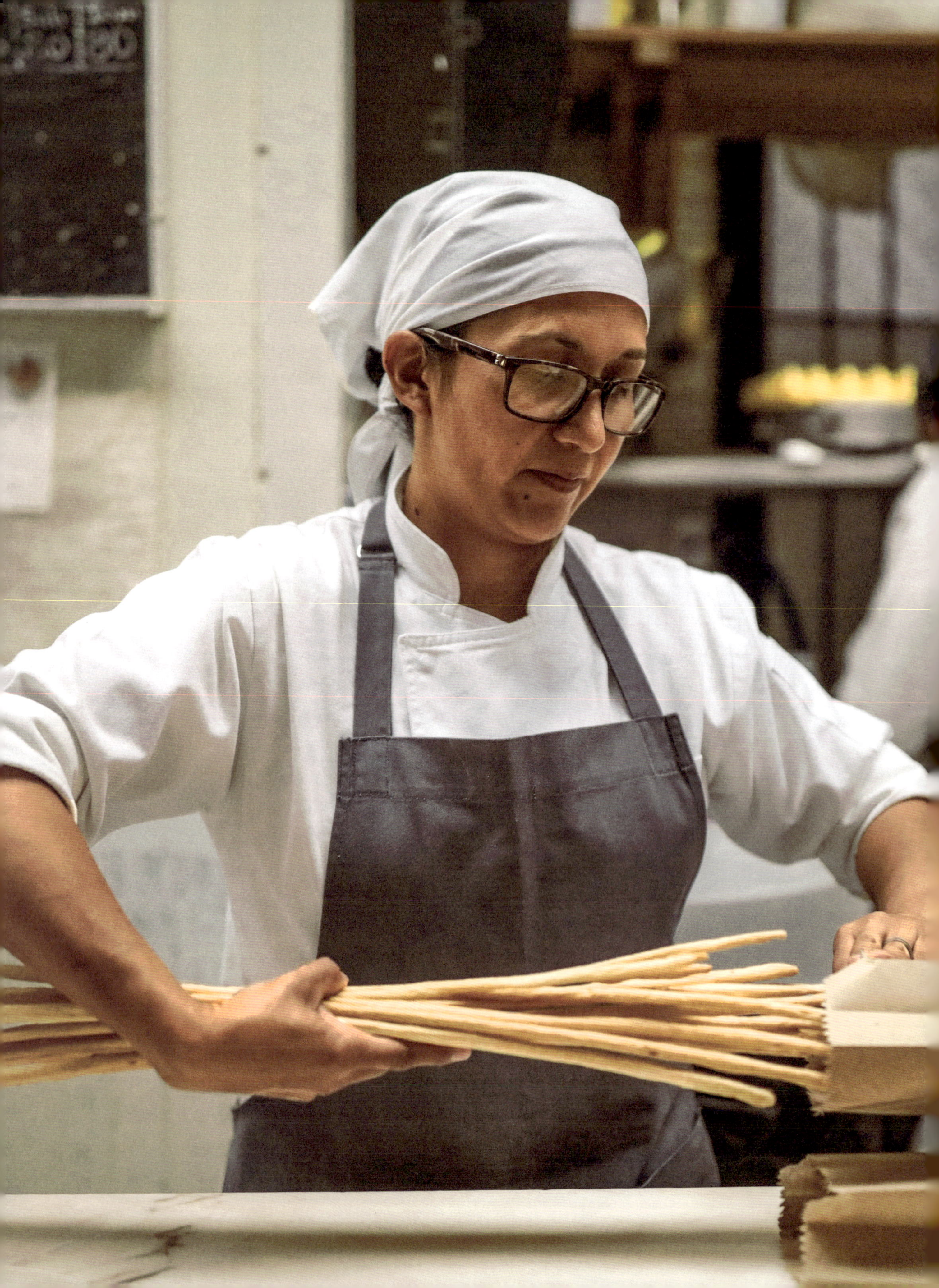

Berry mille feuille

The mille feuille is a classic French cake made with puff pastry, pastry cream, and whipped cream. Depending on the quality of its ingredients, this cake can either be glorious or disastrous. At Rosetta, we make the puff pastry with good butter, the kind that emerges naturally when high-protein milk separates. We make the pastry cream with vanilla seeds from Papantla, Veracruz. And we add just a bit of sugar to the whipped cream.

In theory, a mille feuille should be assembled shortly before serving so that the pastry maintains its texture. Personally, though, I like to serve the cake a few hours after putting it together, because a bit of moisture in the first few layers of the pastry brings all the flavors together.

We've made different versions of mille feuille over time, adding ingredients or altering the flavor of the cream. The variety we make with strawberries, raspberries, and blueberries is incredibly popular. Now we sell it at La Panadería, although we also still make it in the pastry section of the restaurant. One morning, the last slice of mille feuille caused such an uproar that two men ended up flinging coffee onto each other.

Puff pastry

Serves 10

355 grams butter, cubed and at room temperature
440 grams wheat flour
7.5 grams salt
150 grams ice-cold water

Makes 1 kilogram

Using your hands, mix 280 grams of the cubed butter with 110 grams of the flour until you form a paste. Make a 10-by-10-centimeter square and cover it with plastic wrap. Refrigerate for 20 minutes.

Mix the remaining 75 grams of butter with the remaining 330 grams of flour and the salt. Once everything is well mixed, add the ice-cold water all at once. Bundle the dough in plastic wrap and refrigerate for 20 minutes.

Spread out the dough with a rolling pin until you have a 35-by-35-centimeter square. Remove the plastic from the butter and flour mixture and place it perpendicularly in the middle of the dough, so that it looks like a rhombus.

Fold the four corners of the dough toward the center so that you cover the butter and the dough maintains its rhombus-like shape.

Rotate the dough 45° and spread it out with a rolling pin until you have a horizontal rectangle.

Make imaginary vertical lines to divide the dough into 4 equal sections. Take the two edge sections and fold them toward the center. Then fold the dough in half, like a book.

Shift the dough 45° again and repeat the previous step again, folding the dough as if it were a book. Then spread it out with a rolling pin until you have a 35-by-50-centimeter rectangle. Use a fork to prick up and down the entire dough, then refrigerate for 30 minutes.

Remember: if the dough becomes difficult to manipulate during the process, you can refrigerate the dough for a few minutes to make it more malleable.

Place the dough on a baking sheet and bake for 20 minutes at 180°C. Remove from the oven, carefully turn over the dough, and sprinkle evenly with powdered sugar. Increase the oven temperature to 410°C and bake for 5 more minutes.

Remove. Once it has cooled, cut it into 3 sheets, each 10 centimeters wide.

Vanilla pastry cream

150 milliliters heavy cream
150 milliliters milk
½ of a vanilla pod
35 grams egg yolks
35 grams sugar
15 grams cornstarch

Makes 300 grams

Heat the cream, the milk, and the vanilla. When it reaches a boil, remove and let infuse for 20 minutes.

Mix the yolks with the sugar, the cornstarch, and a bit of the milk from the infusion. Whisk until the mixture whitens.

Add the egg yolk mixture to the milk and return the milk to the burner.

Cook until it reaches 85°C or until the first bubbles appear, whisking constantly. Make sure to whisk the entire surface to keep lumps from forming.

Transfer the cream to a bowl and cool on top of a bowl of ice as quickly as possible.

Refrigerate until ready to use.

To Serve

300 milliliters heavy cream
30 grams powdered sugar
500 grams strawberries
3 sheets puff pastry
200 grams vanilla pastry cream
425 grams raspberries
130 grams blueberries

Beat the cream and the powdered sugar until the mixture forms peaks.

Slice each strawberry cross-wise, into quarters.

Place the first sheet of puff pastry onto a cake stand. Using a pastry bag, add strips of vanilla pastry cream. Decorate the entire edge with raspberries. In the middle, lay out a bed of 4 strawberry slices and 4 raspberries, alternating between them.

On top, place the next sheet of puff pastry and decorate it, covering the whole surface with generous pompoms of whipped cream.

On top of that, place the final sheet of puff pastry. Using a spatula, cover the whole surface with a thin layer of whipped cream. Decorate the entire edge with strawberries and arrange the other berries irregularly across the entire sheet.

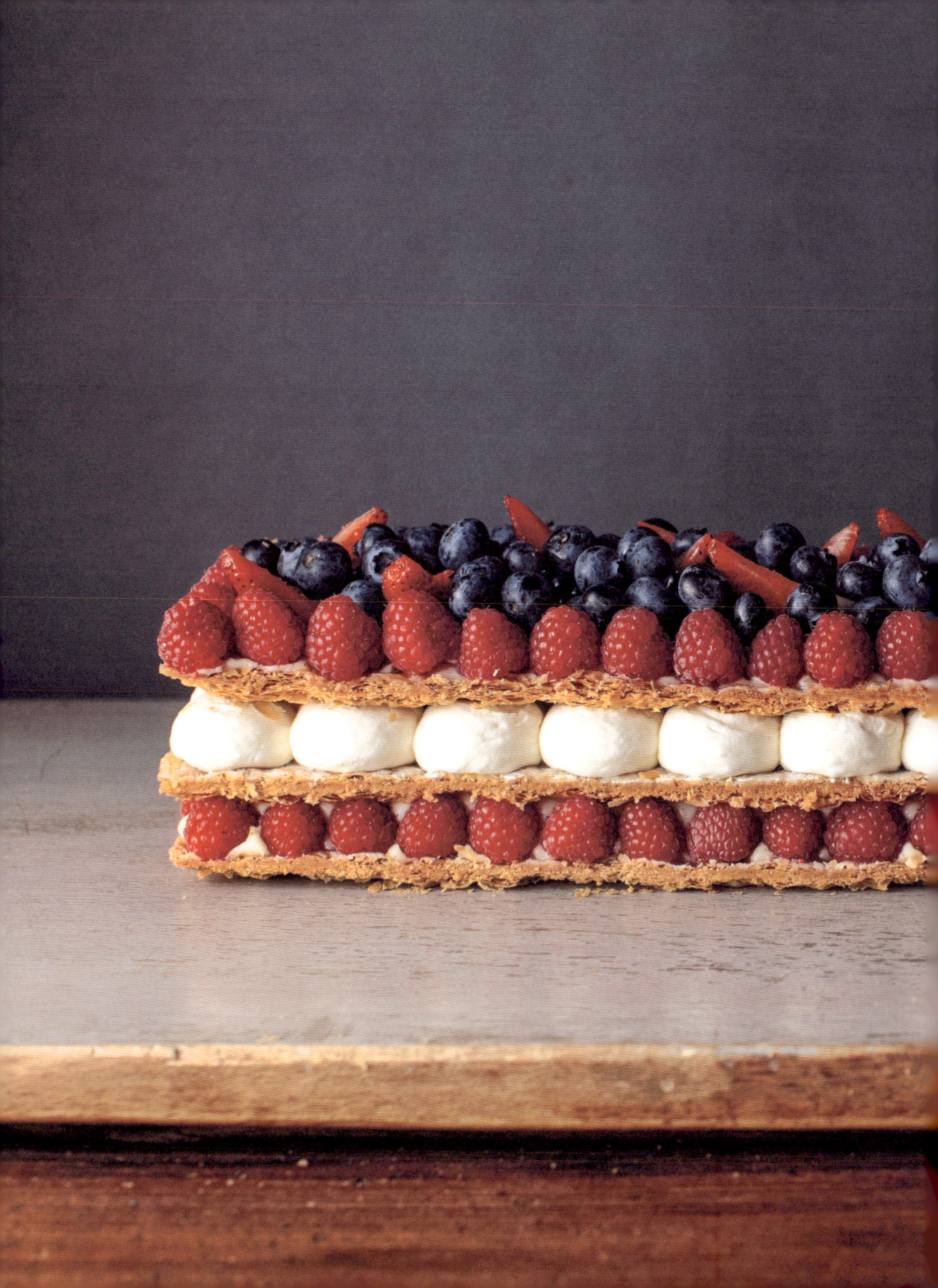

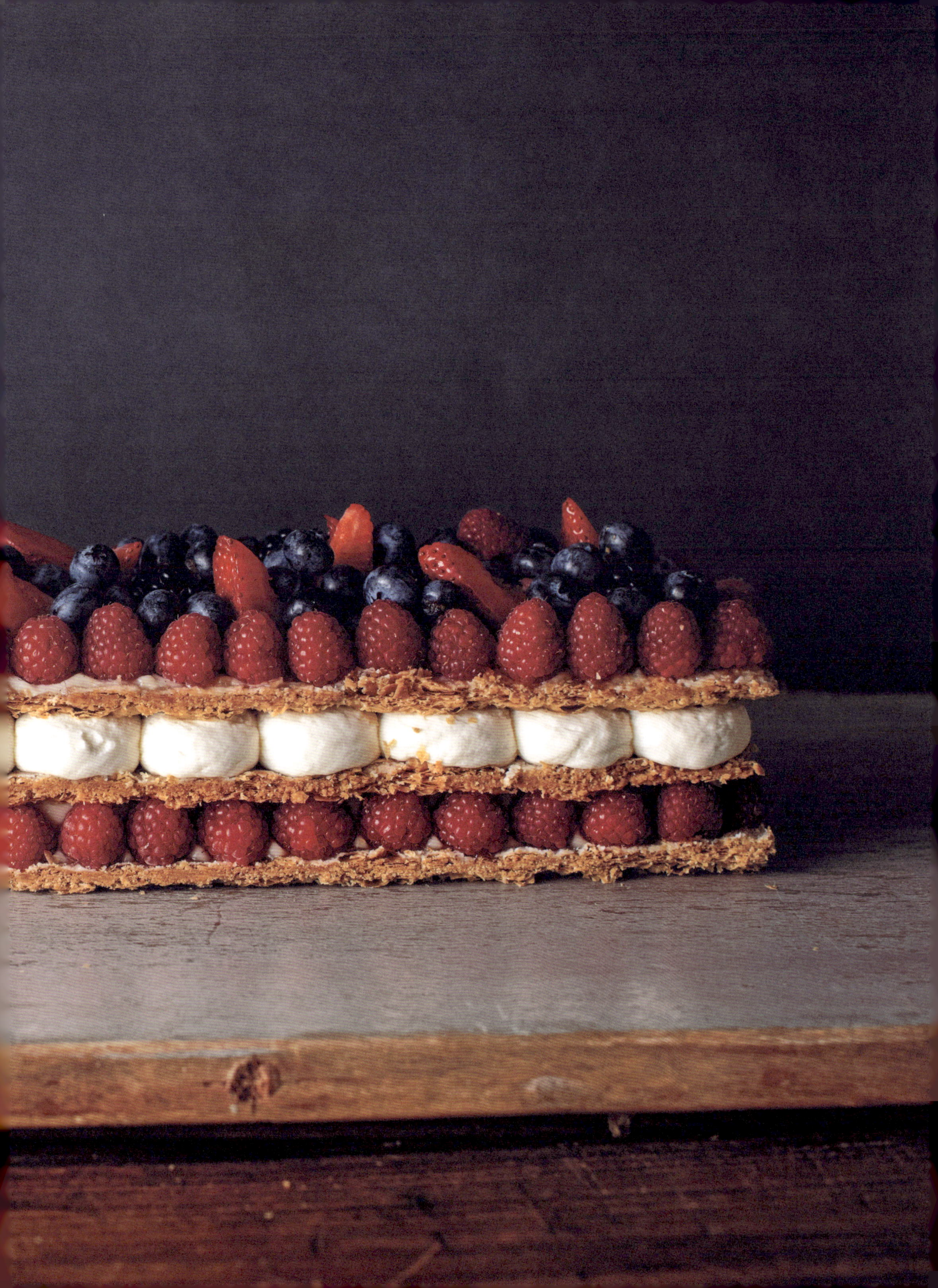

Rosemary bun

The rosemary bun was the first pan dulce we made at La Panadería. We were exclusively making savory bread at the time. This sweet bread isn't especially sweet because it consists of white bread dough that's rolled out and spread with a paste made of lard, sugar, and chopped rosemary. Then it's rolled out again, cut, allowed to rise, and baked.

Lard has been used in baking for ages, though less frequently in recent decades, given its link to cholesterol. Like any fat, it should be consumed in moderation; like any ingredient, too, quality makes all the difference. Good lard is creamy, white, and shiny. When it's fresh, its flavor is almost neutral, its scent almost imperceptible. Lard adds crunchiness to dough and its flavor isn't sweet or dominant, unlike butter.

Rosemary has a fresh, aromatic flavor; it reminds me of pine trees. The combination of rosemary, sugar, and lard makes this pan dulce truly fragrant. It has a light crust on the outside and it's soft on the inside. After we made these buns, we realized that there is a synergy between sugar, fat, and certain herbs. Herbs like rosemary make the fat feel lighter, and the fat steadies the scent and flavor of the herbs. Now we use a wide variety of herbs, both at La Panadería and in the dessert section of the restaurant.

Dough for buns

Makes 12 buns

250 grams wheat flour
6 grams salt
2 grams dry yeast
150 milliliters water
100 grams sourdough starter

Makes 500 grams

Combine the flour and the salt in a large bowl and make a hollow in the middle.

Dissolve the yeast in a little water and pour it, along with the sourdough starter, into the center of the flour. Mix with your fingers, making small circles from the outside in.

Once everything is well mixed, place the dough on a wooden surface and start to knead, striking the dough lightly until it becomes smooth and elastic.

Transfer the dough to a covered bowl for 1.5 hours.

To Serve

75 grams lard
75 grams sugar
5 grams fresh rosemary, chopped
500 grams dough for buns

Mix the lard with the sugar until they make a uniform paste.

Place the dough on a floured surface, spreading it out with a rolling pin, and form a rectangle, measuring approximately 30 by 20 centimeters. Spread the lard and sugar paste onto the dough. Sprinkle rosemary uniformly across it.

Use a pizza cutter to make 12 equally sized squares. Fold each square into thirds, then repeat.

Place the buns right next to each other on a previously greased baking sheet that's approximately 5 centimeters deep. Let them rise for 1 hour in a warm place.

Make a shallow cut with scissor-tips across the top of each bun and bake with steam at 250°C for 15 minutes.

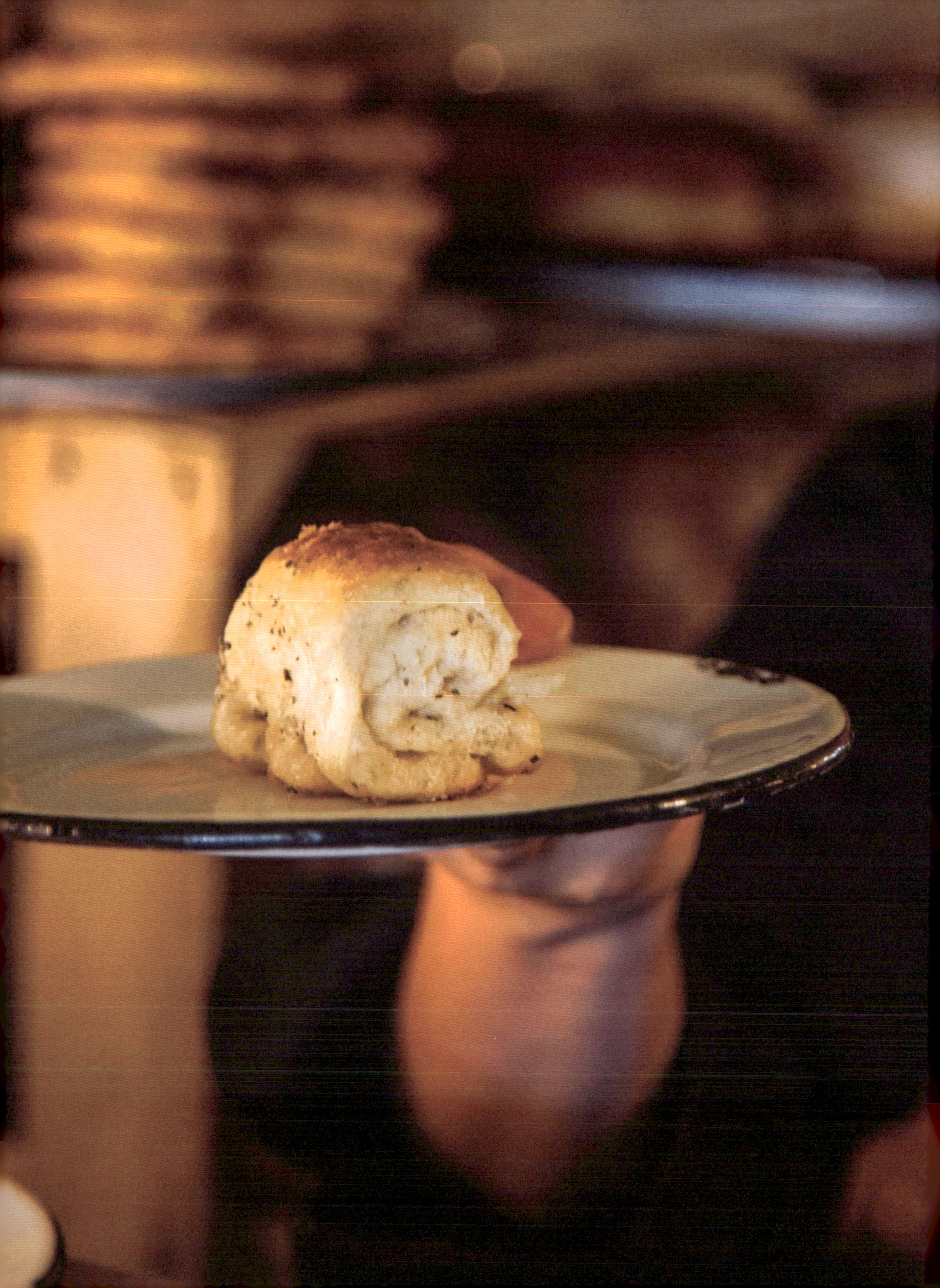

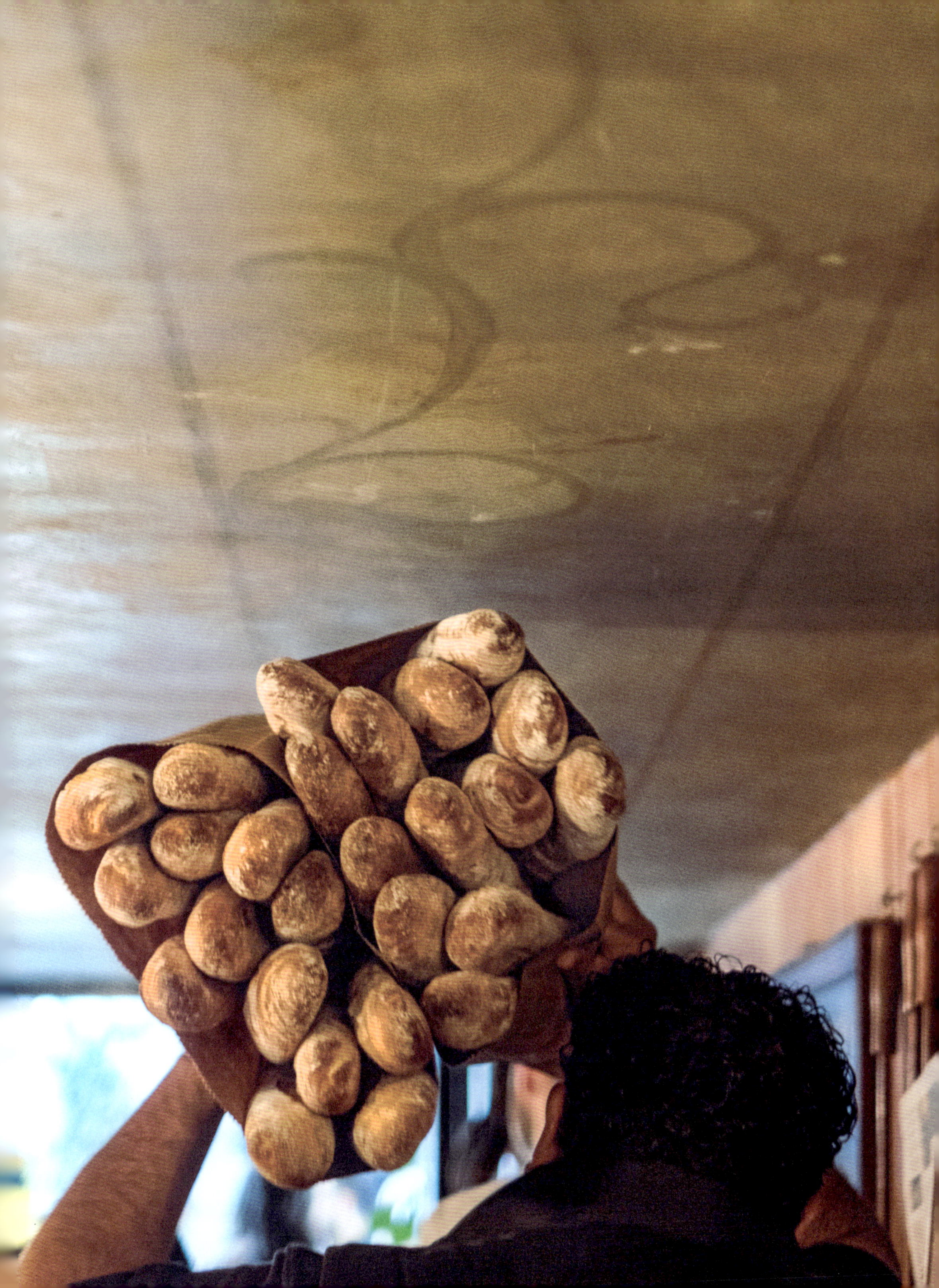

Concha

The concha is among the most emblematic kinds of Mexican pan dulce. It's easy to spot: a round, spongy bun that resembles a seashell, it's characterized by a topping of shortening, flour, and sugar. A concha can be vanilla- or chocolate-flavored. It's everywhere, in every Mexican city and town—both in bakeries and on the street, where people sell them from bicycles with enormous wicker baskets.

Concha dough, like that of the plain white roll called the bolillo, typically contains neither eggs nor butter, although this has been changing. At La Panadería, however, we make our concha dough with butter and eggs but very little yeast. We let the dough sit for quite a while before shaping it into balls. Once shaped, we refrigerate it while we make the sugar topping; our version includes either cocoa or vanilla seeds from Papantla, Veracruz. We make cuts across the topping to form a shell pattern, then let the buns rise slowly for two hours. I'm describing the process in detail because, strictly speaking, what distinguishes our conchas is a question of time. Because we let them rise, we don't need to use much yeast, and the fermentation occurs unhurriedly. In the end, all of these measures ensure that the conchas at La Panadería are light, airy, and easy to digest.

Vanilla topping

Makes 12 pieces

100 grams wheat flour
90 grams vegetable shortening
45 grams powdered sugar
45 grams sugar
2 grams baking powder
0.5 grams salt
½ of a vanilla pod

540 grams wheat flour
6.5 grams dry yeast
80 grams sugar
3 grams salt
45 milliliters milk
155 grams eggs
155 grams butter
1 egg for glazing
280 grams vanilla topping

Makes 280 grams

Combine all of the ingredients in a bowl, adding only the seeds of the vanilla pod. Using a mixer, beat the ingredients at a low speed until well-blended. Once the mixture is uniform, don't beat it for longer than 3 more minutes.

To Serve

Combine the flour, the yeast, the sugar, the salt, the milk, the eggs, and the butter in a large bowl and mix with your hands, making small circles. Once everything has blended together, knead the dough, lightly striking it against the surface until it becomes smooth and elastic.

Place the dough in a bowl and let it sit at room temperature for 1.5 hours. To release the air, fold the dough in half, then in half again, and refrigerate in a covered bowl for 10 to 15 hours.

Divide the dough into 12 pieces and shape them into balls.

Glaze each piece with egg and cover with the vanilla topping. Mark them with a shell-pattern mold or with a knife. Dip each piece in sugar and place them on a baking sheet.

Let them sit on the tray for 2 to 3 hours.

Bake at 175°C for 18 minutes.

Guava roll

The guava roll—a flaky pastry filled with cream cheese custard and guava jam—is currently our most popular pan dulce. Sweet guava paste and cheese are often paired at the end of a meal in Mexico and other parts of Latin America. Adding flaky pastry to this combination was an exciting discovery. So was the concoction of the jam: ripe guavas and sugar, cooked over low heat for several hours, stirring constantly, until they're transformed into a dense brick-colored purée. The rolls are best enjoyed straight from the oven.

Guava jam

Makes 10 pieces

2 kilograms ripe guavas
400 grams sugar
4.75 liters water

Makes 1 kilogram
   Cut the guavas in half, remove the seeds, and set the fruit aside. Transfer the seeds to a saucepan with 1.75 liters of water and boil them for 20 minutes.
   Strain the seeds and press the pulp. Transfer the liquid to a saucepan and add the sliced guavas and 1 liter of water. Add the sugar, too, and cook over low heat, stirring constantly.
   As the liquid is absorbed, gradually add more water so that the fruit continues to cook. Keep stirring it with a scraper or spatula to prevent it from sticking. Let the mixture cook over low heat for 3 or 4 hours, or until it has the texture of jam.
   Remove the saucepan from the heat, let cool, and set aside until ready to use.

Dough for the rolls

250 grams flour
22 grams sugar
5 grams salt
4 grams dry yeast
10 grams sourdough starter
80 milliliters water
80 milliliters milk
220 grams butter

Makes 650 grams
   On a clean surface, make a pyramid with the flour and the sugar. Scatter salt around it.
   Make a hole in the middle of the flour mixture. Put the yeast and sourdough starter inside it.
   Little by little, pour the water and the milk into the middle and mix them with your hands, starting from the center and working toward the edges.
   Once all the ingredients are mixed together, start to knead, striking the dough lightly against the table until it becomes smooth and elastic.
   Place the dough into a container, cover it with plastic wrap, and let it sit for 40 minutes.
   Press on the dough to release the air and freeze it for 25 minutes.
   Spread the butter onto a sheet of plastic wrap, forming a rectangle, and refrigerate it for 5 to 10 minutes. It should be malleable (but not soft), so that the butter won't crack during the filling process.

Lightly flour a clean surface and shape the dough into a rectangle. The rectangle of dough should be 1 centimeter wider than the rectangle of butter and 6 centimeters long.

Lay out the rectangle of dough horizontally. On top of it, place the rectangle of butter—without the plastic wrap—on the left side, leaving a 1-centimeter border of dough around the butter. Fold the three edges of the border inward to keep the butter from slipping out later on.

Make imaginary vertical lines to divide the dough into 3 equal parts. Fold the third part toward the middle, then do the same with the first part. This way, you'll end up with a rectangle one-third the size of what you started with.

Using a rolling pin, make the dough into a rectangle again—a long one now, rolling lengthwise—and shift it 45°. This time, make imaginary lines that divide it into 4 equal sections. Take the 2 edge-sections and fold them toward the middle. Then fold the dough in half, like a book. Repeat this step once more, folding it once again as if it were a book. Stretch it out just a bit with the rolling pin and cover it with plastic wrap. Refrigerate the dough for at least 24 hours before using.

Sweet cream filling

200 grams cream cheese
25 grams sugar
25 grams heavy cream

Makes 250 grams

Whip the cream cheese until its consistency is soft and add the sugar. Add the heavy cream and mix to remove all lumps. Refrigerate until ready to use.

To Serve

650 grams dough for the rolls
250 grams sweet cream filling
250 grams guava jam
1 egg for glazing
30 milliliters milk

On a clean surface, lay out the dough for the rolls, using a rolling pin, until you have a rectangle that's 0.5 centimeter thick. Place the rectangle horizontally and make imaginary lines to divide it into 4 equal sections. Take the two edge-sections and fold them toward the middle. Then fold the dough in half as if it were a book. Lay out the dough lengthwise and shift it 45°.

This time, make imaginary lines to divide the dough into 3 equal parts. Fold the third part toward the middle, then the first part. Stretch it out with the rolling pin until the rectangle is 0.25 centimeters thick. Use a knife to cut the edges, making a uniform rectangle.

Roll up the dough. Paste the edge with a bit of egg to keep the roll from coming open in the oven.

Cut the dough into pieces approximately 5 centimeters thick. Place the pieces on a tray and let them sit until they double in size.

Beat the egg and the milk, then use a pastry brush to glaze the pieces with the mixture.

Use a spoon to flatten the center of the rolls. In each hollow, place a generous spoonful of the sweet cream filling. On top of that, place a spoonful of guava jam.

Bake at 180°C for 20 minutes.

This book was incredibly hard for me to write. I had no idea what it would involve. I went back and forth. I changed my mind a thousand times. It must be because I'm not really used to writing, to thinking analytically about what I do. I'm more intuitive. I don't think about food in conceptual terms. I follow what I feel, what I like. In this sense, there's a quote from Michel Serres that I love: "…knowledge cannot come to those who have neither tasted nor smelled…We were too quick to forget that Homo sapiens refers to those who react to sapidity, appreciate it and seek it out, those for whom the sense of taste matters—savouring animals—before referring to judgement, intelligence or wisdom, before referring to talking man."

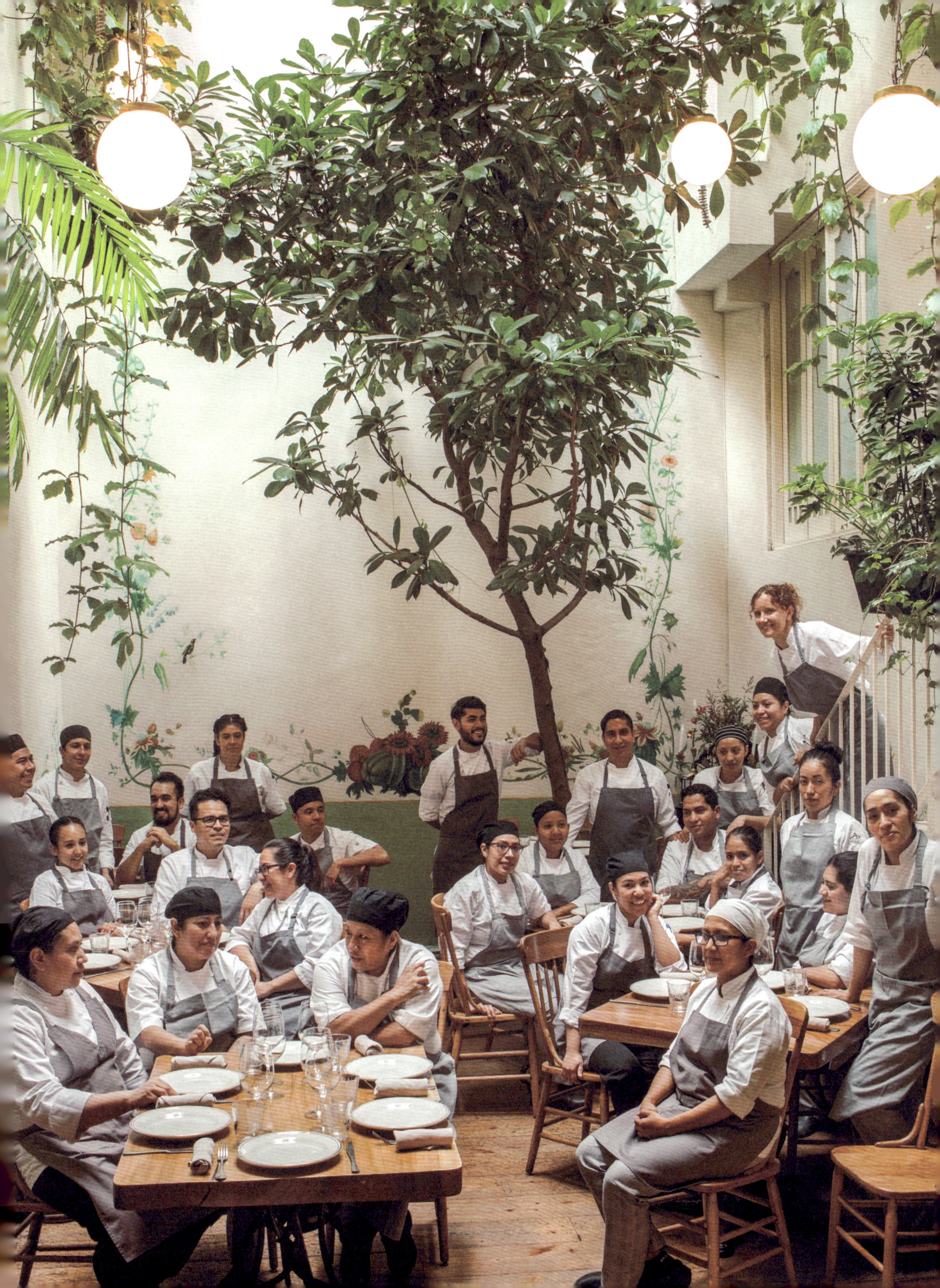

LIST OF
INGREDIENTS

A

Achiote
213, 297

Anchovies
53, 126, 208, 218

Apples
81, 239, 294

Avocado
42, 87, 89, 105, 242, 304
leaf 242, 304

B

Banana
284

Barley
97, 286

Basil
129, 134, 159, 234,
lemon 53

Bass
sea striped 244
sea 186

Beef
chuck flap tail 242
tongue 134, 190
sweetbreads 190, 192

Beet
57, 105, 149, 224, 269

Berries
269, 328

Black cod
211

Bok choy
220

Bottarga
158

Buckwheat
53, 156

Burrata
53, 156

Butter
42, 81, 121, 126,
131, 134, 148, 149,
152, 156, 158, 164,
167, 186, 190, 211,
213, 224, 231, 239,
244, 260, 269, 297,
328, 332, 336

Bottarga
158

Coral
131 *smoked* 121
white 53, 164, 167

C

Cauliflower
81, 211

Carrots
52, 81, 131, 134,
163, 168, 184, 190,
224, 234, 239

Celery
97, 134, 158, 163,
167, 186, 211, 224,
234, 239

Celery root
121

Chamomile
294

Chaya
126, 130, 164, 208,
220, 242

Chayote
242

Cheese
259, 262
cream 338
goat 150, 273
mascarpone 274
Parmesan 126, 129,
152, 156
Ramonetti 126
ricotta 102, 148
sheep's milk 126, 149

Chicatanas
42, 87, 89, 105

Chocolate
81, 105, 282
white 269, 281

Chorizo 229

Cilantro
leaves 49, 79, 101,
134, 136, 243
seeds 81, 224, 239

Cider
239

Citron
53

Cocopaches
41, 105

Cod, rock
220

Corn
121

Crab
101

Cradle, sea
158, 186

Cream
heavy 53, 121, 152,
163, 168, 264, 269,
275, 282, 284, 294,
297, 304 305, 328,
338
sour 267, 275, 277

Cucumber
101, 105, 232

D

Dates
234

Dragon fruit
280

E

Eel, smoked
126

Elderberries
239

Endives
57, 211

F

Farro
97, 131, 234, 273

Fennel
77, 131, 158, 186
frond 89, 98, 208
seeds 81, 148, 239

Flowers
borage 45
hibiscus 269
lavender 286
nasturtium 42, 87, 105, 220
squash 186
turnip 222
yucca 275

G

Gnocchi
126, 129

Grouper
218

Guava
338

H

Hazelnuts
259, 273, 274, 282, 315

Hoja santa
129, 186, 220, 239

Honey
Melipona 294
Tzalancab 273

Horseradish
45

J

Jicama
84, 101

L

Lemon
51, 79, 84, 87, 97, 126, 131, 148, 158, 184, 186, 208, 211, 218, 220, 224, 229, 231, 239, 275

Lemon basil
53

Lentils
184

Lime
42, 49, 51, 77, 79, 85, 87, 89, 148, 191, 243, 281

Lobster
131, 186

Lovage
224, 304

M

Macadamia
284, 291

Mahi-mahi
184

Mamey
297, 315

Mango
101

Merengue, smoked
267

Mesquite
42, 121, 148, 152, 208, 213, 229, 234

Mizuna
220

Mole
81, 105, 269

Mushrooms
chanterelles 273
wild 152

Mustard leaf
234

N

Nanches
275

Nasturtium
42, 87, 105, 220

'Nduja
156

Nicuatole
291

O

Oil
charcoal 81
olive 31, 45, 49, 46, 49, 53, 57, 81, 84, 87, 97, 102, 126, 129, 131, 134, 147, 148, 149, 158, 163, 184, 186, 208, 211, 213, 215, 218, 220, 222, 229, 231, 234, 242, 244, 264, 286

Olives, black
97

Onion, red
49, 79, 101, 213, 243

Orange
51, 57, 77, 97, 101, 213, 239
blood 155

Oysters, Kumiai
45

P

Pápalo
87, 167

Pappardelle
167

Parsley
45, 51, 87, 129, 152, 158, 186, 186, 190, 211, 220, 231

Pear, Asian
79

Peppers
ancho 105, 134, 218
árbol 134, 158, 163, 235
cascabel 134, 220, 244
chipotle 57, 218, 220, 269
cuaresmeño 184, 232
guajillo 105, 218
habanero 49, 51, 79, 81, 84, 213
morita 222
pasilla 105, 222
pink 57, 269

Persimmon
84, 102

Pineapple
244

Pine nuts
57, 82, 129, 211, 269, 305

Pistachios
102

Pixtle
297, 315

Plantain
82

Plum, muscatel
79, 80, 190, 192

Pollen
294

Pomegranate
77, 190

Pork
156, 213, 222, 239, 333

Potatoes
126, 129, 186

Prickly pear, red
280

Pulque
244, 267, 280

Purslane
87, 105

Q

Quail
234

Quelites
87, 167, 260

R

Rabbit
224

Ragù
duck 167
sausage 163

Raisins, golden
81, 211

Ramón
35

Raspberries
269, 328

Ravioli
148, 156

Risotto
134

Romesco
218
black 222
green 220

Rosemary
121, 163, 167, 190, 289, 332

S

Samphire
45

Sardines, pickled
97

Scallop, pen shell
84

Scorpionfish
229

Shisho
102, 239

Shrimp, sweet
51

Snail
49

Snapper, red
231

Sorrel
102, 149, 208, 244, 264

Spearmint
97, 101, 184, 231, 264

Strawberries
269, 328

Suckling pig
213, 269

Sweet potato
213, 215

T

Tagliatelle
152, 163

Tagliolini
158, 167

Tamales
121, 129

Tamarind
231

Tangerine
84

Tarragon
57, 77, 102, 126, 244

Taxcalate
297

Thyme
57, 85, 105, 127, 134, 148, 190, 218, 220, 222, 239, 264, 269

Tomato, grape
126

V

Vanilla
84, 267, 282, 286, 328, 336

Verdolagas
87, 105-106

X

Xoconostle
244, 280

Y

Yellowtail amberjack
79

Yogurt
45, 148, 190, 267, 269, 280, 294, 304

Z

Zaatar
190

Zucchini
43, 89, 158, 242

ACKNOWLEDGEMENTS

Every restaurant is a shared endeavor. Which is why I want to thank each and every person who has made it possible for Rosetta to exist: everyone in the kitchen, everyone in the dining room, everyone in the office. Yet every restaurant also owes its existence to the people who choose to eat there: my heartfelt thanks to all of you, too. Last but not least: I'm so grateful to my family and friends for supporting me in this project, in my life.

ROSETTA

Editor: Diego Rabasa
Editorial coordinator: Andrea Arbide
English translation: Robin Myers
Copyediting and proofreading Spanish: Guillermina Olmedo
Copyediting and proofreading English: Joanna Zuckerman Bernstein
Consultancy: departamento ideológico (d.i.)
Graphic design: Studio Manuel Raeder
(Miglė Kazlauskaitė, Lucas Liccini, Manuel Raeder)
Lithography: max-color, Berlin
Printing: Gutenberg Beuys Feindruckerei GmbH
Third edition: 2024

Published by

Editorial Sexto Piso, S. A. de C. V.
París 35-A
Colonia del Carmen, Coyoacán
04100, Mexico City, Mexico

Sexto Piso España, S. L.
C/ Los Madrazo, 24
28014, Madrid, Spain
www.sextopiso.com

ISBN Spanish: 978-607-8619-02-3
ISBN English: 978-607-8619-03-0

and

BOM
DIA
BOA
TARDE
BOA
NOITE

Rosa-Luxemburg-Str. 17
10178 Berlin, Germany
www.bomdiabooks.de

ISBN: 978-3-96436-001-4

The Deutsche Nationalbibliothek lists this publication in the Deutsche Nationalbibliografie; detailed bibliographic data are available on the Internet at http://dnb.dnb.de.

All rights reserved, including the right of reproduction in whole or in part in any form. No part of this book may be reproduced, transmitted, or stored without written permission from the publisher.

© 2018, Elena Reygadas, BOM DIA BOA TARDE BOA and Editorial Sexto Piso

Photographs on pages 10-11, 12-13, 26-27, 31, 32, 37, 47, 50, 58-59, 70-71, 72, 73, 79, 88, 93, 99, 104, 105, 107, 114-115, 116, 123, 133, 137, 140-141, 144, 151, 174-175, 176-177, 178-179, 180-181, 182, 183, 193, 194-195, 196, 198, 199, 200, 201, 202, 203, 204-205, 206-207, 210, 220, 248, 256, 257, 258, 260, 263, 265, 266, 276, 278, 279, 284, 288, 329, 298, 302, 303, 308, 309, 310, 311, 312, 313, 320-321, 323, 327, 328, 332, 335
© Santiago Arau

Photographs on pages 30, 34, 42 top, 43, 44, 48, 49 top, 51, 56, 66, 68, 77, 78, 84, 86, 97, 100, 110, 120, 124-125, 129, 131, 134, 138-139, 142-143, 148, 149, 156, 157, 160-161, 167, 170, 186, 213, 226-227, 228, 234, 288, 267, 269, 271, 272, 275, 280, 294, 300, 322, 330-331 © Omar Zepeda Vargas

Photographs on pages 14-15, 16, 17, 18, 28, 33, 38, 42 bottom, 49 bottom, 53, 55, 60-61, 65, 67, 80, 81, 83, 90, 94, 95, 96, 97, 102, 108, 109, 119, 120, 146, 152, 153, 158, 162, 165, 166, 184, 186, 190, 208, 216, 217, 218, 222, 224, 231, 233, 237, 242, 244, 246, 247, 251, 252, 263, 268, 273, 283, 286, 290, 296, 297, 306, 314, 230, 324, 326, 334, 336, 339, 340
© Ana Lorenzana

Photographs on pages 69, 74-75, 169, 238 © Ana Hop

Botanical illustrations on pages 62, 76, 86, 154-155, 188-189, 214 © Tiziana Cortese

Map of Mexico, insert © Paloma Contreras, Abraham González Pacheco

Printed in Germany